USA 101

A GUIDE TO AMERICA'S
ICONIC PLACES, EVENTS, AND FESTIVALS

GARY MCKECHNIE

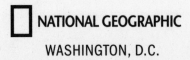

NATIONAL GEOGRAPHIC

WASHINGTON, D.C.

Published by the National Geographic Society

Copyright © 2009 Gary McKechnie

Maps © 2009 National Geographic Books Publishing Group

This 2012 edition printed for Barnes & Noble, Inc. by National Geographic.

ISBN 978-1-4351-3981-7

The Library of Congress has cataloged the 2009 edition of this book as follows:
McKechnie, Gary
   USA 101 : a guide to America's iconic places, events, and festivals / by Gary McKechnie.
      p. cm.
   Includes index.
   ISBN 978-1-4262-0457-9 (pbk.)
   1. United States--Guidebooks. 2. United States--History, Local. 3. Americana--Miscellanea. I. Title. II. Title: U.S.A. 101 III. Title: USA one-o-one

E158.M35 2009
973--dc22

                                        2009001464

The National Geographic Society is one of the world's largest nonprofit scientific and educational organizations. Founded in 1888 to "increase and diffuse geographic knowledge," the Society works to inspire people to care about the planet. It reaches more than 325 million people worldwide each month through its official journal, *National Geographic,* and other magazines; National Geographic Channel; television documentaries; music; radio; films; books; DVDs; maps; exhibitions; school publishing programs; interactive media; and merchandise. National Geographic has funded more than 9,000 scientific research, conservation and exploration projects and supports an education program combating geographic illiteracy. For more information, visit nationalgeographic.com.

For more information, please call 1-800-NGS LINE (647-5463)
or write to the following address:

National Geographic Society
1145 17th Street N.W.
Washington, D.C. 20036-4688 U.S.A.

Visit us online at www.nationalgeographic.com

For information about special discounts for bulk purchases, please contact
National Geographic Books Special Sales: ngspecsales@ngs.org

For rights or permissions inquiries, please contact National Geographic Books Subsidiary Rights:
ngbookrights@ngs.org

Interior design: Cameron Zotter

Printed in the U.S.A.

11/QGF-LPH/1

CONTENTS

NORTHEAST

MID-ATLANTIC

SOUTHEAST

MIDWEST

GREAT PLAINS

ROCKY MOUNTAIN WEST

PACIFIC COAST, HAWAII, & ALASKA

⛊ACROSS AMERICA

With love, appreciation, and gratitude, this book is dedicated to

America, redeemed

Lois Mercier McKechnie

Nancy Howell

Charles Kuralt

and to teachers who have made a difference.

INTRODUCTION

INSPIRED BY CHARLES KURALT, whose "On the Road" features introduced me to our nation's scenic, social, and cultural abundance, in 1998 my wife, Nancy, and I set off on a year-long voyage of discovery for my book, *Great American Motorcycle Tours*. The experience was beautiful, dramatic, and enlightening. With plenty of time to think in those 20,000 miles, I reflected on a previous journey.

A decade earlier, while backpacking across Europe, people who learned I was from the United States switched their natural accent to a curiously broad Texas slang, convinced that all of America was just a widescreen version of *Dallas*. Most Europeans I met couldn't grasp that my one nation was as large and diverse as their entire continent.

This was the genesis of *USA 101*. As I rode America's highways, I wondered: If these people had asked me to educate them on America, what would I have told them? Which things, collectively, would reveal America, generally? I started a list.

I weighed nearly 200 choices I felt had proven themselves for their longevity, access, and role in our cultural composition. With advice from friends, historians, and fellow travelers, I eventually arrived at what I felt was an equitable balance of 101 icons, events, and festivals that encompassed history, faith, art, nature, adventure, sport, leisure, and our favorite pastimes.

With that list in my pocket, once again Nancy and I hit the road. While humbled by the privilege of exploring America, at times I was exhausted by the task. Racing from icon to icon, we'd return home certain that if Miss America saw her shadow, there'd be six more weeks of Mardi Gras. But it was all worth it.

Here's your road map. Travel safe, and God bless America.

Gary McKechnie
www.garymckechnie.com

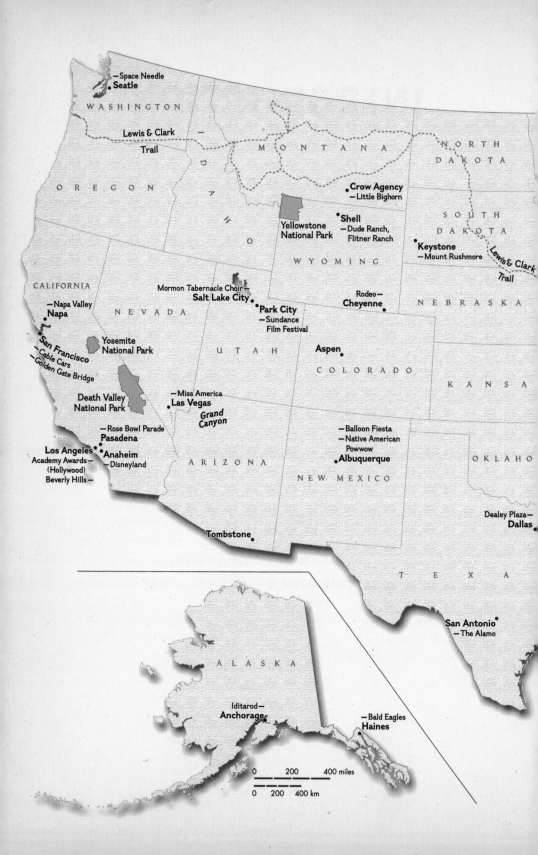

—Space Needle
Seatle

WASHINGTON

Lewis & Clark
Trail

OREGON

MONTANA

NORTH
DAKOTA

Crow Agency
—Little Bighorn

SOUTH
DAKOTA

Shell
—Dude Ranch,
Flitner Ranch

Yellowstone
National Park

WYOMING

Keystone
—Mount Rushmore

Lewis & Clark
Trail

CALIFORNIA

—Napa Valley
Napa

NEVADA

Mormon Tabernacle Choir—
Salt Lake City

Park City
—Sundance
Film Festival

Rodeo—
Cheyenne

NEBRASKA

San Francisco
—Cable Cars
—Golden Gate Bridge

Yosemite
National Park

UTAH

Aspen

COLORADO

KANSA

Death Valley
National Park

—Miss America
Las Vegas

*Grand
Canyon*

—Rose Bowl Parade
Pasadena

—Balloon Fiesta
—Native American
Powwow
Albuquerque

OKLAHO

Los Angeles
Academy Awards—
(Hollywood)
Beverly Hills—

Anaheim
—Disneyland

ARIZONA

NEW MEXICO

Dealey Plaza—
Dallas

Tombstone

T E X A

San Antonio
—The Alamo

ALASKA

Iditarod—
Anchorage

—Bald Eagles
Haines

0   200   400 miles

0   200   400 km

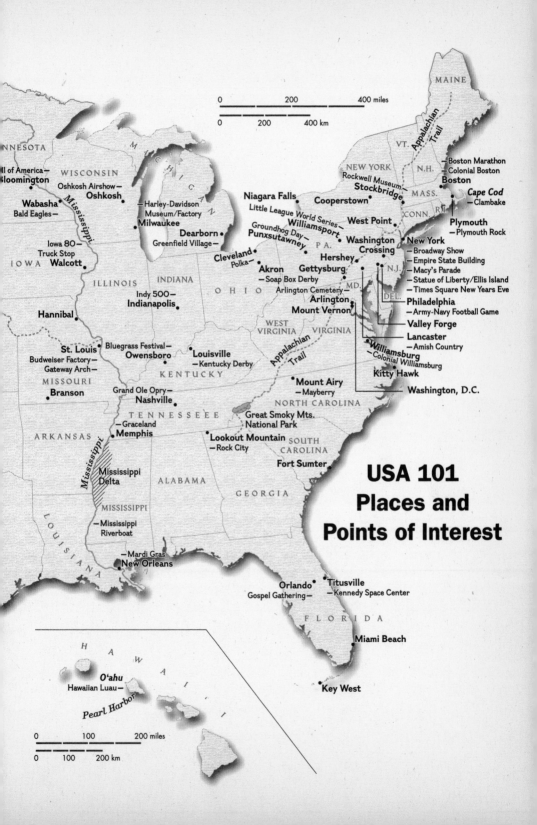

MAINE

0   200   400 miles
0   200   400 km

MINNESOTA
Il of America—
loomington

WISCONSIN
Oshkosh Airshow—
Oshkosh

Wabasha
Bald Eagles—

Mississippi

Iowa 80—
Truck Stop
Walcott

IOWA

ILLINOIS

INDIANA

Indy 500—
Indianapolis

Hannibal

St. Louis
Budweiser Factory—
Gateway Arch—

MISSOURI
Branson

ARKANSAS

*Mississippi
Delta*

MISSISSIPPI

LOUISIANA

—Mardi Gras
New Orleans

Harley-Davidson
Museum/Factory—
Milwaukee

Dearborn
Greenfield Village—

Cleveland
Polka—

Akron
—Soap Box Derby

OHIO

WEST
VIRGINIA

Owensboro

Bluegrass Festival—
Louisville
—Kentucky Derby

KENTUCKY

Grand Ole Opry—
Nashville

TENNESSEE

—Graceland
Memphis

ALABAMA

GEORGIA

*Mississippi
Riverboat*

Niagara Falls
Little League World Series—
Groundhog Day—
Punxsutawney

Gettysburg

Arlington Cemetery—
Arlington
Mount Vernon

VIRGINIA

*Appalachian
Trail*

Mount Airy
—Mayberry

NORTH CAROLINA

Great Smoky Mts.
National Park

Lookout Mountain
—Rock City

SOUTH
CAROLINA

Fort Sumter

Rockwell Museum—
Stockbridge

Cooperstown

Williamsport

West Point

**Washington
Crossing**

Hershey

P.A.

N.J.

MD.

DEL.

NEW YORK

N.H.

VT.

*Appalachian
Trail*

MASS.

CONN.

R.I.

Boston
—Boston Marathon
—Colonial Boston

Cape Cod
—Clambake

Plymouth
—Plymouth Rock

New York
—Broadway Show
—Empire State Building
—Macy's Parade
—Statue of Liberty/Ellis Island
—Times Square New Years Eve

Philadelphia
—Army-Navy Football Game

Valley Forge

Lancaster
—Amish Country

Williamsburg
—Colonial Williamsburg

Kitty Hawk

Washington, D.C.

USA 101
Places and
Points of Interest

Orlando
Gospel Gathering—

Titusville
—Kennedy Space Center

FLORIDA

Miami Beach

Key West

HAWAII

O'ahu
Hawaiian Luau—

Pearl Harbor

0   100   200 miles
0   100   200 km

NORTHEAST

Connecticut, Maine, Massachusetts, New Hampshire, New York, Rhode Island, Vermont

In addition to the calendar pin-up favorites of covered bridges, rocky shores, lighthouses, and an autumnal palette of changing leaves, New England gives you charming two-lane roads that drift through cooling green forests in the summer and sparkling white snow in the winter. Those roads lead to small towns and villages that reflect a sense of calming reassurance and an unspoken self-confidence, passed down from the 1700s when their ancestors let Great Britain know they were capable of taking care of themselves. That sensibility seems to have drifted across to upstate New York, where the pace of life mirrors that of its New England cousins. Farther south, of course, is New York City, which contains the combined energy of New England in a multicultural pocket-sized version of America.

Some of the states here may seem small, but when it comes to scenery, diversity, history, and hospitality, you'll find that the land and its people are larger than life.

1. CLAMBAKE-LOBSTERBAKE
Cape Cod, Massachusetts/Maine Coast

The Patti Page song "Old Cape Cod" brings to mind lovely images of the Massachusetts cape, with its weathered seaside cottages, lighthouses—and clambakes in moonlit coves. Farther north, in Maine, fishermen are checking their lobster traps for the evening's entrée. Get ready to dig a pit—a traditional New England bake is a great way to savor these seaside dinners.

DIG IN

If you're unsettled by the sameness of America, consider our nation's diverse tastes. Thanks to this, certain places will bring a certain food to mind—Idaho potatoes, Hawaiian pineapple, and Rocky Mountain oysters, for example. In New England, primarily on Cape Cod, the feast of choice is called a clambake, while in Maine, it's called a lobsterbake.

Off the northwest tip of Cape Cod is the Stellwagen Bank, a popular feeding ground for whales. Whale-watching charters depart from several towns along Cape Cod—one I can vouch for is Provincetown's Dolphin Fleet (508-240-3636/800-826-9300, www.whalewatch.com). Beautiful and unforgettable.

I'm not sure how long ago folks figured out that clams were so tasty, but Steve Hale, a lobster fisherman from Rockland, Maine, told me it took the lobster countless generations before they became a seafood staple.

"The Indians used to crush them up and use them as fertilizer," he explained. "They'd just toss the chunks into the ground. And settlers in the 1600s would just smash them up and use them as bait to catch herring and mackerel and cod that they could salt and smoke and ship back home. It wasn't until the 20th century that people figured out how to ship lobsters live."

Whether the main entrée was lobster, clams, or a combination with side dishes, the idea for what's become a traditional New England seaside bake was picked up from Indians who knew how to create an oceanfront oven. They'd dig a pit, toss in some rocks, fire it up, toss in the food, and allow the trapped heat to cook the feast. What they invented several centuries ago is still cooking.

DO IT YOURSELF

To be fair, unless you participate in a bake prepared by a local restaurant or can convince a local like James Taylor or one of the Kennedys to fix your meal on a private beach, you may find the permitting process for an authentic bake to be a challenge. (Check ahead; many municipalities have banned beachside fires.) It can also take several hours to prepare the meal, so don't expect to experience a bake on a fast-food schedule. Whether you go it on your own or hook up with a pro, generally here's what happens at an old-fashioned bake:

Believe it or not, one of the most important ingredients is fresh seaweed, which locals also call rockweed. You should be able to collect some along the shoreline and then you can store it in a container of fresh seawater while you gather a few dozen stones together. Meanwhile, your friends should be digging a fire pit about three feet wide and a few feet deep. This is where the stones you've gathered will be placed.

Driftwood, provided it's dry, can be stacked atop the rocks and lighted. It may take a few hours for the wood to heat the rocks to a glowing red. When that's done, rake the coals away from the rocks and sift the embers between the stones to keep them red hot. Add a layer of seaweed over the coals—a step that creates a satisfying sizzle.

Congratulations. You've now built your very own oceanfront oven. If you only had a few more stones, some empty beer cans, and spare radio parts you could have created a microwave. Now, atop the seaweed place your ingredients, which will most likely include fresh-caught lobster, little-neck clams, steamers (soft-shell clams) or mussels, scallops, ears of corn minus the silk but in the husk, new potatoes, onions, and sausage.

In early August in Rockland, Maine, the Maine Lobster Festival (207-596-0376 or 800-562-2529, *www.mainelobsterfestival* *.com*) features the world's largest lobster cooker, cooking contests, the coronation of the Maine Sea Goddess, and the Great International William Atwood Lobster Crate Race, which involves scampering over a string of partially submerged lobster crates until you fall in the frigid water. Record scamper: 4,501 crates.

A cover is necessary to trap heat and steam. Canvas tarps or potato sacks soaked in seawater are often used for this purpose, and are held down with more rocks. If your guests have worked up an appetite from digging the sand pit, add more layers of food atop the cover, followed by more layers of seawater-soaked tarps.

What now? It takes a few hours of steaming before the food is done, so do what people do at the seashore: swim, play, talk, sing…time will pass. When the meal is ready, uncover the tarp and fill your plates.

Then call the Food Network and tell them you want your own cooking show.

CONTACTS

Cape Cod Chamber of Commerce
www.capecodchamber.org
(508) 362-3225
(888) 332-2732

Maine Tourism Association
(207) 623-0363
(888) 624-6345
www.mainetourism.com

Penobscot Bay Regional Chamber of Commerce (Rockland)
(207) 596-0376
(800) 562-2529
www.therealmaine.com

For Lodging and Dining, see pp. 285–286

2. FALL FOLIAGE
New England

While the miracle of fall foliage takes place in North Carolina, Alabama, the Great Plains, the Pacific Northwest, and nearly anywhere there are trees, New England is the region most closely associated with this spectacle. There, millions of acres of forested land present one of nature's most remarkably vivid beauty pageants.

TRUE COLORS

Between spring and late summer most of the nation is accustomed to seeing a landscape that presents a fairly monochromatic palette of green leaves. But, believe it or not, the green leaves are not really green.

This isn't dialogue from *Kung Fu.* It's really true.

While you're in New England, check into the plentiful fall festivals, hayrides, and farmer's markets. Buy some local apple cider or maple syrup or take a walk in the woods.

As the leaves come to life in the spring, they are filled with chlorophyll that gives them the green pigment. Then, toward the end of summer, a layer of cells begins to form at the base of each leaf. With that, the water, minerals, and chlorophyll that once flowed through the veins of the leaf are blocked and the leaf starts to show its true colors—many times brilliant orange, fiery red, or flaming yellow. So why doesn't the government ban chlorophyll so we can enjoy colorful leaves all year long? Well, it takes chlorophyll to capture the sun's rays and convert them into energy that nourishes the tree and helps it grow.

Mother Nature isn't done yet. The brilliance of the autumnal display will be affected by the forest's exposure to the sun, the season's rainfall, and the elevation and chemical composition of the trees. As a rule of thumb, the changes will usually be seen at higher elevations in the north first and then slowly work their way down the hills and mountains, moving southward.

You just need to work your way to the woods.

DO IT YOURSELF

Again, the region most closely associated with the phenomenon is New England. Calendars and postcards have always promoted the season there, showing the warm hues of the leaves surrounding a covered bridge or a simple white church steeple piercing a layer of crimson that cloaks a tiny hamlet.

A handy reference for fall foliage is the *Fall Color Finder,* which identifies more than 150 fall leaves by species in full color. Written by botanists C. Ritchie Bell and Anne H. Lindsey, the pocket-sized guide also identifies America's common native trees by range.

Unless you already live there, call in advance to find out when and where the colors will peak in the area you'd like to explore—and make a hotel reservation, since thousands of other "leaf peepers" arriving from across the U.S. and Canada will be there too. From Maine to Connecticut you can find quiet roads laid across gentle hills; some roads scoot across covered bridges that ford clear streams, while others guide you into sweet villages clustered around old-fashioned town greens.

One of my favorite rides in America is Vermont's Highway 100, a feisty little two-lane road that carves a fairly straight path right through the center of the Green Mountain State. A little to the east, the Kancamagus Highway takes off near Littleton, New Hampshire, and rolls across the White Mountains between Lincoln and North Conway.

No matter where you ride, roll down the windows and let the refreshing chill flood in. Park on the roadside and set out a picnic, sip apple cider, and take time to feast on the glorious colors of autumn that burst from every branch.

CONTACTS

National Forest Service Fall
Foliage Hotline
(800) 354-4595
www.fs.fed.us/news/fallcolors

www.mainefoliage.com
www.vermontfallfoliage.com
www.yankeefoliage.com
www.foliagetrains.com
www.fallinpa.com
www.iloveny.com/foliage

3. COLONIAL BOSTON
Boston, Massachusetts

Today, a town of 15,000 hardly ever makes the news. Travel back a few centuries, however, and the folks in Colonial-era Boston were in the papers nearly every day. They were doing it by changing the world.

STREET FIGHTING MEN

In the American colonies, loyalists appreciated the fact that Great Britain financed their defense and supplied them with goods. Then there were patriots who didn't like living under what they viewed as an occupying force. When the patriots' position grew more popular, there was bound to be a showdown with the British Empire—and the flashpoint was Boston. One little spark ignited one of the most memorable days in history.

On March 5, 1770, wigmaker's apprentice Edward Garrick approached British sentry John Goldfinch at Boston's Towne House (now the Old State House) and demanded that he fork over cash for work his master had done. Goldfinch refused (he had already paid) but it didn't satisfy Garrick, who was joined by a pal who also needled the guard for cash. This was cheap entertainment for hundreds of curious residents who watched reinforcements arrive to protect the sentry. When some Brits were pelted with snowballs and knocked down, they opened fire on the crowd and killed five Boston citizens.

One of the biggest days in Boston is March 17. Not because of its Irish population, but because this is Evacuation Day, a local holiday that marks the day the British forces pulled out of Boston in 1776.

While not a massacre in today's sense, it was good enough for patriots to proclaim the event the "Boston Massacre" to foment more resistance and anger against the British. Despite this, things cooled off until December 1773, when the Crown insisted on imposing a three-pence tax on tea.

Thousands of citizens gathered at the Old South Meeting House to debate this "taxation without representation," but when they learned the royal governor wouldn't stop a shipment of tea from being unloaded and delivered to loyalist merchants, 200 men dressed as Mohawk Indians marched to Griffin's Wharf. There they helped unload 342 chests of tea by cracking them open with hatchets and dumping the contents overboard.

When King George III learned what had happened, he closed the port and imposed martial law in Boston. British troops turned the Old South Meeting House into a makeshift riding stable for their officers. Still, all-out war was more than a year away. For that, you have to move ahead to April 1775, when Gen. Thomas Gage gave secret orders to Lt. Col. Francis Smith and Maj. John Pitcairn to take 700 men and confiscate weapons he believed were being stashed in Lexington, Concord, and Worcester.

William Dawes and Paul Revere rode that night to warn the citizenry, shouting not that "the British are coming!" (there were no Americans then so *everyone* was British), but, more likely, "the Regulars are out!"

> Christened in 1797, the USS *Constitution* is the oldest commissioned warship in the world. It still has a captain and crew.

It was 5:30 a.m. when about 200 soldiers peeled off toward Lexington, but about 80 local militiamen—also known as Minute Men—had been called to arms and were waiting. The two sides faced each other until someone (no one will ever know who) opened fire. Within three minutes eight colonists were dead and nine wounded. The British continued their march to Concord.

As the Regulars entered the town, they were surprised to see Minute Men there to meet them, who then turned and marched ahead of them through Concord and over the North Bridge. Pausing to consider how to handle the situation, the Minute Men looked back toward town, saw smoke and assumed the British were torching the town. Actually, the Regulars were trying to douse an accidental fire, but the Minute Men marched back to the bridge and fired "the shot heard round the world."

From about noon until ten that evening, some 4,000 ordinary citizens from across the countryside kept up a running battle against the British troops all the way back to Boston. The American Revolution had begun.

DO IT YOURSELF

Boston may just deserve the self-proclaimed title "America's walking city." Thanks to the Freedom Trail you can turn yourself loose in the city center and follow in the footsteps of the men and women who helped create our nation. Created in 1958 by William Schofield, a newspaper editor and columnist, the 2.5-mile trail connects significant historic sites such as the Old State House, Paul Revere's house, Boston Common, and many others.

Before getting lost in the city streets, I got my bearings at the Prudential Tower's 50th-floor observation deck, where an audio history and 360-degree view of the city and surrounding countryside helped me understand what I would soon see at street level on a trolley tour. Those tours are great for several reasons. Guides are usually passionate about local history; have primed themselves with stories; and liberally dispense facts every second during the 90-minute tour.

Supplement your self-education with a road trip. About 15 miles outside of Boston is the Minute Man National Historical Park. Near Lexington, the tranquil 971-acre park is found primarily along Route 2A, the Bay Road that Paul Revere, the British, and the Minute Men used that fateful day in 1775.

A few miles away in Concord you can wander around the town on your own; hook up with a local guide to get the lowdown on the decisive battle there; travel up to the Old North Bridge; make a side trip to Henry Thoreau's Walden Pond; and visit Author's Ridge where local residents Thoreau, Louisa May Alcott, Nathaniel Hawthorne, and Ralph Waldo Emerson are buried.

On that April day in 1775, the British left Boston at midnight, certain they could crush the rebellion before it began. They were wrong.

CONTACTS

Greater Boston Convention & Visitors Bureau
(617) 867-8444
(888) 733-2678
www.bostonusa.com

Boston Common Visitor Information Centers
147 Tremont Street
(617) 426-3115

Information Center at Center Court
800 Boylston Street
(617) 867-8389

Minute Man National Historical Park
174 Liberty Street, Concord
(978) 369-6993
www.nps.gov/mima

www.oldsouthmeetinghouse.org

For Lodging and Dining, see pp. 286–287

4. BOSTON MARATHON
Boston, Massachusetts

It seems strange that anyone would base a sport on an event in which the guy who inspired it dropped dead. But for runners and fans, the Boston Marathon is both a race and a block party. On the third Monday in April, the city closes up shop and turns the streets of Boston into a giant jogging trail.

RACING THROUGH HISTORY

No one's exactly sure if it really happened this way, but the accepted version of marathon lore goes back to 490 B.C., when Athenian foot soldier

Pheidippides was told to run to Sparta to seek help after the invading Persians landed at Marathon. In two days, he ran 150 miles. After the outnumbered Greeks beat the Persians at the Battle of Marathon, Pheidippides ran another 26 miles from Marathon to Athens to utter "We have won" or "Rejoice! We conquer!" before he died on the spot.

So here it is, 1897. With memories of the previous summer's first modern Olympics marathon fresh in his mind, Olympic track coach John Graham has created a marathon in Boston. On April 19—Patriots' Day in Boston—15 runners lined up and took off on a 24.5-mile run. Nearly three hours later (2:55:10 to be exact), New Yorker John J. McDermott crossed the finish line to win what was then called the American Marathon. The following year, the winner, a 22-year-old Boston College lad named, believe it or not, Ronald MacDonald, cut the time by a whopping 13 minutes to 2:42. Had that trend continued, today's runners would finish the race more than a day before they started.

> Consider heading a few miles west of Boston to Lexington for the Patriots' Day reenactment of the Battle of Lexington. Like the Minute Men, you'll have to rise early, since the first shots in Lexington were fired at 5:30 a.m.

A longer distance marathon—26 miles, 385 yards—came to the Olympics in 1908, and to Boston in 1924. The extra running was a walk for Clarence DeMar, who, with seven victories between 1910 and 1930, was the Lance Armstrong of marathoners. DeMar, though, couldn't hold a birthday candle to two-time winner John A. "the Elder" Kelley, who ran his first race in 1928 and his last in 1992, at the age of 84.

As decades passed, an increasing number of international competitors ran away with victories. But women were barred for most of that time. In 1966, Roberta "Bobbi" Gibb waited until the race began before slipping into the pack to prove that she could compete. In 1967, Katherine Switzer signed her entry form K.V. Switzer to get a number. Still, she had to run the equivalent of a marathon obstacle course as officials tried to physically drag her out of the race. In 1972, women were finally allowed to enter officially. In 1975, a wheelchair division was added.

Today the Boston Marathon is the gold standard for runners. Whether or not an American comes in first (one hasn't since the 1980s) doesn't matter much to the 500,000 people who line the route to celebrate Patriots' Day and, from the comfort of their lawn chairs, cheer on the sweating, grimacing runners.

DO IT YOURSELF

The Boston Marathon has always taken place in April and, since 1969, on the third Monday in April, known locally as Patriots' Day to mark the day in 1775 when Paul Revere and William Dawes alerted colonists that the British were on the march.

There are other traditions tied into the race, including its route. Passing through rural areas and differing kinds of terrain, it begins in the town of Hopkinton and passes through Ashland, Natick, Wellesley, Newton, and Brookline before entering Boston proper.

If you plan to stay over in Boston on Patriots' Day, be sure to book your room as much as nine months in advance.

Unlike a football game that affords a measly 100-yard viewing area, the Boston Marathon offers 26 miles, 385 yards to choose from. Locals hold marathon-watching parties on front lawns and sidewalks, in open-air cafés and the upper floors of downtown hotels. A popular place to settle is in Newton near the 21-mile mark. There, the rise in elevation known as Heartbreak Hill is the obstacle that knocks many runners out of the race. Every step of the way the runners are cheered and applauded, greeted by screams of encouragement from the Wellesley College women and then, eight miles down the road, by shouts in a lower register from Boston College frat boys.

The most prized real estate is at the finish line. Since so many spectators congregate along the route's last mile, you'll either have to rise very early or train for several years to reach this point. Some motivated fans catch the race over and over by using the subway to leapfrog past the runners and race to stops near the route.

About an hour and a half after the wheelchair athletes leave Hopkinton at their starting time of 9:25 a.m., they roll across the finish line. The elite women runners depart about 9:35 a.m. and it takes about 2:20 for the first of them to finish; the elite men's division that begins at 10 crosses the line about 2:10 later.

An American man last won the Boston Marathon in 1983; an American woman last won in 1985.

So what motivates these runners? It's not the prize money, which is awarded only to a handful of first finishers. At the pinnacle of the world's marathons, the Boston Marathon offers the reward of personal accomplishment in just qualifying for the event and, more importantly, finishing it.

To paraphrase Pheidippides, *"They have won."*

CONTACTS

Boston Athletic Association
(617) 236-1652
www.bostonmarathon.org

**Greater Boston Convention
Visitors Bureau**
(888) 733-2678
www.bostonusa.com

Massachusetts Office of Tourism
(617) 973-8300
(800) 227-6277
www.mass-vacation.com

www.marathonguide.com
www.coolrunning.com
www.runnersworld.com
www.runningnetwork.com

For Lodging and Dining, see pp. 286–287

5. PLYMOUTH ROCK
Plymouth, Massachusetts

Any parent who's ever attended a Thanksgiving pageant has seen kids looking exactly as Pilgrims would have looked had they been seven years old and worn cardboard hats. The funny thing about Plymouth, Pilgrims, the *Mayflower,* and the first Thanksgiving is that the story has become a time-entangled mixture of fact and fiction. Still, quite a lot happened in Plymouth, where American history is hit and myth.

ROCK SHOW

First off, the Pilgrims didn't land at Plymouth Rock. Well, they did, kind of, but only after they had landed at what would become Provincetown, at the tip of Cape Cod. They were 200 miles north of their intended destination, northern Virginia, and winter was approaching. They needed to stop and do laundry. Yes, they did.

When they left Provincetown, shoals prevented the Pilgrims from sailing around the Cape into the Atlantic, so they headed due west to the mainland shore across Cape Cod Bay. On December 17 the *Mayflower's* 102 passengers, only about half of whom were religious pilgrims, dropped anchor. Had they arrived a few years earlier, they would have been met by mainland Wampanoag, a tribe that had been there for about 10,000 years. Unfortunately, English, Spanish, Dutch, and French explorers had arrived earlier, bringing diseases the tribe couldn't combat and reducing their numbers dramatically.

In what would become the capital of the Plimoth Colony, they found a protected harbor, fish and food, high ground, and cleared land. The Pilgrims put aside their prejudices and fears to befriend Indians like Tisquantum (Squanto) who, having been kidnapped and taken to Europe, spoke English. As a trusted adviser, he taught the 50 or so settlers who survived the first winter how to raise crops, catch fish, build warm shelters, and identify edible plants. By 1621, the settlers were so amazed at their bounty and good fortune that they invited Squanto and Massasoit and nearly 100 other members of the Wampanoag tribe to a celebration of the harvest. Future generations called this the first Thanksgiving. Note that this was *their* first Thanksgiving, not the nation's. Spanish explorers had already held them, and English settlers hosted one near Jamestown, Virginia, in 1619.

Still, the fellowship and camaraderie lasted for a few generations. Then others settlers arrived and tried to "civilize" the Indians by pushing them to adopt new clothing, new shelters, and Christianity. Relations between the Indians and the colonists headed south.

Did the Pilgrims call themselves Pilgrims? No. They called themselves "Separatists"—separate from the Church of England which, they felt, was dragging its feet when it came to completing the work of the Reformation. The word "Pilgrim" first appeared in a reference by Plymouth settler William Bradford.

After Plimoth Colony was absorbed into the larger Massachusetts Bay Colony in 1691, Plymouth eased into a commercial groove that would last for more than two centuries. A center for fishing and shipping, the town also became known for producing ropes for sailing ships. But fish and ships and rope couldn't compete with the legend of Plymouth Rock.

In 1741, local resident Thomas Faunce shared a tale about his dad, who arrived in Plymouth in 1623. He claimed a giant boulder in town was the Pilgrims' landing place. Even though it was 121 years after the fact and Faunce was already 94 years old, his story would last for centuries. In fact, it may last longer than the rock.

Locals were thrilled by the story. In 1744 they planned to move the boulder from the shore to the city center, but the rock broke in half. It was later moved a few more times. Souvenir hunters chipped away at it with hammers and chisels. By 1921, what remained of Plymouth Rock was put on the beach, the centerpiece of 11-acre Pilgrim Memorial State Park.

DO IT YOURSELF

I pictured Plymouth Rock as a boulder the size of the White House, but what I saw is an ordinary rock, two-thirds of which, I heard, is buried. It is marked with

"1620," so I guess it's legit. Aside from looking at it and taking pictures of it, there's not much to do with it, so you'll probably soon head over to the *Mayflower II*.

It was built in England in 1956 as a close replica of the 1600s original. In 1957 a hearty crew sailed it across the Atlantic. On the pier placards and displays explain who the Pilgrims were, why they came here, and the conditions they endured on their voyage. On board, crew members explain how the ship was sailed and the sailors' roles and responsibilities. What may astound you is its diminutive size. It's hard to imagine 102 people crossing the Atlantic on a vessel that could fit inside the fitness center of a modern cruise ship.

Each Thanksgiving, there's a traditional Thanksgiving feast at Plimoth Plantation. Several seatings are available...but tickets go fast.

In the center of town, the Pilgrim Hall Museum, founded in 1824, displays an unmatched collection of Pilgrim possessions, including the Bible of William Bradford (who coined the term "Pilgrim"); Myles Standish's sword; a sampler stitched by his daughter, Loara; and a portrait of Edward Winslow (the only Pilgrim who was painted from life). The museum also focuses on the Wampanoag, who helped the settlers when they arrived but were slowly pushed aside by successive generations of colonists.

It wasn't just a rock and a ship that defined the Pilgrims. Head about three miles to Plimoth Plantation, a 130-acre living history museum where the Pilgrims' settlement, circa 1627, and a replica of a Wampanoag homesite have been created. Guides playing the roles of early settlers and their Indian neighbors explain the conditions they faced. This is where you can ask questions that may shed the myths of Plymouth. When you do, you may find that a similar question posed to colonists and Indians can elicit answers that reveal completely different historical perspectives.

It may also solve the mystery of why Plymouth's story has become an entangled blend of fact and fiction.

CONTACTS

Destination Plymouth
(800) 872-1620
www.visit-plymouth.com

Pilgrim Hall Museum
(508) 746-1620
www.pilgrimhall.org

Plimoth Plantation
(508) 746-1622
www.plimoth.org

For Lodging and Dining, see pp. 287–288

6. NORMAN ROCKWELL MUSEUM
Stockbridge, Massachusetts

Norman Rockwell left an extraordinary record of our country in a period of transition. From the covers of the *Saturday Evening Post* to paintings created for the Boy Scouts of America, he could capture in a single image everything we wanted to believe about our nation and ourselves.

MASTERPIECE

For a city boy (he was born and raised in New York City), Norman Rockwell had a gift for painting small-town America. To be fair, he had a gift for painting *anything*.

He sold his first commissioned work at 15, was named art director of *Boys' Life* at 19, and sold his first *Saturday Evening Post* cover in 1916 at the age of 22. There would be more than 300 additional *Post* covers to follow, and each one further secured Rockwell's place as America's favorite artist.

There's much to do in the Berkshires in addition to visiting the Rockwell Museum. Down the street is Chesterwood *(4 Williamsville Rd., Stockbridge, 413-298-3579, www.chesterwood.org),* home of Daniel Chester French, the sculptor who created the Lincoln of the Lincoln Memorial. In neighboring Lenox is Tanglewood *(West St./Rte. 183, 413-637-5165, www.bso.org),* the summer home of the Boston Symphony Orchestra.

"His paintings weren't something people had to go to a museum to see or to be educated to understand," says Corry Kanzenberg, assistant curator of Stockbridge's Norman Rockwell Museum. "Nearly every week they could see his work on the cover of the *Saturday Evening Post,* and then, as now, they saw an idealized America. Rockwell said he painted the best in us."

His first studio was in New Rochelle, New York, which he left for Arlington, Vermont, in 1939. It was in that small village that he created most of the paintings that would come to define his work. In Arlington, and later in Stockbridge, Massachusetts, where he and his family moved in 1953, his models were just friends and neighbors who had the authenticity that professional models lacked. Some earned as much as ten dollars posing for photographs from which he would create the portraits. The sincerity in his work is clearly seen in paintings such as a son leaving for college in "Breaking Home Ties," a little girl daydreaming of her future in "Girl at Mirror," and parents watching over their sleeping children in "Freedom from Fear."

Some critics dismissed him as an "illustrator." In fact, it took decades for some highbrow critics to come around—and some are still mulling it over. The slights don't matter to his many fans. When the first Rockwell museum opened in a small storefront in Stockbridge in 1969, lines trailed down the block. In 1993, a new 12,000-square-foot museum opened nearby to showcase his work. When you arrive there you'll find that, as generations of *Post* readers discovered, it's always a pleasure to take comfort in the works of Norman Rockwell.

DO IT YOURSELF

Stockbridge, Massachusetts, about an hour southeast of Albany, New York, is still a small town. Because it's small, and because it was his last hometown, it is the perfect location for the Norman Rockwell Museum.

Rockwell's original studio was on the south side of Main Street, and the museum is just about two miles north of town. Inside the colonial-style building, begin with an audio tour that guides you to and explains some of the paintings on permanent exhibit. Unless you're an art major or your last name is Wyeth, though, enhance the audio tour with a complimentary guided tour. The docents, some of whom modeled for Rockwell, are gifted at explaining the nuances of his work.

A very pleasing 65-mile drive north of Stockbridge is Arlington, Vermont, where you'll find the charming Norman Rockwell Exhibition (3772 Route 7A, 802-375-6423). There are some rare Rockwell items, including sketches he made for his friends and neighbors. Can't get enough? His former home is now the Inn on the Covered Bridge Green (802-375-9489/800-726-9480, www.covered bridgegreen.com), and you can even sleep in his old studio.

This is the world's largest and most significant collection of work by Norman Rockwell, with more than 700 paintings and drawings and a repository of archival documents. The paintings that most visitors search for, such as the *Four Freedoms* series, are displayed in the center of the museum. Most of the paintings are on permanent display, although some may be on loan to other museums.

When you're done inside, there are 36 acres of grounds to enjoy. Those who travel in high season (May through October) can also step into Rockwell's studio, which still holds his easels, paints, and brushes.

You won't find many museums in the pages of this book, so consider this an exception. At the Norman Rockwell Museum, you'll not just be looking at paintings, you'll be looking at yourself.

CONTACTS

Norman Rockwell Museum
9 Glendale Road, Route 183
Stockbridge
(413) 298-4100

www.nrm.org
www.normanrockwell.com

For Lodging and Dining, see pp. 288–289

7. NIAGARA FALLS
New York

You may have seen them on millions of postcards, potholders, dish towels, color slides, purses, hats, posters, and porcelain plates, but until you see them up close in all their thundering glory (or buy a really, really big plate) you'll never honestly appreciate Niagara Falls.

They always seem to flow into our lives. You know about daredevils and the depressed washing over the falls, but you've also seen snapshots of honeymooners and beautiful scenery there and you wonder if they are really that extraordinary.

Yes, they are.

LIQUID ASSETS

Considering it's taken 12,000 years for them to reach the shape they're in today, it's hard to believe Niagara Falls isn't a government project. But the Niagara River, flowing between the U.S. and Canada, had been on the job for thousands of years when it was first seen by an Iroquois tribe called the Ongiara. They called the water show Onguiaahra (Thunder of Waters). Frenchman Samuel de Champlain showed up in 1604 and laid claim to them—although other explorers, including Finns and Belgians, took credit for "discovering" the falls. They must have looked incredible without utility lines, high rises, or casinos to spoil the view.

Every spring, workers at Cave of the Winds raze and rebuild the ice-damaged boardwalk, fighting cold and wind all the while.

In the 1800s travelers arrived and entrepreneurs built bridges across the falls and railroad companies promoted Niagara Falls as a honeymoon destination. Even if they weren't the highest falls in the world (there are more than 500 waterfalls higher than this), daredevils sealed themselves up in padded barrels or airtight canisters…and sailed over the falls toward certain celebrity or certain death. More often it was certain death.

When the popularity of the falls began to interfere with their natural beauty, representatives of the U.S. and Canada created Free Niagara. Luminaries such as landscape designer Frederick Law Olmsted and Hudson River School artist Frederic Edwin Church teamed up with others to restore and preserve the natural beauty of the area. In the mid-1880s, the Niagara Reservation State Park (U.S.) and Queen Victoria Niagara Falls Park (Canada) were established.

After the turn of the 20th century, interest in Niagara Falls spiked again when Americans took to the roads in their new automobiles. Ever since, interest has seldom wavered. For decades, Niagara Falls was *the* honeymoon destination of America, and even though that status has been challenged by resort capitals like Las Vegas and Honolulu, the falls continue to woo couples. But even if you're not all hopped up on hormones, they are still beauties well worth seeing.

Like other 19th-century travelers, Jean-François Gravelet loved to take walks by the falls. But since he wasn't comfortable in regular shoes, he'd walk barefoot…or with baskets on his feet or on stilts or blindfolded or with a man on his back. Even more unusual was that Gravelet, better known as the tightrope walker Blondin, did all this on a wire suspended 160 feet over the Niagara River.

DO IT YOURSELF

I'm certain that some couples have been torn apart arguing whether the American or Canadian side is more picturesque. But if that's all it took for an argument I'd bet those misfits would have broken up anyway. If that debate comes up, here are some things to consider: The Canadian side offers more spectacular views since Horseshoe Falls is about 2,220 feet across, about 170 feet high, and washes an astronomical 600,000 gallons of water over the edge *every second*. Also, from the Canadian side, you can see from a distance the narrower American falls and the sliver of a flow called Bridal Veil Falls. Canada's downside is a commercial district of towering hotels, casinos, and tourist traps. Oh, Canada.

On the other hand, the American side is enveloped within Niagara Falls State Park, America's oldest state park and, for my money, one of the prettiest. After he tidied up a weekend project called Central Park, Frederick Law Olmsted wrapped the river's sloping banks and rolling terrain into a botanical oasis, shaded by sycamore, maple, and poplar trees.

At the park's visitor center, "Niagara-Legends of Adventure" is a short film that shows some stunning footage. Archival photographs at the center offer a nice contrast to the present-day scene, while geological charts show how, in 20,000 years, the falls will erode as far south as Buffalo. Plan to get there on June 27, around seven-ish. For now here's what you're seeing: After traveling through Lakes Superior, Huron, and Michigan, the water drops more than 300 feet between Lake Erie and Lake Ontario, and more than half of that happens at Niagara Falls.

Next, walk out on the Observation Tower, a 200-foot-high canti-levered structure that extends a boom far over the Niagara River for a great view of the waterworks and early-morning rainbows in the mist. An elevator descends to the base of the tower and to the *Maid of the Mist*, which chugs upriver to Horseshoe Falls, where the captain revs up the engine and forces the bow toward the water. As the ship bobs before the cacophonous gusher, the 300 purple-poncho-clad passengers look like a tugboat full of bouncing blueberries. Adults are mesmerized by the broad wall of water and kids scream just because the water's so loud and because it's fun.

Trolleys circle the park, so after the boat ride hop over to Goat Island, where only a thin metal rail stands between you and eternity. Hang on tight and watch water sloshing over the hard-packed black dolostone and shale (some people take it for granite) before it turns into a frothy white blast as it slams into the 100-foot-high nest of boulders below.

Then jump back on the trolley to reach the Cave of the Winds, the most exciting site in the park. Slap on a pair of sandals (free); don a rain parka; and take the elevator down 170 feet to the base of Bridal Veil Falls. It's just a trickle compared to the others, but still mighty enough that when you follow the boardwalk and the falling water hits nearby, it whips up high-velocity winds and blows out white-cold blasts of water. If you can muscle your way up a flight of stairs, you'll feel the peak force of wind and water at the Hurricane Deck, thoughtfully posted with a "No Smoking" sign.

If your plans include going over the falls in a barrel, pick the Canadian side if you'd like a shot at living. The rocks beneath the American falls will kill you as sure as you're born.

Near day's end, make your way to Three Sisters Island, located far enough away from the main falls to discourage most tourists. Sit in a quiet cove and watch the river. Gaze upstream. Here is Niagara's true beauty, untouched.

CONTACTS

Niagara Tourism and Convention
Corporation
(716) 282-8992
(877) 325-5787
www.niagara-usa.com
www.niagaraparks.com

Niagara State Park Visitors Center
(716) 278-1796
www.niagarafallsstatepark.com

For Lodging and Dining, see p. 289

8. BASEBALL HALL OF FAME
Cooperstown, New York

Of all the people who have every played baseball, about 17,000 were good enough to make it to the major leagues. Of those 17,000, just a shade more than 1 percent were good enough to earn immortalization in Cooperstown's Baseball Hall of Fame.

THAT'S NOT CRICKET

At the turn of the 20th century, sportswriter Henry Chadwick's research led him to conclude that the "all-American" sport of baseball had actually evolved from an English game called rounders. This wasn't good news to Albert Spalding, a retired baseball player, current baseball executive, and sporting goods manufacturer who preferred that the sport have a purely American pedigree.

In 1905, Spalding organized a panel that conducted a three-year study of baseball's origins. Among the pieces of evidence the committee received was a letter from one Abner Graves, who, more than 60 years after the fact, recalled being right there when young Abner Doubleday added a twist to the existing sport of "town ball" by laying out a diamond-shaped field and adding bases. In the committee's final report, it determined "the first scheme for playing baseball, according to the best evidence obtainable to date, was devised by Abner Doubleday at Cooperstown, N.Y. in 1839."

Except for the part about Doubleday and Cooperstown, everything was 100 percent accurate. "He means well," said Chadwick about his friend Spalding, "but he don't know."

> Civil War general Abner Doubleday did a lot for America, but one of the best things he did was to *not* take credit for inventing baseball, and that's good—because he didn't.

In 1934 the Cooperstown snowball began rolling a little faster when a rudimentary baseball was found in a farmhouse a few miles from town. Cooperstown resident and philanthropist Stephen Clark purchased the so-called "Doubleday baseball," which led to an exhibition of baseball artifacts and sparked the idea for a national baseball museum. Clark found a valuable supporter in Ford Frick, president of the National League, who was also thinking of a way to mark baseball's 1939 "centennial" by honoring the game's immortal players. The first five inductees—Ty Cobb, Babe Ruth, Honus Wagner, Christy Mathewson, and Walter Johnson—had been chosen; by the time the National Baseball Hall of Fame and Museum was dedicated on June 12, 1939, 20 more players had been named. Eleven living inductees were at the ceremony; a special baseball postage stamp was released; and, like baseball itself, the Baseball Hall of Fame became part of the American story.

DO IT YOURSELF

Although the links between baseball's true origins and Cooperstown are questionable at best, this town has become the hometown of baseball history over time. Even the nostalgic veneer of Cooperstown, suspended somewhere in the 1950s, seems designed to enhance our idealized image of baseball.

That story begins inside the Grandstand Theater (which recreates old Comiskey Park) where a short film called "The Baseball Experience" takes a look at the game and its cultural impact. The museum itself takes a chronological tour of the game from the 1820s to the most recent World Series through roughly 35,000 items and artifacts that include bats, balls, gloves, caps, helmets, posters, uniforms, shoes, trophies, and awards, plus a collection of about 130,000 baseball cards.

After helping provide America with the Doubleday legend, Abner Graves ended up in an asylum after killing his wife.

In the first-floor Plaque Gallery, where baseball's finest are enshrined, more than 200 Major League Baseball players; 35 Negro Leaguers; 26 baseball pioneers, executives, and organizers; 18 managers; and 8 umpires who've made it to Cooperstown are enshrined. In another part of the Hall, famous sportswriters and broadcasters are honored as well.

Elsewhere, there are exhibits on baseball's role in the movies, baseball in art, women in baseball, the Negro League, team uniforms, baseball statistics, famous ballparks, World Series rings, and an entire exhibit honoring Hank Aaron (the real home run king) and others who've reached the 500-homer club with and without the aid of pharmaceuticals.

If you think the volume of information you've seen so far is overwhelming, wait until you enter the world's largest baseball research library. The librarians catalogue and track 2.6 million items, including more than a half-million historic images of players, teams, ballparks, and other sport-related subjects and approximately 10,000 hours of recorded footage dating back to the late 1800s.

Each year the Hall of Fame's research department answers approximately 60,000 inquiries.

The Hall of Fame draws more than 300,000 visitors a year, but if you'd like to see it minus the crowds, time your visit for September or May while the kids are back in school or waiting to get out for summer. But if this will be a summer excursion, arrive during the last weekend in July—when the Induction Ceremony welcomes the latest legends.

Baseball may not have been born in Cooperstown, but this is definitely the place it calls home.

CONTACTS

National Baseball Hall of Fame and Museum
(888) 425-5633
www.baseballhall.org

For Lodging and Dining, see pp. 289–290

9. WEST POINT
New York

Over the course of four years, cadets are pushed hard to excel intellectually, physically, militarily, morally, and ethically. West Point graduates include Robert E. Lee, Ulysses S. Grant, William Tecumseh Sherman, Douglas MacArthur, Omar Bradley, George S. Patton, Dwight David Eisenhower, Buzz Aldrin, Norman Schwarzkopf, Jr., Wes Clark, and David Petraeus. But graduates also rank among our nation's leading jurists, astronauts, explorers, engineers, inventors, scientists, educators, authors, executives, and athletes.

MILITARY INTELLIGENCE

Along the Hudson River's banks about 50 miles north of New York City is a commanding plateau that provides an excellent line of vision up and down the river. Feeling that this was perhaps the most strategically important site in the Revolutionary War, in 1778 George Washington decided a fortress should be built on its west bank. To design it and supervise its construction he enlisted the engineer and later general Thaddeus Kosciuszko, a Polish immigrant, who had already fortified Philadelphia and helped achieve victory at Saratoga with the construction of several forts and fortified military camps along the Canadian border.

Within a year, soldiers under his supervision had built a series of forts, batteries, and redoubts to monitor the Hudson River. And just to make sure the British behaved, they created the 150-ton "Hudson River Chain" that, when stretched across the river, was capable of blocking any ship.

With its strategic location and defensive capabilities, it seemed West Point could withstand virtually any enemy assault. But what if the enemy was your friend? Enter Benedict Arnold.

Arnold had performed heroically at Fort Ticonderoga and the Battle of Saratoga, but when other officers took credit for Arnold's actions, he was passed over for promotion. It rankled Arnold so much that, shortly after he was awarded command of West Point, he implemented a plan to surrender it to the British. In September 1780, a patrol captured British Major John André carrying notes from Arnold that revealed the plot and the price for treason (about $1 million in today's currency).

You won't find freshmen, sophomores, juniors, or seniors at West Point. Instead they are officially called "fourth class" or "plebes"; then "third class," or "yearlings" or "yuks"; "second class" or "cows"; and finally "first class" or "firsties."

Instead of Arnold surrendering the fort, André was hanged on October 2. Arnold escaped to England, but his name would forever become synonymous with traitor.

The Founding Fathers learned another lesson during the Revolution: America was too dependent on foreign engineers and military experts. Washington and his colleagues agreed the nation needed an institution that could teach the art and science of warfare.

In March 1802, President Jefferson signed legislation that established the United States Military Academy at West Point. It opened on July 4.

When Colonel Sylvanus Thayer was named the Academy's superintendent in 1817, he made civil engineering the foundation of the school's curriculum. Over the next 16 years, the "Father of the Military Academy" graduated cadets who would design and build some of America's first railways, bridges, harbors, and roads.

Some 40 years later West Point graduates matched their military skills against one other during the Civil War. Fortunately, in every conflict that followed, they were fighting on the right side. The same side.

DO IT YOURSELF

Start at the West Point Visitors Center, which features displays and short videos on the school's history. Next door is the Gothic-style West Point Museum, the country's oldest and largest military museum.

There, six permanent galleries showcase weapons and artifacts from prehistoric times to the present. You can see pistols used by George Washington, Geronimo's rifle, Sitting Bull's tomahawk, John J. Pershing's uniform, Eisenhower's sidearm, and George Custer's last message telling Captain Frederick Benteen that he needed help. The message arrived; Benteen didn't. There's also Hitler's pistol, Napoleon's sword and pistol, and Hermann Göring's Reichsmarschall's baton.

> **Cadets are required to adhere to the Cadet Honor Code, which states simply, "A Cadet will not lie, cheat, steal, or tolerate those who do."**

Since 2001 it's been more difficult, but not impossible, to gain access to the Academy itself. Independent of a tour, the general public can travel onto the post only for certain events such as chapel services, football games, or performances at the arts center. Most first-time visitors start at the museum and follow with a bus tour. Two tours—one an hour long, the other two—depart from the Visitors Center several times daily.

The first stop on both tours allows visitors to enter the main Cadet Chapel, the largest of the five on post, with numerous stained-glass windows and the world's largest pipe organ in a house of worship. There are 23,000 pipes hooked up to this monster, and you can hear it live if you attend a chapel service Sunday at 10:30.

The next stop, Trophy Point, takes in cannons captured in battle, 13 links from the Hudson River Chain, and the 1897 Battle Monument commemorating the men of the Army who had fallen in war—all overlooking a breathtaking stretch of the Hudson River. If the scenery looks familiar, you may have seen it featured in works of the art movement known as the Hudson River School.

Across the street, by the Parade Field, you might catch the spectacle of the lunch formation as cadets line up and march to Washington Hall accompanied by a drum and bugle corps and color guard.

The two-hour tour also includes a stop at the Old Cadet Chapel, built in 1837. Examine the wooden plaques and shields that honor American generals who served from the American Revolution to the War of 1812. One, though, is blank. This is the plaque for Benedict Arnold.

This tour ends at the West Point Cemetery, the final resting place of many of America's greatest citizens.

From now on, if anyone asks, you can tell them the truth. You went to West Point.

CONTACTS

United States Military Academy
Visitors Center
(845) 938-2638

West Point Museum
(845) 938-3590

West Point Tours, Inc.
(845) 446-4724
www.westpointtours.com
(photo ID required for visitors over 16)

For Lodging and Dining, see p. 290

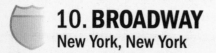

10. BROADWAY
New York, New York

When a television show boasts that it's "filmed before a live studio audience," one thing they don't mention is that the 23-minute show is a painstakingly crafted compilation of multiple takes, camera angles, and recorded music. Attend a Broadway show and you'll witness America's best actors, dancers, singers, and musicians creating three hours of quality entertainment live on stage and right before your very eyes.

RAISING THE CURTAIN

In the 1800s Shakespearean dramas and Victorian melodramas dominated the American stage, but as the calendar flipped into the 20th century, our own performers began gaining the home field advantage. Vaudevillians, minstrel musicians, burlesque comics, and touring performers practiced their craft and aimed for the top: *Broadway*. In New York City's theater district, audiences were ushered into the nation's newest and most ornate theaters to attend shows written by its most gifted playwrights, scored by its most talented composers, and performed by its finest actors. By the 1920s, the curtain had lifted on a new era of purely American theater.

Because most of us live hundreds, if not thousands, of miles from New York City, we think we're unaffected by what happens on Broadway. But Broadway *has* affected us. We're familiar with its history because at schools and community theaters are amateur actors staging shows that premiered more than a half century ago—familiar plays and musicals like *Harvey, Arsenic and Old Lace, Damn Yankees,* and *Annie Get Your Gun.* Some of our greatest actors—Marlon Brando, Meryl Streep, Shirley MacLaine, and the Marx Brothers, to name a few—honed their craft there, while composers like Irving Berlin, the Gershwin brothers, Cole Porter, Richard Rodgers, Oscar Hammerstein, Lorenz Hart, Jerome Kern, and Johnny Mercer contributed their Broadway show tunes to the Great American Songbook.

> Why the name the Great White Way? Early colored lights quickly burned out and were replaced with longer-burning white lights.

Although purists insist that the golden age of the American theater peaked between the 1940s and 1960s, Broadway manages to stay relevant by moving up shows proven "off Broadway," reviving classics, or staging new plays and musical extravaganzas. In the last few decades Andrew Lloyd Webber created a string of new classics with shows like *Cats, Phantom of the Opera,* and *Evita* while intricately exotic musicals based on Disney hits like *The Lion King, Beauty and the Beast,* and *The Little Mermaid* were phenomenally successful.

New York certainly isn't the only place to experience live theater. But night after night (and twice on Wednesdays and Sundays), there's no place like Broadway.

DO IT YOURSELF

While some of the 39 theaters that constitute the theater district are actually found on Broadway, many are found on Manhattan's west side between West 41st and West 51st streets. If you can find Times Square (it's pretty big), you won't get lost. There are a few more things visitors should know:

> I swear I'd love to see men attend the theater wearing top hats and capes and monocles, and women in tiaras and strands of pearls, but aside from an opening-night performance when the audience is dressed to the nines, dress is casual.

• Take advantage of the TKTS booth in Times Square, operated by the non-profit Theatre Development Fund. This is where you can find same-day tickets (or next-day matinee tickets) at discounts of between 25 and 50 percent.

- Some theaters offer standing-room tickets and discounts such as last-minute "rush" or "lottery" tickets. Occasionally I've had luck by asking for a junior citizens discount.

- In general, theaters are "dark" (closed) on Mondays and shows are presented Tuesdays through Saturdays with an 8 p.m. curtain. There are also less expensive afternoon matinee performances at 2 p.m. on Wednesdays and at 3 p.m. on Saturdays and Sundays. Some Tuesday shows may start at 7 p.m. to attract locals, while others (such as shows by Disney), break with tradition and adjust curtain times to attract the largest audience possible. Doors open around 30 minutes before curtain.

> **Standing Room Only tickets are just that—a chance to enter the theater and stand while the show is presented. In exchange for tired feet, you'll only pay between $20 and $30.**

- Stage doors still exist and if you hang out long enough you may meet the cast of the show. You may also bump into the actors in restaurants adjacent to the theaters. That's how I met Savion Glover and Gregory Hines. Really.

- Even if a play's a hit, do your homework. Read the reviews and see if it's something you'd like to invest your time and money in.

CONTACTS

Check these sites out for theater reviews and details on theater etiquette and discounts.
www.nytheatre.com
www.nyc.com/broadway

www.playbill.com
www.theatermania.com
www.broadwaybox.com
www.talkinbroadway.com
www.tdf.org

For Lodging and Dining, see pp. 290–291

11. EMPIRE STATE BUILDING
New York, New York

Taller buildings have been built, but the Empire State Building still stands alone. What it represents helps explain our devotion to it. When it was completed in 1931, the Empire State Building seemed to project the nation's desire to break out of the Great Depression and return to an age of prosperity. Through the decades that followed and the changes they brought, the Empire State Building has done something special.

It hasn't gone away.

A TALL TALE

A race was being run in New York City, but this one was different.

It was being run vertically.

Three companies were intent on constructing the tallest building in the world. The runners-up—40 Wall Street and the Chrysler Building—would each hold the lead briefly before the Empire State Building rocketed past them.

Perhaps the 3,400 workers who built it were just grateful to be employed during the depths of the Great Depression. Maybe it was simply the work ethic of their generation. Whatever their motivation, these men—a mix of native-born Americans, European immigrants, and Mohawk Indians from Canada—were going flat out to shape 370,000 tons of concrete, 70 miles of pipe, 2.5 million feet of wire, and 60,000 tons of steel into a 102-story art deco masterpiece. How fast were they working? *Fast.* Each week, the building would rise another four and a half stories. Between the commencement of construction on March 17, 1930, and the ribbon cutting on May 1, 1931, only 410 days passed.

This was a cutting-edge building. In fact, the Art Deco mast that rose from the rooftop was originally designed as a mooring mast for dirigibles, which were believed to represent the future of aviation. This was a brilliant idea except for the fact that only a handful of people on Earth would agree to step off a swaying blimp tethered at more than 1200 feet.

Webcam views from atop the Empire State Building are available at *www.esbnyc.com*.

In the race to the top, Empire State, Inc., the project's backers, overlooked an important factor: occupants. Much of the building remained vacant during its first year, earning it the nickname Empty State Building. It was so empty that the $2 million generated at the observation decks nearly equaled the income collected through office rentals. It would take another 20 years for the building to turn a profit.

The Empire State Building became an icon of popular culture much sooner. Ashtrays, postcards, figurines, and assorted souvenirs highlighted the high rise. So did Hollywood. By 1933, legions of moviegoers watched King Kong scale the building in a star-crossed attempt to elope with Fay Wray. The building has also been a romantic backdrop in films starring Cary Grant, Deborah Kerr, Tom Hanks, Meg Ryan, Warren Beatty, and Annette Bening, who all appeared without apes.

It was also cast in another starring role. Although it's no longer the world's tallest building, it's now the tallest in New York. It's been that way since September 11, 2001.

DO IT YOURSELF

Visiting the Empire State Building doesn't require much preparation. You go in, get in an elevator, go up and that's it. The only real planning required is when to go. Holiday weekends—Thanksgiving especially—generate crowds that can lead to two-hour lines.

Once you've cleared security, invest in an audio tour. Playing a NYC cabbie, the narrator shares information that is both thorough and thoroughly entertaining as he mixes a general overview of the city's geography and history with detailed anecdotes. From the 86th floor, you can conduct an aerial reconnaissance that takes in parts of New Jersey, Central Park, Staten Island, the Bronx, Queens, and Brooklyn. Soon you'll start to sense that with more then eight million people below, it really does take a building as big as this to tell a story as big as New York's.

The Observation Deck is open from 8 a.m. until 2 a.m. daily. The last elevator goes up at 1:15 a.m.

Time your visit for late afternoon and you'll have the best of both worlds, starting with sunlit views and ending with night skies. On a clear day, visibility can range as far as 80 miles and it can seem as if you're viewing the world on a life-sized movie screen. Starting on the south perimeter, you're shown a view of Little Italy, Chinatown, the Lower East Side, the Financial District, and iconic structures like the 22-story 1903 Flatiron Building, considered one of the world's first skyscrapers. From this angle, you would once have seen the World Trade Center, three miles away.

For an additional $15, you can visit the observation deck on the 102nd floor. The area was designed as the debarkation platform for the fleet of dirigibles that was planned to transport guests here.

In addition to the beauty found in the city below, there is also beauty in the scene around you on the Observation Deck, as people of varying cultures speaking dozens of languages enjoy the shared experience. You'll witness a natural camaraderie as language barriers are overcome by smiles and gestures that indicate someone wants a photo taken or there's something special to see in the distance.

As the sun sets you'll notice a new lighting effect. Bridges reveal looping strands, bulbs peek through the treetops in Central Park, and the taillights from a string of yellow cabs add a trail of crimson to the Big Apple's color wheel. To the northeast the crown of the magnificent Chrysler Building is illuminated. On a perfect night, the moon clears the horizon, hanging peacefully in space.

Eventually, as daylight fades away and the novelty of the views subside, take a moment to reflect: Beneath you is the new *caput mundi*—the Capital of the World.

CONTACTS

Empire State Building   www.esbnyc.com
350 Fifth Avenue   www.skyscraper.org

For Lodging and Dining, see pp. 290–291

12. THANKSGIVING DAY PARADE
New York, New York

It takes quite a bit to create a parade that's as big and bold as America. For that, you need a national holiday, 8,000 volunteers, well over 500 cops, two and a half miles of New York City streets, a route bordered by three million fans, and a lot of helium. That's what Macy's began giving the nation in 1924. Now it's much more than a parade. It's tradition.

AMERICA ON PARADE

Most of the year we'd be content to line the sidewalks for parades that showcase babies or dachshunds or clowns, but on Thanksgiving we won't settle for anything less than the most magnificent procession on earth—and that's where Macy's comes in.

In 1924, some store employees decided to celebrate Thanksgiving Day by re-creating the type of parade they recalled from the Old Country. A procession of marchers, floats, bands, and animals stepped off from West 145th Street in Harlem and marched past a quarter-million people as it shuffled about five miles to Macy's main store at 34th Street and Herald Square. Over the years, the starting point shortened the parade route, first by moving south to West 110th Street and then, in 1945, by moving even farther south to West 77th Street, which is where it still starts today.

In 1927, Macy's followed the lead of Hudson's department store in Detroit and introduced what has since become the trademark of the parade: gargantuan inflated balloons. In 1928, Macy's began inflating those balloons with helium and introduced another spin that would never fly today with the FAA or insurance actuaries. At the conclusion of the parade, they released the balloons, which, eventually, reached higher altitudes and exploded. The following year, safety valves helped prevent that calamity. After the balloons deflated and fell to Earth, the lucky finders would simply mail the behemoth balloon back to Macy's to receive a gift. With luck, it was a new roof.

As the parade grew, so did the crowds. More than a million people were there to see an inflated Mickey Mouse join Felix the Cat in 1934, and people who couldn't make it to Manhattan tuned in as the parade was broadcast on the radio. During World War II, there were better uses for rubber and helium, so the parade passed Macy's by until 1945. Since then it has continued, uninterrupted, to this day.

Why does Macy's use a red star for a logo? When Rowland Hussey Macy was a teenager working on a whaling ship, he had a red star tattooed on his hand.

Certainly the biggest event that threaded the parade into the American fabric came with the release of *Miracle on 34th Street,* which used Macy's and its parade as a backdrop. Popular when it was released as a romantic comedy in the summer of 1947, it later became a television holiday standard.

In the decades since, fans of the parade have increased to an estimated three million on the streets and more than 40 million television viewers tuned to sponsoring network NBC since 1955.

DO IT YOURSELF

Unless your new high-def television is three miles wide and 200 feet tall, watching the Macy parade on television merely hints at the experience of actually being there. You'll want to get an early start, as early as the night before. Why? Because from 77th to 81st streets between Central Park West and Columbus Avenue, machines are already pushing helium into the balloons.

There to witness this are fans who have made the inflation nearly as popular as the parade itself. On Thanksgiving eve, families walk by the balloons, mingle on the sidewalks, drop into corner cafés, and enjoy the pleasure of greeting the holiday season.

Long before the parade steps off at 9 a.m. the next morning, the wide sidewalks and side streets are packed with families bundled up against the cold. Along the parade route—Central Park West from 77th Street to Columbus Circle, then south all the way down to Macy's at 34th Street, and then west to finish at 7th Avenue—are people who have brought ladders or improvised stands to gain some elevation. Everyone is admirably patient while awaiting the parade, but that mood shifts into anticipation when the first chirp of sirens is heard. When you see balloons gliding silently down Broadway, it actually seems surreal, since few things aside from national monuments and the nation's deficit are this huge.

Then there's the rest of the parade. There are celebrities you know and marching bands you've never seen. Only a handful of the 300 bands that apply make it, so you can expect that the performances of the baton twirlers, drum major, flag corps, and the brass, woodwind, and percussion sections are the sharpest; their uniforms the cleanest; and their notes the most precise.

> Although there may be competitors, the *Guinness Book of World Records* claims Macy's Herald Square is the largest department store in the world, with one million square feet of selling space.

Overall, everything moves in slow motion, but it has to. The larger balloons are nearly 70 feet tall, 40 feet wide, and 65 feet long and the balloon handlers beneath them, who carefully spool and unravel their lines as necessary, watch the balloon pilot like violinists watching the conductor. Between bands and balloons and floats are novelty acts like tap dancing Christmas trees, clown troupes, and precision motorcycle drill teams. After a good 90 minutes, you think you've seen enough…but you haven't. The parade keeps coming with more floats and bands and balloons and clowns and elves.

Even though merchants have been pushing you to believe that the holiday season begins in August, you've held firm. You know better. When you look down Broadway and see Santa Claus at the tail end of this most amazing parade, you know that the real holiday season won't begin until he reaches his winter home, right there at 34th Street and Herald Square.

CONTACTS

Macy's Parade Information
(212) 494-4495

www.macys.com
www.nycvisit.com

For Lodging and Dining, see pp. 290–291

13. TIMES SQUARE NEW YEAR'S EVE
New York, New York

Of the thousands of New Year's Eve parties happening across America, there's one that nearly everyone is watching. It's also the one nearly everyone seems to be attending.

It's New Year's Eve in New York's Times Square. As the year comes to a close, a million people there and a few billion more at home believe that what they are witnessing marks the official beginning of the new year.

You know, they're probably right.

RIGHT PLACE, RIGHT TIMES

There's a reason you never tune in to watch the New Year's Eve celebration from Longacre Square.

Adolph Ochs.

The owner of the *New York Times* began the whole kerfuffle as a marketing ploy for the newspaper to promote the grand opening of its new headquarters and persuade the city to change the name of the area in front of its building from Longacre Square to Times Square.

The illuminated ball that had marked every celebration since 1908 was muted in 1942 and 1943 because of WWII "dimout" rules. Even the celebration was more subdued: Crowds observed a minute of silence at midnight, broken by chimes ringing from sound trucks parked at the base of the Times Tower.

Located by the intersection of Seventh Avenue, Broadway, and 42nd Street, the building was the focal point of the area and Ochs was determined to throw a party that would throw a spotlight on the *Times*. Previously, many people had attended a more traditional celebration at Trinity Church in Lower Manhattan, but at the end of 1903 the *Times*'s all-day festival was followed by an all-night party that culminated at midnight with an estimated 200,000 revelers watching a fantastic fireworks show that, not coincidentally, made the morning papers.

"From base to dome the giant structure was alight," the *New York Times* gushed about the *New York Times*'s event. "A torch to usher in the newborn year!"

When the city banned the fireworks display a few years later, Ochs masterminded a new visual to usher in 1908: a 700-pound wood and iron ball lowered from the paper's flagpole exactly at midnight. By 1914, the

Times—a victim of its own success—had moved out of Times Square to a larger headquarters, but the celebration stayed put. They even kept it on the same day.

Today, the event has become the world's indicator of the arrival of the new year, with an estimated billion people watching on television as bands play, celebrities say hello, and the New Year's Eve Ball descends from the flagpole atop One Times Square.

DO IT YOURSELF

If you've never attended a major event in New York City, be prepared. To beat the New Year's Eve street closures and crowds, you'll need to get there early. Like November 8.

Actually, arriving by mid-afternoon should guarantee a good spot. You'll enter what the police refer to as a "pen" which, after it is filled, becomes off-limits to prevent overcrowding.

If you're there—and by "there" I mean Broadway from 43rd Street to 50th Street or Seventh Avenue as far north as 59th Street—by 6 p.m., you'll be able to see the New Year's Eve ball raised to the top of the 77-foot flagpole at One Times Square. The only thing that may interfere with your seeing it drop again six hours later is that there are no public restrooms in Times Square. There are no food vendors, either, although there are hundreds of restaurants. Should you leave in search of food or comfort, chances are you won't be able to reclaim your spot.

Hosting a party for a million or more people takes a lot of preparation, so the Times Square Alliance is always looking for your help with mailings, putting together gift bags, general office support, and much more. For more information write to *volunteers@ timessquarealliance.org*.

Another physical factor is the cold. Temperatures on December 31 usually dip below freezing, so experienced celebrants arrive wearing warm gloves and caps and layers of clothing topped by wind- and water-resistant jackets. Some folks combat the cold by grabbing spots inside nearby restaurants or by reserving rooms at one of the hotels that overlooks Times Square. Others keep warm by staying home and watching it on TV.

After several hours, your endurance is rewarded as midnight approaches. You may have anticipated a lot of things in your life, but now you have the warm glow of anticipation knowing that a million people around you are all waiting for same thing...but you'll have to wait to find a restroom, because it's nearly time for the famous Waterford crystal ball to begin its 60-second descent.

As the clock ticks off the last ten seconds to midnight, all the Whos in Whoville will join you in shouting out the final countdown…

Happy New Year!

CONTACTS

Times Square Alliance
(212) 768-1560
www.timessquarenyc.org

New York Convention
and Visitors Bureau
801 7th Avenue
(212) 484-1222
www.nycvisit.com

For Lodging and Dining, see pp. 290–291

14. STATUE OF LIBERTY
New York, New York

So exactly which 101 reflections of America say it best? No one, including myself, will ever get that right, but in the process of trying to figure it out, I've come to believe one burns especially bright: the Statue of Liberty.

THE FRENCH CONNECTION

Today when someone turns 100, he or she is usually the recipient of a big cake, a story in the local newspaper, and a greeting from Willard Scott. When the 100th birthday of the United States of America was approaching, in the 1860s, some French intellectuals, artists, and politicians held a meeting and decided that America's birthday deserved a gift that would symbolize the friendship between the two countries and their shared love of liberty. The gift would be a magnificent statue.

At that meeting was a young French sculptor, Frédéric Auguste Bartholdi, who then traveled to America for inspiration and to seek a place where the gift could be displayed. He found it on Bedloe's Island in New York Harbor. The statue he would create was in some ways reminiscent of one he had designed a few years earlier for the Egyptian Khedive, Ismail the Magnificent, though "Egypt Bringing Light to Asia" was never commissioned.

It had been agreed that American citizens would pay for the pedestal while French citizens would pay for the statue—and neither side would accept government funds. By 1876 the Union Franco-Americaine (Franco-American Union) had raised enough money on the French side through donations to finish the right forearm, hand, and torch, which were shipped to America in time for the Philadelphia Centennial Exposition that year. By 1880, the sale of small terra-cotta souvenir statues signed by Bartholdi himself and a special lottery helped secure financing for the rest of the statue.

In America, it was a different story. Who wanted to pay for a stupid pedestal? By the end of 1876, not a cent had been collected, so in 1877 a group of prominent New Yorkers created a committee dedicated to raising $125,000 for the cause. It was tough going. Most citizens thought the rich should pay for it all and attempts by the city and state to kick in money died. That's when Hungarian immigrant and newspaper publisher Joseph Pulitzer stepped in. He began running articles in his newspaper that chided his rich peers for not opening their wallets—but he also thumped the middle class for expecting the rich to finance the project alone. After Pulitzer reprimanded the public, donations started coming in, and within seven months *The World* announced that more than 120,000 contributors—80 percent of whom had donated less than a dollar—had raised more than $100,000. Nine months later, in 1886, the pedestal was in place within the star-shaped border of Fort Wood.

Where is the Statue of Liberty? For years a battle brewed between New York and New Jersey, each of which claimed ownership. Its territorial jurisdiction is in New York, although the island and statue are owned by the federal government.

Meanwhile, the French had disassembled the completed statue into more than 300 numbered pieces and transported them to America via the French frigate *Isére*, which arrived in June 1885. The statue was reassembled piece by piece and dedicated on October 28, 1886.

It was the best birthday present ever.

DO IT YOURSELF

At Battery Park on the southern tip of Manhattan is the Castle Clinton National Monument. This is where you'll stand in line for one of roughly 1,500 passes issued for the Statue of Liberty each day; only ticket holders are admitted inside the statue's pedestal.

En route to Liberty Island, captains give the island wide berth so the vessel's arc continually frames the Statue of Liberty in increasingly dramatic points of view. The sight of this national icon, the shifting of the boat in the waves, and the mix of mother tongues spoken by passengers may put you aboard a ship arriving in New York Harbor in 1900.

A small gift shop, museum, cafeteria, and ranger's headquarters are near the landing, but with the statue right in front of you you'll probably bypass all of these and follow the promenade that puts you directly in front of Lady Liberty.

The Statue of Liberty is a big-boned gal: From the base of the pedestal to the tip of the torch the statue is 305 feet, 6 inches. From her feet to the top of her head, she's 111 feet, 6 inches. Her face is more than 8 feet tall. She has a 35-foot waistline and weighs in at a dainty 450,000 pounds.

I had known this face my entire life but had never seen it up close, and it was more than a little breathtaking. By the time I backtracked to join up with a ranger-led tour, I was even more anxious to hear more about the history of the statue, its symbolism, poet Emma Lazurus, publisher Joseph Pulitzer, and the financial and aesthetic challenges that the backers faced.

Inside the museum housed within the pedestal, visitors can see a full-scale copy of the statue's face, Bartholdi's original torch (replaced by a gold-coated torch in the mid-1980s), and a portion of the statue's foot in several stages of construction. A diagram revealing the statue's interior framework looks suspiciously like its designer's future masterpiece, the Eiffel Tower. Because the statue is in the public domain, its image has been reproduced on sheet music, posters, T-shirts, glasses, and nearly anything else with a surface. Many such items are displayed in the museum.

Where the displays end a long staircase leads to the top of the pedestal. There, you can look up through the glass ceiling and see the framework or, better yet, step outside and walk around the parapet for a 360-degree view of the shores of New Jersey and lower Manhattan. To the south is the Verrazano Narrows, the inlet from which immigrants, returning troops, and other shipboard travelers caught their first glimpse of the statue.

The greenish tint is the result of the weathering of the copper that coats the statue.

Later I read about some of the families who were greeted by the Statue of Liberty. I learned that Nicola and Antonietta Iacocca had come from Italy, hoping their children would have a better shot. Their son, Lee, certainly did. He grew up to head Chrysler. There was Josef Korbel, who sailed past the statue and wondered how his daughter would fare in this new country. It turns out that little Madeleine would grow up to become Secretary of State Albright.

Our flag and our Constitution mean something to all Americans, but the Statue of Liberty is different. She *transcends* America. She's a symbol of freedom all around the world.

FOOTNOTE: ELLIS ISLAND

Following your visit to the Statue of Liberty, set sail for Ellis Island, the main arrival center for millions of European immigrants from 1892 to 1954. This is where America welcomed new citizens, first mainly from northern and western Europe (including Germans, Scots, Irish, and British) before the flow switched to central and eastern Europe (Slavs, Jews, Poles, Finns, Greeks, Lithuanians, Ukrainians, and Italians, among others). In total, nearly 12 million immigrants sailed past the Statue of Liberty, checked in here, and were registered as new residents. Ellis Island marked the conclusion of what had likely been a long and arduous journey. At this historical site, you can see the stories of these immigrants, their journeys, their reception by America, and their contributions to their new home. Ellis Island is a national treasure. Don't miss it.

CONTACTS

Statue of Liberty
(212) 363-3200
www.nps.gov/stli

**Statue of Liberty/
Ellis Island Cruises**
(877) 523-9849
www.statuecruises.com

Castle Clinton National Monument
(212) 344-7220
www.nps.gov/cacl

Ellis Island
(212) 363-3200
www.nps.gov/elis

www.statueofliberty.org

For Lodging and Dining, see pp. 290–291

MID-ATLANTIC

Delaware, Maryland, New Jersey, Pennsylvania, Virginia, Washington, D.C., West Virginia

In the American family of states, the Mid-Atlantic region is like the middle child. There's nothing extraordinarily dramatic about it, at least not in a Rocky Mountain sense, but it more than compensates with a wealth of history. Come here and see cities and towns and fields where our nation was born in the American Revolution and nearly died during the Civil War.

Explore the region's rolling hills and coastal plains and drop in on All-American events like the Little League World Series. Discover places where our dynamic drive toward the future is tempered by an awareness and preservation of our past—in Colonial Williamsburg, Amish Country, and the memorials at Gettysburg and Arlington National Cemetery, where those who gave their last full measure of devotion are honored.

The Mid-Atlantic is the Shenandoah Valley. It is Valley Forge, the Delaware River, it is Washington, D.C. It is America.

15. HERSHEY
Pennsylvania

Milton Hershey, by all accounts, was a very sweet man. The character trait seems fitting considering that his breakthroughs as a chocolatier helped finance the creation of an entire candy community in south-central Pennsylvania.

THE CANDY MAN

The late 1800s were an excellent time to be an entrepreneur. Electric lights began to overshadow candles, telephones took over for telegraphs, and horses yielded to automobiles. As an entrepreneur, Milton Hershey worked in a field far more important than any of these. Hershey was a candymaker.

The only surviving child of Henry and Fanny Hershey, he attended seven schools before leaving with the equivalent of a fourth grade education. When he was 14, he was fired from an apprenticeship with a printer but hooked up with a Lancaster confectioner for a four-year apprenticeship. At 18 he took his training to Philadelphia to make his fortune but, after six years, his business failed. Strike one. Milton next worked for candymakers in Denver, Chicago, and New Orleans before starting his own business in New York. Three years later, he was bankrupt. Before risking strike three, Milton returned to Lancaster, where he brushed off his failures and got ready to try again.

In 1886, the 29-year-old convinced his aunt Mattie Snavely that he knew he could be a success and all he needed was a little favor. The favor required her to mortgage her farm and give him the money to open a caramel company.

> To avoid the uniformity of other factory towns, Milton Hershey made sure homes were built in a variety of styles and employed a landscaper to help decorate the yards.

It turns out that Aunt Mattie was as shrewd an investor as her nephew was a savvy inventor. Aware that milk chocolate was a European delicacy, Hershey added milk to his caramels and turned his Lancaster Caramel Company into an outstanding success. In 1900, the 43-year-old Hershey sold out for $1 million—but he wasn't done yet. Convinced he could surpass caramel's success by creating a new recipe for milk chocolate, Hershey needed a ready supply of fresh milk, an active labor force, and close proximity to railroads. With proceeds from his caramel company, he purchased 40,000 acres about 45 minutes north of Lancaster near the rural hamlet of Derry Church.

By 1900, the five-cent milk chocolate Hershey bar was on the shelves. By 1907, Hershey Chocolates was producing conical-shaped treats called Kisses, and by 1908 Americans were enjoying Hershey bars with almonds.

Just as he had revolutionized the chocolate industry, Hershey, raised a Mennonite, approached his corporate responsibility with an equally innovative philosophy: He believed that a nice living environment created better, more dedicated, and more productive employees. He invested much of his company's profits into a model town he created to benefit and house his workers. He added public transportation and a library, a community building, and a stadium where needy youth could play.

There are a lot of different theories why the chocolate Kiss is named a Kiss. The most common explanation is that the name comes from the smooching sound the chocolate makes as it's distributed onto the machine belt during the manufacturing process.

With no children of their own, Milton and his wife, Kitty Hershey, in 1909 endowed the new Hershey Industrial School for orphan boys with $60 million. Graduates would learn a trade and leave with $100. Today, with the endowment approaching $8 billion, graduates—including girls—still receive $100, plus a suit, a computer, and an opportunity to receive a scholarship to a college or trade school.

During the Great Depression, Milton initiated construction projects that would keep his workers employed. Hershey's largesse continued in World War II, when GIs were given more than three billion chocolate Ration D and Tropical bars that became a goodwill greeting around the world.

Hershey, an American original, passed away at the age of 88 in 1945. Chocolate bars are only part of his legacy.

DO IT YOURSELF

I was more than a little perplexed and disappointed when I learned Hershey doesn't offer a tour of its chocolate factory. Since the factory tour ended years ago, the company added a complex called Hershey's Chocolate World, which has gift shops, a few rides, and a 3-D movie that deals with chocolate. This may entertain the kids for a bit, but it's also fitting to learn more about the man who made all of this possible. That's done at the new interactive Hershey Story museum that opened in January 2009, which tells the rags to riches story of Milton's life and legacy.

Then there's the town itself; the town that Milton Hershey built. On the trolley tour that departs from Chocolate World, you'll roll around the central district and see the iconic Hershey Kiss lampposts and then head into cute as a button residential neighborhoods.

The town's biggest draw is Hersheypark, which offers nearly a dozen roller coasters, water rides, a miniature train, Ferris wheels, stage shows, and kiddie rides. A short drive away is Hershey Gardens, which was created by Milton in memory of his wife, Kitty, who died of pneumonia in 1915 at the age of 42. The garden opened in 1937 and covers 23 acres dappled with 275 varieties of roses, a children's garden, and a butterfly arboretum. Near the garden entrance is a wonderful promontory that overlooks Hersheypark.

The 107 Kiss-shaped lampposts alternate between wrapped and unwrapped, and were designed in 1962 when Hershey's CEO was Samuel Hinkel—earning them the nickname "Hinkel's twinkles."

It's especially charming as night falls and the lights sparkle below. In the quiet evening you see just a fraction of Milton Hershey's legacy. He was a man who might have left the world as a two-time failure...if he hadn't tried a third time.

CONTACTS

Hershey Entertainment and Resorts
(800) HERSHEY (437-7439)
www.hersheypa.com

www.hersheygardens.org
www.hersheys.com
www.hersheypark.com
www.hersheystory.org

For Lodging and Dining, see pp. 291–292

16. AMISH COUNTRY
Lancaster County, Pennsylvania

Few of us mind letting technology enhance our lives. We no longer churn butter; we buy it. We don't hang wash on the line; machines dry it. The Amish do it differently. If a new i-product sells on eBay hours after it's released, the Amish don't care. They're indifferent to "progress" and have been for centuries. The Amish possess a force more powerful than the pressures of the outside world: their inner faith.

THE AMISH, PLAIN AND SIMPLE

Like their better-known counterparts aboard the *Mayflower*, the Amish also sought religious freedom in America. These Christian Anabaptists left Germany during the late 1600s and early 1700s, settling first near Lancaster and then elsewhere in Pennsylvania. Over time, the Lancaster area became known as Pennsylvania Dutch Country—despite the fact that no Amish here, or anywhere, are of Dutch descent. One guess is that somewhere along the way, the word Deutsch—German—was mistranslated as Dutch.

The settler's descendants have branched out into different regions (such as Ohio and Indiana) as well as denominations, including the Mennonites and the Brethren. Today it is the Old Order Amish who most uphold the traditions of their predecessors. Members forsake cars in favor of horse-drawn buggies; they use candles and lanterns instead of electric light; and their schools provide Amish children with an education only up to the eighth grade.

Their appearance reflects their austere lifestyle. Amish woman seldom cut their hair, which is generally kept cloaked by a prayer shawl or bonnet. The men's dark suits are modest, with straight-cut coats and lapels. They wear no belts or ties, but use suspenders. Colorful patterns are shelved in favor of solid blue, black, or white shirts. Hats are broad-brimmed black or straw. It may all look like a costume to outsiders (usually referred to as the "English") but Amish apparel is really a visible representation of their faith.

> The Amish tradition of *Rumspringa* allows adolescent men free rein to leave the church and community. During their sabbatical, they'll face many temptations, but should they submit, they face shunning from their community. Once shunned, they become outcasts, and cannot return to the community—or the church.

For a culture so deeply rooted in religion, it seems odd there are so few churches in the community. Realize though that in Amish society churches don't have ostentatious steeples, Gothic arches, or televised sermons sold on DVD. Like their lifestyle, church is a simple affair. Services, which are only open to members and last about three hours, are held every other Sunday in church families' homes.

DO IT YOURSELF

One of my favorite Amish communities lies about ten miles east of Lancaster, Pennsylvania. It's the small village of Intercourse and I love it here because the name provides enough material for my own comedy special, and also because the Amish and English here co-exist.

Outside the towns, the horizon is largely uncluttered by telephone poles and utility towers, and farms operate without the use of combines and tractors. Amish country suggests an America that existed in the 1800s, but remains here today. The Amish themselves are as natural and photogenic as the setting. But don't take that picture. The bottom line is that the Amish do not want to be the subject of curiosity.

Amish country boasts an abundance of food I've not seen anywhere else. In Lancaster County there are standout restaurants like the Bird-In-Hand Family Restaurant, Stoltzfus Farm Restaurant, Miller's Smorgasbord, and the awe-inspiring Plain & Fancy Farm, where platters are stacked with chicken, ham, pork, apple butter, sweet potatoes, corn, roast beef, mashed potatoes, bow-tie noodles, homemade breads, soups, sauerkraut, lima beans, roast turkey, sausage, applesauce, baked apples, fish, sautéed mushrooms, baked cabbage, chicken pot pie, cakes, ice cream, and cherry crumb, apple crumb, and fresh shoo-fly pie.

After waddling back to town, surrender to the local pace. A hectic schedule may be as simple as strolling over to visit the shops at the Kitchen Kettle Village or dropping in at the circa 1909 W. L. Zimmerman market. Another diversion is exploring some of the most beautiful roads in America, all laced within a rectangle created by Highways 340 and 23 on the south and north, and Springfield and Mount Sidney roads on the east and west. On these soft and slow country roads you are led back in time to where tobacco cures in the fresh air, where Amish children stare in wonder at passing cars, and where you may spy the communal phone families share only when absolutely necessary.

Lancaster's Central Market is America's oldest continuously operating farmer's market. English, Amish, and Mennonite families have been coming here since 1730 to sell farm-fresh produce and handmade crafts.

Awed by the roads during the day, I returned at night and rode in darkness so deep that a two-story farmhouse surprised me when it appeared just a few yards away. I parked my motorcycle and let my eyes adjust until, standing quietly in the middle of the road, I could survey the hills, barns, and pristine countryside.

It was a calming experience that followed me into the next morning. Rising early on Sunday, I again rode out into the country, where the Amish were on their way to worship, either on foot or riding buggies. I again parked the bike and watched them from a distance. I saw vapor rising from a dew-coated covered bridge and a spider spinning its web as I listened to the steady rhythm of hooves on the pavement.

For me it was not a typical Sunday. Curiosity had taken me to Lancaster County. Lancaster County was taking me back.

CONTACTS

Lancaster County Conference
and Visitors Bureau
(717) 299-8901
(800) 723-8824
www.padutchcountry.com

Mennonite Information Center
(717) 299-0954

Amish-Mennonite Information Center
(717) 768-0807

www.padutchcountry.com
www.amish.net
www.amish-heartland.com

For Lodging and Dining, see pp. 292—293

17. LITTLE LEAGUE WORLD SERIES
Williamsport, Pennsylvania

The summer sight of kids on the field, fans in the stands, and families on blankets spread out beyond the outfield is pure Americana. Sure, every community in America has a Little League team, but the Little League World Series is where the best of the best kids from across the nation and around the world play baseball because—well, just because they love to play baseball. Go to Williamsport in August and you can watch it live.

PLAY BALL!

Baseball had been around for nearly a century before Little League showed up. Before that, kids used streets and sandlots instead of real fields and stadiums, fielding hits caught in worn gloves and throwing balls patched together with tape. Then in 1938 a 28-year-old lumberyard clerk named Carl Stotz had an idea. His two nephews loved to play ball, so with help from them and some other kids around Williamsport, he created rules, equipment, and a playing field that would fit their skills and size. The name of the organization, Little League, was a natural, and so was Stotz's goal: to teach the boys of Williamsport sportsmanship, fair play, and teamwork.

The following year, Stotz's wife, Grayce, recruited friends George and Annabelle Bebble, and Bert and Eloise Bebble, to become managers for three charter teams sponsored by three local businesses: Lycoming Dairy, Lundy Lumber, and Jumbo Pretzel. The first game was held on June 6, 1939, with

Lundy Lumber defeating Lycoming Dairy 23-8, but Dairy came back at the end of the season to win the series 3-2.

By 1946 there were 12 leagues in Pennsylvania, and the following year it crossed state lines with the formation of a team in Hammonton, New Jersey. That same year, the Maynard Midgets won the first National Little League Tournament (later renamed the Little League World Series) by defeating the Lock Haven All-Stars, 16-7.

> **One thing that surprises first-timers is that there are no scalpers on the streets, and no tickets being sold online. Every game is absolutely free.**

Soon national corporations became interested in sponsoring teams, and after a 1948 *Saturday Evening Post* article appeared, so did newsreel footage of the Little League teams. Within days Stotz was fielding calls from would-be participants across America. In 1950, the first international Little League team was formed in Panama, and today nearly 200,000 teams play in all 50 states and more than 80 countries.

Each August the best of them arrive in Williamsport.

DO IT YOURSELF

I'm not sure what happens in Williamsport when it's not August, but I'm sure whatever happens is nice. This is a typical American town with a cute downtown, some independent restaurants, and a pleasant location in the Susquehanna Valley of central Pennsylvania.

With 16 teams in contention (8 from the United States and 8 international teams), the ten-day competition takes place at the Howard J. Lamade Stadium and the adjacent Little League Volunteer Stadium. The first five days are pool play, and the second five are single elimination rounds. For

> **The Little League Pledge:**
> **I trust in God**
> **I love my country**
> **And will respect its laws**
> **I will play fair**
> **And strive to win**
> **But win or lose**
> **I will always do my best**

parents and players, the first five days are thrilling enough, but most fans arrive on the days leading up to Championship Weekend.

From the stands I watched several semi-final games and it was just like watching Major League baseball… but friendlier. When a player on either team got a hit, stole a base, or dinged a homer that cleared the fence at 225 feet, everyone cheered and applauded. If any kid got tagged out, popped out, or whiffed at three pitches in a row, everyone sighed…and applauded.

During the tournament, this unexpected sense of, well, *decency,* was noticeable throughout the game and around the entire town. At restaurants and on sidewalks, people would talk about games they had seen and compliment players from both teams. One game no one would forget is Saturday afternoon's Challenger Game—and you must see this. There are 28,000 kids in Little League's Challenger Division, and a handful were there: kids on crutches, kids in wheelchairs, kids who need assistance to reach first base. All are first helped to home plate, where a buddy helped them hit the ball off a tee. After the game, the teams lined up on the baseline and were awarded medals by the president of Little League International. Their faces swelled with pride, and in the stands fans and families wiped away tears.

That same afternoon the International Championship was played. As the sun went down and the stadium lights came up, the mood and atmosphere reminded me of a county fair. About 45,000 fans laid out blankets on the berm past the outfield while, in the stands, the parents of kids on competing teams created cheering sections, their enthusiasm spilling over to the strangers beside them.

After the teams recited the Little League Pledge, a dignitary threw out the first pitch, and six innings of quality baseball began. While the players were less than half the size of the pros, their determination and emotion were larger than life.

When the bases were loaded, when there was a full count, when there was a close play at home plate, you could tell everyone was holding their collective breath. When it came down to a final out, you knew that one team would soon be carrying the pennant around the bases to tell the world they were the champions, and one team would be in the dugout wondering why they had come this far to lose.

When the Little League Baseball World Series was first shown on *ABC's Wide World of Sports* in 1963, only the championship game was televised. Today, ESPN broadcasts every single game in the tournament.

They weren't old enough to realize they really hadn't.

Note: The following day, the United States Championship team would face off against the champion International Team to determine which would return home with the title World Champions. On that day you could witness all of the emotions of Saturday's games…magnified.

CONTACTS

Little League International
(570) 326-1921
www.littleleague.org

For Lodging and Dining, see p. 293

18. GETTYSBURG
Pennsylvania

I'll never know whether the soldiers at Gettysburg had any idea that their individual efforts—fighting for a hill, killing someone to capture a few yards, firing a cannonball into dozens of men—would help this nation survive its darkest days. But the nation would be saved because of what happened there.

WAR AND WORDS

Like boxers circling each other in the ring, 97,000 Union soldiers under the command of George G. Meade and 75,000 Confederate soldiers under Robert E. Lee had feinted and jabbed at one another throughout the spring of 1863 through skirmishers who would fight and retreat. That all started to change on June 30, 1863.

Legend has it that a band of Confederate soldiers searching for shoes near Gettysburg was spied by an advance team of Union scouts. Alerted to each other's presence, the two armies spread out over 25 square miles to engage in a three-day battle. It was a horrendous display of savagery that produced an astonishing 51,000 deaths and injuries. Lee's army retreated, pursued by the victorious Union Army.

Rangers at the Museum and Visitors Center offer free tours, but can also arrange in-depth battlefield tours. Arrange in advance by calling 877-874-2478 or visiting www.gettysburg foundation.org.

Over the summer, corpses rotted in the searing heat and were plucked clean by looters and animals. That's when the United States government determined that their sacrifice warranted the creation of a permanent resting place on part of the battlefield. Looters were pressed into service to scour the field for bodies while gravediggers emptied the earth to create the Soldiers' National Cemetery.

In town, 32-year-old local attorney David Wills was tasked with organizing a dedication ceremony, scheduled for November 19, 1863. Having already lined up Edward Everett, the leading orator of his day, Wills asked President Abraham Lincoln to come to Gettysburg to make a few "appropriate remarks." Lincoln accepted.

In a guest room at Wills's home, he polished his address. The following day, he sat patiently as Everett delivered a two-hour, 13,000-word speech. When Everett was done, Lincoln waited through a musical interlude and then stood to deliver his remarks.

Some in attendance had no idea he had even addressed the crowd, because just two minutes later the speech was back in his pocket and Lincoln was seated. Fortunately for the nation, Lincoln made every word count as he spoke of America's past, its current struggle, and his hopes for its experiment with democracy.

THE EXPERIENCE

For the two million tourists who visit each year, the most important site is the cemetery itself, but it's something you may want to see only after touring the broader area with a guide—and they are legion. An inexpensive choice is Gettysburg Battlefield

Tours to the Eisenhower National Historic Site depart from the new Museum and Visitors Center. The farm home of President Eisenhower remains as it was when the President lived there. Visit *www.nps.gov/eise*.

Tours, which takes visitors past Pickett's Charge, Little Round Top, the Peach Orchard, and other sites aboard a double-decker bus. You can also purchase an audio tour for a self-guided visit or hire a licensed guide or historian who will ride along in your car for a private, personalized tour.

On any tour you'll likely reach Little Round Top, which overlooks a sunken glade known as the Valley of Death, in memory of the Southern soldiers picked off by Northern troops who held the high ground. Nearby, Devil's Den is a mass of boulders that offered protection to Confederate riflemen. At the infamous Wheatfield, roughly 4,600 Union and Confederate soldiers were killed, wounded, or captured during just four hours of bloody charges and countercharges.

Back at the new $110 million Gettysburg Museum and Visitor Center, rangers and exhibits pick up where the tour guides leave off. After that you may want to spend some time alone at the cemetery before driving back to the town square and its pleasant collection of shops, pubs, taverns, restaurants, and bookstores.

Don't miss the David Wills House, the home where Lincoln stayed on November 18, 1863. Restored in 2008, the museum includes six galleries and the bedroom where Lincoln finished revising the Gettysburg Address.

The next morning I was up before sunrise and was soon back at the peak of Little Round Top. Standing beside the statue of Gouverneur Kemble Warren, the Union "hero of Little Round Top." I could now look across the Valley of Death uninterrupted by other bus passengers. I watched the day break and through the morning mist thought I could see soldiers engaged in their doomed assault on the hill.

After sunrise I rode out among the town's 1,328 monuments, searching for one in particular. Built of Maine granite and Alabama limestone, the Eternal Light Peace Memorial was paid for by aging soldiers of the North *and* South and dedicated in 1938 at the 75th anniversary of the battle. The inscription at its base reads: PEACE ETERNAL IN A NATION UNITED.

CONTACTS

Gettysburg National Military Park Visitor Center
1195 Baltimore Pike
(717) 334-1124
www.nps.gov/gett

Gettysburg Battlefield Tour Center
778 Baltimore Street
(717) 334-6296
www.gettysburgbattlefieldtours.com

Gettysburg Convention & Visitors Bureau
102 Carlisle Street
(717) 334-6274
(800) 337-5015
www.gettysburg.travel

www.gettysburg.com
www.gettysburgaddress.com

For Lodging and Dining, see pp. 293–294

19. GROUNDHOG DAY
Punxsutawney, Pennsylvania

Take an old German tradition and a frozen west Pennsylvania winter. Add a groundhog to the mix, and what do you have? The foundation of what has become the silliest holiday on the American calendar.

GET YOUR PHIL

Perhaps Clymer Freas, editor of the *Punxsutawney Spirit,* was just looking for an excuse to party when, in 1886, he began promoting his variation on a German holiday known as Candlemas. Tradition held that if the weather was clear on February 2—the midway point between the winter solstice and the spring equinox—there would six more weeks of winter. Then Freas added a *Marmota monax*—a groundhog—to the event for a frivolous and fun masterstroke. Indeed, it was more than enough to power the small-town celebration clear to 1993, when the hit movie *Groundhog*

Day confirmed Punxsutawney's celebration as the Queen Mother of all Groundhog Days.

It defies explanation, but each and every February 2 the nation's media head to Gobbler's Knob to monitor the prognostications of Punxsutawney Phil, the George Clooney of all groundhogs. With as many as 40,000 people expected for the celebration, members of the hallowed Inner Circle (Groundhog Day's de facto board of directors) work year-round before Punxsy Phil, heralded as the "seer of seers, the prognosticator of all prognosticators," makes his annual prediction.

At Gobbler's Knob between 3 a.m. and daybreak the temperature averages in the mid-20°s—but with the wind chill it will feel like a balmy 12°.

Charged with protecting and perpetuating the legend of Punxsutawney Phil, the 15 local residents take their mission seriously. Judging by their formal top hats and tails, maybe too seriously.

"Phil sits at the absolute pinnacle of the animal kingdom," explains Inner Circle member Mike Johnston with suspect sincerity. "You wouldn't see hand servants around the King of England dressed in jeans and T-shirts, would you? So it's only appropriate that we maintain the level of respect of which Phil is deserving."

I hate to admit it, but maybe he does deserve it. Phil has been the star of every Groundhog Day celebration since 1886. Aside from a sedentary lifestyle and a balanced diet of dog food and ice cream, what's the secret of his longevity? At a grand picnic banquet each September, Phil is given a sip of the "Elixir of Life," which extends his life by seven years. It may also enhance his powers of prediction. An unbelievable run of 100 percent accuracy through the years has made him the nation's most reliable weather forecaster, although some doubting statisticians calculate his accuracy at a shade less than 40 percent.

"Clearly," sniffs Johnston, "if you question the science, you miss the point. Phil is never wrong."

DO IT YOURSELF

It may involve a touch of sleep deprivation and near frostbite to experience Groundhog Day the way locals do, but it's worth it. At least once.

On February 1, try starting at the Chamber of Commerce on West Mahoning Street to peruse groundhog-centric postcards, posters, T-shirts, sweatshirts, key chains, and random souvenirs. Then walk down the street where 32 larger-than-life fiberglass "Phantastic Phil" statues guide you toward Barclay Square. There you can fill up on hot food and subs and pizza. Over at the Community Center on Jefferson Street, the basketball court has become a showroom for crafters selling groundhog puppets, caps, banners, candles, tea cozies, yard ornaments, and, my favorite, a groundhog particle accelerator.

The Chamber of Commerce lists a wealth of other activities, but as night falls you could just as well hang out with the locals at the Pantall Hotel's Coach Light Bar, or attend the Annual Groundhog Banquet, the highlight of Punxsutawney's social season. Though society mavens believe it's worthy of the Waldorf-Astoria, the event has been held for decades in the Punxsutawney High School cafeteria.

For about $25, you can join the tuxedoed men and bejeweled women as they arrive to the sounds of a 95-year-old playing sax while his father joins in on keyboards. As you dine, the Inner Circle's emcee introduces dignitaries, such as the newly crowned Groundhog King and Queen, and asks those in attendance to join in repeated choruses of the stirring chant "Groundhoooooog! Gro-ow-ownd-haaaawg!" After guests have fled the paparazzi, the film *Groundhog Day* is shown in the Community Center at midnight. That not only puts you in the spirit, but also helps pass an important 101 minutes inside a warm building. You may squeeze in a short nap before 3 a.m., when buses begin running the 1.5-mile route to Gobbler's Knob, Punxsutawney's own Mount Olympus.

Current Inner Circle president William Cooper observed that "there are a lot of important events in life—and Groundhog Day is not one of them."

It'll be dark and cold and at least four very long hours before Phil appears. Don't even count on staying close to the stage, since the call of nature or the warmth of a roaring bonfire will lead you away. Members of the Inner Circle do their best to keep the crowd active and stave off frostbite by firing T-shirts from an air cannon, playing music (the "Pennsylvania Polka" is a traditional favorite), and occasionally ceding the stage to men who sincerely believe their girlfriends are aching for a surprise engagement at Gobbler's Knob.

Finally, around 7:20 a.m., the entire Inner Circle begins its formal procession to the stage, where the president welcomes the "true believers." Minutes later he wields his magic acacia wood cane (the cane that makes him the only member conversant in Groundhog-ese) and raps on an old oak stump. After Phil is roused from his slumber within, two members of the Inner Circle present him to the cheering crowd before placing him upon on a red carpet atop the stump. The president leans over to focus on the consultation and the crowd grows quiet…

Depending upon how vigorously Phil wants to communicate, the consultation lasts anywhere from a few seconds to several minutes. The president nods and expresses his interest until he captures the gist of Phil's prediction. He then gestures to one of two scrolls held by the vice president and reads the long-awaited prognostication.

If the prediction is six more weeks of winter—as has been the case most of the time—count on a chorus of boos; if an early spring, a chorus of cheers. Either way, part of the crowd then shuffles to the road for the mile and a half walk back to town; another group scoots to the restrooms; and an impressive contingent of diehard true believers flock around Phil.

> Feel your life lacks a certain something? Consider membership in the Punxsutawney Groundhog Club. Visit *www.groundhog.org* for information.

No one questions the science. This morning, everyone gets the point.

CONTACTS

Punxsutawney Area
Chamber of Commerce
(800) 752-PHIL (7445)
www.punxsutawney.com

www.groundhog.org
www.punxsutawneyphil.com

For Lodging and Dining, see p. 294

For Lodging and Dining, see p. 294

20. VALLEY FORGE
Pennsylvania

In 1963, Martin Luther King, Jr., observed that "If a man has not discovered something that he will die for, he isn't fit to live." He could have been referring to the situation at Valley Forge in the winter of 1777 and 1778 when about 12,500 volunteers in the Continental Army proved that they were willing to die for something.

America's liberty.

WINTER CAMP

Although the British occupied Philadelphia and Washington's troops hadn't tasted a major victory in a year, in late 1777 the morale of the men under his command was up. Battles in Saratoga, New York, had led to the defeat of the British there and the finest American soldiers were now en route to Washington's winter encampment at Valley Forge. Located about 25 miles northwest of Philadelphia, it was close enough for Washington to attack Philadelphia if he wanted to but far enough away to retreat if the British had similar intentions.

In the museum, be sure to see Washington's own campaign tent and banner.

Within a week of arriving on December 19, men began digging trenches and constructing about a thousand cabins that could house a dozen men each. But, as winter progressed, the troops became disillusioned by the lack of food, clothing, shelter, and support from the local population.

As the temperature fell, many of the men succumbed to illness. Their uniforms were tattered, leaving them only rags and blankets to use as shoes and clothing. Even Washington was discouraged, writing to Congress that "unless some great and capital change suddenly takes place…this Army must inevitably…starve, dissolve, or disperse, in order to obtain subsistence in the best manner they can."

The transformation began in March. It wasn't just the arrival of spring, but the arrival of new people and provisions. A new quartermaster was able to procure wagonloads of food and clothing; bakers arrived and began serving the soldiers the daily pound of bread they had been promised; men were catching fish in the Schuylkill River; and even local farmers were ready to share their bounty with the soldiers.

The greatest change came with the arrival of a disciplined 47-year-old Prussian former captain, Friedrich Wilhelm Ludolf Gerhard Augustin Stuebe (aka Baron von Steuben). At Valley Forge he found undisciplined soldiers who gambled, fought, went AWOL, sold their equipment, couldn't march, and used their bayonets as meat skewers. Washington named him Acting Inspector General.

The cumulative effect of "intolerable smells" led Washington to order that soldiers who relieved themselves anywhere but in "a proper Necessary" receive five lashes.

With translators to interpret his commands (he couldn't speak English), the Baron began by first turning 100 men who had trained under a variety of manuals into a force that reflected one united system. Those 100, in turn, were expected to teach others their newly acquired skills in marching, loading their weapons, and using a bayonet. With the troops lacking a standard infantry manual, von Steuben worked each day on a new book: *Regulation for the Order of Discipline of the*

Troops of the United States. Every evening, his manuscript was translated into English and copied by an officer in each brigade.

Washington, understandably, was proud of von Steuben and his new army of fighting men. "To see the men without clothes to cover their naked-ness, without blankets to lie upon, without shoes, without a house or hut to cover them until those could be built, and submitting without a murmur," he wrote, "is a proof of patience and obedience which, in my opinion, can scarcely be paralleled."

By May the passionate but fragile army that had arrived more than five months earlier had become one of confident, disciplined, and determined men who now had something else on their side.

France.

After its alliance with the United States was announced, the soldiers would receive new French-made uniforms and military gear. The news had a different effect in Philadelphia, where the British recognized they would no longer be able to defend the city and left for New York.

Despite the loss of thousands of men to disease that winter, 14,000 soldiers and as many as 5,000 support personnel marched out of Valley Forge in early June. They were an army transformed. A new spirit had been forged.

THE EXPERIENCE

Valley Forge was named a state park in 1893 and a National Park Historic Site in 1976. The biggest attraction is a circle tour of its nearly 3,500 acres, which you'll want to embark upon after first stopping at the visitor center to watch "Valley Forge: A Winter Encampment," a short film. Next, stop at the museum where displays, illustrations, artifacts, and historical reproductions show the type of conditions the men and women endured. Yes, women were there, contributing to the success of the encampment by doing laundry, caring for sick men, fixing weapons and equipment, guarding baggage trains, and working in Washington's spy network. For this, they received half pay and half rations.

A variety of living history programs are presented at Valley Forge throughout the year. Visit *www.nps.gov/ vafo* for more information.

One option for touring the grounds during the summer is a 90-minute narrated trolley tour, offered on weekends only in April, May, September, and October. Option two is picking up one of the National Park Service pamphlets for a leisurely do-it-yourself drive around the park. Along the way you'll pass white-tailed deer, statues, and reconstructions of the log cabins the men built. You'll see monuments from the 11 states the soldiers came from, and the restored colonial era home used by George Washington as his headquarters during the encampment.

Towering above the grounds is the National Memorial Arch, dedicated to the officers and private soldiers of the Continental Army. Completed in 1917, it is inscribed with Washington's tribute to his troops' perseverance and devotion to the cause of liberty.

> NAKED AND STARVING AS THEY ARE
> WE CANNOT ENOUGH ADMIRE
> THE INCOMPARABLE PATIENCE AND FIDELITY
> OF THE SOLDIERY.

CONTACTS

Valley Forge National Historical Site
(610) 783-1077
www.nps.gov/vafo

Valley Forge Convention and Visitors Bureau
(610) 834-1550
www.valleyforge.org

For Lodging and Dining, see pp. 294–295

21. WASHINGTON CROSSING
Pennsylvania

If your perception of George Washington crossing the Delaware is based on the famous and improbable image of Emanuel Leutze's 1851 painting, wait until you hear what really happened that night.

AGAINST THE ODDS

It was Christmas Day 1776. Just six months earlier, the Second Continental Congress had declared America's independence. But when the sun came up on that Christmas morning, the thought of independence was fast slipping away.

The British had pursued George Washington's Continental Army across New Jersey into Pennsylvania. Many of the nearly 20,000 troops Washington had commanded in Boston and in New York had been killed, captured, wounded, or had deserted. Fewer than 5,000 were still fighting. When enlistments ran out at the end of the week, only about 1,400 men would remain and they had minimal training, makeshift uniforms, and little support from the people or Congress. Washington confessed in a letter to his brother Augustine, "I think the game is pretty near up."

In a last-ditch gamble, Washington and his generals agreed that three units would deploy across the Delaware River late on Christmas evening. They would capture towns and bridges and after everyone—including horses and men and artillery—had reached the other side, Washington's men would march through the night and surprise about 1,500

David Hackett Fischer's Pulitzer Prize–winning account of those Ten Crucial Days, *Washington's Crossing*, turns great history into great reading.

Hessians (German mercenaries) at Trenton. It would be a tough fight. The Hessians were well-financed, properly armed and outfitted, disciplined to fight with crisp efficiency, and ready to face whatever a demoralized pickup army could throw at them.

Things started to unravel on Christmas Day. The weather was horrendous. It rained, then sleeted, then snowed. It was so cold and so brutal, and the water so fierce and choppy, that neither Gen. John Cadwalader, who was supposed to attack and capture the British at Bordentown, New Jersey, nor Gen. James Ewing, who was supposed to capture a key bridge and prevent the enemy from escaping, were able to make it across the river.

Although alone, Washington pressed on, backed by bookseller-turned-chief artillery officer Henry Knox. The 2,400 men were loaded into Durham boats (normally used for hauling pig iron across the river) at McKonkey's Ferry. Horses and artillery were put aboard ferries and as night fell the sky was as black as the river. A passage from the Washington Crossing Historic Park's website describes the scene:

Directly across the river is the other half of the Washington's Crossing National Historic Landmark, New Jersey's 3,100-acre Washington Crossing State Park (609-737-0623).

"What did they see? Gusts of breath billowing from the nostrils of agitated horses being loaded this dawn onto ferry boats. Ice floes clogging the Delaware and the river's choppy water churning past. What could they hear? The poles of Glover's Marblehead sailors penetrating the water with frigid splashing and oar-thwacks as they maneuvered the Durham boats across the inky river. They heard Colonel Knox's booming voice giving orders, rising above the confusion, as to how the assembled 2,400 troops, cannons and equines should be shuttled across the Delaware...."

The plan was to be across by midnight and in Trenton before dawn. But it was already 3 a.m., and there were still nine miles to march through the snow and ice along a rugged New Jersey road marked by the tracks of wagons and cannons, the hoofprints of horses, and the bloody footprints left by the marching men. Cadwalader's and Ewing's men were still on the Pennsylvania shore. Only Washington's men were in the position to do the impossible.

No one will ever know the name of every man who was along on that mission, but it's said that among those who crossed the Delaware that night were future President James Monroe, future Vice President Aaron Burr, future Chief Justice John Marshall, and future Secretary of the Treasury Alexander Hamilton.

They arrived in Trenton after sunup and pointed their cannons into the heart of town. When the Hessians woke up on that December 26 they found a belated Christmas surprise: 2,400 exhausted but determined men who, with the fate of the new nation depending on them, did something unbelievable. *They won.* Washington's men captured not only a treasury of food, supplies, and munitions, but also 896 officers and men. Enlistments rose; Congress was convinced; and once again citizens believed in the cause.

This was the beginning of the first day of the fabled Ten Crucial Days—and it all began at Mc-Konkey's Ferry on a snowy Christmas evening in 1776. Washington's troops had given the colonies a great gift: a fighting chance.

THE EXPERIENCE

Washington Crossing is surrounded by a picturesque 500-acre national landmark. Before strolling across the grounds, step inside the visitors center, where guides will fill you in on the details of the mission, point you toward some informational displays, and invite you to watch "Of Dire Necessity," a fascinating video presentation about the long odds faced by Washington and his men.

Their decision to press on is a testament to their courage and to the character of George Washington. How did he get his men to believe in what seemed a lost cause? How did he keep his own fears and doubts in check as he led them through the night? We may never know, but we'll always be grateful.

CONTACTS

Washington Crossing Historic Park
1112 River Road (Route 32)
Washington Crossing
(215) 493-4076

www.ushistory.org/washingtoncrossing
www.tencrucialdays.com

For Lodging and Dining, see pp. 295–296

22. COLONIAL PHILADELPHIA
Pennsylvania

Based on memories of elementary school films, you may picture Philadelphia as a colonial community where carriages whirl past and people write with quill pens. To its credit, Philadelphia has never forgotten the role it played in the founding of the nation more than two centuries ago.

MAKING A BREAK

By the 1770s Philadelphia was fulfilling the vision of its founder, Quaker William Penn, whose ideal of a City of Brotherly Love had drifted down through the generations. It was a welcoming place for scientists, philosophers, inventors, publishers, musicians, writers, politicians, and philanthropists—but Ben Franklin wasn't the only one who lived there.

When the First Continental Congress convened in Philadelphia in September 1774, it organized an ultimately ineffective boycott of British goods. But after April 1775, when British regulars and Minute Men fired at each other at Lexington and Concord, there was added urgency to convene a second Continental Congress at the Pennsylvania State House.

At the corner of Second and Market you'll find the 1695 Christ Church (215-922-1695, www .christchurchphila.org), where 15 signers of the Declaration of Independence, including George Washington and Benjamin Franklin, worshipped.

It would take another year and great debates before the Virginia Convention advised its congressional delegation to propose that the colonies declare independence from Great Britain. After the resolution was introduced in the Assembly Room of the State House (later Independence Hall), 33-year-old Thomas Jefferson was drafted to write a declaration that said as much. The young politician blended ideas from existing declarations of rights, thoughts shared by his fellow countrymen, and concepts advanced by the English philosopher John Locke, among others, to open his work with this immortal passage:

"We hold these truths to be self-evident, that all men are created equal, that they are endowed by their Creator with certain unalienable Rights, that among these are Life, Liberty and the pursuit of Happiness…"

Years later Jefferson observed that the declaration was "intended to be an expression of the American mind, and to give to that expression the proper tone and spirit called for by the occasion."

His first draft was presented on June 28, 1776, when the delegates questioned whether the colonies should even pursue independence without first lining up some allies to help out. After they agreed to the separation, they turned to Jefferson's document and after several days of debate and editing (to pacify Southern delegates, sections that criticized the slave trade were excised), the document was approved by the Congress and sent to the printer for publication.

It was July 4, 1776.

DO IT YOURSELF

The district known as Old City, although surrounded by a modern metropolis, preserves many key sites in close proximity. Within a few minutes you can walk to the Betsy Ross Home, to Benjamin Franklin's gravesite, to the Quaker Meeting House, to Christ Church, and to Independence Mall, which holds the Independence Visitor Center, Independence Hall, the Liberty Bell Center, and the National Constitution Center. Arrive early—the limited tickets to Independence Hall go fast during the busy spring and summer months. (Another incentive: The quiet you can experience around daybreak makes it far easier to imagine this setting as it once was.)

The Mall's layout will nudge you toward the Liberty Bell, a symbol of America as a nation and faulty metallurgy as a trade. A small museum dedicated to it shows how its image was used to inspire Americans; exhibits historical documents; and pays off with the bell itself, centered in a small glass-enclosed room. Beyond, Independence Hall creates a picture-perfect backdrop.

Sending a postcard? Mail it from 316 Market Street, where Franklin was postmaster—the postmark "B. Free Franklin" is still used to cancel stamps. It's the only active post office in the United States that doesn't fly an American flag, as there was no flag—or America—when it was built in 1775.

Inside the Hall, rangers put the impact of the Declaration into context as they step back in history to discuss the Boston Massacre, the Boston Tea Party, George Washington's appointment to command the Continental Army, his retreat across New Jersey, and the revitalizing advance across the Delaware. The British, you're reminded, didn't take insurrection lightly, and even carrying a copy of the signed Declaration was a capital offense. Every man who signed the Declaration of Independence was effectively signing his own death warrant. *These were brave men.*

A little more than a decade later, in 1787, many of those same patriots were among the 55 delegates who rose to the occasion in the same place to create the Constitution of the United States, a document strong enough to represent millions of people but flexible enough to change and to give "we, the people" power over our government. After hammering out the Constitution, they worked the Bill of Rights into shape. For this amazing story, walk across the street to the National Constitution Center.

A must-see for every citizen, especially those who hold or seek public office, the Center presents a multimedia presentation that illustrates vividly how this document was created and explains the challenges the framers of the Constitution faced during the sweltering summer of 1787. As they alternated between confrontation and compromise, everyone understood that the idea of a government ruled by the people was ambitious—and no one knew if it could work. Eighty-one-year-old Ben Franklin was one who was willing to try.

> When you're ready to win a bet, ask someone to tell you when the Declaration of Independence was signed. It wasn't July 4. That's the day it was adopted, but the signers had to wait until it was "engrossed on parchment," and that wasn't completed until August 2. *That's* when John Hancock signed his John Hancock.

"I confess, that I do not entirely approve of this Constitution at present," he declared. "But Sir, I am not sure I shall never approve it…Thus I consent, Sir, to this Constitution, because I expect no better, and because I am not sure that it is not the best."

Well, it was the best, so thank you, Mr. Franklin.

And thank you, Philadelphia.

CONTACTS

Independence National Historical Park
143 South Third Street
(215) 965-2305
(800) 967-2283 (advance tickets)
www.nps.gov/inde

Independence Visitor Center
6th and Market
(800) 537-7676
www.gophila.com

www.phillyhistory.org
www.ushistory.org

For Lodging and Dining, see pp. 296–297

23. ARMY-NAVY FOOTBALL GAME
Philadelphia, Pennsylvania

As football becomes increasingly high tech and marketing-heavy, it's nice to recall the old-fashioned gridiron classics played when the game was more sport and less commercial entertainment. On the first Saturday each December, the United States Military Academy and the United States Naval Academy engage in a rivalry that's been going on since the autumn of '90.

1890.

FIELD MANEUVERS

Back in 1890, football was a novelty. There was no NFL, no sexy cheerleaders, no stadiums that could hold 100,000 people. The sport had only recently evolved from rugby, and while the game may have been recognizable, it wasn't exactly what we're used to seeing today.

Army had the home field advantage, but Navy had better plays and players. Four quarters later, Navy left the field with a 24-0 victory, bragging rights, and a series lead of 1-0. At Annapolis the following year, Navy had the home field advantage but were sunk by Army 32-16. The series was tied at 1-1.

Navy sailed off with a victory in the next two match-ups. Following a six-year hiatus, the teams played not at West Point or Annapolis, but at the football equivalent of neutral Switzerland: From then on, Philadelphia would be the most frequent site of showdowns. Bragging rights seesawed between the two for decades. Throughout the 20th century—*an entire century*—the teams were seldom more than three games apart.

> It's unlikely Army or Navy players will reach the NFL, but there have been a few notable exceptions. Perhaps top of the pack is Heisman trophy–winner and Dallas Cowboys quarterback Roger Staubach (Navy '65), two-time Super Bowl champ and MVP of Super Bowl VI.

While there have certainly been amazing plays and hard-fought games, both Army and Navy often lag behind the top college football programs when it comes to recruiting the best football players. Not only must their players fulfill extremely high academic entrance requirements and adhere to established height and weight limits (no 300-pound tackles here), but even the most talented know they won't be signing a multimillion-dollar contract and an endorsement deal from Nike when they graduate. They'll leave with an obligation to fulfill a multiyear commitment to the nation.

For fans in the stands and those watching at home, the likelihood that a potential Heisman winner won't be playing on Saturday doesn't matter. They know these young men are playing for the love of the game and the honor of carrying on the tradition of an American football classic.

DO IT YOURSELF

Most Army-Navy games have taken place in Philadelphia, but it's possible that future contests may be hosted at other venues. Wherever game day lands, it will likely follow a routine long established in Philly.

Fans arrive early: The stadium parking lot opens around 6 a.m. With 20,000 spaces available, the lot has plenty of room for tailgate parties. Granted, it's much too early to set up the grill, yet passionate fans are here to wring every minute they can out of this day.

When the stadium gates open at 8 a.m., it's still four hours until kick off, but returning fans are anxious to claim their seats. They know from experience that what happens prior to the game is nearly as thrilling as what can happen during the game.

> The U.S. Air Force Academy football team is also in competition against Army and Navy. Whichever of the three teams wins more games than the others is presented with the Commander in Chief's Trophy.

At about 9 a.m., the Navy Brigade of Midshipmen conducts the "March On." With fans standing at attention, the midshipmen walk onto the field—and on and on and on until some 4,000 of them occupy 100 yards of turf. There is no music, no singing, no national anthem, only the spectacle of seeing them take the field. Half an hour later, the field is cleared for 4,000 members of the Army Corps of Cadets who, like their counterparts, parade in formation onto the field where they, too, stand in silence.

An hour or so before kick off, both teams take the field to warm up. Then, weather permitting, Army's Golden Knights and Navy's Leap Frogs parachute onto the field. Flyovers by Navy and Army aircraft punctuate the singing of the national anthem. And there's still a football game to watch.

At halftime, the teams' bands take the field for anyone who hasn't cut out for the concession stands. Folks who stick around can witness another halftime tradition: If he's there that year, the President will

> As of 2008, Navy maintains a 53-49-7 lead in the series.

leave his seat and walk across the field to sit with the opposing team for the second half.

When the game is over, the 8,000 midshipmen and cadets who have remained standing throughout the entire game become the focus of attention, as each team gathers beneath their fellow soldiers and sailors in the end zone. Turning to the winning team, the losing cadets or midshipmen sing their alma mater to the victors, who stand at attention. The winning team then returns the honor.

Americans can learn a lot from a football game.

CONTACTS

Tickets for the Army-Navy game are sold only through the athletic department of each academy. A donation above and beyond the ticket price benefits each school's athletic programs. Tickets go on sale when season tickets become available in the spring, and go fast. To purchase your tickets, contact:

West Point
(877) 849-2769 (TIX-ARMY)
www.goarmysports.com

Naval Academy
(800) 874-6289 (US4-NAVY)
www.navysports.com

For Lodging and Dining, see pp. 296–297

24. WASHINGTON, D.C.

Don't let *who's* in Washington detract from *what's* in Washington. The first time you stand at the Capitol at dusk and look down the Mall and see the slender Washington Monument and the outline of the Lincoln Memorial framed in the glow of the setting sun, you'll see not just American icons, but the promise of America.

A MONUMENTAL PLAN

The Washington most tourists see is the one you'll see, with wonderful museums, monuments, green space, galleries, and federal buildings. The Washington our Founding Fathers saw was quite different. In fact, it didn't even exist.

Laid out in the nation's new Constitution was authority for the government to establish a federal capital. In the end, James Madison, Alexander Hamilton, and Thomas Jefferson pounded out a deal that would place the capital in what was considered the South. In September 1791, the Federal City was named Washington in the territory, not district, of Columbia.

Once the nation had the land, the government needed a civil engineer to design the capital. That man was Pierre Charles L'Enfant, who, just six months after being hired in March 1791, delivered his vision of a grand city with broad avenues, public buildings, and public green space in circles, parks, and squares. Unfortunately, L'Enfant's desire to see it built all at once ran contrary to the position of the three commissioners he worked for, as well as that of Secretary of State Thomas Jefferson. A year after he was hired, L'Enfant was fired and spent the rest of his life fighting for the money and recognition he believed was his. But Washington had kept a copy of L'Enfant's original plans, which were modified and later used as the basic blueprint for the city's design.

Would you like to see your government at work? That makes 300 million of us. Actually, to see Congress or the Senate in session, call your senator or congressman and get a gallery ticket to sit and watch Congress in action. Or inaction.

What Congress, L'Enfant, and subsequent planners envisioned is still the main stage of American history. Think of the success and failures of every president, marches on Washington, attacks on Washington, Supreme Court decisions, landmark legislation, and thousands of other historic events—it all happened here. In Washington, D.C., you'll see where American history is still running on the fast track.

DO IT YOURSELF

In general, Washington is a fairly simple city to navigate. Between the Washington Monument and the White House is a 52-acre green space called the Ellipse. To the west is the Lincoln Memorial and to the east is the Capitol Building. The open area between these two points is the National Mall. Bordering the Mall you'll find the National Archives, many federal buildings, the Department of Justice, and several museums of the Smithsonian Institution. Across the Tidal Basin to the south stands the Jefferson Memorial.

If you're a fast walker and a quick study, you should be able to cover these few sites in about a month and a half. With so much to see and so much ground to cover, start with a bus tour of the city to gauge the city's layout, distances, and sites that catch your interest.

Even after your bus reconnaissance, you won't be able to do nearly as many things in a day as you hope. A pass is required to enter the Washington Monument. On busy days, the daily allotment can be distributed as early as 9 a.m. If you have the good fortune to get inside and to the top, from about 555 feet you'll see one of the greatest views in the nation.

To the east, the new U.S. Capitol Visitor Center opened in late 2008 and, as at the Monument, advance tickets are required for tours. They are available through your congressman or senator (although a limited number of same-day tickets is handed out). Likewise, if you'd like to enter the White House you can either win your party's nomination or arrange well in advance for a free, self-guided tour offered mornings only between Tuesday and Saturday. Available for groups of ten or more only, passes for these tours can be obtained from your senator or congressman up to six months in advance. They may also be able to combine groups of fewer than ten to reach the minimum number.

South of the Mall, just across the Tidal Basin from most of the action, stands the impressive rotunda of the Jefferson Memorial. Modeled after the Pantheon in Rome, the monument commemorates our country's richly accomplished third President. It was dedicated in 1943.

You won't need passes or pay fees to enter any of the Smithsonian museums (American History, Natural History, American Indian, Air and Space, and more than a half-dozen others), or the National Archives, which is the home of the original Declaration of Independence, Constitution, and the Bill of Rights.

West of the Washington Monument is one of the more recent but long overdue memorials: the classically inspired National World War II Memorial, which opened in 2004. Visiting the Memorial offers the added bonus the opportunity to meet—and the honor to thank—WWII veterans, many of whom arrive in wheelchairs and on walkers. From there, walk along the Reflecting Pool to the somber Korean War Memorial before entering the Lincoln Memorial and the powerful presence of President Abraham Lincoln. On the north wall, read the Second Inaugural Address; on the south wall the Gettysburg Address describes in 271 words Lincoln's eloquent vision.

The Vietnam War Memorial is to your left as you leave the Lincoln Memorial. Directories near the entrance contain the names of 58,249 men and women who died in that conflict.

The monument's wide "V" design draws you to its center while its black granite surface reflects your image in the roster of names engraved on it. It's a sad experience to look down and see the photographs, dog tags, beer cans, and other personal tributes that are often left at its base—but the saddest are the simple notes written decades after the fact to buddies who didn't make it home.

CONTACTS

Destination D.C.
(202) 789-7000
www.washington.org

D.C. Visitor Information Center
(202) 289-8317
(866) 324-7386
www.dcchamber.org

White House Tour Information
(202) 456-7041
www.whitehouse.gov

U.S. Capitol Tours
www.visitthecapitol.gov

Vietnam Veterans Memorial
www.nps.gov/vive

Washington Monument
www.nps.gov/wamo

Jefferson Memorial
www.nps.gov/thje

National Archives
www.archives.gov

Smithsonian Museums
(202) 633-1000
www.smithsonian.org

For Lodging and Dining, see p. 297

25. ARLINGTON NATIONAL CEMETERY
Arlington, Virginia

More than 300,000 headstones cross 624 acres at Arlington National Cemetery. Every day, caretakers honor the memory, service, and sacrifice of the men and women laid to rest there, but it is Memorial Day that best symbolizes their devotion.

A GRAVE MATTER

Back in 1861, citizens living in Washington, D.C., could look across the wide Potomac River and see the estate home of a man intent on dismantling America. That property was the home of Robert E. Lee, who, while awaiting the decision of his beloved Virginia to secede or not, had already turned down President Abraham Lincoln's offer to lead the federal Army. So when Virginia said farewell to the nation, Lee said goodbye to the Union Army and accepted a commission with the Army of Northern Virginia.

Nearly 30 funerals take place on any given day except weekends and federal holidays.

Lee would soon learn a lesson in repercussions. As the war dragged on far longer than either side had predicted, the Confederate Army, under Lee's command, contributed heavily to the crowding of the capital's hospitals and cemeteries. That's when the Union's quartermaster general, Montgomery C. Meigs, came up with a novel idea: Since Lee hadn't paid his property taxes, the United States of America should be entitled to commandeer the Lee property. Its highest and best use? A cemetery filled with Union war dead.

By the end of 1864, those who had expended their "last full measure of devotion" were beginning to fill the grounds of the Lee estate. Four months later, as Lee was signing papers at Appomattox, more than 16,000 men were resting beneath the ground at Arlington. Lee never returned to his former home.

Today, the cemetery is the final home of more than 300,000 soldiers, statesmen, presidents, and others. Supreme Court justices share ground with such notable Americans as Audie Murphy and Joe Louis. Generals George Patton and Omar Bradley are buried there, along with those under their command.

THE EXPERIENCE

Every day is an appropriate day to visit Arlington Cemetery, but on Memorial Day, special ceremonies take place at the Tomb of the Unknowns and in the adjacent Memorial Amphitheatre. Trams take guests up Sheridan Drive near the graves of President John F. Kennedy and his brother Robert and past rows of evenly spaced headstones. Each is marked by a small American flag placed by members of "The Old Guard," the Third U.S. Infantry.

The inscription on the Tomb of the Unknowns reads "Here Rests In Honored Glory An American Soldier Known But To God." This was true until 1998, when the remains of Air Force 1st Lt. Michael Joseph Blassie were identified through DNA testing. Blassie died in Vietnam in 1972.

Approaching the services, you'll pass members of honor guards and color guards, veterans, and active military personnel. The main ceremony is held inside the amphitheatre; behind it a set of marble steps faces the Tomb of the Unknowns. Part of this plaza is reserved for dignitaries and honorees, including Congressional Medal of Honor recipients, leaving a modest amount of room for other visitors. But it's worth remaining there even if you can't find a prime spot.

One of the highest honors for the soldiers serving in the Army's Third U.S. Infantry Regiment is the mission to guard the Tomb of the Unknowns. Every minute since July 2, 1937, they have upheld an inspiring tradition. Each and every day and without variation, the sentinel charged with protecting the 79-ton tomb takes exactly 21 strides; turns and faces the tomb for 21 seconds; turns again and places his rifle on the opposite side of the tomb; and takes 21 steps to return.

> **For information on laying a wreath at Arlington, call 703-607-8559, although requests must be made in writing: Arlington National Cemetery, Attn: Public Wreath Ceremonies, Arlington, VA, 22211.**

Then, every 30 minutes in the summer and every hour between September and April, you'll witness another spectacle of military precision. The relief commander arrives in tandem with the replacement guard reporting for watch. In a ceremony lasting roughly ten minutes, the commander will inspect the replacement guard and his weapon before signaling to the guard on duty that he is relieved. More than seven decades of scuff marks on the marble reveal the path the soldiers will walk, and the procedure—executed with split-second timing and without a sound—is equal parts mysterious and fascinating.

As it approaches eleven o'clock, honor guards representing the Army, Navy, Air Force, Marines, and Coast Guard—the five branches of the United States Armed Forces—step up to the plaza. Next, the Army band plays "The Star-Spangled Banner," accompanied by the people gathered here. No applause or cheers follow the anthem.

Next, the President arrives and stands before the wreath, which is moved into place by the honor guards before a bugler blows Taps.

Within seconds, the President and honored guests have departed, escorted into the Memorial Amphitheatre for the main ceremony.

Behind them, the sentinel continues his watch.

CONTACTS

Arlington National Cemetery Visitor Information
(703) 607-8000
www.arlingtoncemetery.org

Internment Services Branch
(703) 607-8585

www.arlingtoncemetery.net

For Lodging and Dining, see p. 297

26. MOUNT VERNON
Virginia

Anyone who has traveled long and far carries a longing to get home. George Washington was no different. Time and again he stepped forward to serve his country and each time he did he looked forward to the day he could return to Mount Vernon.

MIND YOUR MANOR

The Mount Vernon estate on the Potomac River had been in the family since 1674, when the land was acquired by George Washington's grandfather John and passed down to his father, Augustine, who, in the 1740s, built a new house that he would leave to Washington's half-brother, Lawrence. But in July 1752, Lawrence, who had stepped forward to guide George after their father's death, was himself dead of tuberculosis.

Washington had been living at Mount Vernon and supervising its operation since 1747. In 1754 he acquired the estate from Lawrence's widow, Anne Fairfax, and committed himself to life as a gentleman farmer or, more precisely, one of America's premier scientific agriculturalists. Washington learned how to cultivate crops; map out fields and orchards; and apply his surveying skills to the creation of what would grow from a 2,000-acre estate to an 8,000-acre estate.

The one thing that surpassed his love of Mount Vernon was his love of country. And because no one in the colonies possessed his charismatic combination of heritage, stoicism, stature, and leadership, he was repeatedly called to serve.

Each morning the American flag is raised above the Main Gate at Mount Vernon. Contact *groups@ mountvernon.org* for information about performing the honor.

In 1775 he was in Philadelphia to meet with the Second Continental Congress when he was appointed Commander in Chief of the Continental forces. For the next eight years he was mostly away from home as he engaged the British, but in 1783 the war was won and Washington retired to Mount Vernon. Four years later, though, he was called back to Philadelphia, where, during the long, hot summer of 1787, he presided over the committee that crafted the United States Constitution. Washington returned again to Mount Vernon—but his nation called yet again. In 1789, the 57-year-old Washington learned he would become the first President of the United States. During the next eight years he would spend only 15 months at Mount Vernon.

Whatever Washington sacrificed for his nation, he always had Mount Vernon. Whether at home, at camp, or forging a new government, it would remain his sanctuary. While there he supervised the expansion of the residence from a seven-bedroom, one-and-a-half-story home to a two-and-a-half-story mansion with an extensively redecorated interior. Having witnessed the horrors of war, Washington was determined that the setting of his Georgian-style home would be serenely harmonious. Gardens, walkways, and outbuildings were both practical and aesthetically pleasing. The modest frame exterior of the mansion was given the look of stone by being covered with bevel-edged pine blocks coated with a mixture of paint and sand. He added a two-story porch that overlooked the Potomac, and then capped the mansion with a cupola adorned with a weathervane topped with a dove of peace.

The Donald W. Reynolds Museum and Education Center at Mount Vernon features 23 galleries, educational videos, and hundreds of artifacts. Don't miss the three stunning likenesses of Washington: As an adventurous 19-year-old surveyor, forceful 45-year-old general, and finally as the dynamic 57-year-old president.

DO IT YOURSELF

Mount Vernon is about 16 miles south of Washington, D.C., on the banks of the Potomac River. Although it's about 7,500 acres shy of what Washington owned, it still tells a story.

The story begins at the Ford Orientation Center, where a dramatic introductory film, "We Fight to Be Free," highlights pivotal moments in Washington's life. Whether you're a kid or an adult, watch this and you'll realize that the elder statesman we thought we knew was actually one of America's first action heroes. Washington was *cool.* The center also features "Mount Vernon in Miniature," an exquisitely crafted model of the mansion created in 1/12th scale. Had they made a dozen they could have had a full-size spare.

Tree-lined walkways lead from the center onto the well-manicured grounds of Mount Vernon, past the upper garden (part of 50 acres of gardens) and the expansive bowling green. The mansion itself is the only site here where you'll join a guide. The mansion is furnished with replica and original items, some owned by the Washingtons themselves. As the tour leads through the first and second floors (occasionally the third floor is open to guests), think of how Washington felt about his home:

"I can truly say I had rather be at home at Mount Vernon with a friend or two about me," he wrote, "than to be attended at the seat of government by the officers of the State and the representatives of every power of Europe."

Beyond the mansion, there are forest trails to explore, along with outbuildings including a stable, slave quarters, servants' hall, and coach house. Past the fruit garden and nursery is the tomb of George and Martha Washington. It's worth a long look. When you consider that if there had been no George Washington, there might have been no United States, you may want to carve out a few minutes to attend the daily wreath-laying ceremonies, too.

> **Three miles west of Mount Vernon is a reconstruction of Washington's distillery. The whiskey produced is sold (only) at the gift shop there.**

CONTACTS

Mount Vernon
(703) 780-2000
www.mountvernon.org

For Lodging and Dining, see pp. 297–298

27. COLONIAL WILLIAMSBURG
Williamsburg, Virginia

Thanks to the vision of one determined clergyman and the fortune of one passionate Rockefeller, what existed in Williamsburg, Virginia, in the 1700s survives. Within the historic district the past is reflected in the buildings and in the people living and working here. What it lacks in flash, it makes up for in content. Not only does Colonial Williamsburg reveal how far we've come as a nation, it reminds us that the challenges our ancestors faced in nurturing a democracy are the same ones we face today.

THERE GOES THE NEIGHBORHOOD

For some residents of Jamestown, it was about time. It was 1699 and the capital was moving less than ten miles west to Williamsburg. When the relocated residents compared their new inland home to the swampy quagmire they had lived in, the governor was delighted to marvel that the "clear and crystal springs burst from the champagne soil."

In 1903, the Reverend Dr. W.A.R. Goodwin was also pleased with the town. When he arrived to become rector of the town's Bruton Pastor Church,

Williamsburg was seemingly frozen in time. Homes, shops, and other buildings that were there after the government relocated to Richmond in 1780 were still there—and showing their advanced age. Goodwin had the notion to preserve the colonial community by restoring significant buildings—he placed the Bruton Parish Church, the Capitol, and the Governor's Palace at the top of his to-do list. Goodwin raised funds for restoration with some success until he was transferred to another parish in 1917. When he returned to Williamburg in 1924, he picked up where he left off. In fact, he was soon miles ahead of where he left off because he had a secret weapon: John D. Rockefeller, Jr.

Responding to Goodwin's invitation, Rockefeller visited Williamsburg. Intrigued, Rockefeller suggested that instead of just a few sites, he might buy and preserve the *entire town*. For a year and a half, Rockefeller secretly snagged buildings that architectural historians he employed had identified as worth saving.

Things couldn't stay under wraps forever, though. At a town meeting on June 12, 1928, Goodwin proposed a deal to 200 townspeople: Rockefeller would buy their homes, fix them up, and offer the residents life tenancy. In exchange, ownership would pass to the Colonial Williamsburg Foundation upon their death. All but two homeowners approved.

Make an annual donation of at least $100, and you'll be granted admission to the St. George Tucker House. Donors can rest there, get refreshments, and receive special services such as hotel reservations.

Meanwhile, the more modern elements of the town disappeared. A gas station, a Baptist church, and an elementary school were razed. The median along Duke of Gloucester Street was removed; electrical lines were buried; and the town began falling backward in time. Eighty-eight buildings and more than 450 other structures spread across 301 acres were preserved and restored to their original uses. Former taverns were once again taverns; the old stores became stores again; and the foundry began striking pewter, silver, and gold dinnerware.

This is where our nation's forebears first wrestled with some of the challenges of self-governance. When you come, you may the find the past as relevant as the present.

DO IT YOURSELF

It's not unusual for some visitors to question the entertainment value of Colonial Williamsburg. It's a long one-mile walk between the modern world and the old Capitol, and you can go for days without seeing a single flume ride or roller coaster.

But just suspend disbelief, place yourself in the 1700s, and immerse yourself in the illusion. Talk to tradesmen who shoe horses and the women who spin wool or serve meals in the old taverns. Let the interpreters take you back. A reference guide lists five key sites for first-time visitors and suggestions if you're interested in a particular trade or craft.

In addition to must-see sites like the Governor's Palace, the Courthouse, or the Capitol, there is also large-scale street theater presented in "Revolutionary City." In scenes based on historical records, a wife and husband argue over his enlisting in the Army just because it's the best-paying job he can find. She'd rather have him stay home and stay alive. In another scene, a mob threatens to tar and feather a merchant after he's discovered hoarding flour.

> According to Virginia Snyder Lee of the Colonial Williamsburg Foundation, Colonial Williamsburg welcomed municipal leaders from former Soviet bloc countries after the fall of the Soviet Union. Tasked with creating free and open cities, they came here to pick up some fundamentals of democracy.

Make reservations for dinner in a tavern. Sit in on a witch trial. Have a conversation with George Washington and Thomas Jefferson and discover what they feel is needed to sustain America's experiment with democracy. They should know.

They've done it once already.

FOOTNOTE: THE HISTORIC TRIANGLE

Colonial Williamsburg is only one point in what is known as the Historic Triangle. The other two are Jamestown and Yorktown.

Nine miles from Williamsburg, Jamestown was founded in 1607, 13 years before the Pilgrims arrived in Massachusetts. It served as Virginia's first capital until 1699. There's a re-creation of an English fort and an Indian village, and replicas of three English sailing ships—the *Susan Constant, Godspeed,* and *Discovery.* Nearby, on Jamestown Island, more than a million artifacts have been recovered by the Jamestown Rediscovery Project.

> To sustain the illusion of a colonial community, the re-enactors actually live in the homes along Duke of Gloucester Street.

Fourteen miles southeast of Williamsburg is Yorktown, where George Washington pinned down the British army under Gen. Charles Cornwallis. When Cornwallis realized he wouldn't be rescued by Maj. Gen. Henry Clinton, on October 17, 1781, he offered to surrender unconditionally. Afterward he would claim he was too ill to meet Washington and surrender his sword. When he sent his second in command, Washington countered the slight by refusing to meet with the subordinate and had *his* second in command accept the surrender. The Treaty of Paris wouldn't be signed for another two years, but it was at Yorktown that the British realized they could no longer force American loyalty to the Crown.

CONTACTS

Colonial Williamsburg Foundation
(757) 220-1000
(800) HISTORY (447-8679)
www.history.org

City of Williamsburg
www.visitwilliamsburg.com

Jamestown-Yorktown Foundation
(757) 253-4838
(888) 593-4682
www.historyisfun.org

Historic Jamestowne
www.nps.gov/jame

For Lodging and Dining, see p. 298

28. APPALACHIAN TRAIL
Appalachian Mountains

Only a relative handful have ever traveled the entire length of the Appalachian Trail. But even if you have no plan to embark on an epic journey from Maine to Georgia (or vice versa), at least set off on a short walk. Step by step through its colorful range of ranges (including the White Mountains, Green Mountains, and Blue Ridge Mountains) you'll get a glimpse of America's majesty. Go the distance and you'll see 2,176 miles of it.

A RIDGE TOO FAR

New Englander Benton MacKaye loved the outdoors and was awed by the realization that a single mountain chain could rise in the hills of north Georgia and run all the way to Maine. In 1921 he wrote an article that envisioned identifying and protecting a collection of hiking paths, shelters, stores, and camps that would link the Appalachian ridge from end to end.

This idea, as simple as it was grand, fired the imagination of supporters. The first link in MacKaye's chain opened on October 7, 1923: an 18-mile section that ran from Bear Mountain to Arden, New York. In 1925 MacKaye worked to keep up enthusiasm for his project by hosting a meeting in Washington that created the Appalachian Trail Conference. Soon, though, reality hit Benton MacKaye.

A few practical volumes to read before you walk: *Thru-Hiker's Companion,* the ATC's official guide, available at *www.appala chiantrail.org;* the *Official AT Databook* which includes mileages, road crossing, and locations of water and the Trail's 200-plus shelters; and *The Thru-Hiker's Handbook* by Bob McCaw.

His vision was inspiring, but creating the numerous shelters, stores, and camps would be a major undertaking. In the late 1920s a trail enthusiast and retired judge named Arthur Perkins proposed downscaling MacKaye's idea to include only hiking trails. MacKaye resigned in protest. Then Perkins's friend, Myron Avery, an attorney and advocate of the trail-only concept, began to walk, blazing a trail, mile by mile. The first person to walk the entire route, Avery soon realized it would require the care of volunteer "trail clubs" to maintain their assigned sections of the path. So Avery got busy and helped create those.

Interest in the Trail waned during World War II but rose again in 1948 when WWII vet Earl Shaffer set out solo. He had lost a friend in the war; to fulfill their pact that they would hike the Trail together, Shaffer spent the next four months becoming the first person to complete a thru-walk of the Appalachian Trail.

Environmental awareness helped pass the National Trails System Act of 1968. With that, the framework was in place to provide protection for the Trail. A decade later, an amendment to the Act provided the Department of the Interior the funds needed to acquire a 1,000-foot-wide corridor that ran the entire length of the Trail. At 250,000 acres, the Appalachian Trail became the nation's longest and skinniest national park. The staffing is just as thin: Fewer than ten National Park Service staff members and just 45 Appalachian Trail Club staff members are assigned to the Trail—although more than 6,000 volunteers tend to it.

When hiking during hunting season, it's best to wear a fluorescent "blaze orange" vest.

Nearly a century after MacKaye saw a path leading across a swath of America and Avery made his contribution by assigning volunteer clubs as its stewards, the Appalachian Trail is still there, a uniquely American project that offers everyone an opportunity to tap into the frontier spirit.

DO IT YOURSELF

I've never thru-hiked the Appalachian Trail and probably never will unless they add a separate lane for motorcycles. Despite my absence, as many as four million people a year take day trips or longer treks. Who can tackle the Trail? Anyone.

"Several blind people have thru-walked the Trail," says Laurie Potteiger of the Appalachian Trail Conservancy. "We've had single and double amputees walk it and kids as young as six and as old as 81 thru-hike. The Trail is there for everyone."

With hundreds of access points along its length, hikers can enter the Trail at different locations for an array of different experiences. But iconic white Trail markers called "blazes" keep just about everyone on the right path.

"There's something thrilling about seeing your first white blaze," says Potteiger. "It's just a block of paint but if you follow blazes in one direction they'll lead you to Maine. The other, you'll go to Georgia. Blazes tell you that you are now part of something magnificent and great."

Like Potteiger, Bob McCaw, editor of *The Thru-Hiker's Handbook,* has thru-hiked the Trail.

"When you're on the Trail, there's a change in perspective," McCaw explains. "Like in the book *Walden,* we find the things that we feel we're dependent on may not be as important as we think. It's corny, but there's also the universal experience of people showing you acts of kindness that renew your faith in humanity."

The heroes of the Trail are volunteers affiliated with 30 Trail Clubs. You can join a club and volunteer time to keep the Appalachian Trail maintained and ensure that those who follow in your footsteps will enjoy an equally wonderful walk. Contact www.appalachiantrail.org.

Preparing for your own excursion requires an understanding of your physical limitations, the gear you'll need, a guidebook, and an awareness of plants and animals you may encounter. Why go to the trouble? Why subject yourself to bad weather and insects and the chance of encountering ticks, snakes, and bears? Because the risks of the Trail are far outweighed by its rewards.

"When you spend six months by yourself," says McCaw, "you work through why your girlfriend dumped you when you were 17 and why you didn't get that grade in college—you have time to figure out and sort through every problem you've had. Once you've hiked 15 or 20 miles and set up camp, it's just you there alone and all you hear is the forest."

But you don't have to be a thru-hiker to realize the magic of the Trail.

"In the midst of some very developed areas is a strip of land that is an oasis," observes Potteiger. "It transports you into a different world of quiet and silence and beauty. You see the whole spectrum of society where people leave their status and beliefs behind so you are simply a fellow hiker who is unplugged and outside enjoying the physical and spiritual beauty of the woods."

Let's go for a walk.

CONTACTS

Appalachian Trail Conservancy
(304) 535-6331
www.appalachiantrail.org

Appalachian Trail Park Office
(304) 535-6278
www.nps.gov/appa

Appalachian Trail Thru-Hikers Guide
www.trailplace.com

www.whiteblaze.net
A community of Appalachian
Trail enthusiasts

www.atctrailstore.org
An assortment of maps, books,
and accessories

For Lodging and Dining, see "Across America" p. 285

SOUTHEAST

Alabama, Florida, Georgia, Kentucky, Louisiana, Mississippi,
North Carolina, South Carolina, Tennessee

There's an image of the American Southeast that, I'm afraid, is not always flattering. But that image of kudzu and clay roads is just an overlay; an overused caricature of what is really a varied, pretty, and remarkable region.

To fully appreciate the Southeast you'll have to factor in cosmopolitan cities like Miami as well as the hundreds of miles of Atlantic Ocean and Gulf of Mexico coastlines. You'll have to take into account the natural beauty of the Great Smoky Mountains and the fiery bluegrass music of Kentucky. Then consider the peace you'll discover in rural mountain towns that give you a chance to do something rare. To stop. To simply stop and enjoy the perfume of citrus blossoms and gardenias and night blooming jasmine; to listen to a locomotive whistle off in the distance; to watch the flickering glow of fireflies in the night.

The Southeast is a patchwork quilt of cultures and experiences. Get wrapped up in it.

29. KENTUCKY DERBY
Louisville, Kentucky

The Kentucky Derby clocks in about four hours shy of the Super Bowl, but seems to contain nearly the same level of excitement. Add in the fact that several million dollars are being won and lost on the performance of a three-year-old, and you can understand its reputation as the "most exciting two minutes in sports."

THE GREAT RACE

Like Bigfoot and the state of Washington, horses and the state of Kentucky are forever intertwined. Jockeys were racing horses on Louisville's Main Street back in 1783, and over the next century several public and private tracks cropped up in town. The best was yet to come.

Traveling abroad in the early 1870s, Col. Meriwether Lewis Clark (grandson of the explorer) had an idea: He would create the Louisville Jockey Club to showcase the quality of Kentucky horses. By June 1874, Clark and his backers had announced their grand plan. Combining his own vision and his investors' money (320 membership subscriptions sold at $100 each), Clark leased 80 acres owned by his uncles, John and Henry Churchill. He began building a track, a clubhouse, grandstand, porter's lodge, and six stables. In May 1875, 10,000 fans watched as 15-year-old African-American jockey Alonzo "Lonnie" Clayton rode Aristides, a three-year-old chestnut colt, to victory in the inaugural Kentucky Derby.

A government wartime ban on horse racing in 1945 threatened to interrupt the 70 straight runs of the Derby. Fortunately for Churchill Downs, V-E Day was declared on May 8. The race was run on June 9.

It took a while for Churchill Downs (as the *Louisville Courier* dubbed it in 1883) to become profitable. Clark himself lost most of his money in the Crash of 1893; reduced to being a steward at racetracks, he killed himself in 1899. Had he stuck around until 1902, he would have seen a new set of owners turn a profit on the track. How'd they do it? Perhaps it was that rare flash of genius that told them if they could rent out Churchill Downs for the Kentucky State Fair, 50,000 people would pay to watch a head-on collision between two steaming locomotives. Yes, really.

By 1915 bans on horse racing in other states helped make the Kentucky Derby one of the nation's premier sporting events. Listeners across the country avidly anticipated the "run for the roses," named for the blanket of 554 roses draped across the winning horse.

The Kentucky Derby thundered ahead with landmark events. Beginning in 1952, television audiences could see the nation's fastest horses charging around the track. Bettors watched Secretariat break the two-minute mark in the mile and a quarter in 1973. In 1988, Churchill Downs hosted the Breeders' Cup, the most prestigious day of American racing, for the first of several times.

Churchill Downs is on the register of National Historic Landmarks—exactly where it deserves to be. On the first Saturday in May, you deserve to be there, too.

DO IT YOURSELF

It takes about two minutes for the field to circle the track, but the spectacle of the Kentucky Derby lasts much longer.

Kicking off several weeks before Derby Day, the Kentucky Derby Festival puts the city in a festive mood with fashion shows, parties, golf tournaments, Derby balls, volleyball tournaments, parties, food festivals, a marathon road race, poker tournaments, bed races, more parties, and the massive Pegasus Parade. Above the Ohio River, fans can see Thunder Over Louisville, a fireworks spectacular synchronized to explode to an accompanying music track, and the skies are filled with balloons competing in the Great Balloon Race. If there's time, they may even have a horse race.

On Friday, the day before Derby Day, about 100,000 people arrive at Churchill Downs to see a full card of races, highlighted by three-year-old fillies running in the Kentucky Oaks, known as the mini-Kentucky Derby.

On Derby Day, gates open at 8 a.m. Depending on your budget, you may sit in the grandstands with the deep-pocketed celebs, VIPs, and sponsors who are ushered into one of two premier seating areas known as Millionaire's Row. If you invest about $40 on a general admission ticket, you'll have access to the track's first level, saddle paddock, and infield. Wherever you sit, you'll discover more action than you've seen on television.

If you ever plan to drink a mint julep in your life, now's a good time and a good place to do it. Served in a souvenir glass, the traditional beverage of the race mixes Early Times Kentucky whiskey with crushed ice, sprigs of fresh mint, and a sugary syrup.

Starting at 11 a.m., races run every half hour until it's time for the big one, Race 10. Before it begins, there'll be about an hour's break while everyone rushes to place their bets on the horse they *know* will be the winner.

Just after 6 p.m. anticipation builds as the track bugler blows the traditional "call to the post." Then, 20 of America's fastest horses saunter from the saddle paddock to the gate, welcomed by the University of Louisville Marching Band playing "My Old Kentucky Home," just as they've done every year since 1921.

As at England's Ascot, ladies arrive at the Kentucky Derby wearing elaborate hats.

The atmosphere is electric as more than 150,000 people focus on the starting gate. When it opens, the pack stays fairly close for more than a minute—everyone's still sure that he or she holds a winning ticket. Hearts are pounding, hoofs are pounding, and adrenaline is surging in humans and horses.

In the final 30 seconds the pack starts to break but some horses are still in it until the heart-stopping finish. As the winning horse trots toward the Kentucky Derby Winner's Circle, there's a thunderous ovation for the horse and its rider, and even the luckiest of bettors will watch the ceremony from the grandstand before collecting their winnings. But even if you don't have the good fortune of cashing a ticket, you won't be disappointed. When it comes right down to it, Derby Day isn't about winning or losing.

The Kentucky Derby is about witnessing one of America's greatest events.

CONTACTS

Churchill Downs
(502) 636-4400
www.kentuckyderby.com

Kentucky Derby Festival
www.kdf.org

For Lodging and Dining, see pp. 298–299

30. BLUEGRASS MUSIC
Kentucky and Across America

A band can feature guitars, an upright bass, banjo, and a fiddle and what you'd hear would sound like country music. Add a mandolin and what you've got is bluegrass. The subtle difference makes a big difference because the sound captures the feel of rural America in general and Kentucky in particular. When virtuoso pickers go flat out with crisp, bullet-fast notes and seamless harmonies, it's as pure and clear as a cold Kentucky stream.

THE MONROE DOCTRINE

If your iPod held 20,000 bluegrass tunes, not for a single moment would Bach or Vivaldi cross your mind. But they're in there. At least that's what Gabrielle Gray says. She's a classically trained musician and executive director of the International Bluegrass Museum in Owensboro, Kentucky.

"There are definite classical influences in bluegrass," she insists. "Classical music influenced Celtic music—music from Scotland and Ireland—and that's the music that influenced bluegrass."

When immigrants from Scotland, Ireland, England, and Wales settled in the Appalachians and American South, their folk music, lyrics, and instruments brushed up against the folk music and instruments played by immigrants from Africa. One day it would all lead to bluegrass.

"You had the banjo from Africa and the African stomp beat and that developed into gospel and the blues and jazz and ragtime," Gray says. "You had country music that evolved from the Celts. Those were the roots of the tree that Bill Monroe coalesced into the trunk of the tree called bluegrass."

That's right, Bill Monroe is the man who created bluegrass…sort of. In the same way Elvis didn't create rock 'n' roll by himself, Monroe was influenced by many others before becoming the first to plant his flag on bluegrass mountain.

Born in 1911, he grew up in rural Rosine, Kentucky, and studied under the guidance of the area's best music teachers: his parents and his uncle Pen, Pendleton Vandiver. After his older brothers had

> One of Elvis Presley's first hits was a remake of Bill Monroe's "Blue Moon of Kentucky" in which he turned the plaintive waltz-time bluegrass tune into rock 'n' roll. You can understand why he was a little nervous when he encountered Monroe at the Grand Ole Opry. It turned out that Monroe really liked it, and told Elvis that his own up-tempo version was going to be released the following week.

snagged the guitar and fiddle, little Bill, the youngest of eight, was left holding the mandolin. His mother died when he was ten and his father six years later; by the time Monroe was 18 he had let music take a back seat to manual labor. But even while they worked at an Indiana oil refinery, the talented Monroe Brothers were soon making cash at dance hall gigs.

Bill Monroe's definitive sound was still decades away. Until it arrived, he performed on radio shows, landed a recording contract, and turned out hit singles. In 1939 he and his new group, the Blue Grass Boys, earned a regular spot on the Grand Ole Opry. Real success was now seven years away.

If you've ever watched the *Beverly Hillbillies* or *Bonnie and Clyde,* you've heard Earl Scruggs. In 1946 the 21-year-old banjo prodigy joined the Blue Grass Boys and his lightning-fast picking helped accelerate the tempo of Monroe's songs to speeds the country audiences had never heard. The rush of the tempo was balanced by pitch-perfect harmonies complemented by staggering solo breaks. With Monroe on his Gibson F5 mandolin, Scruggs fueling things with three-finger rolls on his banjo, Lester Flatt flatpicking guitar, Howard Watts thumping his bass, and Chubby Wise slicing notes out of his fiddle, they set the Opry on fire.

Before the name "bluegrass" was applied to the style in the 1960s, it was generally known as "old-time mountain hillbilly music."

This lineup was known as the Original Bluegrass Band, but, surprisingly, it recorded fewer than 30 songs. By the time Monroe found the style's classic "high lonesome" sound, America's tastes had changed. Bluegrass would soon be pushed aside to make room for rock 'n' roll.

But just listen to what Monroe crafted in the mid-1940s through songs like "Blue Grass Breakdown," "Molly and Tenbrooks," and "Blue Moon of Kentucky" and you'll get the picture. It's a picture of the American countryside.

DO IT YOURSELF

With more than 1,000 bluegrass festivals taking place every summer, it's easy to plunge into the world of bluegrass. Just check some of the websites below and you'll find a few hundred. Where are they? All over Kentucky—and all over America.

"Kentucky may have birthed it," says Gray. "But it certainly doesn't own it."

One place you should go is the last place you'd expect: San Francisco. The Strictly Bluegrass Festival began in 2001 before the name was changed to the *Hardly* Strictly Bluegrass Festival two years later when its founder, Warren Hellman, featured acts that purists didn't think were thoroughly traditional. It doesn't really matter, because each October more than one million people head to Golden Gate Park to take in three days of free bluegrass music.

During the last weekend in June the International Bluegrass Museum in Owensboro hosts the River of Music Party (ROMP), which features bluegrass pioneers, including some players who performed with Bill Monroe. They'll still take the stage to re-create what they helped create more than half a century ago, joined by younger performers who have been handed the torch.

Sliding down the scale, head to the Barn at Rosine. Located about 40 miles southeast of Owensboro, it's just about a mile from the Monroe Home Place where Bill Monroe was raised and where he and his relatives—including Uncle Pen—are buried. Each Friday evening, inside a weather-beaten old barn, musicians armed with fiddles, mandolins, banjos, basses, and guitars fire up the night. There's an open mic session to get things going and then the players kick in around 7 or 8, digging into the bluegrass as buck dancers stomp and shuffle around the dance floor.

Out here along a remote road in Kentucky, in the twilight beside an old barn, musicians are hooking up with pickup bands in the parking lot and creating music from scratch. After a while a few will set down their instruments and head over to the general store for some fried catfish.

Some things just don't change. Thank goodness.

CONTACTS

International Bluegrass Music Museum
207 East Second Street
Owensboro, Kentucky
(270) 926-7891
(888) 692-2656
www.bluegrassmuseum.org

Too large for Rosine (Bill Monroe's birthplace), this Owensboro museum includes interactive exhibits, costumes, jam sessions on Thursdays, and a collection of videotaped oral histories of first generation bluegrass musicians.

Radio Bluegrass International
24-hour Internet radio station
www.bluegrassmuseum.org/rbi.html

www.bluegrassfestivalguide.com
www.bluegrassworks.com
www.bluegrasslist.com
www.worldwidebluegrass.com

For Lodging and Dining, see p. 299

31. KITTY HAWK
North Carolina

The story of Wilbur and Orville Wright is extraordinary. Without assistance from any individual or institution, the soft-spoken bicycle mechanics took flight apart piece by piece and solved dozens of problems that had stalled experts for centuries. They did it all from the workshop of their bicycle business in Dayton, Ohio, and then proved it on the sands of Kill Devil Hills, North Carolina.

THE WRIGHT STUFF

How, in just a few years, did two guys who never finished high school perfect each component system needed for three-axis flight? Not only that, how on earth did two guys wearing *suits* haul a 600-pound flying machine up and down the deep sand dunes of the North Carolina coast?

A quarter century after the first flight, photographer Daniels recalled that before the flight, Wilbur and Orville stepped away from the group, shared a few words, and shook hands as if maybe they'd never see each other again. As Orville slid into the hip cradle atop the lower wing, Wilbur told the group to cheer and wave to keep his brother's spirits high.

Prior to 1900, Wilbur and Orville Wright were publishing a little newspaper and running a bicycle shop in Dayton, Ohio. Over in Europe, the "German glider king" Otto Lillienthal had published data on wing design that everyone agreed was the model to follow. It wasn't. In 1896, he died when a gust of wind stalled his craft and it crashed. Wilbur, who was intent on making some contribution to humanity, felt the tragedy gave him a chance to uncover the secrets of flight.

The self-taught engineer and scientist wrote to the U.S. Weather Bureau for a rundown of the windiest places in America. For its privacy, open space, and consistent breezes he chose the sixth windiest place: Kitty Hawk, on the Outer Banks of North Carolina. It was four miles south of there, at Kill Devil Hills, that Wilbur and his younger brother, Orville, began creating gliders they could test on the sand dunes.

For four years beginning in 1900 they traveled to Kitty Hawk and contended with sand fleas, freezing weather, storms, and, memorably, the unsuccessful 1901 season that nearly defeated them. Realizing the Lillienthal design was wrong, the brothers began carving miniature wing shapes out of old hacksaw blades; mounted them on bicycle spoke perches; and tested them in a handmade wind tunnel until they had tested more than 200 versions. The most promising was a breakthrough design used on a 1902 glider that also included an "elevator" to help control the aircraft and a rudder that would stabilize the steering system, called wing warping. Oh, and since no propellers existed, they had to invent their own and then carve them by hand. On top of that, they needed an engine that could power the craft. But since none of the 15 automobile companies they contacted knew how to make one, they asked Charlie Taylor, the master machinist at their bicycle shop, to build one. He did it from scratch. In six weeks.

Between 1900 and 1903, the Wright Brothers invested about $1,000 in their tests.

When the Wrights returned to Kitty Hawk in September 1903, broken propeller shafts delayed their tests as they awaited replacements from home. But the replacements arrived broken, so Orville packed his bags, headed back to Ohio, built his own shafts, and headed back to Kitty Hawk. There was another delay on Sunday, December 13, since they had promised their father, a church bishop, that they wouldn't fly on the Sabbath. A minor accident on the 14th postponed things until the 17th, when it was Orville's turn to fly.

Guards from the nearby lifesaving station arrived to help move the machine into place. Wilbur placed lifeguard John T. Daniels at a camera and told him to squeeze the bulb when the craft was aloft. When Orville released the restraining wire around 10:30 a.m., the *Wright Flyer* lifted into the air. It flew 120 feet in about 12 seconds and was the world's first powered and controlled flight of a heavier-than-air craft. Daniels was so excited, he couldn't tell Wilbur if he had snapped the photo, but Wilbur was so excited that when it was his turn to fly he soared 175 feet. That was soon eclipsed by Orville's second flight of 200 feet. Not to be outdone, Wilbur took off again…and kept going. His second flight covered 852 feet in just under a minute. Before the fifth flight a gust of wind flipped the *Wright Flyer* and damaged it beyond repair, but it didn't matter. The Wright Brothers had invented a machine that proved powered, controlled flight was possible. And they had proof.

Daniels had taken the picture.

> Why'd they do it? As Orville noted years later, "We did it for fun. We were trying to have fun." Wilbur agreed: "From the time when we were children, my brother Orville and I always worked and played together."

DO IT YOURSELF

The landscape in the 1903 image of Orville sailing over the sand is not what you'll see today. Kitty Hawk is jam-packed.

Once you've adjusted to the passage of time, you'll appreciate the small museum at the Wright Brothers National Memorial. Looking out through bay windows you see markers that show the distances flown in 1903. Before stepping outside, attend a presentation in the Flight Room. Before a full-size model of the 1903 *Wright Flyer*, the rangers share the dramatic story of the Wrights' years of experimentation, failures, and success.

Outside, near the markers, are re-creations of the rustic camp buildings where the Wrights lived. You can only imagine what it must have taken for those two to leave home year after year and rough it in such Spartan conditions, not knowing whether their efforts would lead to success. Walking onto the field you can also see marker "4" nearly 300 yards away—without a word many visitors begin walking the entire length of the field.

A quarter-mile to the south is Big Kill Devil Hill, atop which stands the grand monument dedicated to the brothers in 1928. Some people walk there and others drive, but all are impressed by its aeronautical art deco design, the busts of Wilbur and Orville, and the expansive view from the top of the 90-foot hill. Walk around the monument and read the inscription that wraps around its base:

"In commemoration of the conquest of the air by the brothers Wilbur and Orville Wright, conceived by genius, achieved by dauntless resolution and unconquerable faith."

CONTACTS

Wright Brothers National Memorial
(252) 441-7430
www.nps.gov/wrbr

Outer Banks Visitors Bureau
(252) 473-2138 or (877) 629-4386
www.outerbanks.org

For Lodging and Dining, see pp. 299–300

32. MOUNT AIRY (MAYBERRY)
North Carolina

In every city and town between Savannah and San Diego, any conversation that touches upon the virtues of a small town will invariably include the name Mayberry. Although it's a fantasy, Mayberry has become a real part of America, thanks to Andy Griffith and his memories of his hometown.

RETURN TO MAYBERRY

Andy Griffith had already honed his craft as an actor portraying Sir Walter Raleigh in *The Lost Colony* before turning to Broadway and motion pictures in the 1950s with comedies like *No Time for Sergeants* and the drama *A Face in the Crowd*. But an entirely new level of stardom was around the corner.

In 1960, on an episode of *The Danny Thomas Show*, Griffith played a small-town sheriff who pulls Thomas over for speeding. The casting and the story worked so well that by the following October *The Andy Griffith Show,* television's first spin-off series, was airing on CBS.

Right away, Mayberry seemed like a real town with real people. Viewers knew Sheriff Andy Taylor, a widower, was raising Opie with help from his aunt Bee and that his deputy, Barney Fife, carried only a single bullet in his pocket. The lawmen got their hair cut at Floyd's Barber Shop; had Gomer Pyle check out the squad car at the filling station; and often took their girls, Helen Crump and Thelma Lou, down to the diner for the blue-plate special. When duty called, they'd occasionally have to lock up rock-throwing Ernest T. Bass or Otis Campbell, the town drunk.

It was a television sitcom, but it felt...*different.* Because Griffith was a storyteller, characters didn't speak in punchlines. He told writers if something sounded like a joke, toss it out. Each episode was scripted and shot like a thirty-minute movie with a balance of gentle humor and pathos that would have viewers laughing and crying in the same half hour.

Over eight seasons and 249 episodes Mayberry seemed so real that, a half century later, fans of the show included Oprah Winfrey, Garth Brooks, R.E.M, and Bill Clinton (each of whom are members of The Andy Griffith Show Rerun Watchers Club).

Further evidence that Mount Airy may indeed be Mayberry is found in a listing of local businesses, which includes Mayberry Auto Sales, the Mayberry Motor Inn, Mayberry Mall, Mayberry Alarm Company...and Wedding Chapel, Campground, Country Store, Five and Dime, Learning Center, Consignments, Embroidery, Flea Market, Kountry Kitchen, Pharmacy, Waterworks, and Septic Pumping Service.

You may not be able to get to Mayberry, but if you get to Andy's hometown of Mount Airy, you'll be pretty close.

DO IT YOURSELF

Andy Griffith spent years insisting that Mount Airy was not Mayberry and he could have spent 100 more years pushing the point, but fans and folks still living in his hometown begged to differ. People were so anxious for America to have a real Mayberry that over time the fantasy of Griffith's program and the real-life Mount Airy merged into one.

To be honest, this isn't a bad place to put a fantasy town. Located just south of the Virginia border, Mount Airy's in the foothills of the Blue Ridge Mountains and only a few miles from the beautiful Blue Ridge Parkway. The town of Pilot Mountain (remember Mount Pilot?) is nearby, Raleigh's a little farther, and there's a prevailing sense of the South all around.

You'll get this feeling when you arrive and see that things haven't changed much since the days of black-and-white television. A molasses-slow pace coats the town. Walk down Main Street and drop by Snappy Lunch, which fans claim was the inspiration for Mayberry's diner. Oprah has eaten here and so has Aneta Corsaut (Helen Crump) and Hal Smith (Otis); they and nearly every other patron have ordered a pork chop sandwich. If you're feeling shaggy, a few doors down is Floyd's City Barber Shop (two chairs!) and the barber's likely to ask you if he can take your picture to post with thousands of others he's collected over the years.

Even if Andy Griffith had been born in New York, Mount Airy would still be known for the world's largest open-face granite quarry; Donna Fargo (the Happiest Girl in the Whole USA); and Chang and Eng Bunker, the original Siamese twins.

Super fan Wes Collins restored a circa 1937 filling station and created Wally's Service Station, a great place to dip into the soda pop cooler and pick out an RC Cola or Nehi and then just sit a spell in one of the rocking chairs and nibble a Moon Pie. In the old Studebaker dealership next door, Collins also created a brilliant replica of Sheriff Taylor's Mayberry Courthouse so fans can sit at Andy's desk or lock themselves in Cell Number One or Cell Number Two. Fellow fan Mike Cockerham tricked out a fleet of vintage Ford Galaxie 500s (based at Wally's), each customized as a Mayberry squad car, and stands ready to take you on a tour of the town.

Griffith's finger-pickin' guitar and the mighty strange Darling family proved that music and Mayberry belonged together. That's true in Mount Airy. Every Saturday morning folks head on over for a free show at Main Street's Downtown Cinema. It's the WPAQ "Merry-Go-Round," a broadcast of live bluegrass that's been going out over the airwaves since 1948.

Continue your fall back through time at the Bright Leaf Drive-In out on Andy Griffith Parkway (Highway 52 North).

To witness the town's crowning achievement, make plans to be here the last full weekend in September. To help promote those Mayberry Days, the Surry County Arts Council publishes the annual *Mayberry Confidential*, a newsletter that includes vital news about Aunt Bee's bake sale and details on the Little Miss Mayberry pageant. About 30,000 fans from around town and the world arrive to see folks connected to the show; watch the parade on Main Street; compete in checkers and horseshoe tournaments and an apple-peeling contest; listen to more bluegrass; enter a pie eating contest; socialize at Mrs. Wiley's Tea Party; and snap photos with fans dressed as Barney, Floyd, Gomer, Otis, Opie, and other favorite characters.

Even after the festival's over, fans and the idly curious head over to the Andy Griffith Playhouse. Inside is the world's largest collection of Griffith memorabilia, some of it donated by fans and townsfolk and some contributed by Barney and Thelma Lou—Don Knotts and Betty Lynn. On the third Saturday evening of each month, red-hot pickers play at the long-running bluegrass jam session there.

Nearby is the statue that TV Land unveiled in 2004. It's a statue of Andy and Opie hand in hand, just a father and son carrying their poles and heading to the ol' fishin' hole.

A lot of us wish we could tag along.

CONTACTS

Mount Airy Visitors Center
200 North Main Street
(336) 786-6116
(800) 948-0949
www.visitmayberry.com

Mount Airy Chamber of Commerce
www.mtairyncchamber.org

The Andy Griffith Show Rerun Watchers Club
www.mayberry.com

Mayberry Squad Car Tours
(336) 789-6743
www.tourmayberry.com

Andy Griffith Playhouse
218 Rockford Street
(336) 786-7998

For Lodging and Dining, see pp. 300–301

33. GREAT SMOKY MOUNTAINS
Tennessee/North Carolina

Researchers have theorized that the Garden of Eden was in Iraq, Scotland, northeast Africa, or somewhere along the Persian Gulf. My educated opinion is that it still exists, and it straddles the border of Tennessee and North Carolina.

The Great Smoky Mountains are home to more species of trees than the European continent. Drive the roads or walk the trails and you'll glimpse trout lilies, yellow trillium, flame azaleas, rhododendrons, mountain laurels, fire pinks, and more than 1,600 other types of flowers. Living here are animals found nowhere else on the planet, roaming across ecosystems that range from wetlands, grassy balds, and spruce forests to cove hardwoods and the only remaining old-growth forest east of the Mississippi.

No wonder this is America's most visited national park.

ENVIRONMENTAL PROTECTIONS

Today's environmentalists face constant uphill battles, so you can only imagine how challenging things were for conservationists in the 1920s. It was up to them to save the Great Smoky Mountains from destruction. Logging companies were ripping apart huge chunks of forest, which loosened the soil, polluted the rivers, and set the stage for erosion and mudslides. Judging by photographs from the era, it was a horrific scene.

Because this is the most visited national park in the U.S., plan your visit wisely. If you arrive in peak season, the odds of enjoying a peaceful retreat are greatly diminished.

Sprouting from the ruin was the farfetched idea that it could be saved. A unique confederation comprising Tennessee and North Carolina state governments, the federal government, John D. Rockefeller, Jr., and private citizens gathered money (Rockefeller alone kicked in $5 million) and bought parcels of land piece by piece until they had saved 800 square miles from destruction. What was lost in the rescue was several mountain communities. More than a thousand people moved out and left behind nearly 80 now-historic structures including grist mills, schools, and barns. Also uprooted were family histories, stories, folk songs, and ways of life that had existed there for well over a century.

President Franklin Roosevelt dedicated the Great Smoky Mountains National Park in 1940. Since then, this magnificent wilderness has become an easy day's destination for tens of millions of residents of the southeastern United States: solo travelers, couples, and families wishing to find themselves by getting lost in nature.

DO IT YOURSELF

The easiest and most popular activity is a casual drive along the more than 270 miles of roads that crisscross the park. Splitting the park horizontally, from east to west, is Highway 441, a smooth road that winds through forests and broad valleys, opening vistas that stretch clear to the horizon, uninterrupted by any trace of civilization.

On the North Carolina side of the park, the towns of Cherokee and Bryson City are near the eastern entrance, but odds are you'll start at the western entrance at Gatlinburg, a town that's a clutter of tourist traps, fudge shops, and gawdy gift boutiques that, surprisingly, are all super enjoyable. A few miles past the Gatlinburg entrance is the largest of the visitors centers, known as Sugarlands, which offers maps, brochures, and information on activities like camping, fishing, and horseback riding.

Past Sugarlands, it's about 25 miles to Cades Cove where many pioneer families once lived. The Little River Road, which leads there, follows the river's slow and graceful turns to create an experience Germans call *fahrvenügen*.

Or, you could stick with 441 for the entire 40 miles to the North Carolina entrance. The speed limit is just 35 mph and the mountain road is as pleasing and curvaceous as Mamie van Doren. Pullouts and scenic vistas remind you to take your time because there, especially, the pleasure is in the journey, not the destination. You'll be tempted to stop and explore forest paths and clear streams that inspire you to ditch your planner and enjoy your planet.

> **Surrounding the Smokies are whitewater rivers like the Nantahala, Ocoee, Big Pigeon, and Lower Pigeon. A few, but not the only outfitters, are: Rafting in the Smokies (865-436-5008 or 800-776-7238, www.raftinginthesmokies.com), River Thunder (800-408-7238, www.rollingthunder riverco.com), Wildwater Ltd. (800-451-9972, www.wildwaterrafting.com), and the Nantahala Outdoor Center (888-590-9268, www.noc.com).**

At Newfound Gap at the North Carolina–Tennessee border, you've reached 5,046 feet, and there are wonderful views all around. Definitely worth a stop, the Gap is just a few miles shy of the entrance to Clingman's Dome, an even higher peak—6,634 feet—accessed by a spur road that brings you to lookouts that are even more impressive.

From there, gravity, not gas, can take you on a steady descent from the mountains into the eastern regions of the park. Stick around the Smokies for a few days and use part of your life for camping out, riding horses, birdwatching, photographing waterfalls, cooking out, hiking in the woods, picnicking, or fishing. Or, simply invest your time in doing something really extraordinary…

Absolutely nothing.

> **Why Smoky? A natural bluish haze settles over the hills and ridges, the result of hydrocarbons released by vegetation. With higher levels of pollution filtering in, they may one day have to rename them the Smoggy Mountains.**

CONTACTS

Great Smoky Mountains National Park
(865) 436-1200
www.nps.gov/grsm

Cherokee (NC) Chamber of Commerce
www.cherokeesmokies.com
(877) 433-6700

Gatlinburg (TN) Chamber of
Commerce
(800) 588-1817
www.gatlinburg.com

Bryson City (NC) Chamber of
Commerce
(828) 488-3681
www.greatsmokies.com

For Lodging and Dining, see p. 301

34. FORT SUMTER
Charleston, South Carolina

For nearly a century after American became a nation, politicians had passed the buck when it came to slavery. Until 1861 no one faction was willing to put the nation's unity at risk over it. Now the battle had to begin somewhere. That somewhere was Fort Sumter.

SHOWDOWN IN THE SOUTH

No one knew where America would go to war with itself, but the folks down in Charleston, South Carolina, were beginning to get the idea it would begin there.

The state had already let it be known that if antislavery candidate Abraham Lincoln was elected president, they would divorce themselves from America. Lincoln was, in November, and so on December 20, 1860, South Carolina made good on its threat and seceded from the Union. The news sounded warning bells to Robert Anderson, an Army major in command of approximately 80 men at Fort Moultrie on Charleston Harbor. For their own safety, he and his men rowed across the harbor and moved into Fort Sumter, a more defensible island stronghold still under construction after thirty years.

Abner Doubleday, who is known (incorrectly) as the man who invented baseball, was stationed at Fort Sumter when the war began.

Anderson's men were already at a disadvantage. Only 60 of the fort's planned 135 guns were in place, and Anderson's troops could only man 15 cannons at a time.

Charlestonians didn't want a bunch of uninvited Yankees living in their harbor. Negotiations with Anderson began, but the major (who had no authority to surrender the fort) played for time by sending messages to the War Department in Washington. Also stalling for time was President James Buchanan, who wanted to postpone major decisions (aka pass the buck) until Lincoln assumed the presidency in March.

By January, South Carolina and several other states had become the Confederate States of America. When a Union supply ship appeared in the harbor, cadets from the Citadel fired on and damaged the *Star of the West*. The showdown started shaping up.

Lincoln made it clear he didn't recognize the Confederate States of America or their right to secede. He ordered ships to Charleston, but storms split up the flotilla and fractured this show of force. When several of the ships reached Charleston near midnight on April 11, 1861, the last day of peace the nation would know for four years had ended.

Around 4:30 a.m. a ten-inch mortar shell fired by Confederate Lt. Henry S. Farley exploded over Fort Sumter. All the other batteries then let loose. According to legend, civilian Edmund Ruffin, one of the state's most passionate secessionists and proponents of slavery, fired the first shot. The story goes that the 67-year-old was granted the honor of lighting the fuse on a cannon aimed straight at Fort Sumter by troops at the Ironclad Battery. Historians side with Farley, but Ruffin's consolation prize was being one of the Civil War's final casualties. After the Confederacy was vanquished in 1865, he blew his brains out.

When the shells began hailing down upon Fort Sumter, Lt. Norman J. Hall saw the Stars and Stripes knocked off the flagpole. Knowing that this would be seen as a sign of surrender, Hall picked up the flag and, exposing himself to fire on the highest walls of the parapet, put the flag back in view on a makeshift pole. The flag is on display in the fort's museum.

Inside Fort Sumter, Anderson and his men were besieged by a 33-hour bombardment of cannonballs and mortar shells that came across the harbor. On shore, Charleston bluebloods enjoyed the sight from the waterfront Battery, sipping cool drinks as they watched shells land on the fort.

Anderson's men tried to answer the assault, but they knew they were outmanned and outgunned. By April 13, Anderson accepted the inevitable and surrendered Fort Sumter. Within hours, the Confederates took the fort.

Major Anderson took something just as valuable. He took the flag.

THE EXPERIENCE

Throughout the war, the Union Army repeatedly and unsuccessfully attempted to retake Fort Sumter. When it finally got the fort back in 1865, four years of war had wrecked it. It was used as a lighthouse station for the rest of the 19th century. In World War I it was used again as a fort. During World War II it took on its current role as a tourist attraction administered by the National Park Service.

The mainland Visitors Education Center is the best place to begin your tour, with exhibits that catch you up on the story of what you are going to see. From there, it takes about half an hour to travel the three-plus miles across the harbor to reach Fort Sumter. An audio history played en route fills in more blanks.

In peak season, visits are limited to about an hour—you should be selective about how you choose to spend your time. You can invest about 15 minutes listening to a ranger deliver a history of the fort and its battles; you can spend a little time going through the museum; and you can spend the rest of your time on a self-guided tour across the parade ground and atop the walls.

> When the Confederates controlled Fort Sumter during the Civil War, they, too, were under blockade. To get supplies to the troops, Confederate blockade runners sailed at night to avoid the omnipresent Union guns.

What you see at Fort Sumter today is only a small fraction of what was once here. On July 10, 1863, the Union began shelling the fort and, in seven days, had dropped more than half a million pounds of shells atop it. The siege of Fort Sumter lasted a total of 587 days and pounded the fort nearly to the ground. Before the Confederates finally called it quits on February 17, 1865, they had been subjected to an assault that threw an estimated seven million pounds of shells weighing from 30 to 440 pounds.

That may have savaged most of the fort, but it was another vital step in saving the Union.

CONTACTS

Fort Sumter National Monument
(843) 883-3123
www.nps.gov/fosu

www.spiritlinecruises.com

For Lodging and Dining, see pp. 301–302

35. GRAND OLE OPRY
Nashville, Tennessee

Of the hundreds of musical styles competing for attention on the air-waves and Internet, country music is the most popular. It began with Irish and British immigrants who arrived with a treasury of folk music that later mingled with African-inspired slave spirituals. This hybrid found new expression on handmade banjos, guitars, autoharps, and fiddles. Since 1925, the Grand Ole Opry has chronicled and celebrated the development of country music. By paying tribute to country music's many intertwined roots as well as its new branches, the Opry remains timeless.

MUSIC FOR THE HOME FOLKS

Elvis Presley gets the credit for creating rock and roll and W. C. Handy gets a bow for inventing blues. Is there also one person who can be considered the genius behind country music?

Credit goes to quirky Appalachian fruit tree salesman Alvin Pleasant (A.P.) Carter of Maces Springs, Virginia. While on sales calls through the Clinch Mountains and Poor Valley in the 1920s, he heard mountain families singing songs that had been passed down over generations. Haunted by these melodies, he'd transcribe the music and lyrics as best he could when he got home. Then he'd teach them to his wife, Sara, and her cousin Maybelle. In 1927, the women joined A.P. in Bristol, Tennessee, for a recording session arranged by Ralph Peer, a traveling producer for Victor Records. By the end of the session, the Carter Family had recorded songs Peer could sell. The trio later added to the foundation of country music with songs like "Wildwood Flower," "Can the Circle Be Unbroken," and "Keep on the Sunny Side."

Also discovered at the Bristol sessions was another pioneer of country music—Jimmie Rodgers, known as the "singing brakeman." Soon, at barn raisings and house parties and local dances and on crystal radio sets across America, the songs of the Carters and Rodgers and their peers were being heard. In the sinful fast-paced Jazz Age, these down-home tunes reassured anxious families that the nation was still both moral and rural. Radio stations, primarily in the South, began broadcasting "barn dances" featuring hillbilly comics and musicians. It just so happened

When buying your ticket, try to get a seat on the left side of the auditorium, where the performers enter. Remember, too, that you're allowed to approach the stage and take pictures anytime.

that one of these shows, the "WSM Barn Dance," grew up to become the "Grand Ole Opry."

First broadcast on WSM (650 AM) on November 28, 1925, "Grand Ole Opry" is the world's longest-running live radio show. The Opry has presented the biggest names in the business, welcoming Roy Acuff, Minnie Pearl, George Jones, Ernest Tubb, Hank Williams, Loretta Lynn, Patsy Cline, Garth Brooks, Reba McIntire, Faith Hill, and Carrie Underwood—and thousands of others.

"I think country music was designed for people who worked hard all week in the fields or the factory or wherever their jobs were," muses country music scholar and star Marty Stuart. "The Grand Ole Opry gave people a sense of community and gave them a reason to get together and have fellowship. And it was a reason to get up and forget your troubles and kick up your heels and hear fiddle tunes and square dance tunes and sing songs about real life. And that's what you still hear at the Grand Ole Opry."

Everyone on tonight's bill understands this. When a performer is asked to appear on the Grand Ole Opry, they know they've earned the equivalent of a country music gold medal.

DO IT YOURSELF

Twenty minutes northeast of Nashville, the modern retail and hotel complex known collectively as Opryland is a far cry from the fabled Ryman Auditorium in downtown Nashville. Originally a tabernacle and the Opry's home from 1943 to 1974, it is known as the "mother church of country music." Opry shows are still held at the Ryman during the wintertime.

While in Nashville, don't miss the Country Music Hall of Fame (222 Fifth Avenue, 615-416-2001, www.countrymusichalloffame.com). Its collection includes Bill Monroe's mandolin, Maybelle Carter's guitar, and Webb Pierce's stylized Cadillac with a bullhorn hood ornament and pearl-handled revolver door handles.

Opryland is a new 4,424-seat venue where the wide open stage, red barn backdrop, and church pew seats pay tribute to Opry's days at the Ryman. At center stage, where the lead singer stands, is a circular section of wood cut from the old Ryman stage.

Thanks to a program that places country music legends on the same bill as newcomers, gospel groups with square dancers, and bluegrass musicians with Cajun singers, you'll rarely see the same show twice. But the amount of talent you'll see is phenomenal.

All of this is a live radio show divided into four thirty-minute segments. The whole shebang kicks off with an energetic "Let 'er go, boys!," followed by a blast of music. The on-stage announcer then reads the lineup of performers and thanks the sponsors before bringing out the first act.

After the first performers have delivered two songs, they stick around to host the next half-hour, retreating to the wings as the second act takes center stage and delivers their two numbers. Once in a while the announcer pitches Cracker Barrel or Martha White biscuit mix or some other product that's been around for generations while the audience catches its breath. As that's going on, the stage crew adjusts a stage full of equipment and instruments and microphones in a matter of seconds.

> How do you write a country song? Hank Williams, arguably one of the most influential musicians in any genre, thought it was simple: "A song ain't nothin' in the world but a story wrote with music to it."

The show's timing is precise, and some performers have been demonstrating their precision for more than fifty years. But as far as country music artists are concerned, the Grand Ole Opry is the pinnacle of their profession, so you can bet your bottom dollar that even if they made their debut in 1958, they're going to put on the best show they can every time.

The sheer exuberance of the performers syncs up with the enthusiasm of the audience throughout the night. When bluegrass legend Bobby Osborne takes the stage and flies through a lightning-fast rendition of "Rocky Top"; when The Whites throw the audience into overdrive with the rocking gospel tune "Big Wheel"; when The Isaacs have 4,000 people on their feet with "Walk On" and then, minutes later, have them sitting hushed in their seats during an a cappella spiritual, you'll look around and understand the soul of country music and the unique power of the Grand Ole Opry.

CONTACTS

Grand Ole Opry
(615) 871-6779 (OPRY)
www.opry.com

Nashville Chamber of Commerce
www.nashvillechamber.com

Nashville Convention and Visitors Bureau
(615) 259-4700
(800) 657-6910
www.visitmusiccity.com

For Lodging and Dining, see pp. 302–303

36. TENT REVIVALS
Tennessee and Across the American South

Supplanted by the broad reach of radio, television, and the Internet, only a dwindling band of itinerant preachers still takes to the road to pitch a tent and deliver the Word. While it's a method of communication rooted in tradition, so is their message.

A MESSAGE FROM CAMP

Beginning around 1800, missionary groups eager to spread the Gospel and social activists revved to preach against slavery, alcohol, and a multitude of sins introduced a new style of delivering deliverance called a camp meeting.

Settlers in remote areas would congregate in a clearing and watch as tag-team preachers conducted religious services that could last for days. Preachers addressing a flock that hadn't enjoyed much entertainment for months were generally able to work bored, curious, cynical, or faithful worshippers into fits of dancing, shouting, and singing. When they were emotionally spent and spiritually ecstatic, they'd be ripe and ready for repentance.

After the Civil War, memories of camp meetings followed families as they traveled into the American West. Settlers were confident that God was willing to attend a service whether they sat in church pews or set up a makeshift open-air service on the plains. These services seemed akin to those of former slaves who, for obvious reasons, often had to conduct worship covertly.

But even after towns had been settled and churches constructed, the simplicity of these open-air services held its appeal. As America closed in on the 20th century, camp meetings evolved into tent revivals: Traveling preachers issued dire warnings of the Second Coming, appeared to cure someone through the strength of their faith, and inspired the congregation to speak in tongues.

Despite novels like *Elmer Gantry* that targeted unscrupulous ministers, tent revivals held on until the advent of radio, when some preachers folded up their tents and took to the airwaves. Fast forward to the 1950s, when former tent preachers like Oral Roberts and Billy Graham became televangelists. In their wake, ministers of a new generation stepped into the breach to preach.

While today's tent revivals are generally more subdued than those of the past, drop in and you can see the modern equivalent of the old camp meetings of the early 1800s.

DO IT YOURSELF

The first trick to attending an old-fashioned tent revival is finding one. Your chances improve in the Deep South or around the southern Appalachians, but some small-tent preachers and larger road shows roam outside these regions to share their spiritual message.

Many itinerant preachers rely on word-of-mouth advertising as well as assistance from local churches to announce their arrival. That's how Pastor Anthony Wynn of Athens, Tennessee, does it six months a year.

"A tent is an awesome tool to reach people," he explains. "There's no commitment, nothing real formal, just the presence of Jesus. People who may not feel comfortable going into a church will walk into a tent."

Wynn arrives in town with his tent, chairs, staging, lights, and a PA system. A few dozen friends who've seen him preach are there to help pitch the tent. When the sun has set, and the congregation is seated, the local pastor begins the service with singalong standards like "Amazing Grace" and "What a Friend We Have in Jesus." Then members share personal stories of redemption. To a chorus of "Amen!" and "Thank you, Jesus," Pastor Wynn takes the microphone and leads the congregation in song. Soon he gets down to the business of saving souls.

"I like to preach heaven and hell because if I don't reach people that night, then I don't know how long it'll be until they go to another service," he explains. "I have just one sermon to tell them that you're not going to stay here forever so you have a choice: You may break an appointment with a doctor or a lawyer, but you can't break an appointment with Jesus Christ."

It's not just parishioners in the folding chairs who are getting emotional. Even Pastor Wynn is weeping and crying because he knows that lives are on the line and he wants people to get right with God. He preaches and reads Scripture and pretty soon the service starts to slow down and people bow their heads as music plays and hands are raised. "Who is lost?" asks Pastor Wynn. If anyone is lost and needs guidance and a helping hand, he can walk to the altar and repent and accept Christ as his personal savior. It's obviously a special moment for the lost soul as well as for the man at the pulpit.

For an in-depth account of tent revivals, find a copy of Patsy Sims's 1996 book, *Can Somebody Shout Amen! Inside the Tents and Tabernacles of American Revivalists*.

"This is always a real sacred moment," Wynn shares. "The atmosphere is electrified but it's also very solemn and sincere."

"I don't make very much doing this," he reflects. "But I'm a country boy and it doesn't take much to make me happy. I'm just a builder making a difference one soul at a time. This isn't to build my ministry. It's to build the Kingdom of God."

CONTACTS
Pastor Anthony Wynn
www.holyghostonline.com

For Lodging and Dining, see p. 285

For Lodging and Dining, see p. 285

37. GRACELAND
Memphis, Tennessee

From obscure and impoverished roots, Elvis Presley rose to global fame and immense wealth. Sadly, the fame draped upon Elvis was a burden so heavy it crushed him. He died in isolation at Graceland at the age of 42, proving it can be dangerous to get all you want—but not all you need. The King is dead; long live Graceland.

A DIAMOND IN THE ROUGH

Until you can get to the bookstore to buy Peter Guralnick's brilliant *Last Train to Memphis,* here's a thumbnail sketch of Elvis.

He was born on January 8, 1935, in Tupelo, Mississippi. His twin brother, Jesse Garon Presley, was stillborn; that may have led his mother, Gladys, to erect an obsessive wall of protection around her only surviving child. Elvis grew up sheltered and extremely poor. Things stayed that way even after his father, Vernon, moved his family out of their shotgun shack and to Memphis, Tennessee, in 1948. There, Elvis carried his guitar to Humes High School and listened to blues, R&B, and gospel records at Poplar Tunes (he couldn't afford to buy them). He also began sporting a greased-up James Dean hairstyle with trucker-inspired sideburns. How many times the oddball teenager got his ass kicked, no one knows.

If you're more interested in paying your respects than paying admission, plan to arrive at Graceland at 7:30 a.m., when folks can visit the family cemetery in Meditation Garden free of charge.

Somehow, Elvis found enough inner confidence to participate in a school talent show, try out for football, and enroll in ROTC. In July 1953, the 18-year-old high school grad even had the brass to drop by the Memphis Recording Service and record himself singing and playing guitar on "My Happiness" and "That's When Your Heartache Begins." Marion Keisker, the secretary, thought she heard something in the boy's voice and kept a duplicate recording. Keisker's hunch paid off a year later when producer Sam Phillips (who was always searching for a "white man with a black man's voice") invited Elvis to jam with musicians Scotty Moore and Bill Black. At the end of a plodding and disappointing session, Phillips was changing tapes when Elvis tried to break the tension by vamping on the blues song "That's All Right (Mama)." When Moore and Black joined in, the trio had fused hillbilly with blues and gospel to create a hybrid called rock 'n' roll.

Visit Memphis's Sun Studio (706 Union Avenue, 901-521-0664/800-441-6249, www.sunstudio.com), where Elvis, Jerry Lee Lewis, Carl Perkins, Johnny Cash, Roy Orbison, and others recorded their first tracks. You can even record a song here yourself at the birthplace of rock 'n' roll. A must-see.

Phillips had never heard anything like it—and neither had anyone else. When "That's All Right" was released, no one knew if the singer was black or white; that song and Elvis's follow-up Sun recordings turned the established music scene upside-down. And when Presley's stage fright caused his legs to quiver during live shows, he inadvertently created a sexy burlesque to go with his looks and his voice. His talent was undeniable. From the road to television to the movies, Elvis was unstoppable. Until 1977.

Fame came so easy that Elvis's life became too hard. The lack of challenges and his dependence on drugs and yes-men killed him. When he died on August 16, 1977, his manager observed that it didn't change a thing and, in a way, he was right. Even though he was gone, fans could still see his stuff— and there was so much of it.

The most important piece of memorabilia Elvis left behind was Graceland, his home for 20 years. It has become the gathering place for mourning fans and the merely curious.

DO IT YOURSELF

Now that you've primed yourself with Elvis lore, it's time for the payoff. By the spring of 1957, Elvis felt he needed privacy and he found it at Graceland. The 22-year-old paid $100,000 for the home and its 14 surrounding acres. After he and his family moved in, things seemed to imitate the Beverly Hillbillies. His mother, Gladys, furrowed out some ground to plant her snap beans and his grandmother Minnie Mae moved in. While Elvis was in the Army, Gladys died. From then on the mansion was a private retreat for a rich young man, his sycophants, and assorted starlets. From recording albums to lavish living to all night parties, it's impossible to list everything that occurred at Graceland.

It turns out that Elvis's finances, like his body, had been greatly depleted. After his death, ex-wife Priscilla arrived to transform Elvis's legacy into an empire. The gates of Graceland opened in 1982 and it soon became the second-most visited home in America (just after the White House).

Bring a Sharpie on your trip. On the wall fronting Elvis Presley Boulevard, fans scrawl notes to Elvis. You can do the same, adding your sentiments alongside notes like "Elvis didn't die, he just went home." And "Elvis is my personal Jesus."

The Platinum Tour includes a self-guided audio tour of his home and his planes and cars. There are wings in the home that feature walls of awards, racks of costumes, and fleets of cars. The ostentatious Jungle Room, dining room, and living room reveal how one wealthy person who remembered what it was like growing up poor would decorate a house in tacky 1970s style.

Outside the mansion, the former racquetball court now holds an extensive showcase of Elvis's personal memorabilia. There you can glimpse his old Army uniform, movie costumes, paperwork, canceled checks written to hundreds of charities, and a dazzling array of awards and gold records. The final stop on the tour is Meditation Garden, the final resting place for Elvis and his family. Having seen what he achieved, it's strange that it all ended here so soon. An eternal flame, fresh and faded flowers, and a heartfelt inscription written by his father adorn his grave.

At this point, even the merely curious stand as solemnly as his devoted fans do.

CONTACTS

Graceland
(901) 332-3322
(800) 238-2000
www.elvis.com

Memphis Convention and
Visitors Bureau
(901) 543-5300
www.memphistravel.com

For Lodging and Dining, see p. 303

38. MISSISSIPPI DELTA
Northwest Mississippi

A century ago it seemed even hope was a luxury for black fieldhands and sharecroppers trying to make a living in the Mississippi Delta. Their songs were their emotional outlets. Eventually, the music of men like Robert Johnson, Muddy Waters, Son House, and Elmore James was heard in juke joints and on jukeboxes far beyond the Delta's fields and shacks.

THE ORIGINAL HOUSE OF BLUES

In 1900, there wasn't much in the Delta of northwest Mississippi. A handful of automobiles, dead-end jobs, poor schools, and little opportunity. No television, certainly, and it was far too early even for radio. If you wanted to travel, you could hitch a ride on a freight train, but more often your range was generally limited to how far you could walk.

But with a guitar, fiddle, banjo, harmonica, a box to beat on, or a tool to provide a rhythm, people could sing about love, despair, heartbreak, hope, oppression, sex, or any topic that could fit into a 12-bar rhythm. Their Southern mix of African spirituals, minstrel show standards, gospel numbers, and field songs was about to be folded together into the foundation of a new type of music.

For a complete roster of local juke joints, contact the Delta Blues Museum. In Clarksdale you'll find the Ground Zero Blues Club, Red's Lounge, Club 2000, and Sarah's Kitchen. Down in Merigold, check out what some consider to be the last true juke joint, Po' Monkeys.

Up in Memphis in 1909, musician W.C. Handy was approached by E.H. Crump, a mayoral candidate who needed a campaign song. Handy, recalling rhythms and melodies played by other Southern blacks at train depots and parties, wrote "Mr. Crump Don't Like It." The catchy tune helped the politician win office; after Handy renamed and rereleased it as "Memphis Blues" in 1912, it helped him win the title "father of the blues."

As blues songs started to drift out of the Delta, outsiders were pulled in by humorous and often raunchy lyrics as well by as stories and images that were exotic to most Americans. One classic tale could have been invented by a Hollywood press agent. The story goes that no one knew much about Robert Johnson's past, but everyone knew he was so determined to become a great blues musician that one midnight he stood at the crossroads of Highways 61 and 49 in Clarksdale, Mississippi. Satan appeared and after Johnson promised him his soul, the Devil tuned Johnson's guitar and granted him the gifts that would make him the King of the Delta Blues Singers.

Lacking surveillance tapes, we can only assume this is partially a folktale, but Johnson did set the standard for generations of blues musicians and artists. Even Johnson's death was emblematic. While playing at a juke joint in 1938, he drank a bottle of poisoned whiskey offered by a jealous husband. Johnson was only 27.

I guess that's why they call it the blues.

DO IT YOURSELF

It's been said that the Delta begins in the lobby of Memphis's Peabody Hotel and ends on Catfish Row in Vicksburg. Now I was on that route, riding Highway 61 south of Memphis. There were no trees, no buildings, no people, and all that broke the horizon were billboards promoting the casinos of Tunica, Mississippi. With no turns to contend with, I slipped into the pace of the highway and pictured people so far removed from civilization that music became their lifeline.

Maie Smith of the Delta Blues Museum points out: "No one can tell you or teach you how to play the blues; it has to be in you so you don't look like you're trying to put on an act. You'll notice when a lot of blues musicians play, it looks effortless. That's because it comes naturally to them. If someone's making it up, they look tired."

It was 75 long and lonely miles to the crossroads in Clarksdale where Robert Johnson received his talent in exchange for his soul. Clarksdale, therefore, is the right place for the Delta Blues Museum.

If you think the blues have had no effect on you, this place will set you straight. If it weren't for the blues, chances are Elvis would be a retired truck driver and Mick Jagger would be singing Dean Martin tunes in a lounge. The blues influenced Buddy Holly, Chuck Berry, Jerry Lee Lewis, the Beatles, the Rolling Stones, Bob Dylan, Jimi Hendrix, Eric Clapton, and Led Zeppelin (whose founding members, Robert Plant and Jimmy Page, dropped by the museum in 1998 and had their picture taken for the Clarksdale *Press-Register*).

The museum's collection includes guitars played by John Lee Hooker, B.B. King, and Big Joe Williams; there's an exhibit on Big Mama Thornton and the "Three Forks" sign from the juke joint where Robert Johnson played his last gig. There's the "Muddywood" guitar created and donated by ZZ Top's Billy Gibbons from wood from the log cabin Muddy Waters was raised in—as well as the entire log cabin. Blues concerts are performed during April's Juke Joint Festival and the Sunflower River Blues and Gospel Festival takes place in August.

Back on Highway 61, you're back to the empty flatlands. Heading south, I rode through Shelby, which flared up and fizzled, and then I recall Merigold as a bustling place where a crawfish cooler was the local business enterprise, and then there were more small towns interrupted by long stretches of nothing.

The Delta looked empty, but its fields were filled with sound.

CONTACTS

Mississippi Delta Tourism Association
(877) 335-8267
www.visitthedelta.com

Delta Blues Museum
(662) 627-6820
www.deltabluesmuseum.org

For Lodging and Dining, see pp. 303–304

39. MARDI GRAS
New Orleans, Louisiana

If you compared two of the nation's most famous parades—New Orleans' Mardi Gras and New York's Macy's Thanksgiving Day spectacle—you'd realize there's really no comparison. What New Orleans's bacchanal has going for it is a degree of outrageousness that places it on a throne of hedonism and debauchery. Need proof? Has a woman ever pulled up her top when Popeye floated by?

KREWE CUTS

It was all a matter of timing. The day a group of French explorers arrived at the site 60 miles below where New Orleans would be built was March 3, 1699: Mardi Gras. The group's leader checked the calendar and pronounced the campsite La Pointe du Mardy Gras. By recognizing the holiday, the explorers carried over a tradition that had begun in France centuries earlier. By 1743, Carnival balls were taking place in New Orleans. On February 24, 1857, the Mistick Krewe of Comus introduced traditions that were the prototype for today's parades, with themes, floats, costumes, masks, and celebratory balls. By 1875, the event was so firmly established in Louisiana culture that legislators declared Mardi Gras a state holiday.

Although wars canceled celebrations, weather never has. The clearest display of the city's dedication to Mardi Gras and its value to the city came in 2006. The previous August, Hurricane Katrina had swamped the city, yet even as its residents were drowning in a sea of bureaucratic incompetence, they felt that Mardi Gras was their lifeline.

"This was one of the most important celebrations ever," explains Mardi Gras historian Arthur Hardy. "Six months after Katrina, the citizens demanded that it happen. We chose to celebrate rather than surrender."

In 2006, evacuees showed their solidarity by returning to the Big Easy to celebrate what may have been one of the most heartfelt, emotional, and needed celebrations in New Orleans history.

DO IT YOURSELF

Mardi Gras, or Fat Tuesday, is the day before Ash Wednesday, which is 40 days before Palm Sunday, which is seven days before Easter, and about a month or so before my birthday.

Who's building those incredible floats? Many are created by Blaine "Mr. Mardi Gras" Kerns at Mardi Gras World (233 Newton Street, 504-361-7821/800-362-8213) across the river in Algiers. A free ferry and shuttle take you to the warehouses, where the monumental floats are built. You can even try on carnival costumes for one of the most fantastic photo ops in America.

When you reach the city, find your feet and then find a copy of Arthur Hardy's *Mardi Gras Guide* to map out the time and route of the next parade. There are also barbecues and cotillions and Bals Masque (masked balls) attended by the city's debutantes and bluebloods, but since you won't be invited to any of these, just focus on the parades.

Parades fuel the festivities, and the epicenter of the processions is Canal Street, the wide boulevard that borders the 50-block French Quarter. For 12 days, official Mardi Gras parades take place nearly every hour from as early as 8 a.m. to as late as 10 p.m. Gigantic floats carry hundreds of Krewe members, who fling thousands of strands of beads and toss a treasury's worth of doubloons. On Mardi Gras itself—Fat Tuesday—the oldest and most historic parade of all, Rex, takes place. When you see parades like this rounding the corner for hours on end, you'll begin to understand the colossal nature of Mardi Gras.

After the parades have left the streets and darkness has fallen over the city, it's time to experience the flip side of the French Quarter. On this last evening, your enjoyment of what's ahead will vary based on your level of tolerance for alcohol, huge crowds, hustlers, street fights, and the aromatic triple threat of piss, puke, and stale beer. The most devout revelers are focused almost solely on Bourbon Street, so if you have only a few hours to witness the Mardi Gras of your imagination, this is where those few hours should be spent.

Anticipating that the night would reveal a multitude of sins, I intended to last until midnight, when mounted police and street sweepers closed down the party by marching down Bourbon Street. Here's what I could recall through hypnosis:

About 8 p.m. I navigated around two street fights and worked my way about 15 blocks into the French Quarter via Royal Street. Backtracking on Bourbon Street, I passed a man dressed as Christ, who stepped aside for a man dressed as Elvis, who gave way to a bloodied, shoeless, shirtless, handcuffed redneck being led away as he sang "Take Me Home, Country Roads." Over the next few blocks I passed a woman whose outfit was a sheen of body paint; cowboys wearing leather chaps and nothing else; a fat man in a coconut bra, red hula skirt, and blond wig; a 50-something woman leading a line of young men attracted by her inner beauty or exposed breasts; and a topless octogenarian sporting painted leopard spots, T-strap thong, and Lady Godiva wig.

For a taste of pure jazz, drop into the French Quarter's Preservation Hall (726 St. Peter Street, 504-522-2841, www.preservation hall.com). This is really just a small room with no dance floor, food, or drinks—but nightly you will hear some of the finest traditional New Orleans jazz by some of the best musicians in town. Get there early; they don't take reservations.

Lacking a cold compress or a sedative, I knew I wouldn't make it until midnight. I was in a centrifuge of weirdness that was spewing out a new universe born of hedonism. Still, my grit and determination pushed me to run the gauntlet back to Canal Street and as I pushed through the crowds, one sight caught my attention. Was it the diaper the man was wearing? His gold glitter paint? His fake breasts? The devil horns?

Nope. It was the fact it was my grandpa.

CONTACTS

New Orleans Convention
and Visitors Bureau
(800) 672-6124
www.neworleanscvb.com

www.nola.com/mardigras
www.mardigrasguide.com
www.mardigras.com

For Lodging and Dining, see p. 304

40. ROCK CITY
Lookout Mountain, Georgia

Kitsch, cool, and an American original, Rock City is America's minimalist theme park. There are no fireworks, no virtual reality games, no stage extravaganzas or thrill rides. The sales pitch is equally streamlined. Few Madison Avenue ad campaigns can compete with the park's simple barn roof request that you "See Rock City." Imagine how successful Microsoft could have been had Bill Gates just painted a few barn roofs.

GNOMES, SWEET GNOMES

It was May 1932 and smack dab in the middle of the Great Depression, but Frieda and Garnet Carter had no shortage of entrepreneurial ideas. They had already decided to turn a portion of their mountaintop estate into a "fairyland" for visitors, complete with gnomes and other vestiges of European folklore. Part of that "fairyland" would include a golf course. When Garnet realized an actual golf course wouldn't fit, he scaled it down, franchised the concept as "Tom Thumb Golf," and created the nation's first miniature golf course.

That would have been enough success for some folks, but Frieda had also decided that she wanted to create a botanical garden and nature walk. She knew just the right spot. Within their estate was a magnificent rock outcropping visible for miles. The Carters modified the Fairyland concept, laid out a walking path, planted some flowers, and began advertising the place they named Rock City. Not willing to lavish money on a fancy ad campaign, they enlisted their friend Clark Byers to roam the South with a few dozen gallons of black and white paint. With the permission of farmers, Byers painted "SEE ROCK CITY" on more than 900 barn roofs across 19 states.

Garden gnomes were first created in Germany in the 1800s, based on folklore that suggested that gnomes have a talent for gardening. There are actual (tongue-in-cheek) groups determined to free gnomes from their horticultural captivit. In France, it's the Front de Liberation des Nains de Jardins, and in Italy the Garden Gnome Liberation Front rescues garden gnomes and returns them to the wild.

Soon travelers heading through Dixie made it their mission to discover this out-of-the-way attraction.

Thanks to the Carters, Clark Byers, and an anonymous paint supplier, to this day nearly everyone in America is aware of Rock City.

DO IT YOURSELF

From the mountains just over the Georgia border, a few miles south of Chattanooga, Tennessee, you'll follow a series of antique directional signs through the Carters' original fairytale-themed neighborhood to Rock City's small entrance plaza. Take a moment and take in what surround you: architecture designed by the Brothers Grimm and a robot gnome that ceaselessly plucks a lute and sings Burl Ives's "Big Rock Candy Mountain." This lute-playing gnome is a clear indicator that the simple pleasures of Rock City have begun.

Rock City is just one-third of a kitsch trifecta. Nearby are two other old-fashioned attractions: Ruby Falls (423-821-2544, www.rubyfalls.com), and the Lookout Mountain Incline Railway (423-821-4224, www.ridetheincline.com). Combination passes for the three will save you a little money.

Past the turnstiles, a waterfall flows and a waterwheel spins and a flagstone walk descends to chasms and cliffs and gardens. The path winds around lichen-covered rocks, Canadian hemlocks, sweetgum trees, autumn ferns, and purple azaleas and, even though you may have arrived to poke a little bit of fun at Rock City for being what you thought it was, you sense that it's actually very serene and sweet. Families are here and kids accustomed to thrill rides and sensory overload seem just as content to walk the trails and peer across overlooks.

Past grottoes and alcoves and narrow clusters of rock with names like the Needle's Eye and Fat Man's Squeeze, the gardens slowly reveal themselves. Eskimo vibernum, mayapple, and flowering dogwood speckle the paths that rise and fall to places like Gnome's Overlook and Goblin's Underpass, Eagle's Nest, and Cliff Terrace. At Seven States Flags Court, you can supposedly view Alabama, Georgia, Kentucky, North Carolina, South Carolina, Tennessee, and Virginia—though you may need a remarkably clear day and a powerful telescope.

Occasionally, you're reminded why this is one of the most kitsch tourist attractions in America. Rainbow Hall? Several pieces of colored glass that tint the vista. Diamond Hall? A small cavern where thousands of pieces of cheap coral are glued to the walls. Fairyland Caverns features garden gnomes that tend a moonshine still, and in Mother Goose Village fairy-tale dioramas are presented beneath the glow of black lights.

It may not be flashy, but it *is* calming. Sometimes that's just what you need.

So, please, see Rock City.

CONTACTS

Rock City Gardens
Lookout Mountain, Georgia
(approximately six miles from
downtown Chattanooga, Tennessee)
(706) 820-2531
(800) 854-0675
www.seerockcity.com

www.chattanoogafun.com
www.lookoutmtnga.com

For Lodging and Dining, see pp. 304–305

41. KENNEDY SPACE CENTER
Titusville, Florida

How, in less than a decade, did America go from exploding rockets on the launch pad to putting men on the moon? Through a combination of science, technology, competition, and spirit. That's what it took for America to face off with the Soviets in the Space Race—and win.

The launch pad for this story? Florida's Kennedy Space Center.

LAUNCH TIME

Following World War II, Americans had plenty of souvenirs to bring home from Europe. Flags, swords, pistols, cuckoo clocks, and some V-2 rockets, along with the scientists who designed them. By the 1950s scientists had made major improvements in aerodynamics, telemetry, rocket propulsion, and tracking.

Cape Canaveral, Florida (renamed Cape Kennedy from 1963 to 1973), was selected as America's portal into space thanks primarily to a safety zone provided by the Atlantic Ocean and 15,000 acres of wetlands. Only pride would be harmed if an unmanned rocket exploded—and they did. Just two months after the Soviets launched Sputnik I in October 1957, America responded with the Vanguard TV3, which reached an impressive altitude of 24 inches before exploding on live television. The media dubbed it "Stay-putnik" and "Flopnik."

The government redoubled its efforts with the formation of the National Aeronautics and Space Administration (NASA) on October 1, 1958. So began a high-flying international rivalry between capitalist monkeys and

communist dogs that lasted until NASA recruited seven military pilots—
the Mercury Seven—who would be launched into space inside their tiny
Mercury capsules, both named for the Roman god
associated with speed.

The single-man Mercury missions were followed by two-man Gemini missions, which tested
the crews' endurance on extended space missions
and advanced the art of docking two spacecraft
traveling at more than 17,000 miles per hour. It
all laid the groundwork for the Apollo program,
which reached its peak both literally and symboli-
cally when the crew of Apollo XI landed on the
moon in July 1969.

For launch viewing, most places along the Indian River on US 1—especially near Highway 50 in Titusville—offer an unobstructed view of the Vehicle Assembly Building, as does Highway 528 and the Beachline Expressway.

Even when the public's attention strayed, NASA remained focused—on
Skylab, Apollo-Soyuz, more than 100 successful space shuttle flights, the
Hubble Space Telescope, the International Space Station, and hundreds of
satellites, probes, landers, Mars rovers, and spacecraft that have sailed beyond
the fringes of our solar system.

Nearly every one of them slipped the surly bonds of Earth...from the
Kennedy Space Center.

DO IT YOURSELF

If you've timed your visit for a launch day, your visit to the Kennedy Space
Center Visitor Complex may be a little more restricted, but the bonus is
that you'll get to see a rocket launch, which isn't a bad deal at all. Launch
or not, there's always enough to keep you occupied for at least a day and
maybe more.

Get your maps and bearings at the information center near the entrance.
Once inside you'll see the Rocket Garden: a collection of surplus rockets
that shows the significant leaps from the Redstone
rockets of the 1950s to the Saturn 1B of the 1960s.
You can even walk across the gantry arm that Armstrong, Aldrin, and Collins used to reach the capsule
of Apollo XI.

The space shuttle had no brakes. It rolled to a stop within three miles of landing.

In the nearby IMAX theater, sail through space courtesy of mind-blowing
3-D footage shot by teams of space shuttle astronauts, and step on the moon
with Tom Hanks's "Magnificent Desolation: Walking on the Moon 3-D."
For a 4-D flight sensation, the Shuttle Launch Experience starts with a

fascinating step-by-step shuttle launch sequence simulation and segues into a re-creation of an explosive vertical ascent into space. Nearby is the Astronaut Memorial. The massive granite memorial, created after the *Challenger* shuttle disaster of 1986, includes the names of all astronauts who died in the pursuit of space exploration.

One of the coolest things I've ever found is the Astronaut Encounter. Every day a real live astronaut fields questions from the audience. Make advance reservations and you can even join them for lunch.

So far you've only seen half of the Center. Bus tours depart for the far side of the space center. Along the way you'll be able to ascend the 60-foot-tall LC-39 Observation Gantry, which presents a great view of historic launch pads 39A and 39B. The tour swings past the fantastic Vehicle Assembly Building, where the Saturn V and entire shuttle fleet were readied for launch. The ultimate stop is the Apollo/Saturn V Center and the Firing Room Theater, which re-creates the launch of Apollo VIII with eerie realism. It reminds you that for a launch to be successful, millions of separate systems, parts, pieces, valves, pumps, and chips need to perform flawlessly and in unison under extremely high stress. NASA's rockets do this regularly.

As you exit the Firing Room theater, you see a 6.2-million-pound, 363-foot-long surplus Saturn V rocket. Built for a mission that would never take place, it's now displayed horizontally in the long hall. They tell me it can still fly but I didn't have any luck jumpstarting it. Keep in mind that to get something this size into space it took nearly eight million pounds of thrust and the intellectual clout of thousands of scientists, engineers, and technicians.

> **NASA's Vehicle Assembly Building is, in volume, the fourth largest building on Earth. The largest is the Boeing plant in Everett, Washington, with 472,000,000 cubic feet of space atop nearly a hundred acres of land.**

In this grand hall you'll see an actual Apollo capsule, the transport van that carried astronauts to the launch pad, and visit the extraordinary Lunar Surface Theater. Through audiotapes from the Apollo XI landing on the moon, you're reminded of the high-tension drama unfolding as Armstrong and Aldrin made their descent onto the moon. Their computers malfunctioned and a field of boulders forced them to bypass their original landing site. The tapes reveal that their desperate search ended when the astronauts landed with less than 30 seconds of fuel to spare.

It takes stories like these to remind us that routine space travel is never routine. It takes the Kennedy Space Center to remind us what we're capable of.

CONTACTS

Kennedy Space Center
(407) 452-2121
(800) KSC-INFO (Florida only)
www.kennedyspacecenter.com

Space Coast Office of Tourism
(321) 433-4470
(877) 57-BEACH (572-3224)
www.space-coast.com

For Lodging and Dining, see pp. 305–306

42. BLACK GOSPEL
Orlando, Florida, and Across America

Filling in the awkward silence of offices, malls, and elevators is a kind of musical vapor that offers little to grasp and nothing to feel. Gospel music—especially black gospel—is quite different. With its spiritual message and emotion, gospel is meant to be felt and heard because its purpose is to fill your soul.

TO KNOW HIM IS TO LOVE HYMNS

Why no one's ever done a movie about Thomas Andrew Dorsey (1899–1993) is beyond me, so from now on if anyone *does* make a movie we're in halfsies.

Although he had been raised in Georgia, Dorsey was growing up fast in Chicago playing barrelhouse piano at speakeasies and after-hours parties as "Georgia Tom." Fast living led to a nervous breakdown at the age of 21 and while Dorsey was recuperating in Atlanta, his Baptist minister father and his church organist mother advised him to slow down. Dorsey had other plans. He returned to Chicago and put together the Wild Cats Jazz Band for the "mother of the blues" Ma Rainey, and got back to business.

As prolific as he was gifted, Dorsey composed nearly 500 jazz and blues songs. In 1928, he had his biggest hit to date, a raunchy multimillion seller called "Tight Like That." Success came at a price. When another nervous breakdown knocked him back for two years, he considered suicide, visited doctors, and saw a faith healer. Finally, he realized that he just needed to listen to his folks. He chose to lose the blues and serve the Lord—at least most of the time. When his spirituals proved too tough to sell, Dorsey drifted back into the blues. The two disparate styles began to merge until his songs of hope and affirmation were being composed with the syncopated eight-bar blues beat.

Gospel, as it was called, was a new approach to what was known as sacred music, but it didn't fly with old-school pastors who believed Dorsey was writing "the devil's music." Their lack of understanding and a similar lack of sales began to push Dorsey back toward the blues, but those difficulties were nothing compared with what came next. In August 1932 his wife and son died during childbirth. The next day Dorsey was at his piano, pouring out his anguish through music, when he (and God, he said) composed what would become the most popular gospel song ever, "Take My Hand, Precious Lord." Recorded by Mahalia Jackson, Dorsey's message of helplessness and dependence on a higher power resonated with millions of people whose faith was being challenged by personal tragedy and the Great Depression.

> **Each summer, the Gospel Music Workshop of America (313-898-6900, www.gmwanational.org) hosts an annual convention (in various cities) that draws about 15,000 of its members. During the convention, as many as 3,000 vocalists get together to create the National Mass Choir. If you can't make it to an AME church, give this one a try.**

Despite Dorsey's obvious gifts, traditional music publishers dismissed gospel as "race music." Dorsey worked around this by creating his own music publishing company. Dorsey also formed his own gospel choir at Chicago's Pilgrim Baptist Church and became co-founder and first president of the National Convention of Gospel Choirs and Choruses.

With hundreds of spirituals to his credit, Dorsey is considered the father of gospel music, and it all began with a plea he wrote from the depths of his despair. Today, that song, and the style of music Dorsey created, is found in hymnbooks across America.

DO IT YOURSELF

Gospel music's offshoots include contemporary gospel, Southern gospel, and a branch known as praise or contemporary Christian music. But for the exuberant rocking style that'll get you out of your seat and on your feet, find yourself at an African Methodist Episcopal church. I've been to a lot of different churches, but I'd never been to one like St. Marks AME in Orlando, Florida, where the message was delivered with the passion of a Billy Graham Miracle Crusade, the groove of a Stevie Wonder jam, and the volume of a Led Zeppelin stadium show.

Only a few of the pews were filled when the service began with Bishop Dorothy Jackson Young stepping to the pulpit with an enthusiastic "Amen!" and a "Praise Jesus!," which she followed with a reminder that all of us needed to "get right with God!" That was the cue for the Voices of Praise choir to crank up the volume on "Get Right with God" with drums knocking out a beat, hands clapping in time, and the swirl of the organ wrapping everything together. When the song ended 15 minutes later I wanted a lighter to flick for an encore.

Reverend Young asked the congregation to "make a joyful noise," which it did as the Voices of Praise next sang "Let It Rise," another tune that moved members of the congregation (and the choir) to tears. "Our God Is an Awesome God" asked worshippers to "high five" or "do your dance" if they loved Jesus—

If you're unfamiliar with good black gospel, test the waters by listening to Mahalia Jackson, the Dixie Hummingbirds, Alphabetical Four, or the unparalleled Golden Gate Quartet.

and they did. The impact of the music climaxed when the choir's version of "Go Tell It on the Mountain" felled a member of the choir who, overcome with emotion, folded like a damp rag. Her friends simply fanned her until she could stand and then they carried her off.

For three hours that day I had the chance to "make a joyful noise" with the Voices of Praise choir and my fellow parishioners. I was extremely happy that I did.

CONTACTS

African Methodist Episcopal Church
500 8th Avenue South
Nashville, TN
(615) 254-0911
www.ame-church.com

St. Mark's A.M.E. Church
1968 Bruton Boulevard
Orlando, FL
(407) 422-6941
www.stmarkameorlando.org

For Lodging and Dining, see p. 306

43. MIAMI BEACH
Florida

No other beach in America offers the feeling of Miami Beach. On a typical evening along Ocean Drive, swaying palms are silhouetted against the fabled "moon over Miami," couples in open-air cafés watch an endless parade of bronzed women and buff Latin playboys as surf rolls in on the shore. All of this is accented by the Kodachrome colors of restored the art deco hotels beyond.

VICE MAKES NICE

A string of barrier islands runs along Florida's southeast coast and on just one sliver of one island is South Beach, the quintessential Miami Beach hotspot.

That's the beach you have to experience—thanks to Julia Tuttle.

If you like your coffee thick and black and your sandwiches flat and hot, order up a Cuban *tinto* (a potent espresso) and a Cuban sandwich at any sidewalk window in SoBe.

In 1895, the 47-year-old widow owned 640 acres downtown on the Miami River and she wanted to see her city grow. When a February freeze hit the rest of the state, she plucked a few live blossoms from an orange tree and mailed them to oil millionaire turned Florida developer Henry M. Flagler to prove Miami was frost-proof. Flagler, who had already built a railroad line to link his resorts along Florida's Atlantic Coast, arrived in March. That's when Tuttle sweetened the deal by offering to *give* Flagler the land he needed for a hotel and a railroad station. Then she threw in half of the rest of her land for good measure. Flagler accepted.

Over the next three decades, Flagler and other developers began building Miami. Some headed out to the barrier islands, dredging sand and heaping it atop the mangrove trees. Bad for the environment, but good for business. By the 1920s, tourists and the "smart money"—speculators, salesmen, shysters, and developers—were heading for Miami. Everyone was happy until September 1926 when the "No-Name Hurricane" thundered in and wiped out Miami.

Rebuilt, the city served as a favorite stop for folks on the way to Havana's casinos and nightclubs. Then, in 1959, Fidel Castro took power and the flow of travel reversed. Cuban refugees created their own neighborhood in Miami, dubbed Little Havana. In 1980 the origi-

To really appreciate the art deco heritage of Miami Beach, attend the Art Deco Weekend held every January, a festival of parades, music, film, lectures, and architectural tours.

nal refugees got company when Castro temporarily allowed Cubans to leave the island. During the so-called Mariel Boatlift, a new wave of 125,000 refugees, including newly freed prisoners and mental patients, arrived in Miami. At the same time, the city's "cocaine cowboys" were giving the law a run for their money, and crime spiked. Fortunately, two cops were about to ride to Miami's rescue. When

Miami Vice premiered in 1984, Crockett and Tubbs showed America an MTV version of Miami that revolved around cool clothes, brilliant pastels, and beautiful people.

Helping also to repair Miami's image was a feisty retiree named Barbara Baer Capitman. Capitman recognized the value of the art deco hotels of Miami Beach (and South Beach in particular), which had become flophouses and seedy retirement homes. Through the 1970s, Baer stared down the bulldozers until South Beach became the first 20th-century district to be named to the National Register of Historic Places in 1979. In the 1980s, the hotels began to attract fashion photographers who felt Miami's weather and architecture made it the hottest and hippest backdrop on earth. After that, hoteliers and restaurateurs and entrepreneurs and celebrities arrived to put their own polish on these once-faded jewels.

The café society they introduced is still here today.

DO IT YOURSELF

It looks almost like a Busby Berkeley extravaganza. Roller-skating women glide by in their bikinis. There are students with tattoos and pierced body parts and gay men wearing thongs and tourists adorned in Bermuda shorts and tropical shirts. Welcome to South Beach, also known as SoBe.

The pulse of SoBe is Ocean Drive, the waterfront avenue that runs parallel to Lummus Park between 5th and 15th streets. The best place to start is the Art Deco District Welcome Center at the corner of Ocean Drive and 10th Avenue. This is where you can pick up souvenirs and sign up for a tour of the Deco District. The guided walking tour lasts about 90 minutes and costs $20 bucks ($15 for a self-guided audio tour), but if you'd prefer to save your cash, set off on your own to catch a few highlights.

Crimes against tourists have dropped significantly, but don't be foolish. Avoid back streets and areas too far removed from the central tourist areas.

Lummus Park has everything you need for a perfect day at the beach: changing facilities, volleyball nets, curving sidewalks for skating or jogging, and soft sand. If surf and sand itself isn't your thing, head two blocks west to reach SoBe's Washington Avenue, a working-class street cluttered with delis, restaurants, clothing stores, and nightclubs. Heading north on Washington, pass 14th Street and turn left on Espanola Way. In the 1930s, young Desi Arnaz was here creating a sensation by popularizing the conga in America. The shops, galleries, and youth hostel here give it a special energy.

One block up Espanola Way, turn right on Meridian Avenue and head three blocks over to the Lincoln Road Mall. After falling into disrepair, the pedestrian mall was resurrected in the 1990s and rivals Ocean Drive for its sidewalk cafés, shops, and entertainment. At its east end, the mall joins Collins Avenue, and if you want to see a hotel that embodies Miami's style and attitude, turn left on Collins and drop by the Delano Hotel. Like Alice, you'll travel through the looking glass and maybe end up by the poolside bar alongside floating lawn chairs and mirrors resting on the lawn.

If it all seems exotic, it should. You're kicking back in the northernmost capital of South America.

CONTACTS

Greater Miami Convention & Visitors Bureau
(305) 539-3063
(800) 283-2707
www.miamiandbeaches.com

Miami Beach Visitor Information
(305) 672-1270
www.miamibeachchamber.com

Art Deco District Welcome Center
1001 Ocean Drive
(305) 672-2014
www.mdpl.org

For Lodging and Dining, see pp. 306–307

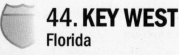

44. KEY WEST
Florida

Sorry, but it's just a legend that Ponce de Leon went to St. Augustine seeking the Fountain of Youth. If he really had been looking, he would have been better off sailing to Key West, at the tip of a string of barrier islands that arc into the Straits of Florida. This is where Ponce's spiritual descendants renew their youth through a special potion. It's an elixir known as a margarita.

THE KEY TO THE CITY

Key West had been home to Calusa Indians for centuries before they were bumped out when the Spanish showed up. In 1815 the Spanish governor of Cuba deeded it to Juan Pablo Salas, a naval officer. But after the United States acquired the Florida territory, Salas was so anxious to unload his island he sold it. Twice. First to a guy who gave him a sailing sloop and then to a different guy who gave him $2,000. Sloop guy sold "his" island to the former governor of South Carolina but the $2,000 buyer claimed it first.

For such an out-of-the-way place, Key West has always been coveted. It attracted Bahamian immigrants known as Conchs, freed African slaves, Cubans fleeing wars at home, and entrepreneurs who saw promise in the island. In the early 1900s, even Henry Flagler wanted to cash in and connected the mainland to Key West via the 128-mile Florida Overseas Railway. Although chunks of the railway were washed away by a 1935 hurricane, a highway would soon replace it. Ernest Hemingway was there in the 1930s, attracted to an island where he could do manly things like drink at Sloppy Joe's and go deep-sea fishing. While there he also had a setting that helped him complete classics including *For Whom the Bell Tolls* and *A Farewell to Arms*.

Playwright Tennessee Williams arrived in 1941 and was followed by an even bigger celebrity, President Harry S. Truman, who arrived in late 1946 and established Key West as his winter White House. The press showed him wearing tropical shirts, fishing for marlin, and lazing in the shade of coconut trees. The images helped Key West become a vacation destination that would later seduce a Mississippi-born musician who envisioned himself passing the hat on a Key West dock.

When Jimmy Buffett arrived in the early 1970s, Key West, like his career, was drifting through time. But when Buffett crafted his own blend of calypso, island, folk, country, and pop, he created real and imagined images of Key West that were easy to understand, easy to love, and easy to sell. Any problem, it seemed, could be solved with a visit to Key West. The promise of this paradise was a double-edged sword. Corporations anxious to capitalize on the fantasy threw up resorts to sell an odd hybrid of preplanned and packaged spontaneity.

While this type of development threatens to turn Key West into a parody of itself, it seems like the island will always be a haven for oddballs, dropouts, nonconformists, free spirits, sportsmen, and freaks. Join them.

After the U.S. Border Patrol blockaded US 1—the only road in and out of the Keys—in April 1982, furious residents of Key West seceded from the Union and declared themselves the Conch Republic. A minute later they surrendered and asked for $1 billion in reparations. In 1984 the federal government declined to recognize the secession—but the county did. Residents hold dual citizenship in the United States and the Conch Republic. Read all about it at *www.conch republic.com*.

DO IT YOURSELF

Since the island's only about two miles wide by four miles long, you may be overwhelmed by the number of things to do in a place so compact. Provided you don't instantly succumb to the lifestyle and start carving wooden flutes for tourists, determine what to do and where to go by boarding the high-kitsch Conch Train to get a sense of history as well as a sense of direction.

On the western end of the island is the commercial district, which contains most of what you'll want to see, including Harry Truman's Little White House. There's the Mel Fisher Maritime Museum, which tells the story of the chicken farmer–turned–treasure seeker who discovered the *Nuestra Señora de Atocha* in 1985, and then had to fight the state and federal governments for the right to keep what he found. Part of the $450 million treasure of gold, emeralds, and silver that he found is displayed there.

The Hemingway House is one of the island's most popular tourist attractions, but in peak season it can become a tourist trap as guides rush through as many tours as they are able to. To experience the natural pace of Key West, slip into the waters on a diving trip. During the day, charters set sail to the stunning coral reefs that surround the island, and fishing charters head out a bit farther. Some charters split the day, departing for an afternoon dive then switching gears at sunset for a celebration that may include sea shanties and frosty draft beer to make the shanties sound better than they really are.

Key West has a busy festival calendar. Among the most popular events are Key West Literary Seminar (January), Conch Republic Independence Celebration (April 23), PrideFest (June), the Hemingway Days Festival (July), and Fantasy Fest (October).

The biggest sunset celebration takes place each evening at Mallory Square. There, every tourist in the Lower 48 arrives to be entertained by a carnival of street performers, vendors, and local characters hustling for hat money. There are fire jugglers and gymnasts, magicians and performing dogs, trained cats and men with pierced nipples carrying iguanas, and pot-bellied women in bikinis toting pot-bellied pigs in their bicycle baskets. Dress is casual.

At night, Duval Street is the site of the Duval Crawl, a tour of the commercial district's bars and restaurants. At the corner of Duval and Greene, Sloppy Joe's is the island's most popular retreat—partly for its history, partly for its T-shirts, and partly because the bands perform for college kids and cruise ship passengers, who can all get drunk together and yell at once. Around the corner is Captain Tony's (the original Sloppy Joe's that Hemingway frequented), which has somehow evaded the crush of tourism and remains a real watering hole with a décor of bras, business cards, and dollar bills.

Then there are local bars like the Green Parrot and the Bull. And there are walking tours, art galleries, scooter rentals, and quiet neighborhoods where locals laze in hammocks, distracted by nothing but soft sea breezes, the brilliance of tropical flowers, and the sight of pelicans diving for a fresh fish dinner.

Say…maybe this really *is* Margaritaville.

Snorkeling, scuba diving, and schooner trips are highly recommended. Various excursions depart from Mallory Square; discount coupons can be found in local publications.

CONTACTS

Key West Visitors Bureau
(305) 294-2587
(800) 527-8539
www.keywestchamber.org

Key West Welcome Center
(800) 284-4482
www.keywestwelcomecenter.com

Florida Keys and Key West
(800) 352-5397
www.fla-keys.com

For Lodging and Dining, see p. 307

MIDWEST

Arkansas, Illinois, Indiana, Iowa, Michigan, Minnesota, Missouri, Ohio, Wisconsin

While progress is generally good, sometimes it has the unintended consequence of turning something worth saving into something obsolete. That's what's nice about the Midwest. Many of the things that *were* good still *are* good because the places and events that define this part of the country are very nearly the same things that defined it 75 or 175 years ago. Kids are still rolling derby cars down a hill in Akron, Ohio, just as they were in the 1930s, and passengers are still floating down the Mississippi River as they did in the 1830s. There is a thread of consistency that appeals to me: It can be as simple as tuning into downhome music and comedy in Branson, Missouri; digging into a meal at a truck stop diner; snagging a beer right off the factory floor in St. Louis, Missouri; or heading to a Great Lakes city to hit the dance floor for a polka.

There's much more here than meets the eye—because there are so many things that evoke a wonderful sense of America's traditions.

45. SOAP BOX DERBY
Akron, Ohio

"It's all for the kids."

That's what Larry Gallimore told me. He had volunteered at the All-American Soap Box Derby for more than 30 years. He had seen the glory days of the races and had kept coming when other fans were diverted to malls and movies. Every year he was back because he enjoyed watching parents and their kids working together on their derby cars; sharing the butterflies that come with competition; and meeting after the race to hug because the kid scored a victory or had simply run a good race.

GREAT ROLL MODELS

In 1933, Myron Scott, a photographer for the *Dayton Daily News,* had an idea. Kids would build a cheap cart out of junk wood or scrap metal, climb in, and roll down a hill. Within a few years he would see his idea develop into the All-American Soap Box Derby.

Following an inaugural run in Dayton, the race moved to a more suitable home in hilly Akron. At the time, the Great Depression was a mixed blessing, with the upside being that the Works Progress Administration (WPA) pitched in to build Derby Downs. Since 1936, it has been the official hill and home of the races.

With Chevrolet's early and earnest sponsorship, the event gained traction. Each year, the national media followed the competition and the results were broadcast live on the major radio networks. Akron's glory days coincided with that of the Derby. In the 1950s and 1960s, more than 40,000—some say 50,000—fans would arrive each August to watch the races, making it one of the five most popular sporting events in the nation. In attendance were celebrities like Indy 500 drivers, Ronald Reagan, and Jimmy Stewart who was such a fan he postponed his honeymoon to go there.

For a history of the race, read Melanie Payne's *Champions, Cheaters, and Childhood Dreams: Memories of the All-American Soap Box Derby.*

Little by little, the national media found more important things to cover but they returned in 1973 after a young racer and his uncle, an engineer, secretly crammed an electromagnet in the nose of their car. Attracted to the steel starting gate, the car was propelled into an insurmountable head start.

Aside from Watergate and Spiro Agnew pleading nolo contendere to bribery, it was the biggest scandal of the year.

It also seemed to mark a turning point in the race. Today, the races are scratching to gather 5,000 fans and I wonder why. The All-American Soap Box Derby may be the most heartwarming, decent, and unselfish sporting event you'll ever see.

DO IT YOURSELF

A new champion is crowned at the Soap Box Derby on Saturday afternoon, but if you have time to arrive early, do so, since test runs and special races are run Wednesday through Friday. You'll also witness parents and kids tinkering with their cars and attending seminars like "Building a Master Car—YES YOU CAN!"

On Saturday morning, the grandstands fill and some folks set up lawn chairs on the grass, unpacking picnic lunches and looking forward to eight hours of racing. As racers and parents are channeled toward the starting line, fat kids, short kids, and gangly kids even longer than their cars squeeze into the fiberglass capsule, cinch their helmets tight, and wait anxiously. Standing at the midway point, I would watch three racers at a time fly past me at 30 miles per hour. After a while I could close my eyes and hear the low hum of rubber that told me the gate had dropped and then the receding whir that said the racers had sailed down the 989.4 feet and had crossed the finish line. Sometimes, though, a silence descended on the heats when the race was too close to call and the crowd waited for the verdict. When the winner was finally declared, the sound I'd then hear was that of an elated parent at the top of the hill.

Arrive early and sign up to help as a flag carrier during the opening ceremonies. Volunteers gather beneath a huge American flag and march it down the hill and past the grandstands to signal the start of the races.

I asked a waiting parent what's so special about this race? About this event?

"You're with your child," he explained. "You work together, you race together, you build cars together, and you form a bond that is greater than anything else. There is nothing that comes close to this to bring us together. You are teaching kids sportsmanship and something about just being a person."

Some of the most memorable moments take place just past the finish line in the area known as the run out. For the losers, a defeat can be difficult. I noticed one man consoling a sobbing ten-year-old boy.

"You've just rolled down the All-American hill," he reminded the racer. "How many races did you have to win to make it all the way here? To make it all the way to the national championships? Don't ever forget that you *are* a champion."

Enter "1951 Soap Box Derby" on *youtube.com* to see a three-part documentary with classic footage.

It was great fatherly advice, but when the man put the cart onto a trailer and walked away, I realized it wasn't the kid's father after all. It was Larry Gallimore, the longtime volunteer who knew that at this track, the young racers face perhaps the first of what will be many losses.

It's not just the kids who are winners in Akron.

CONTACTS

All American Soap Box Derby
(330) 733-8723
www.aasbd.com

For Lodging and Dining, see pp. 307–308

46. POLKA DANCING
Cleveland, Ohio, and Across America

I'm not a doctor, but if I had to prescribe an antidote for depression I'd recommend that my patients dance a polka. Polka is the bipolar opposite of the blues. Even though they contain the same exact eight notes found in every song from Beethoven's "Moonlight Sonata" to the Sex Pistols' "Anarchy in the U.K.," polka tunes manage to put them into an order that creates just about the happiest melodies on earth. Magnifying the ebullience of the songs are the musicians who seem as jovial as their audience does.

Maybe it's something in the kielbasa.

POLKAPALOOZA

America loves to take credit for inventing things, but we can't take credit for the polka. Polkas were played at Polish, Czech, and Slovak dancehalls and *biergartens* in the mid-18th century. Even composers Johann Strauss I and II were motivated to set aside their last waltz and write polkas. Shostakovich and Stravinsky wrote polkas. Polkas even appeared in opera, slipped into scenes like Bedřich Smetana's *The Bartered Bride*. Musician Cszlky Szklpwcycz became a legend when he sold all the vowels in his name to buy a concertina on which he composed polkas of incredible beauty.

Polka might have remained a European phenomenon, if not for the Poles, Slovaks, Czechs, and Germans who left their countries and came to ours, bringing with them drums and tubas, concertinas and button boxes. In cities like Cleveland, Chicago, Buffalo, and Milwaukee they unpacked their bags and begin playing the music they knew.

While native-born Americans could only hear one pace in polka, there were nuances hidden within them that were soon enhanced by trumpets, clarinets, and saxophones. Polkas and shuffling waltzes and *polka schnell* numbers accelerated the music and dancing grew popular. Still, most of us also lived woefully unaware of polka superstars and innovators like Eddie Blazonczyk, Li'l Wally Jagiello, Lenny Gomulka, and America's Polka King, Frankie Yankovic (no relation to Weird Al). Only a relative few of us were within the televised signal of Cleveland's *Polka Varieties,* which showcased top polka bands and performers every Sunday from 1956 to 1975.

> Bandleader and accordionist Lawrence Welk always included polkas in his repertoire. He was inducted into the Polka Hall of Fame in 1994.

With the success of the world's first International Polka Convention in 1963, some of the finest minds in the nation realized that in addition to the pursuit of space exploration and improved race relations, America really needed an organization to "promote, maintain, and advance public interest in polka entertainment." In 1968, their dream became a reality with the formation of the International Polka Association (IPA). Thanks to the IPA, our nation has a Polka Music Hall of Fame (Chicago) and a National Polka Month (January). Dances take place all across the nation.

Now all you have to do is *niech dobre czasy zwijajsiê*—let the good times roll!

DO IT YOURSELF

Although polka took root mainly in the Midwest, polka power flexes its muscle at festivals all across America. At the United States Polka Association's (USPA) Polka Festival and Convention in Cleveland, attendees can dance and eat cabbage rolls and witness the crowning of the Junior Miss and Teen Miss United States Polka Association, each of whom has demonstrated her polka skills and completed a 50-word essay on why she seeks the title. Sound familiar? Prior to 1928 our Constitution required the same of presidential candidates.

If you're just testing the waters, visit one of the websites below to locate a polka club that hosts dances. Are you welcome? Why, *öczywicie jeste*—of course you are!

When a fashion trend became popular at the same time as polka dancing did, the style had a new name: polka dots.

"We always get out-of-towners who are looking for a place to polka," explains Barbara Haselow, president of the USPA. "People are really drawn by the camaraderie and the love of the music so we have dances every month and even a picnic in June. And we really love the Polish polka—it draws young people. It's happy music!"

A Czech style of "happy music!" also attracts people to the National Polka Festival which, believe it or not, is held deep in the heart of Texas. As many as 50,000 fans travel south of Dallas to the Czech-rich town of Ennis for the annual hullabaloo held at three dance halls during Memorial Day Weekend.

Starting Friday evening, polka club members arrive in a caravan of cars and buses rolling in from Wisconsin, Minnesota, and Illinois and race to reach the main hall in time for the King and Queen Dance. With polka bands in overdrive, costumed dancers displaying the greatest polka proficiency are presented with a sash that confirms them the weekend's goodwill ambassadors—King and Queen of the Polka Fest. In reality, it looks like everyone's a goodwill ambassador.

"You've never seen so many happy people in one place," gushes Gina Rokas, Ennis's tourism director. "Their mood matches the music. It's happy!"

The festival really kicks into gear on Saturday morning with the Polka Fest Run. That is followed by a polka-themed parade starring participants in Czech costumes; Czech bands riding polka floats; and horses sporting polka dots. After everyone's sashayed down Ennis Avenue, polka fanatics may not hang out too long at the downtown Arts and Crafts Show because they know that about ten bucks will buy one of America's best bargains: a full day of polka.

Today, Jimmy Sturr and His Orchestra is arguably the most popular polka band in America. In addition to performing several sold-out shows at Carnegie Hall, the band are in the Top Ten list of all-time Grammy Award winners.

"On Saturday, dances begin at 11 a.m. and go until well past midnight," explains Rokas. "Oh, is it fun! Polka Dot the Chicken visits each hall; Czech Republic soldiers who were at Fort Hood came over once to polka; and people who know how to polka take beginners under their wing and teach them how to dance. And the kids love it! You should just see our junior polka dancers—the Little Ennis Czechadees!"

Between a day of dancing that requires flurries of steps, jumps, kicks, and spins, whirling dervishes can get rested and recharged over a meal of klobase, dumplings, cabbage rolls, pork roast, and sauerkraut. As the peal of the clarinets and boom of the tubas ring across the floor, folks are back at it, swept up in the madness of the dance.

Everybody polka!

CONTACTS

United States Polka Association
www.uspapolkas.com
www.nationalpolkafestival.com
(440) 886-6157

International Polka Association
(800) TO-POLKA (867-6552)
www.internationalpolka.com

www.247PolkaHeaven.com
With links to local clubs, dances,
festivals, and music.

Polka America Corporation
www.polkaamericacorporation.org

For Lodging and Dining, see p. 308

Cleveland-Style Polka Hall of Fame
www.clevelandstyle.com

Pulaski Polka Days
www.pulaskipolkadays.com
Midsummer festival in Pulaski,
Wisconsin

Ennis Convention and Visitors Bureau
(972) 878-4748
(888) 366-4748
www.visitennis.com

47. GREENFIELD VILLAGE
Dearborn, Michigan

What if you grew up in a place that you loved and then, through a combination of your talent and the times, made an enormous fortune but also managed to erase the world of your childhood? Wouldn't it be something if you could somehow recapture the past?

That's just what Henry Ford did. At Greenfield Village he preserved the past so that every day is yesterday.

FORWARD INTO THE PAST

Sometime in the 1940s, a youth named John Dahlinger met with an elderly Henry Ford. Frustrated by the industrialist's traditional views on education, he upbraided Ford. "Sir, you forget that this is the modern age."

That was enough. Ford cut him off with this simple explanation: "Young man," he said, "I *invented* the modern age."

Ford indeed played a defining role in creating the world we live in, and to his credit he had the vision and capital to preserve the world that *he* had lived in. Starting in the 1920s, he dispatched historians, researchers, and work crews to locate, disassemble, and then reconstruct historically significant treasures at a place he called Greenfield Village. Thanks to Ford rescuing once-endangered sites, since 1933 visitors have been able to walk into Edison's Menlo Park laboratory, the Wright Brothers' home and bicycle shop, and the courthouse where Abraham Lincoln argued cases as a young trial lawyer.

Talk to the staff. They're all specially trained in relevant subjects, and some have advanced degrees in American history. You'll gain a wealth of knowledge if you ask questions.

There are also original slave cabins, schoolhouses, farmhouses, windmills, a steamboat, a locomotive, and taverns that belonged to no identifiable historic figure but only to a historical period. Along with the superb Henry Ford Museum next door, this presents 300 years of history not on an academic level, but on a practical level. You will see how people lived and worked as the nation moved toward Henry Ford's modern era.

DO IT YOURSELF

From the entrance plaza, only a trace of the 90-acre parklike Village is visible. A smart idea is to step aboard a renovated 1931 Model AA bus (one of only three in America) and, for 50 cents, ride it to the far end of the park, letting the driver fill you in on the Village's layout, history, and significant buildings. At the terminus is the Daggett Farmhouse, where women in period costume may be preparing supper (what we call lunch), working in the garden, or otherwise tending to the day's chores as if living in a different era. You can hear the buttermilk sloshing inside the churn and feel the heat of the oven fire as women sift for recipes in a 1750s cookbook.

Down the lane, Model Ts pass and honk. Horse-drawn carriages ease through a covered bridge while schoolchildren in the shade of a weeping willow chase geese by a quiet pond. A few doors down, on the porch of Noah Webster's home, a traveling schoolmaster holds an impromptu spelling bee. At the Eagle Tavern, it's always 1850 and the barkeep is ready to prime the pump with ale or stout, chilled atop a cake of ice.

Of course, the times were not all idyllic. Ford deserves credit for showing us the stifling slave cabins that housed as many as ten people—including the ingenious Henry "Box" Brown, who boxed himself up and shipped himself to Philadelphia—and to freedom.

On a casual stroll you'll follow attorney Abe Lincoln to the plain Logan County, Illinois, courthouse and then visit Menlo Park, New Jersey, where, amid the gears and generators, belts and lathes, Edison failed some 6,000 times before he finally developed an efficient lightbulb. Then, in a section called Liberty Craftworks, watch potters create exquisitely designed commemorative pie plates, urns, and face jugs. In the neighboring weaving shop, sawmill, printing office, tin shop, and glass shop, craftspeople constantly spin, twist, blow, and press one-of-a-kind items.

Adjacent to the Village is another of Ford's gifts to America. When combined with the Village, the Henry Ford Museum occupies more space than the Smithsonian and is second to it in the number of displays. And what displays! Entering the museum is like walking into an enormous time capsule. You'll see JFK's limousine from Dallas and the bus civil rights icon Rosa Parks rode the day she was arrested in Montgomery. There's a complete room from an old Holiday Inn, a 76-foot-long steam locomotive, a Texaco station, and the Oscar Meyer Weinermobile, not to mention assorted dishwashers, stoves, bathtubs, vacuums, and Ford's Quadricycle. "Henry's Treasures" include a copy of the Declaration of the Independence, George Washington's travel kit, and, possibly, Thomas Edison's last breath.

Some wealthy people collect art, some opt for rare jewels. Henry Ford had them all beat. At Greenfield Village, he collected America.

CONTACTS

Greenfield Village
(800) 835-5237
www.thehenryford.org

For Lodging and Dining, see pp. 308–309

48. HARLEY-DAVIDSON
Milwaukee, Wisconsin

Several hundred companies manufacture motorcycles, but most Americans can name just one: Harley-Davidson.

Even motorcyclists devoted to their own brand can't deny Harley's renown or resilience. Born in a Milwaukee shed, the motorcycle corporation managed to weather the Great Depression, a sullied reputation, and disastrous management, and each time it rebounded until it was reestablished as something better.

Harley-Davidson became America's motorcycle.

TWO WHEELS GOOD

In the early 1900s, Milwaukee was known for three things: beer, bratwurst, and beer. Nothing marked Milwaukee as the future Mecca of Motorcycling, the Valhalla of the V-Twin.

Then came 1903 and two young tinkerers, William Harley, 21, and Arthur Davidson, 20, began thinking about ways to "take the work out of bicycling." In their first year, the factory output—to be more accurate, the *wooden shed* output—of the Harley-Davidson Motor Company was three. Not an impressive start to be sure, but each year revealed new improvements in motorcycle design and technology.

York, Pennsylvania (30 miles east of Gettysburg) is known as the "factory tour capital of the world," you can visit nearly two dozen factories that produce products from potato chips, chocolate, and Pfaltzgraff dinnerware to... Harley-Davidson motorcycles. Harley-Davidson's Vehicle Operations (*Route 30 at 1425 Eden Road, one mile east of I-83, 717-848-1177/877-746-7937*) offers a one-hour weekday tour.

By 1909, Harley and Davidson were able to unveil a model tricked out with a seven-horsepower V-twin engine that could rocket riders up to 60 miles per hour. Their bikes began growing larger and more powerful. During WWI, Harley-Davidsons shuttled soldiers along the Maginot Line. During the Jazz Age, cops astride Harleys chased down bootleggers. The company continued to innovate, introducing the teardrop gas tank and popular V-twin knucklehead, shovelhead, and panhead engines.

Technical strides were only half of Harley's legend. In 1947, a motorcycle rally in Hollister, California, changed the public perception of riders from wholesome adrenaline seekers to gutless punks in leather jackets. After beer and brawls spun a Fourth of July motorcycle rally out of control, the media reported that bikers had terrorized an entire town during what was dubbed the "Hollister Riot." A film loosely based on the rally, *The Wild One*, starred Marlon Brando as Johnny, the leader of the Black Rebels Motorcycle Club. That was good enough for real-life riders, and when motorcycles became associated with rebellion, Harley-Davidson became the bike of choice for real-life gangs.

In 1969, Harley-Davidson merged with the American Machine and Foundry Company (AMF), a company more accustomed to producing bicycles. Throughout the 1970s Harley's reputation suffered from a triple threat of poor management, poor quality, and poor design. In mid-1981, 13 Harley-Davidson senior executives bought back the company, streamlined its manufacturing process, improved quality controls, and started the Harley Owners Group (HOG), whose membership rose from about 60,000 in the mid-1980s to more than a million worldwide today.

Also in the 1980s, the public perception of bikes changed again when Malcolm Forbes, one of the world's most affluent capitalists, began showing up in magazine articles that highlighted his many motorcycle journeys.

When celebrities began buying bikes, nearly everyone else did, too.

DO IT YOURSELF

There are a few ways to increase your understanding and appreciation of Harley-Davidson motorcycles. The first way I would recommend is by buying one. After that, go to Milwaukee and visit the Harley-Davidson Museum. The 130,000-square-foot museum opened in July 2008 to display more than 100 years of Harley history.

Even before you enter the building, artist Jeff Decker's larger-than-life sculpture celebrates a Harley-riding hill climber and expresses the passion of motorcycle enthusiasts. Inside, the Archives, which takes up a complete section of the museum, contains rare documents, historical photographs, thrilling videos, cool apparel, and more than 450 motorcycles. An audio tour complements the displays, as riders and experts share stories that illustrate America's long fascination with motorcycles.

Themed exhibits include a special section on Elvis, whose 1956 kH, on display, was purchased two weeks before the release of *Heartbreak Hotel*. As much an Elvis fan as a motorcycle fan, I'm still trying to figure out how to pull off a heist. Motorheads are fascinated by the Engine Room, which reveals the science that enables a 600-pound machine to transport middle-aged riders back a few decades. Special programs, both free and for a fee, provide behind-the-scenes information as well as in-depth explanations of H-D's iconic logo design; the history of the black leather jacket; and how the sport of board track racing accelerated Harley's ascent.

You don't have to spend $20,000 to know what it's like to ride a Harley. Many Harley dealerships rent motorcycles. Visit www.harley-davidson.com. Another rental operation, Eaglerider (310-536-6777 or 888-900-9901, www.eaglerider.com), has locations all over the world.

After the museum, head over to Harley's Capitol Drive Powertrain Operations a few miles west of downtown Milwaukee in Wauwatosa. After a short and impressive film on the company's history, a one-hour guided tour takes you out onto the factory floor where workers are creating the "chrome and black miracles" that power certain Harley models.

In *The Wild One*, Marlon Brando didn't ride a Harley. He was on a 1951 Triumph Thunderbird 6T.

At first you may not be impressed watching machinists fiddle around with some chunks of metal, but as the tour continues those little chunks of metal pick up an assortment of pistons and rods and washers and nuts. By the time you reach the end of the line, you'll see what began as an unrecognizable assortment of parts has climbed engineering's evolutionary ladder to become the V-twin powerhouse for a brand-new motorcycle.

And perhaps the very one that'll end up on your own Harley.

CONTACTS

Harley-Davidson Museum
6th and Canal Streets
(877) 436-8738
www.h-dmuseum.com

Harley-Davidson's Capitol Drive
Powertrain Operations
11700 West Capitol Drive
(414) 535-3666
www.harley-davidson.com

For Lodging and Dining, see p. 309

49. OSHKOSH AIRSHOW
Oshkosh, Wisconsin

Americans have never been content to stay put. Whether for work or a new home or vacation, we like to go different places. Perhaps that's why folks invested so much effort in aviation. Planes get us places faster than nearly anything.

But it's not just speed we love. There's something about the style, innovation, boldness, and mystique of aviation. To celebrate this, each July pilots and aviation enthusiasts land in Oshkosh, Wisconsin, to display in the air and in the fields everything from classic warbirds to cutting-edge aircraft. You'll see nearly the entire history of American aviation here—and you won't have to pay extra for a pillow.

PREPARE FOR TAKE OFF

When you get right down to it, experimental aircraft have been around since the 1700s, when the Montgolfier brothers were floating above Paris in their hot-air balloons. But the Experimental Aircraft Association took off in 1953, created for people who were building or restoring their own recreational aircraft. Since the late 1960s, its annual Fly-In Convention has been held in Oshkosh, Wisconsin.

What began as an event for hobbyists to hang out and chat about flying is still that, but now there are more than 10,000 aircraft coming in, which means that when the show is going at full throttle, the control tower at the modest Wittman Regional Airport becomes the busiest in the world.

Even if you're not a pilot, this is one place where you can wander around the most diverse gathering of aircraft in the world and see some of the most beautiful machines to ever touch the sky.

DO IT YOURSELF

While pilots, obviously, will get the most out of an air show, in Oshkosh even the most casual visitor will find something to enjoy.

There's a parking fee, naturally, as well as admission, around $35 per day for non-EAA members (and about $210 for a weekly pass), and then it's all yours. After passing the front gate, you'll encounter so much eye candy so quickly you'll be tempted to examine every airplane. Organizers have positioned aircraft of a specific era or style at different parts of the airport, so you can head to the planes that move you.

In enormous and segmented clearings far larger than a football field are biplanes, WWII Liberators, classic Ford Tri-Motors, cute Piper Cubs, seaplanes, and sailplanes. There are Japanese Zeroes and Russian MiGs and American P-51s and ultralights and one-of-a-kind aircraft built not on an assembly line but in the garage of some tinkerer. With so much to see, even with the convenience of a courtesy tram, there's an incredible amount of walking involved. Or you can just swipe an airplane and do a flyover.

There are more flight opportunities than you'd expect. Sign up and you can fly in a M*A*S*H-style helicopter, or perhaps take a spin in a sweet 1929 Ford Tri-Motor.

Some pilots, especially those marketing smaller planes and ultralights, offer free test rides (!) that not only get you one step closer to your dream of becoming a pilot, but also give you an impressive aerial view of the entire spectacle. Just look for a line forming on the grounds and you'll know you're near a sign-up sheet.

By now, the sight of this massive air fleet may have inspired you to leave a downpayment on a Sopwith Camel. If your budget is more modest, vendors sell a wonderful assortment of aviation paraphernalia, including aviation art, leather flying jackets, vintage propellers, books, model airplanes, videos, flight suits, sunglasses, and caps. You may find a war ace or original Tuskegee Airman signing copies of his book.

For a few bucks extra you can visit one of the world's great aviation museums, the EAA AirVenture Museum. More than 130 aircraft are on display.

You'll also want to refer to your schedule for the starting time of the day's air show. But even if you've lost your schedule and your watch has stopped, all you have to do is listen for the squeezing, labored breath of cylinders coaxing a propeller into life. That plus the ensuing drone alerts you that a squadron of planes is taking off. Head over to the runway and sit in the shade of a military C-5 and take in the show. Already impressed by the number of planes on the ground? Now you'll be in awe of the number of planes in the sky. There are Bearcats and Wildcats and F4 Corsairs sailing past, the world's best aerobatic pilots thrilling the crowd, and special flyovers by specialty aircraft like the Harrier Jump Jet.

American aviators were the first to fly, at Kitty Hawk; the first to fly solo across the Atlantic; and the first to fly nonstop around the world. At Oshkosh, American aviators are still pushing the envelope.

CONTACTS

Experimental Aircraft Association
(920) 426-4800
(800) JOIN-EAA (564-6322)
www.eaa.org

www.airventure.org

For Lodging and Dining, see p. 309

For Lodging and Dining, see p. 309

50. MALL OF AMERICA
Bloomington, Minnesota

Most any convenience store carries the staples we really need. Specialty items? A strip mall should suffice. Outfitting a house? The local mall could have it all. But what if your shopping list includes a flight simulator? A wedding chapel? A miniature golf course? That's when you head to the Mall of America.

A MAXIMUM MALL FOR MINNEAPOLIS

Often, when a community finds it's about to lose what it thinks is its life-blood—a factory, a military base, an aging grand hotel, for instance—residents go through a period of anxiety as the community tries to come up with something to compensate for the loss. Many times, the process works well. A military base becomes a planned community; a textile factory is turned into condos; and the aging grand hotel also turns into condos to compete with those lousy condos in the old mill down the street.

In the Minneapolis suburb of Bloomington, the process of recycling worked extraordinarily well. In 1982, both the Minnesota Twins and the Minnesota Vikings packed up and headed to a new stadium in downtown Minneapolis. In their wake, they left behind 78 acres of prime real estate, right beside the nexus of four major highways and close to the international airport.

For losing one of the biggest draws their town ever had, Bloomington's consolation prize was this vacant land. In 1985, the Bloomington Port Authority began kicking around ideas about its future. Offices, condos, and a convention center were considered but fell short when placed beside the idea of a combination retail/entertainment center.

Opportunities like this don't come along often, so it was clear that the design of the project would have to deliver far more than an ordinary mall. Why not build a big mall, someone asked? Why not build an even bigger mall, others countered. Hey, kids! Let's build the biggest mall in America!

Tasked with the responsibility were the Ghermezian brothers, who, not coincidentally, had just finished building the world's largest retail and entertainment center in Alberta, Canada. Their partner, Melvin Simon and Associates, was one of the largest developers of shopping centers in the United States. When they broke ground on June 14, 1989, 35-miles-per-hour wind gusts blew across the vacant land. The next morning headlines asked "Why Minnesota?" It would take three more years, but people would find out why.

In August 1992, the $650 million Mall of America opened with ten thousand employees working at four anchor stores and 330 other stores. Just 20 minutes from downtown Minneapolis, it was a destination that brought in curious browsers and hardcore shoppers who would charter buses from as far away as Chicago and Canada for a full day of shopping. To this day, a group of Icelandic shoppers flies in and reserves a suite of rooms at a local hotel—and also rent the hotel's conference room so they have a place to stash their overloaded shopping bags.

More than 5,000 couples from around the world have been married in the Chapel of Love Wedding Chapel.

So in the end, the MOA has delivered consistently better seasons than the Twins and Vikings combined. It's been featured in movies and on national and international news, and it has been the focus of documentaries. Each year, 40 million people visit the mall and pump nearly $2 billion into the state's economy.

DO IT YOURSELF

It's an unusual experience to arrive at the Mall of America and find that, even before the stores opens, more people have arrived to walk the mall for exercise (or, in winter, to stay warm,) than would be at the average mall all day.

As you adjust your mindset to the size of the place, consider that it's not just one mall—in a way, it's actually four. While the footprint of the mall covers just over a million square feet, there are four levels under one roof. And as you get your bearings and look at the upper levels, you'll realize that you've stepped into the retail equivalent of an M.C. Escher drawing. Walking just the interior circumference of these levels will put more than two miles under your belt.

There are other noticeable differences between the Mall of America and an ordinary mall. Ordinary malls don't employ 11,000 people (13,000 during the holidays) and they don't offer a shooting arcade or a babysitting service or a water flume ride or a calliope. Few malls,

If you have a layover in Minneapolis, it takes only ten minutes for the Light Rail to run out to the Mall of America from the airport.

or cities for that matter, have nearly 20 sit-down restaurants; 30 fast-food restaurants; 40 specialty food stores; and a college campus. The MOA also features Nickelodeon Universe, which is the nation's largest indoor theme park; a 1.2-million-gallon aquarium at Underwater Adventures; a 14-screen theater; and the Lego Imagination Center. This all starts to indicate that this is more county fair than suburban mall.

At the stage in the center of the mall, you may watch Highland dance championships or a celebrity book signing or a fashion show or an A-list musical act. Time it right and you may hit the jackpot: Mariah Carey may dance a jig in her Stella McCartney original before signing copies of her autobiography.

In a day that should wear out your wallet and your walking shoes, it's possible, though not probable, that you'll get lost. Color-coded numeric maps should keep you on track. Still, you may feel like you're lost when you pass your 30th shoe shop or 40th fashion boutique, but stick with it.

Now you're ready to head up to level two.

CONTACTS AND SITES

Mall of America
(952) 883-8800
www.mallofamerica.com

Meet Minneapolis
(888) 676-MPLS (6757)
www.minneapolis.org

For Lodging and Dining, see pp. 309–310

51. TRUCK STOPS
Walcott, Iowa, and Across America

If you only visit your corner gas station to fill up, grab a snack, and go, take a detour the next time you hit the road. Pull up beside the big rigs at a truck stop; hang out with your fellow travelers; and feast on the hearty foods that fuel the drivers.

A FORK IN THE ROAD

At the turn of the 20th century the arrival of the automobile caught a lot of people unprepared. Primarily drivers. Those early explorers could go for long stretches without finding gas or a restroom, which, after a few days or a glass of tea, became a matter of great urgency.

The people who were most affected by all of this were professional drivers. As the nation was being connected by networks of blacktop, those men needed real food and ready fuel. The same way transportation was evolving from simple trucks to the Dodge Power Wagon—the first commercial four-wheel drive—America's highways were evolving as well. Starting in the 1950s, nearly every major American city became connected to the grid known as the Interstate Highway System. Larger and more powerful trucks were built to help drivers cross those long expanses, so stations had to mature from ramshackle cabins in the middle of nowhere into large food and fuel stops that could accommodate 70-foot-long, 80,000-pound semi-tractor-trailers.

For decades many smaller operations clung to their few diesel pumps and mom-and-pop diner, where waitresses poured enough black coffee to keep drivers wired for the ride ahead. You can still find old-fashioned, independent truck stops, but they're now taking a back seat to large corporate operations like Pilot, Flying J, and TA that have the resources to provide the space and equipment drivers need.

DO IT YOURSELF

My favorite truck stops are still the authentic truck stops (as opposed to so-called travel centers) and you can find those through some of the websites below. If you'd rather not go off the beaten path, you're bound to find a travel center along an interstate that'll give you a glimpse of the trucker lifestyle— but you may have to make an effort to introduce yourself to a trucker. Fueling stations are divided into regular gas stations for ordinary motorists and separate wide-open areas fielding an array of dual diesel pumps for the big semis' twin tanks. Even the entrances and amenities are divided. Your side probably doesn't have a lounge or a small theater or showers, a game room, a laundry area, masseuse, barber shop, or, for the growing number of female truckers, a beauty salon. Theirs does. Skeet shooting and Olympic pools are next.

Where the twain meet is inside the convenience stores, food courts, and restaurants that cater to both truckers and casual travelers. If you left your television set at home, you can buy one there, along with a refrigerator, chrome accessories, CB radios, microphones, lights, medicine, whip antennaes, maps, souvenirs, groceries, books, videos, audiobooks, video games, and DVDs.

Why is all of it there? Some truckers' rigs are literally mobile homes, so their extended sleeping cabs (especially the 155-inch versions) can be equipped with a washer and dryer, king-sized bed, flip-down 52-inch plasma TV with continuous satellite tracking, shower, toilet, computer center, and a full kitchen with cabinets, oven, and a microwave.

Trucks and truck stops are far larger than you may recall and if you roll into the small town of Walcott, Iowa, you'll find the largest truck stop in the world. The Iowa 80 Truckstop welcomes about 5,000 people a day, which

Since 1979, the Iowa 80 Truckstop has hosted the Annual Walcott Truckers Jamboree, held on the second Thursday and Friday in July. Thousands of drivers head in to show off their rigs—some of which are contestants in the Super Truck Beauty Contest. It's a showcase of real Americana with more than 200 antique trucks, a pork chop cookout, the Trucker Olympics, bands, carnival games, and fireworks.

surpasses the population of Walcott by more than four times. And it's big. A lot bigger than when it opened in 1964, when there was just a small store, a lube bay, and a mom-and-pop restaurant. Today there's the Iowa 80 Kitchen, a 300-seat restaurant that's open 24 hours a day. There's the Truckers Warehouse Store, more than two dozen private showers, a movie theater, an embroidery center, vinyl graphics department, an engraving service, a barber, a dentist, a cell phone store, thousands of DVDs and CDs, a food court, a service center, and the Iowa 80 Trucking Museum.

> **One thing you won't find at Iowa 80? Front-door locks. They've been open every minute since 1965.**

If you ever wanted to know what it's like to sit behind the wheel of a semi, climb into the cab of a Freightliner, Kenworth, or the Peterbilt truck called the Cornpatch Cadillac. Sit at the wheel and glance at a cluster of gauges that could have been borrowed from a 747. Look in back and you'll find the type of sleeping quarters Donald Trump would buy if he only had the cash.

Unlike many truck stops, Iowa 80 is still family-owned. Bill Moon's daughter Delia Meier and her brother Bill Moon, Jr., literally grew up there and each understands the appeal of the American truck stop.

"Truck stops are strictly an American phenomenon," Delia explains. "They're built for everybody. It's a safe place where truckers are working and families are here and everyone is happy because they are *on the road*. They are going places. And it's a diverse group because everyone here is going to or coming from somewhere else. On top of that, people are happy because they are in control. It's not like an airport where you're dependent on someone else for transportation. When you're on the road, *you are in control.*"

When you're at a truck stop, you're declaring your independence. You're part of a select group of adventurers—on the road and ready to discover America.

CONTACTS

Iowa 80 Truckstop
I-80, Exit 284
Walcott, Iowa
(563) 284-6961
www.iowa80truckstop.com

www.trucker.com

www.truckstopinfoplus.com

America's Independent Truckers' Association
www.aitaonline.com

For Lodging and Dining, see p. 285

52. INDIANAPOLIS 500
Indianapolis, Indiana

The Indianapolis 500 holds the pole position as America's Great Race. Each May on the Sunday before Memorial Day, the Indianapolis Motor Speedway hosts the largest one-day sporting event in the world. In addition to a quarter-million fans in the stands, another 100,000 are camped out around the infield. So even if NASCAR has lapped the Indy Racing League in terms of television viewers and marketing, from a standpoint of pure Americana the Indy 500 remains well in the lead.

RACE RELATIONS

It's natural to wonder why 33 men (and occasionally a woman) would spend more than three hours making 800 left-hand turns. When my grandfather tried that, we had to find him a home. Of course when there's about $15 million in prize money on the line, you're bound to find a lot of people anxious to get in the race and follow the path blazed by racers starting way back in 1911.

Before or on Race Day, see the Indianapolis Motor Speedway Hall of Fame Museum, which is located in the infield. This features every bit of Indy 500 trivia, cars, and photos you'd expect.

The first long-distance race—known then as the International 500-Mile Sweepstakes Race—attracted more than 80,000 fans who paid a dollar each to fill the stands and watch automobiles rocket around the oval track at speeds surpassing 70 miles per hour. The performance of the racing cars improved each year with technological breakthroughs like rearview mirrors, fuel injection, and a legendary engine called the "Offy," named after engineer and mechanic Fred Offenhauser. The four-cylinder power plant was so far ahead of the competition that it's credited with winning a record 27 victories, 18 of them consecutive. Try as they might, engineers could never find room for multiple cup holders.

With few exceptions, American drivers and American cars dominated the race until the late 1970s, when more European chassis and engines were being used and then, in the 1980s, when more foreign-born drivers got behind the wheel. Get ready for drive time.

DO IT YOURSELF

On a practical level, watching 33 highly skilled drivers rack up 500 miles takes about three hours. But you don't go to the Indy 500 on a practical

level. Look at this on the once-in-a-lifetime level so you can fully experience the complete scope of events taking place at the track and around the city.

Part of this involves investing about $100 on a Bronze Badge, which is the automotive equivalent of a Wonka Golden Ticket. With it, you can attend three full weeks of events before the big day, and that includes the practice runs and qualifications that determine a driver's starting position. You can spend time getting access to the garages on Gasoline Alley to watch crews working on team cars, firing up the engines, and rolling the racers to the track.

> **With the power to generate 5,000 pounds of downforce, at 220 mph the 1,600-pound cars can run upside-down. It doesn't make sense to me either.**

The Friday before the race is a fan favorite, Carburetor Day, reserved for the race teams' final practice runs. The name gives a nod to the days when pit crews actually had carburetors to adjust (which hasn't been the case since 1963). By Saturday, drivers have fine-tuned themselves and their cars so perfectly that the track closes up and everyone drives downtown to the must-see parade.

Early on the morning of Race Day the stands start filling up—but you won't need to rush in since your seat is reserved. Considering that your Bronze Badge expired the day before, spend time around Gasoline Alley to look for cars and racers and hang out by the Pagoda to watch VIPs and celebrities arrive.

Everything you'll see this morning—the fans at Gasoline Alley, the line of bricks that marks the finish line, the bagpipers who parade before the race—is part of Indy tradition. Finally, the release of a year's worth of accumulated anticipation is ignited with the announcement, "Gentlemen…start your engines!" That's when the combined energy of 33 675-horsepower racers and 350,000 fans explodes around the 2.5-mile track.

> **The cars get less than two miles per gallon. Then again, they can accelerate from 0 to 100 miles per hour in less than three seconds.**

When they round Turn 4, the green flag snaps and what sounds like the muscular drone of a swarm of 1,600-pound metal hornets screams past the stands, releasing the most hellacious noise since the latest *American Idol* soundtrack. It is very loud and very scary and extremely exciting.

After the drivers make the first hundred or so left turns, though, the thrill of the noise and motion may dissipate, since you see the cars only briefly before they disappear down the track. But when they race out of sight at 220 miles per hour, drivers cover 2.5 miles in a flash and you'll see them again in about 40 seconds. That impressive speed can be neutralized by delays when they race under the yellow caution flag or a wreck happens or rain falls and the action comes to a relative standstill and you think you're watching the world's slowest fastest race.

But when the racers are running full bore and driving just inches apart, covering the length of a football field *every second* and skimming past the next fastest racer to inch up to the head of the pack, you're watching exactly what fans have loved since 1911: the Greatest Spectacle in Racing.

CONTACTS

Indianapolis Motor Speedway
4790 West 16th Street
(800) 822-INDY
www.indianapolismotorspeedway.com

www.indycar.com
www.indy500.com

For Lodging and Dining, see p. 310

 # 53. GATEWAY ARCH
St. Louis, Missouri

You may have seen it on postcards and coins, but only when you stand near the banks of the Mississippi River and look at the Gateway Arch does it truly project the boldness and spirit of America's pioneers. Simple and symbolic, this enormous span of steel recognizes the role St. Louis played as America's portal to the west.

DESIGNING MEN

Why St. Louis? Why an arch? Good questions.

One of the first boomtowns of the new American West, St. Louis was the jumping off point for mountain men, traders, and pioneers ready to load up and head into more than 800,000 square miles of new land opened through Thomas Jefferson's Louisiana Purchase in 1803. The city would grow dramatically. Prior to 1840, the population was less than 20,000, 20 years later the arrival of European immigrants had pushed the population past 160,000. St. Louis had become the New York City of the frontier, with the nation's second busiest port giving berth to flotillas of steamboats.

Adventure and opportunity propelled St. Louis into a great American gateway. In 1947, a competition began to create a monument in St. Louis that would honor the ingenuity, vision, and persever-ance that helped settle the West.

In short order, the seven-man jury was unfurling 172 plans that showcased the usual suspects: Greek columns and temples, an Egyptian obelisk, and majestic horses. But there was one design the judges had examined that was clearly the most ingenious, symbolic, and artistic. Choosing it as a semifinalist,

Some 26,000 tons of concrete were poured to support the arch. Even so, it can still sway up to 18 inches, in a 150-mile-per-hour wind.

the panel sent a telegram of congratulations to the home of gifted architect Eliel Saarinen, who was thrilled that his design had been selected. In reality, Eliel's design had been rejected—the note was meant for his son, the appar-ently even more gifted Eero Saarinen, who had submitted what would become the winning design.

Saarinen the Younger's spectacular inverted catenary arch was 630 feet high and 630 feet across. The majestic span would frame the city center and mall, with its historic Old Courthouse, and, beyond, the western horizon. The design was approved in 1948, and work on the foundation began on February 12, 1963. On Thursday, October 28, 1965, the final section was put in place before noon.

Minutes later, it was an American icon.

DO IT YOURSELF

Even if you'd get lost in a one-room schoolhouse, you won't get lost looking for the Arch. More than 60 stories high, it makes an impressive first impres-sion when you enter the Jefferson National Expan-sion Memorial, the park that also features several historic sites and a museum.

The Arch is surrounded by expansive green space, so my first inclination (and it was a good one) was not to rush inside but to wander across the park. It was like an optical illusion: The Arch

During the planning of the project, the insurer predicted that 13 workers would die during the arch's construction. None did.

seemed to twist into a new and fascinating design with every step I took. The biggest surprise was its size. Its sleek appearance belies the fact that it weighs as much as an aircraft carrier (albeit one equipped with optional chrome trim). Because it is so massive, it's anchored an astounding 65 feet beneath the ground.

A historical museum, theaters, and gift shop are also underground. After you drop downstairs head straight to the 35-minute film "Monument to a Dream." The film follows engineers who worked through brittle winter frosts and searing summer heat to build the monument. Approaching from opposite directions, they relied on extremely delicate instruments to determine how to keep the two sides lined up. The narrowing gap had to be kept accurate to within 1/64th of an inch; if it wasn't, the arch could have been off by nearly a foot by the time the two sides met at the top.

> Eero Saarinen was also the architect behind the Trans World Airlines Terminal at Kennedy Airport in New York City; Dulles International Airport near Washington, D.C.; and the General Motors Technical Center near Detroit. He certainly would have done more, but he died at 51.

This was a team that had to devise solutions for an ever-confounding list of challenges. Because heat expands metal, measurements were taken at night.

To creep up the side of the ever-leaning and ever-rising arch, a special crane had to be invented to lift pieces into place. When the keystone—the final insert—was put in place, fire hoses sprayed water on the arch to keep the joints from expanding.

After the film, you'll want to head down the ramps to the north or south trams. If you're familiar with bank canisters being sucked through a tube, the sensation here is nearly the same. Squeeze yourself into a tiny white pod and the entire seven-car string of this ingenious elevator is tugged along the curve of the arch to deliver you to the summit.

What looks like a thin, fragile twist of airborne ribbon from the ground is actually a wide hallway that offers room for 150 people, all of whom are peering through porthole-sized windows. Reaching up, you can easily touch the ceiling.

Walk from window to window and look around. To the east, past the Mississippi River, are America's origins. To the west, you can see what Jefferson envisioned: the gateway to America's future.

CONTACTS

Jefferson National Expansion
Memorial
(314) 655-1700
www.nps.gov/jeff

Gateway Arch
(877) 982-1410
www.gatewayarch.com

www.explorestlouis.com

For Lodging and Dining, see pp. 310–311

54. ANHEUSER-BUSCH FACTORY
St. Louis, Missouri

Every year, Americans drink the equivalent of 67 billion cans of beer, double that if you factor in what's consumed in frat houses. A trickle of it comes from microbreweries, a flood from regional breweries, and a whole gullywasher from the Anheuser-Busch factory in St. Louis, Missouri.

BUSSSSSCH!

To trace the history of beer you'd need a pretty long calendar, probably one that went back about 8,000 years. Archaeologists have found wooden models of ancient Egyptians brewing beer; they've also uncovered a prayer to Ninkasi, the Mesopotamian goddess of beer, which was a clever device to remember how to brew the stuff. Babylonian king Hammurabi's rules for brewing beer were in his law code circa 1760 B.C.

But if you ever come across an unopened bottle of ancient Babylonian, Egyptian, or Mesopotamian beer don't drink it—even if it's chilled and sitting beside a platter of chips and salsa. You wouldn't recognize that beer or the beers that were brewed in Europe before immigrants brought their recipes to America and adapted them to American tastes.

In the U.S., most breweries cropped up where German immigrants settled. Milwaukee, for one, and St. Louis, for another. In St. Louis, the Bavarian Brewery wasn't doing so well until a soapmaker named Eberhard Anheuser bought it in 1860. Lacking any practical brewing experience, he teamed up with his son-in-law Adolphus Busch, whose business skills helped turn the local product into a national one. How'd they do it? For one, Busch applied the process of pasteurization to the beer so he had a product that would travel well without spoiling. After that he introduced artificial refrigeration, refrigerated railcars, and rail-side icehouses. In 1876, Anheuser-Busch unveiled the first national beer brand, Budweiser, followed 20 years later by Michelob.

> Milwaukee is another of America's great beer-producing cities—several tours are available at micro-breweries and at the city's landmark Miller Brewing Company (4251 W. State Street, 414-931-2337, www.millerbrewing.com).

Anheuser-Busch also understood promotion. A highly popular series of lithographs highlighted the pulchritude of the Budweiser Girl; there were giveaways like logo-adorned cork pulls and pocketknives; and guests were invited to tour the breweries. As Anheuser-Busch hit the million-barrel-a-year mark in 1901, things were running like a well-oiled beer factory. That changed on January 6, 1920, when Prohibition put beer and other alcoholic beverages on ice.

For 13 years Anheuser-Busch waited it out by expanding into other products, including a nonalcoholic beer called Bevo, soft drinks, ice cream, and even truck bodies. When it turned out the only folks benefiting from Prohibition were gangsters and folks who craved Bevo, the ill-fated law was repealed on April 7, 1933. By 1936, metal cans were replacing wooden kegs and the same wave of growth that propelled America after World War II swept Anheuser-Busch along as well. In the 1950s, the company became the leading brewer in the United States.

Half a century later they're still in the lead and they want you to see how they do it.

DO IT YOURSELF

OK, you're right. While Anheuser-Busch is still the largest brewer in America, it's no longer an American company. In 2008, it was sold to the Belgian corporation InBev. But dozens of free walking tours (and a special fee tour, see sidebar) still depart from the Tour Center every day. While you wait for your guide, admire the displays of gorgeous steins, bottles, taps, photos, a race car, and assorted memorabeerlia.

From there, follow your guide and your nose to the Clydesdale stables, home of the famous draft horses that pull the Budweiser beer wagon. I'm still not sure how Clydesdales became affiliated with a brewery since they aren't from Germany (they're from the Clyde River Valley of Scotland). Maybe they had a strong union. Anyway, they successfully reflect Budweiser's heritage and the sight of them and the 1885 stables, which are a National Historic Landmark, is memorable.

Upgrade to the two-hour Beermaster Tour ($25 adults, $10 ages 13-20) for behind-the-scenes opportunities, including a chance to sample some brew straight from the tank.

The tour continues at the chilly Lagering Cellar and then moves to the circa 1891 Brewhouse (another National Historic Landmark), which has been restored to its Victorian splendor and features giant brew kettles tended by brewmasters who can explain the process of making beer.

After passing the 1868 Lyon Schoolhouse, where the Busch children attended school, you'll arrive at the packaging plant and see where your favorite brews are bottled. From a gallery overlooking the factory floor, you witness the whirring, spinning, blurring spectacle that moves beer from pasteurization to labeling. Remember, the equivalent of up to 800,000 cases, packaged in cans, kegs, and bottles, is being filled each day during the summer, so in just five minutes you could be looking at about 50,000 bottles' worth of beer being processed below. Take one down, pass it around...49,999 bottles of beer on the floor.

> **Beyond the 6.3 million cases the St. Louis factory produces each year, a worldwide network of Anheuser-Busch factories generate an additional 155 million cases annually.**

You've walked several blocks to get there, so a trolley is waiting to take you back uphill to the Tour Center, where everyone of legal age enjoys the payoff. Into the Hospitality Room, you can kick back, choose two samples, sip the beer, and propose a toast.

To Eberhard Anheuser and Adolphus Busch!

CONTACTS

Anheuser-Busch
(314) 577-2626
(800) DIAL-BUD (342-5283)

For Lodging and Dining, see pp. 310–311

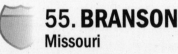

55. BRANSON
Missouri

Something's missing in Branson, Missouri. You won't find trams or monorails or robotic characters. There are no fairy-tale castles and it's a challenge to find high-priced tickets, overpriced concessions, or long lines. Although it lacks the flash of Disney and Vegas, no one seems to mind. In the Ozarks of southern Missouri, you'll find something even better than fireworks and flashing lights. A Great American Vacation.

HEAD FOR THE HILLS

How did Branson become the Chosen One? The place where performers could come off the road, open a theater, and perform two shows a day for busloads of tourists? Part of it goes back to the late 1800s, when a local geological attraction called Marvel Cave made Branson a tourist destination. Then with the 1907 release of the popular novel *The Shepherd of the Hills*, even more tourists dropped in.

Over the next half-century, local entrepreneurs devised new ways to draw in tourists, including a Nativity scene placed atop Mount Branson and square dances held at Marvel Cave, which were broadcast on Red Foley's *Ozark Jubilee* radio and television programs. In 1959, Branson's first stage show, the "Baldknobbers Jamboree," premiered at the town hall to an audience of only 50.

Hugo and Mary Herschend had made Marvel Cave one of Branson's most popular attractions. After Hugo passed away in 1955, Mary and their sons created Silver Dollar City, a make-believe mining camp staged so shopkeepers, cowboys, and saloon gals could entertain tourists in an old-fashioned frontier setting. It was all a precursor to Branson's Big Bang when, in 1983, musician Roy Clark bought and opened the Roy Clark Celebrity Theatre, which inspired other performers to follow suit. In 1985, Boxcar Willie (of the Philadelphia Willies) became one of the first performers to establish a permanent show schedule there. Other show folk came off the road and built their own theaters. In the 1990s the national media caught wind of Branson. Here was a destination where families could enjoy a quality vacation that didn't break the bank. Naturally, critics piled on and argued that Branson was just a hillbilly heaven of lowbrow entertainment, cut-rate tourist traps, and molasses-thick traffic.

Hardly any of that is true. Except the molasses-thick traffic.

You don't have to be a Boxcar Willie to perform in Branson. Youth groups, church groups, and student groups are often presented on Branson stages to open shows and perform during intermissions. To find out if there's room on the stage for your group, call the Director of Meeting and Convention Sales at the Branson Chamber: (800) 272-6766.

DO IT YOURSELF

Of all the ways to see Branson, the best advice I got was the recommendation that I "sample a little bit of everything." So my schedule was a grab bag of live shows, general sightseeing, and much-needed downtime. After three days, I had gotten a fair sense of what Branson's about, watched multigenerational families having a blast, and signed a multiyear contract to open for Andy Williams.

Pleasing memories of an old Florida attraction called Six Gun Territory pointed me toward Silver Dollar City. As at Six Gun, there's everything from log flume rides and Ferris wheels to roller coasters and a steam train. My personal favorite was the Silver Dollar Saloon, where sassy saloon gals trade barbs with dimwitted cowboys in a thoroughly entertaining old-fashioned musical comedy revue. And them saloon gals? Cute! The park is filled with friendly street performers, folk musicians, silversmiths, coppersmiths, soapmakers, jerky vendors (ostrich, elk, alligator, kangaroo, wild boar), and assorted crafters—while at the Wilderness Chapel you can attend Sunday-morning services, renew your vows, and even get hitched.

Be wary of offers for discount tickets. If you'd rather not see a timeshare in order to see a show, check in at the Branson Welcome Center on Highway 248 where attendants can give you the lowdown on discounts that are on the up and up.

Silver Dollar City can fill a day, but save time for the Roy Rogers Museum, which displays Roy's horse Trigger (or at least his taxidermied remains), saddles, boots, rifles, the family dining table, pocketknives, and anything else Rogers ever came in contact with. Rogers achieved stardom by founding the Sons of the Pioneers, and although Roy has ridden on, his harmonizing descendants have made Branson their summer home; their show centers around a chuckwagon feast at the Shepherd of the Hills outdoor theater. The Pioneers' flawless harmonizing on standards like "Cool Water," "Lilies Grow High," and "Tumbling Tumbleweeds" will make you want to quit your job and become a singing cowboy.

Whether it's Andy Williams, the Presley Family Jubilee, the Oak Ridge Boys, Japanese fiddler Shoji Tabuchi, Jim Stafford, or Yakoff Smirnov, some stars have been in business in Branson long enough to justify their name on a theater's marquee. Other theaters present traveling acts such as the Osmonds and Tony Orlando—but every performer has learned to include a "Salute to America" grand finale to guarantee at least one standing ovation.

Highway 76 can be stuck solid with traffic. Running parallel are several alternate routes that can bypass the bottlenecks. Detailed maps provided by the Chamber help you navigate your route.

On a visit years earlier, one traveling show caught my attention: "The Rat Pack: Live from Las Vegas." Dying to see Frank and Dean and Sammy, I arrived early and took my seat that Saturday when the curtain rose at ten o'clock. That was *10 a.m.* I know; it would have been challenging for the *real* Rat Pack to fill a theater this early on a Saturday morning, so my hat's off to the trio that packed the 1,500-seat theater with 150 early risers. I had to suspend disbelief to enjoy the show (which I did), especially when "Frank" finished a tune and proclaimed with cool assurance, "Branson, Missouri…That's where it's at, baby."

Branson *is* where it's at, baby.

CONTACTS

Branson Chamber and Convention and Visitors Bureau
(800) BRANSON (272-6767)
www.explorebranson.com

For Lodging and Dining, see pp. 311–312

56. HANNIBAL
Missouri

The town of Hannibal was to Mark Twain what the sled Rosebud was to Charles Foster Kane. In lives that knew stratospheric fame and great disappointment, these links to childhood were never forgotten.

Everyone, especially those of us who had the good fortune and the good sense to grow up in a small town, has a Hannibal. The difference is that none of us will ever be able to recall those years with the same vividness, perspective, and humor as Mark Twain did… So that's why you're going to his hometown.

MISSISSIPPI YEARNING

If not for a kid blessed with a sense of adventure, an eye for detail, and a gift for expression, Hannibal, Missouri, would have receded into history as just another anonymous and overlooked American town. But Samuel Clemens— better known as Mark Twain—grew up in this "drowsing town" on the shores of the wide and mysterious Mississippi River. Although he left Hannibal in mid-1853 at the age of 17, he never left his hometown behind.

He worked as a printer's assistant, steamboat pilot, journalist, and public speaker. When he wrote best he was writing about his real-life experiences, such as his time as a pilot in *Life on the Mississippi*, his adventures in the American West in *Roughing It,* and his grand tour of Europe in *The Innocents Abroad.* This gift flowed into his fact-based works of fiction. Memories of his childhood in Hannibal resurfaced in *The Adventures of Tom Sawyer* and *The Adventures of Huckleberry Finn.* Through these and other works he became, as William Faulkner noted, the "Father of American Literature."

If you've read Twain you've probably already walked through the caves with Tom and Becky, whitewashed a picket fence, or floated down the Mississippi River on a raft with Huck and Jim. So even if you're visiting Hannibal for the first time, in a way you are going home.

DO IT YOURSELF

It's been well over 150 years since Samuel Clemens was drifting through childhood there, so it's almost certain the Hannibal you visualize won't be the town you'll see. So adjust your perceptions and begin.

Start at the Interpretive Center, where you'll pick up a ticket for a self-guided tour of the eight properties run by the Mark Twain Foundation. The center offers a nice overview of Twain's life and accomplishments, with books and memorabilia and awards he won on display. You'll find more details through the back door, which leads into Twain's childhood home. It doesn't take much imagination to picture Aunt Polly and Sid in the parlor while Tom sneaks out a window to hook up with Huckleberry Finn.

It's a short walk to other sites, including the Huckleberry Finn House and the childhood home of Laura Hawkins, the little girl who became Twain's Becky Thatcher. At the north end of Main Street, a statue of Tom and Huck has stood at the base of Cardiff Hill since 1926, and you can drive up or take the stairs all the way to the summit to see the Mississippi River below. It's natural to imagine what this view meant to young Clemens, who surely wondered what was beyond the river bend.

When you backtrack along Main Street, you'll probably stop at one of the several gift shops, where you'll be stymied by the choice of editions of *Tom Sawyer* to add to your collection. You should also drop into an old department store that is now the Museum Gallery. Inside is the mother lode of Twain memorabilia, including the gown he wore when receiving an honorary doctorate at Oxford in 1907, his writing

Mark Twain could recite a grocery list and it'd still be worth quoting. Here are a few of his finest:

- Reader, suppose you were an idiot. And suppose you were a member of Congress. But I repeat myself.

- Honesty is the best policy—when there is money in it.

- Clothes make the man. Naked people have little or no influence on society.

- There's one thing wrong with the younger generation, and that's that we're not part of it.

- Get your facts first and then you can distort 'em as you please.

desk and chair, his pipe, his typewriter, a complete set of first editions of all of his works, and 15 original Norman Rockwell paintings created for special editions of *Tom Sawyer* and *Huck Finn.* On the mezzanine, a re-creation of a steamboat pilothouse lets you stand at the wheel; another display puts you aboard a raft with Huck and Jim. They even have one of the author's famous white suits—the only one still in existence.

If you can travel around the Fourth of July and don't mind seeing the town with as many as 100,000 other people, the biggest annual event in Hannibal is Tom Sawyer Days. Local kids compete for the honor of being goodwill ambassadors Tom and Becky, and they have contests complete with jumping frogs and whitewashed fences.

A trolley tour winds around downtown and into a hillside neighborhood of Victorian homes before heading about a mile south of town to the Mark Twain Cave, which attracted young Samuel Clemens. He later immortalized it as the labyrinth that trapped Tom and Becky and killed Injun Joe. The guides are well-versed in its literary and geological history and will point out soot marks on the ceiling left behind by cave explorers and the "sign of the cross" that revealed the hiding place of Injun Joe's treasure.

There should be time for one more fantasy. Back in town a small paddlewheeler slaps its way a few miles upstream and then down the Mississippi River. Modern Hannibal disappears and ahead is 1,000 miles of muddy water and endless trees. Let your imagination drift with the current and turn this paddlewheeler into a log raft. As you float down the river, it's just Tom Sawyer, Huck Finn, Mark Twain… and you.

CONTACTS

Hannibal Convention
& Visitors Bureau
505 North 3rd Street
(573) 221-2477
(866) 263-4825
www.visithannibal.com

Mark Twain Boyhood Home &
Museum
120 North Main Street
(573) 221-9010
www.marktwainmuseum.org

www.marktwaincave.com
(800) 527-0304
(573) 221-1656

www.marktwainriverboat.com
(573) 221-3222

For Lodging and Dining, see p. 312

57. MISSISSIPPI RIVERBOATS
Minnesota to Louisiana

When someone wants to brag about something that's not exactly the first or best or biggest thing in the nation, they can qualify it by saying that at least it's the first or best or biggest thing "east (or west) of the Mississippi." The Mississippi River is the nation's natural dividing line, but when you travel its waters you'll discover it's much more than that.

GATHERING STEAM

How do you channel 2,350 miles of Mississippi River into a bathtub-sized compendium of facts and history? You talk to a river historian like Bill Wiemuth. Having spent years paddling up and down the Mississippi River aboard the legendary *Delta Queen*, Wiemuth has a way of impressing upon you not just the significance of the river, but its magnificence.

"You have to think of the Mississippi River as the Nile of North America," he suggests. "Between the Appalachians and Rocky Mountains more than 200 tributaries drain into the Mississippi and it carries all of that water into the Gulf of Mexico. The Mississippi River drains more than 40 percent of the entire nation."

From its headwaters at Lake Itasca in Minnesota, where it's about 3 feet deep and 20 feet wide, the Mississippi stretches as wide as a mile across in Alton, Illinois, and as deep as 200 feet in New Orleans. Each day it dumps enough sand, gravel, and mud near the Gulf of Mexico to fill a freight train 150 miles long.

Prior to trains and highways, this incredible river was America's interstate, but it was all one-way traffic. Until the early 1800s, boatmen had no engines to rely on, so while they had a relatively easy task heading to New Orleans on barges, flatboats, rafts, and canoes, they had no way to make it back.

"People tried to drag and pull or roll their vessels north, but it took tremendous physical exertion," Wiemuth explains. "So most crews would just get to New Orleans, sell their cargo, and then sell their vessels for scrap lumber. Folks in New Orleans used all that wood to build houses and buildings there."

So New Orleans is where boatmen became footmen. A trail called the Natchez Trace led all the way to Pittsburgh, a long six months' walk away.

> It takes about three months for water from Lake Itasca, Minnesota, to reach the Gulf of Mexico.

After making it north, the boatman would rest a few months before embarking on a 950-mile voyage on the Ohio River back to the Mississippi. After three months he'd reach New Orleans again. In other words, a hearty boatman could rack up roughly one round trip per year.

Going fishing? There are 241 fish species in the Mississippi River and its tributaries.

Everything changed in 1811, when a steamboat called the *New Orleans* became the first in what was then considered the American West. Now that riverboats were capable of making round trips, an armada of steamboats helped carry the nation's economy from infancy to manhood. With more than 14,000 miles of navigable waterways branching off the Mississippi River, steamboats also penetrated other regions of America via rivers like the Ohio and Missouri.

"It looked like a Currier and Ives print," suggests Wiemuth. "In the most historic section, between Memphis and New Orleans, were moss-draped southern oaks and riverboat gamblers on board and pie-shaped plantations so everyone had access to the Mississippi. If someone at a plantation wanted a steamboat to stop, they'd go to the bank and wave a handkerchief to flag them over. River traffic all seemed slow and casual."

It was also dangerous. The river was rife with deadly currents and submerged snags that could sink a boat. Pilots with steady nerves dealt with all of these natural hazards, but they couldn't deal with Civil War skirmishes on the river. After the war, railroads begin traveling to places steamboats couldn't. By the dawn of the 20th century, steamboats were reduced to pushing cargo-laden barges.

But even though the paddlewheelers you imagine were lost to another time, a small fleet of them is hanging around to bring that time back.

DO IT YOURSELF

Just a few dozen iconic paddlewheelers slap their way up and down the waterway today. Christened in 1926, the legendary *Delta Queen* is the last of the authentic steamboats, but—due to its age and wooden superstructure—it requires a congressional exemption from a 1966 Safety Act for it to continue its overnight voyages, and its future is imperiled. However, several other Mississippi River paddlewheelers depart for multiday excursions, day trips, and dinner cruises.

As you do your homework, consider which part of the river you want to explore. The Lower Mississippi, which starts at the confluence of the Ohio and Mississippi rivers below Cairo, Illinois, sparks the fantasies of most travelers.

Vanessa Bloy of Majestic Cruises has sailed this region on the *Delta Queen*'s excursions in the Deep South. "The experience takes people back to the riverboating days of the 19th century," she explains. "The *Delta Queen*'s theater is very ornate, like Ford's Theatre in Washington. There's a Ladies' Parlor and a Gentlemen's Card Room. You can sip a mint julep in the Grand Saloon; rock in a rocking chair on the deck; listen to Dixieland jazz; and watch the river and landscapes of the Old South."

In the evening the glow of small, sleeping southern towns can be seen from the decks, with daylight hours reserved for visits to ports of call like Memphis, Vicksburg, Natchez, St. Francisville, and New Orleans. On cruises along the Upper Mississippi River, notes Wiemuth, the sights and the communities are equally All-American.

"People don't realize how pretty it can be in the interior of America," he points out. "There are quaint communities right at the river's edge, little midwestern towns in the heartland that look just like Norman Rockwell paintings. It's all cute and picturesque and looks like something we thought we had left behind in the 1950s. At night the sky is white with the Milky Way and you can see the lights on towboats and barges floating past."

For Wiemuth, Mississippi River paddlewheers are a novel way of introducing passengers to a much larger story.

"The Mississippi River contains history and literature and stories of America's drive west. Lewis and Clark traveled this river; battles in the Civil War took place along these banks; Mark Twain introduced it to the world. When I'm on the Mississippi River, I feel a sense of America's heritage."

In the 1840s, panorama artist John Banvard traveled along the Mississippi River, sketching the banks as he sailed. When the voyage was over, he started to paint. And paint. And paint. His completed work was 12 feet high and up to three miles long. Banvard would haul it from town to town and, for two hours, would have stagehands unwind it to give audiences the sensation they were sailing along the Mississippi River.

CONTACTS

www.steamboats.org
A comprehensive guide to today's paddlewheelers, their locations, and history.

www.experiencemississippiriver.com

For Lodging and Dining, see "Across America" p. 285

GREAT PLAINS

Idaho, Kansas, Montana, Nebraska, North Dakota, Oklahoma, South Dakota, Texas, Wyoming

Unfold a map and peek at the Great Plains and you'll recognize that this is a generous portion of American real estate. Considering that, in books and movies and television, the legends of America's Indian tribes and frontier families are still being told, maybe it needs every square mile to capture and convey what we need to know.

This is land that has largely remained unchanged for centuries. You'll find Yellowstone pretty much as it was before any white man knew it existed. Although there are highways around Little Bighorn, and markers to show where men died, the same winds still blow across the grassy prairie where Custer breathed his last.

You'll notice, too, that the stereotypes that have evolved from this region—the dedicated farm families of Kansas, the taciturn cowboys of Texas and the Dakotas, the proud Plains Indians, and the independent spirit found in Wyoming and Montana—are all pretty much on target. I'm glad they are. You'll be glad, too.

58. LEWIS AND CLARK TRAIL
Great Plains–Pacific Northwest

In the early 1800s, nearly the entire western half of the continent was a great mystery. Its geography, geology, waterways, wildlife, and ways of life were completely unknown to America's white population. After traveling for more than two years, Meriwether Lewis and William Clark returned from our farthest shores with some answers and a road map to a larger national destiny.

SEE THE USA

What was west of the Mississippi River? When 18th-century cartographers reached that point on the map, no one really knew. In 1803, President Thomas Jefferson asked Congress to pony up $2,500 to finance a group of explorers, a Corps of Discovery, to search for an all-water route to the Pacific Ocean and to document the land's botany, wildlife, geography, geology, climate, and Indian cultures along the way.

Jefferson found a perfect team to lead the expedition. Meriwether Lewis, 28, was Jefferson's former neighbor and current secretary, and William Clark, 32, had been raised in a frontier family that had lived off the land. Both men were proven soldiers, leaders, and outdoorsmen. Their sense of curiosity and skills of observation made them ideally suited for the task. Like an astronaut in training, before they set out, Lewis studied navigation, medicine, and natural sciences. Unlike an astronaut, he could bring a pet. Seaman, a $20 "dogg of the Newfoundland breed" would join the expedition.

When the weary and worn Corps of Discovery arrived back in St. Louis on September 23, 1806, they had covered more than 8,000 miles in two years, four months, and nine days.

In December 1803, Lewis and Clark and roughly 45 soldiers, outdoorsmen, and boatmen they had recruited reached the staging area near St. Louis. Six months later, on May 14, 1804, they broke camp and began traveling west on the Missouri River. Almost from the beginning, there were challenges from rough waters and heavy rains to deserters, mutiny, and a death. They conducted courts-martial, and in what would become South Dakota, tensions ran high during a face-off with Teton Sioux Indians.

Fifteen hundred miles and 164 days later they built their winter encampment near what is now Washburn, North Dakota, and during the next five months Indians and French-Canadian traders provided them with information about the territory ahead. One of the traders, Toussaint Charbonneau, was accompanied by his pregnant wife Sacagawea, a Shoshone Indian who had been kidnapped by Plains Indians five years earlier. Agreeing to join the expedition when it left in April 1805, the pair (soon to be a trio) would prove invaluable if only for the fact that the couple's new baby, Jean Baptiste Charbonneau, could prove to suspicious tribes that they were a peaceful research party.

They canoed by the White Cliffs region of Montana before reaching sight of the Rocky Mountains. They labored for more than a week wondering which river branch ahead was the real Missouri River, and then had to portage their boats for miles around a series of waterfalls. There were hailstorms and thunderstorms, open prairies to cross, and more forks in the Missouri River before they reached the Continental Divide. Then came a startling twist of fate.

On August 17, 1805, they encountered Shoshone Indians near the border of present-day Montana and Idaho. Sacagawea was reunited with her brother Cameahwait who was now a chief. The familial link provided the Corps the chance to trade for horses, so the men would be on horseback as they crossed the bitterly cold and snowy Bitterroot Mountains into present-day Idaho. By October they would follow the Snake River to the Columbia River where they once again faced fearsome rapids. Then, in early November, Clark was overjoyed to write in his journal, "Great joy in camp. We are in View of the Ocian, this great Pacific Octean which we been So long anxious to See."

Not quite. They had arrived not at the "great Pacific Octean" but at the tidewater of the Columbia River, a massive estuary that looked as large as the sea. They would face another nine days of unrelenting rain and storms before the Corps of Discovery finally stepped foot upon the Pacific shore 554 days and 4,132 miles after they had left St. Louis.

Four months later, they would turn around and start walking back home.

> **What did the Corps of Discovery accomplish? Aside from surviving, it catalogued and described 178 plants and 122 species and subspecies of animals; mapped a large portion of the rivers and mountain ranges in the American West; and established relations with Indian tribes. Their diaries stand as a permanent record of one of mankind's greatest explorations.**

DO IT YOURSELF

To faithfully follow the Lewis and Clark Trail, you'll need a kayak since the explorers traveled mostly on rivers and waterways. The National Park

Service oversees the Trail and can provide you with maps that reveal the footpaths and water routes, but if there's no time for extensive walking and hiking, in states they traversed, the highways closest to their route are now designated the Lewis and Clark Highway. Pullouts and interpretive signs along the Highway tell you when they passed through the region as well as provide descriptions of the people they met and wildlife they saw.

Just before the expedition set out, France sold the United States 828,800 square miles of land. The Louisiana Purchase doubled the size of the young nation and allowed the explorers to enter freely what had formerly been French territory.

"People use the Trail as a multidisciplinary learning resource, for improving skills in writing, math, science, art, language, geography, geology—all things the Corps of Discovery had to master," points out Wendy Raney of the Lewis and Clark Heritage Trail Foundation. "There are a lot of parents who have their kids keep a journal as they follow the Trail, and have them collect things along the way just like Lewis and Clark did."

With thousands of miles to explore, it's no surprise that some portions of the Trail have remained little changed since Lewis and Clark traveled through more than 200 years ago. There are sections of Montana and Idaho where you can canoe or kayak and camp for days and only see few signs of modern civilization. In the southwest corner of Montana there's the Lolo Motorway which, while sounding like a feat of German engineering, is actually Forest Road 500, a thoroughly rough and rugged highway best covered on horseback.

"To really understand what you're seeing," advises Raney, "travel with a copy of their journals. Gary Moulton edited a thirteen-volume set of the journals of Lewis and Clark and also released a condensed version of the expedition's highlights. Read *Undaunted Courage* by Stephen Ambrose. Try to understand what they did.

"A lot of kids think Lewis and Clark just went out for a walk," she continues. "In Great Falls, Montana, they were pelted by hail that caused welts. They were eaten alive by mosquitoes, they walked across prickly pear cactus that shredded the soles of their moccasins. There was a lot more to this than simply working their way around waterfalls.

"Reflect on what they were going through and what they were thinking. When you put yourself in their frame of mind, and in their time, you'll just begin to understand what a great undertaking and magnificent accomplishment this was."

CONTACTS

Lewis & Clark Trail
(402) 661-1804
www.nps.gov/lecl

Lewis and Clark Trail Heritage Foundation
(406) 454-1234
(888) 701-3434
www.lewisandclark.org

Lewis & Clark Fort Mandan Association
www.lewis-clark.org

Lewis and Clark Journals
http://lewisandclarkjournals.unl.edu/

www.lewisandclarktrail.com

For Lodging and Dining, see "Across America," p. 285

59. MOUNT RUSHMORE
Keystone, South Dakota

Until you go to Mount Rushmore, you cannot fully appreciate the skill, nerve, daring, and determination of those who labored to create this monument—or this nation.

ROCK STARS

In 1923, Doane Robinson, the superintendent of the South Dakota historical society, had a vision. In the Needles—the towering granite spires of his state's Black Hills—he saw a caravan of Indian leaders and American explorers. Fortunately for Robinson, U.S. senator Peter Norbeck shared the same vision.

He suggested that Robinson look up Gutzon Borglum, a Parisian-trained sculptor who was working on a monumental bas relief of Confederate generals and soldiers on the face of Georgia's Stone Mountain. After hearing Robinson's pitch, Borglum went AWOL from the Confederacy and headed for the Black Hills.

The scale of the project was discussed and debated and altered until the three agreed that the memorial would include four presidents who represented the birth, growth, preservation, and development of a

Cher once admitted that she was so naïve that her husband Sonny Bono convinced her Mount Rushmore was a natural rock formation.

nation dedicated to democracy and the pursuit of individual liberty—to wit, George Washington, Thomas Jefferson, Abraham Lincoln, and Teddy Roosevelt.

After weeks of researching mountain sites, Borglum saw that a broad wall of exposed granite on 5,725-foot Mount Rushmore (known by the Lakota Sioux as the Six Grandfathers) faced southeast. The artist realized that the wall would catch light and change with the seasons; from spring's golden glow to a wintertime dusting of powdery snow.

President Calvin Coolidge's dedication on June 15, 1927, kicked off more than 14 years of blasting, drilling, sculpting—and begging. The Great Depression forced Borglum to hit the road to cajole and wheedle cash from congressmen, cabinet members, and other officials. To supplement his own income, Borglum solicited personal commissions in Europe, returning to Mount Rushmore to inspect its progress; argue with the executive board; and fire qualified workers, who later had to be rehired by his son, Lincoln, who was supervising the project.

Gutzon Borglum died on March 6, 1941, just eight months before America's Shrine to Democracy, as it was once called by Franklin Roosevelt, was formally dedicated on October 31, 1941.

My God, is it beautiful.

DO IT YOURSELF

The closest city to Mount Rushmore is Rapid City, about 25 miles northeast. The closest small town is Keystone, a jumble of gift shops and restaurants on Highway 244, just a couple of miles from the main entrance to the Mount Rushmore National Memorial.

At the Crazy Horse Monument (Highway 385, 605-673-4681, www.crazy horse.org), **a dedicated team of artists continues to work on a massive project begun by sculptor Korczak Ziolkowski in 1948: carving into the side of Thunderhead Mountain their impression of Oglala Lakota leader Crazy Horse (he was never photographed).**

Mount Rushmore is such an iconic part of American culture that I wonder why anyone just snaps a few photos and leaves. Instead, invest an afternoon at the Lincoln Borglum Museum and see original models and sketches, and listen to taped firsthand accounts about the construction. Stay and watch the short film "Mount Rushmore—The Shrine" and play with an exhibit on dynamite (hey, kids!) that lets you push a detonator to trigger a video view of the exploding mountainside. Stay and read passages from Calvin Coolidge's 1927 dedication: Silent Cal spoke volumes on how our nation's experiment in democracy was nurtured under the care and guidance of four extraordinary Americans.

For a while I sat outside with others at the park's most popular gathering place, the Grandview Terrace, but when I saw throngs of people arrive and simply stare, pose for a snapshot and leave, I realized I needed privacy. I wandered down a half-mile trail that branches off the terrace to Borglum's studio and offers some close-up views near the base of the mountain. It was there that I was able to truly contemplate and appreciate the monument.

If your timing is right, you can return any evening between May and September for a most American event. About 45 minutes before sunset, take a seat in the 2,500-seat amphitheater to hear patriotic music fill the valley as dusk falls. About 8 p.m. a park ranger (who arguably has the best job in the world) comes out to field questions and introduce a short film, "Freedom—America's Lasting Legacy" before the four faces are gradually illuminated. Then, as "The Star-Spangled Banner" plays, voices echo in song, which often inspires an uncommonly powerful wellspring of pride. To wrap it all up, active and retired military personnel are invited to the stage to assist during the flag retreat.

A monumental grand finale.

In late September, wranglers and onlookers gather at nearby Custer State Park for the annual Buffalo Round Up. You'll have to wake before sunrise, but you can watch as wranglers on horseback and in trucks herd more than a thousand bison across the plains and into the corrals.

CONTACTS

Mount Rushmore National
Monument
(605) 574-2523
www.nps.gov/moru

South Dakota Department
of Tourism
(800) 732-5682
www.travelsd.com

For Lodging and Dining, pp. 312–312

60. RODEOS
Cheyenne, Wyoming, and Across America

It's basic, sometimes brutal, but always impressive. No matter how many times you go to a rodeo and watch a cowboy latch onto a buckin' bronco or see one leap off his horse to wrestle a steer to the ground, you know you're getting your 100 percent recommended daily allowance of adrenaline.

RODEO DRIVE

On July 4, 1882, Buffalo Bill Cody threw a party in his hometown of North Platte, Nebraska. At this event, the showman awarded prizes for roping, shooting, riding, and bronco breaking. Fifteen years later some friends in a little cow town called Cheyenne, Wyoming, decided to begin their own showcase of cowboy feats by presenting contests that would celebrate their lifestyle.

Was there really a reason why cowboys needed to wrestle a steer to the ground? Strap themselves to a horse that would rather not be ridden? Not really, but it was what most of these men did when they were working. Now here was a way they could do it for fun and maybe even win some money.

The Cowboy Code: To offer guidance to his young radio listeners, Gene Autry created the Cowboy Code. Some of his musts include:

• The Cowboy must never shoot first, hit a smaller man, or take unfair advantage.

• He must never go back on his word, or a trust confided in him.

• He must not advocate or possess racially or religiously intolerant ideas.

• He must keep himself clean in thought, speech, action, and personal habits.

They didn't know it, but they were following the trail of Spanish cowboys who had been holding competitions like this for centuries. And 4,000 years earlier on the island of Crete, Minoans were displaying their courage by jumping over charging bulls. But even Spaniards and Cretans might have been impressed by America's fascination with what were known early on as cowboy contests, stampedes, and, as they called them in Cheyenne, frontier days.

In the beginning, the rules were as random as the name. Cowboys (and some cowgirls) often showed up at competitions without knowing what events they'd compete in, which led to injuries and even fatalities. In 1929, Western ranchers attempted to form a tighter, more regulated industry by forming the Rodeo Association of America.

It worked. By the mid-1930s, rodeos had spread even to New York, where rodeo producer Colonel William T. Johnson advertised $40,000 in prize money at the World Championship Rodeo at Madison Square Garden.

In the 1940s, Gene Autry combined his Hollywood celebrity, business acumen, and production skills by stocking rodeos with livestock and buying into a rodeo company that produced contests across America. With showbiz flair, the return of female contestants, and his own star power, the Singing Cowboy helped root rodeo in the American culture.

Rodeos are still a combustible mix of energy, action, grits, and guts. Go to one and even if you're a lily-livered tenderfoot, you may just have the hankerin' to become a hell-roarin', whip-crackin' cow puncher.

DO IT YOURSELF

According to the Professional Rodeo Cowboys Association (PRCA), there are more than 600 sanctioned rodeos and hundreds of intercollegiate and amateur rodeos all over the country each year. The largest of them all is Cheyenne Frontier Days, which draws as many as 300,000 folks to town each July. It's much more than a rodeo; it's a celebration of a lifestyle, with musical acts, food vendors, and an Indian village.

Here, as at all PRCA events, there are standard categories of competition. I was bucked off a carousel horse at age 38, so I asked Kevin Whaley, a real cowboy, about the events.

Bull Riding

"Bullriders try to stay on for eight seconds, holdin' on with one hand. You can't touch the animal with the other hand. If you do, you're disqualified. Some bulls spin around; some kick like a horse; some of the hardest to ride take two jumps out of the gate and turn around real quick. The rider needs to stay on the front rope. It's a pretty tough sport 'coz they're pretty strong, them ol' bulls."

Bareback Riding

"Riders have to stay on for eight seconds. The cowboy's judged on how he spurs the horse and if he stays on his back and keeps his feet out front. That takes power. Your arm takes all the pull and a lot of guys tear their arms all to pieces."

Steer Wrestling

"The bulldogger—the guy who wrestles the steer—waits behind a barrier on his horse. After the steer leaves the chute and reaches the score line, the barrier's released and the bulldogger takes off. He gallops alongside, hangs off his horse, and grabs the steer. Then he puts one hand on the steer's nose, twists it up, grabs his horns and flips 'im over. It ain't cruel to the steer. You're talking about a 200-pound man fighting a 700-pound animal."

One of the first superstars of American rodeo was Bill Pickett (1870–1932). An African American, he sometimes had to compete by claiming to be of Comanche heritage. In 1994 he was honored on a postage stamp as a Legend of the West and today the Bill Pickett Invitational Rodeo (*www.bpir.com*) is the nation's only touring black rodeo.

Tie-down (aka Calf Roping)

"This is the hardest. You have to ride 50 or 100 times to learn to do this and you need a good horse that can do this without thinkin'. The cowboy's gonna rope the calf, throw 'im down, and tie three feet up. Just tie three and that'll make 'im stay down. But it has to stay tied for six seconds. If the calf gets loose, they lose."

Saddle Bronc Riding

"The cowboy's on a saddle that doesn't have a horn to hold on to and it has shorter stirrups. The horse can do whatever it wants. Some are born to buck. It can hurt you in the chute or it can fall backwards and knock you into a metal gate. But you gotta stay on for eight seconds."

Barrel Racing

"This is for women riders. They set up barrels in a clover-leaf pattern and the object is for riders to go around the barrels as fast as they can. They can go through the whole pattern in about 17 or 18 seconds, depending on the length of the run. Y'know, some of 'em will pay a lot of money for a good barrel horse and it's good money because the national champ can win millions."

Team Roping

"This is like steer wrestling. The first guy's the header. He goes out first and whips a lariat around the steer's head to pull 'im around. Then his partner— he's the heeler—hooks the back feet. After that, the riders turn their horses around and face each other. The fastest time wins, yep."

CONTACTS

Cheyenne Frontier Days
(307) 778-7200
www.cfdrodeo.com

Professional Rodeo Cowboys Association
(719) 593-8840
www.prorodeo.com

Wrangler National Finals Rodeo
www.nfrexperience.com

Women's Professional Rodeo Association
www.wpra.com

College National Finals Rodeo
www.cnfr.com

National High School Rodeo Association
www.nhsra.org

Professional Bull Riders
www.pbrnow.com

For Lodging and Dining, see p. 313

61. DUDE RANCH
American West

The images of America that stir my soul are most often visions of the American West. I'm seduced by the magnificent desolation that's foreign to my everyday life. Maybe I've picked up the connection to the Native Americans who created nations in this endless land, or just admire the pioneers who continued driving West not knowing whether life would get any better even if they survived the journey. When you invest some time at a dude ranch, a little imagination can take you back to the days of the wide-open West.

HOMES ON THE RANGE

Talk to a cowboy, a *real* cowboy who rides all day and rounds up dogies (a motherless calf) and pushes cattle and sleeps outdoors and returns to the ranch with a face tanned like leather, and odds are he'd wonder why on earth anyone would *pay* to sample a taste of his lifestyle. It's unlikely any cowboy would pay to trade places with us, which explains the absence of cowboys in cubicles.

But because wide-open plains and prairies and mountains evoke the sense of freedom the rest of us crave, paying to play is worth the cost. It's nothing new, either. As far back as the late 1800s, ranchers with plenty of land were looking for a new cash stream. The first part of the puzzle was the cows and horses and cabins they already owned. The second piece was the hemmed in city folks back East, looking for an escape. The final piece was transportation.

By 1869, there was a way to get out West that didn't require a stagecoach or Conestoga wagon. The merging of the Union Pacific and Central Pacific created the first transcontinental railroad capable of moving passengers from the East Coast to the Dakota Badlands in just a few days. But when they arrived, what did these tourists find? Howard Eaton's Custer Trail Ranch in the Dakota Badlands offered basic meals and lodging and hunting excursions for ten dollars a week. But few ranches could extend the level of comfort these "dudes" were accustomed to.

Cowboy hat hints for the uninitiated:

- Always handle a hat by the brim, and never the crown. A brim can be reshaped, but a crown can't be replaced.

- Remove your hat when the colors parade or a flag is raised.

- Never wear a hat in a residence, a court of law, or a house of worship.

By 1926, ranchers in the Yellowstone area realized this way of vacation-ing was here to stay, and created the Dude Ranchers' Association. Over time, dude ranches have evolved to provide this new breed of tenderfoot with clean accommodations, good food, and a taste of the ranching lifestyle. Today, at more than 100 member ranches, a new generation of drugstore cowboys are saddling up and bonding with hosts and fellow cowpokes, singing campfire songs, and dipping their boots into the cowboy life. Before you go, research different ranches and see if you'll just watch cowboys at work or be in the saddle "pushing cattle" across the range yourself.

DO IT YOURSELF

Whether you spend a few days or a week or more out West, its vastness will give you a glimpse of how our nation may have looked before 300 million of us had to share it.

As you plan your trip, keep in mind that dude ranches reflect their owners' personalities, so quality and comforts can range from ordinary to luxurious. I lassoed the latter option and headed to the Hideout, a dude ranch within the 300,000-acre Flitner Ranch in Shell, Wyoming (pop. 50). According to the more experienced dudes (and dudettes) vacationing there, I had made a smart decision: The Hideout offers a perfect blend of riding time, hard work, and well-deserved rest. What's more, this is an actual cattle ranch as opposed to merely a ranch with cattle, so we'd work hard on the range to earn the privilege of a hot shower, an outstanding dinner, and a soft bed in a beautiful log cabin.

When you travel to a dude ranch be sure to pack jeans, boots, sunglasses, sunscreen, long johns, a warm jacket, chaps (optional), and a cowboy hat (de rigueur).

The Hideout, like most dude ranches, follows a schedule that has groups arriving on Sunday, getting acquainted at an evening social, and waking early on Monday to get saddled up. Remember, when settling in at your dude ranch and being outfitted with a horse, you'll need to be honest about your level of riding experience. If you ride, tell them so and you'll be fine. If not, tell them that as well and they should pair you up with a gentle horse and make sure you have breaks from time to time. I don't ride but gave it a go and was soon far out on the prairie, searching for stray calves, rounding up dogies, pairing them up with their mothers, and leading the entire herd miles across the open range to a reservoir. *That* was a magical, purely Western experience, heightened when a cow bolted from the herd. It's not often I'm asked to gallop across the plains, cowboy hat in hand, and shout "Yip!" and "H'yah!" and "Gid'up!" to head her off and bring her back, but now that I have I'd be pleased to do it again if anyone asks.

Still, the actual experience is far different from the sanitized version you see on television. It's impossible to ride alongside 200 head of cattle without noticing their tendency to poop, piss, and moo with amazing gusto and frequency. Then there's the dust and grit and caked mud and dried sagebrush around you, although it's softened by the sight of canyons, buttes, mesas, and beautiful vistas over yonder.

Dude ranches like the Hideout provide numerous sublime moments. Physically, emotionally, spiritually, and socially you will sense a change. Friendships are formed on the range and superficial talk gives way to meaningful discussions. The absence of strip malls, signs, and traffic settle you down. Released from the office and granted a reprieve from workplace politics, you'll gain a new sense of purpose as your goal is not to please a client, but to please yourself.

Then at dusk, you'll return to the lodge and sit down for dinner with new friends and maybe later listen to a cowboy singing trail songs and then watch the soft autumn glow of sunset and realize the world never seemed so lonely...or so lovely.

CONTACTS

Dude Ranchers' Association
(307) 587-2339 or (866) 399-2339
www.duderanch.org

www.ranchseeker.com
www.duderanches.com

The Hideout
3170 Road 40 1/2
Shell, Wyoming
(307) 765-2080
(800) 354-8637
www.thehideout.com

62. YELLOWSTONE
Wyoming

In the middle of nowhere is one of the most beautiful places on earth. You may see only a portion of Yellowstone's 3,500 square miles of pristine and undeveloped wilderness, but even a glimpse of it will remind you that our nation is truly blessed with incredible real estate.

HIDDEN TREASURE

More than 11,000 years ago, aboriginal Americans were fishing and hunting in the Yellowstone region and most likely doing it without a permit. Incredibly, up until the early 1800s, few were aware of the geological grab bag that existed here.

A mountain man named John Colter, who had been a member of Lewis and Clark's Voyage of Discovery, later spoke of a place where super-heated rivers produced steam; trees were made of stone; and boiling mud bubbled out of the ground. It would be nearly half a century before Colter's claims were backed up by Jim Bridger, another mountain man, who went to the area in 1865 and confirmed reports of geysers and boiling waters. Bridger's veracity was doubted even by his close friends.

The park has several full-service gas stations, auto repair facilities, restaurants, stores, and a free newspaper that lists information about park facilities and programs.

The 1870 Washburn-Langford-Doane Expedition, which included Cornelius Hedges, a lawyer and writer, corroborated what Bridger had said. Hedges's letters and articles were seen by railroad executive William "Pig Iron" Kelley, who supported efforts to turn the area into a public park. The drive gained momentum after the 1871 Hayden Expedition brought back paintings and photographic proof of what was hidden within the region. When the images reached Washington, D.C., President Ulysses S. Grant signed a bill that created Yellowstone National Park.

The park had a rough start, with scant funds to protect its resources and wildlife. It wasn't until 1886, when the U.S. Army established Camp Sheridan (renamed Fort Yellowstone in 1891), to protect the park from poachers, vandals, and robbers, that things finally began to settle down. The Army kept things under control and even stuck around for a few years after the National Park Service took over in 1916. The Civilian Conservation Corps built new roads, visitor centers, and campgrounds during the 1930s, but as at other national parks, Yellowstone's breakthrough came in the 1950s, when middle-class Americans made it a favorite vacation destination.

As many as 3,000 earthquakes shudder under Yellowstone each year.

Today, rangers are doing their part to accommodate three million visitors a year, so you do yours. Take only pictures, leave only footprints, and give yourself the time to see some of the most beautiful places in the world.

DO IT YOURSELF

I'm convinced that the best time to see a popular place is just before or after peak season, when the staff is around, the rates are lower, and the roads less crowded. This is true at Yellowstone.

Yours to discover are 60 percent of the world's active geysers and two million acres of volcanic plateaus. As you explore, you may spy some of the park's nearly 300 species of birds, 12 species of trees, more than 80 types of wildflowers, and nearly 60 species of mammals. There are waterfalls twice as high as Niagara and five distinct "countries," including Roosevelt Country in the northeast, which rekindles images of the Old West, and Geyser Country in the southwest, which contains Old Faithful, fumaroles, mud pots, and hot pools. You can travel to the northwest's Mammoth Country and see a thermal area of limestone terraces and hot springs and a grazing area for elk and bison. In the southeast is Lake Country, which includes delightful trout-filled Yellowstone Lake, which is patrolled by osprey, bald eagles, moose, bison, and bear. In the center of it all is Canyon Country, where you'll visit the Lower Falls, Hayden Valley, and the Grand Canyon of the Yellowstone.

In the north end of the park, at the Albright Visitors Center in Mammoth Hot Springs, you can pick up guidebooks as well as hiking maps that outline more than 1,200 miles of marked trails. You can sign up there for free ranger-led programs, sightseeing tours, fishing, boating, and horseback riding, and if you tell the rangers how much time you have, they'll tell you how much you can pack into your trip.

If you plan to visit Yellowstone and other national parks within the same year, invest in a National Park pass—otherwise you'll pay individual admission to each. Visit *www.nps.gov.*

There's not enough space to tell you about everything you can see, but I can tell you that the roads around Yellowstone are shaped like a figure eight. As you cruise those twin circles you'll cross the 45th parallel (the midway point between the North Pole and the equator) and also see Steamboat Geyser. This is the world's largest and tallest geyser, exploding with infrequent, unpredictable eruptions that reach 400 feet.

In the middle of the figure eight, the road east to Canyon Village will take you to the Grand Canyon of the Yellowstone, a 24-mile-long rainbow-hued canyon of orange, yellow, pink, white, and tan that includes the majestic 308-foot-tall Lower Falls. Miles ahead, Yellowstone Lake is the visible remnant of a volcanic crater that was filled in by glaciers about 12,000 years ago. You may want to spend the night at the Lake Hotel and then several more years there, or, if you have the energy, keep looping up the road and cruising beside the calm and picturesque lake as you head up and around the park toward Old Faithful.

When you reach Old Faithful you've arrived at one of the nation's most spectacular natural wonders. When the geyser is about to go, which is roughly every 90 minutes, it'll let you know by tossing up a few thousand gallons of steaming hot water as an opening act. Then comes a full-throated eruption of hydraulics that blasts several thousand gallons of water about 150 feet into the sky.

Guess what? Everything you've just seen—from Mammoth Hot Springs to the Grand Canyon of Yellowstone to Old Faithful—is contained in less then two percent of the park.

That means Yellowstone is nearly 100 times more amazing than you can imagine.

CONTACTS

Yellowstone National Park
(307) 344-7381
(307) 344-2107 (visitor services)
www.nps.gov/yell

www.travelyellowstone.com

For Lodging and Dining, see p. 314

63. LITTLE BIGHORN
Crow Agency, Montana

Was it bad intelligence? Hubris? Karma? Whatever it was, on June 25, 1876, fate descended like a hammer on the soldiers of the Seventh Cavalry. Ironically, the battle known as Custer's Last Stand also signaled the last stand for the nomadic lifestyle of the northern Plains Indians.

AGAINST THE ODDS

It would take volumes to compile the lies, half-truths, and broken treaties white settlers and the United States government foisted off on America's Indian tribes. In the late 1800s they were still flying fast and furious.

The Indians' hunting grounds, sacred land, and established treaties didn't matter to settlers heading west. To ease friction between settlers and

the tribes that lived there, in 1868 a new treaty established a reservation in eastern Wyoming for Great Plains tribes, including the Cheyenne and Lakota—but it didn't stand a chance after gold was discovered on the reservation in the Black Hills in 1874. Prospectors pushed for ownership of this land, but were rebuffed by the Lakota and Cheyenne, who reacted by raiding frontier towns and travelers. The Commissioner of Indian Affairs issued an ultimatum: Return to your reservation by the end of January 1876 or be treated as hostiles. After they refused, the Army was on its way.

By June the Seventh Cavalry had arrived near the Bighorn River in Montana, joined by Arikara scouts and friendly members of the Crow tribe. An encampment of Lakota Sioux, Cheyenne, and Arapaho had been spotted in the Little Bighorn River Valley and above them, Maj. Marcus Reno, Capt. Frederick

To ensure future victories, the Indians made sure the soldiers wouldn't be able to fight in the afterlife. They cut off soldiers' fingers so they couldn't shoot again; mutilated their feet so they wouldn't be able to march; and, believing a man's spirit was in his hair, scalped their fallen foes so their bodies would wander for eternity.

Benteen, and Gen. George Custer could see what they thought were the dust clouds of fleeing Indians. They wanted to attack and destroy the target before the warriors dispersed.

Custer calculated that 650 men divided among himself, Reno, and Benteen could overwhelm 800 warriors. He could have been right, but his count was wrong. Custer didn't know that as many as 2,000 warriors were in the valley below and that the swirling dust wasn't from warriors on the run; it was from thousands of warriors getting ready to fight. So when Reno launched the attack around 3 p.m. on June 25, he and his men were pursued by warriors under the leadership of men like Sitting Bull, Crazy Horse, Lame White Man, Chief Gall, and Two Moons. As Reno made a break for woods by the Little Bighorn River, the Indians spied Custer.

Attempting an orderly retreat from the valley, Custer's two companies were blocked by the river. With Benteen missing and Reno seeking cover, Custer and his men became the target of advancing warriors. Below them, at what future generations would remember as Last Stand Hill, warriors would rise, fire their arrows and Winchester repeating rifles, and then disappear into the deep prairie grass. With no defensive shelter, cavalrymen shot their horses in a last-ditch attempt at cover.

No one knows for certain what happened next, but by 6 p.m. Custer and the 209 men under his command were dead. When Custer's body was found two days later, it was peppered with bullet wounds, including one in his temple. Did he kill himself? Again, no one knows.

As for Benteen and Reno, they hooked up and formed a perimeter on an exposed hill, listening to the Indians celebrate victory in what they called the Battle of the Greasy Grass. It would be one of their last military victories. The following year the tribes would be pushed back to the reservation and two years later the War Department designated the site as the Custer Battlefield National Cemetery.

Black Elk, a 14-year-old Lakota Sioux, helped strip the fallen soldiers. Years later he spoke of the sight of the Indians swarming over the bodies, recalling, "It looked like thousands of dogs would look if they were mixed up in a fight."

In 1881, a memorial over the mass grave of the Seventh Cavalry soldiers and scouts was erected. As for the Indians, it would take until 2004—128 years after the battle—for the United States government to establish a memorial honoring them.

THE EXPERIENCE

Little Bighorn is not easy to reach. Because it is so remote, attendance falls sharply between October and May and rangers may not be presenting their talks, but whenever you arrive at the visitor center and museum, a short film will catch you up on the conflict and its characters. The museum displays the weaponry of both sides, and illustrations and dioramas convey the battle's passion, confusion, and desperation.

There is a ghostly silence atop Last Stand Hill. Many of the headstones surrounded by a tall black metal fence are engraved with the simple inscription:

US SOLDIER
7TH CAVALRY
FELL HERE
JUNE 25, 1876

One, outlined in black, stands out. It is a headstone for Custer who was later disinterred and buried at West Point. Beyond, a road divides the Seventh Cavalry Memorial and the Indian Memorial and leads five miles to the Reno-Benteen Battlefield, where the pair managed to save themselves and most of their men.

From a 21st-century perspective, it's possible to dismiss the fate of the soldiers of the Seventh Cavalry, but a line in the orientation video may temper that opinion. No matter how we feel today, it suggests, those soldiers, who believed they were doing their duty, were prisoners of their own time.

CONTACTS
Little Bighorn Battlefield National Monument
I-90 (exit 510) and Highway 212
Crow Agency, Montana
(406) 638-3204
www.nps.gov/libi

For Lodging and Dining, see p. 314

64. DEALEY PLAZA
Dallas, Texas

JFK was killed in the middle of downtown Dallas. To this day visitors come to Dealey Plaza to see where the future of a nation changed in a dramatic 4.6 seconds nearly a half-century ago.

HERE...AND GONE

It was a full year before the elections of 1964, but John Kennedy knew he needed to mend fences between factions of the Texas Democratic party. He'd go to Texas with his wife, Jackie, who was traveling with him for the first time since the couple lost their newborn son three months earlier.

They arrived in Texas on Thursday, November 21. The following morning JFK spoke at the Fort Worth Chamber of Commerce before flying to Love Field in Dallas. Supporters who had waited all morning at the airport were delighted when the President and First Lady spent a few minutes shaking hands and saying hello. It had rained earlier, but the weather cleared and the bubble top of the president's 1961 Lincoln Continental limousine wouldn't be needed. With Texas governor John Connally and his wife, Nellie, in the front seat and JFK and Jackie in the back, the motorcade set off.

The Warren Report, which examined the murder of the President, was delivered in September 1964. It ran 20,000 pages and included 10.4 million words—but has never satisfied those who believe there was a conspiracy to murder JFK.

Crowds were already gathered downtown along Main Street and as far west as Dealey Plaza, where Main, Elm, and Houston streets converge at a triple underpass. On the north side of the plaza, the Texas School Book Depository stood along the motorcade route. Lee Harvey Oswald, a $1.25-an-hour clerk hired at the Depository five weeks earlier, found himself a cozy spot in the southeast corner on the sixth floor and turned it into a sniper's nest.

As the President's motorcade drove west down Main Street, the crowd's enthusiasm dispelled earlier anxieties that JFK wouldn't be welcomed in Dallas. The limousine turned right onto Houston Street and a block later nearly slowed to a stop to navigate a 120-degree left turn onto Elm Street, in front of the Texas School Book Depository. Seconds later some in the crowd thought they heard a firecracker. Others thought it was a car backfiring. It was actually the report of a $20 mail-order Mannlicher-Carcano rifle.

Abraham Zapruder sold his film to *Life* magazine for $150,000. He gave the first payment installment of $25,000 to the family of Dallas policeman J.D. Tippit, whom Oswald murdered after fleeing the depository.

No one could be certain if it was the first or second shot that pierced the President's back and ripped through his neck, but it was devastatingly clear that Oswald's third shot, which hit Kennedy in the head, had done its job.

From a clear vantage point ahead of the limousine, local businessman Abraham Zapruder filmed the entire grisly sequence. Supplying critical split-second by split-second evidence of a murder, his recording is the most important and carefully studied 26 seconds in motion picture history.

The President was declared dead a half-hour later at Parkland Hospital. Within 48 hours, Oswald would be dead as well, murdered on live television by local nightclub owner and Kennedy admirer Jack Ruby.

The tragic saga all began in Dealey Plaza, the "front door of Dallas."

THE EXPERIENCE

There's a sense of the surreal when you enter Dealey Plaza. Even if you've never been here before, chances are you'll know its layout. You'll be able to point to the grassy knoll, the triple underpass, the sixth-floor window. Before walking around the plaza, start your tour inside the 9,000-square-foot Sixth Floor Museum, which presents dozens of displays, 45 minutes of film footage, and more than 400 photographs. An audio tour guides you through the story of JFK's life from his boyhood to his burial at Arlington National Cemetery.

Oswald's sniper's nest has been re-created and shielded behind glass. The most moving presentation may be the ten-minute montage of worldwide newsreel footage. An old woman leaning on a cane and a young man in a motorcycle jacket cry as they view the funeral bier in the Capitol Rotunda; Jacqueline Kennedy kisses the flag-draped coffin; and young John-John salutes his father's casket as a steady rhythm of the drums mark the cadence of the funeral cortege.

The museum addresses the raft of conspiracy theories, now mostly discredited, and treats a sensitive event with care and class to the point of offering "memory books" for visitors to record their thoughts and feelings.

Outside on the plaza, vendors sell novelty newspapers chronicling the assassination. Stand on the grassy knoll, near where Zapruder stood (and from where, many conspiracy theorists believe, a second gunman fired). From across the street you can look up at the 6th floor and wonder what Oswald was thinking as he saw the motorcade approach. Try not to be one of the tourists who smile and pose near the painted Xs that mark the pavement where the President was shot.

Several onlookers actually saw Oswald in the window with his rifle. No one reported it—they assumed he was a Secret Service man.

Meanwhile, a nearly continuous line of traffic descends beneath the overpass. That unforgettable image of a limousine disappearing beneath it on that November day closed an act in American history.

CONTACTS

Sixth Floor Museum at Dealey Plaza
411 Elm Street
(214) 747-6600
www.jfk.org

Dallas Convention and Visitors Bureau
(214) 571-1000
(214) 571-1300 (tourist info center)
(800) 232-5527
www.visitdallas.com

For Lodging and Dining, see pp. 314–315

65. STATE FAIRS
Dallas, Texas, and Across America

What I like about state fairs is that they're consistent. There are always Ferris wheels and funhouses; livestock competitions and baking contests; and concession stands filled with cotton candy, funnel cakes, ice cream, and lemonade. State fairs project a purely American kind of nostalgia.

FARMING, FOOD, AND FUN

Credit one of the first American fairs to Elkanah Watson, a Massachusetts farmer and businessman who, about two centuries ago, got his fellow farmers interested in raising more Merino sheep by displaying his own flock in downtown Pittsfield.

When judged by attendance, the State Fair of Texas is America's largest, with nearly three million visitors annually.

While he can't take credit for inventing the corndog (that was Edison's idea), the "father of agricultural fairs" established an easy-to-follow concept: farmers could display livestock, the womenfolk could try to outdo their neighbors' homemade gooseberry pies, and kids could experience rides that were the rural equivalent of astronaut training. The nation's first state fair was held in Syracuse, New York, in September 1841; a state fair showed up in Wisconsin a decade later, followed by the Indiana State Fair; and in 1854 the Iowa State Fair, in Fairfield, set the stage for what is today known as America's Classic State Fair.

In a sense, little has changed. Contestants pit their produce, pies, preserves, and other foods against others' in cooking competitions. All state fairs also whip up foods that are a delicious part of a well-balanced diet—provided that diet includes food on a stick. Cotton candy, corndogs, kebabs, ice cream, corn on the cob, and even stick-stabbed salads, fried pineapple, and deep-fried candy bars remind you that the word "fair" is derived from the Latin word for "feast." *Frumentum caninus* is Latin for corndog.

When cotton candy was introduced in St. Louis in 1904, it was called fairy floss.

Over at the livestock pavilion, farmers, ranchers, 4-H students, and Future Farmers of America are anxious to see if they've raised a blue ribbon winner and how much ol' Bessie will draw at the auction. On the Midway, state fairs present ingenious thrill rides designed to separate you from your lunch. Some whirl like the spin cycle on a super-sized washing machine; others clamp you inside a metallic cage that rocks back and forth until the whole shebang flips over at 100 feet; and some put you in a metal globe and launch you from a gigantic slingshot.

When you've returned to earth, find your feet and enjoy the fair.

DO IT YOURSELF

It had been decades since I visited a state fair, and while Iowa's may be America's Classic State Fair, my schedule took me to Texas. Based on attendance, this state fair is the nation's largest. Based on my aching feet, I think I walked a fair portion of the state.

Meeting me at the turnstiles were the familiar smells of a fair: the popcorn, curly fries, fried dough, and cotton candy. I watched men test their skills on games of chance in hopes of winning a stuffed animal for their wives or girlfriends. There were kids grabbing strips of coupons from their parents and racing toward rides that promised a brush with vertigo. There were daredevil shows and trained animals and live music.

Then, as night fell, the 20-story-tall Texas Star Ferris wheel was outlined in cool blue lights while the sparkling bulbs on the tilt-a-whirl and bumper cars flashed with the intensity of a miniature Las Vegas. There were bells ringing and music playing and buzzers buzzing. The workday over, more families were arriving, with every member determined to cram in as much food and fun as possible.

Walking beneath the gondolas of the Texas Sky-Way, I was soon at Big Tex Circle, which is lorded over by Big Tex himself. The towering 52-foot-tall statue has been the emblem of the State Fair of Texas since 1952. Slightly spooked by Big Tex (he looked like my uncle Frank), I walked on while enjoying a four-course meal (corndog, pretzel, cotton candy, soda pop) and dropped in on exhibitions of cars and trucks and tractors.

> To really get involved in a state fair, find out which competitions are open to a person of your talent. A victory in cooking or raising livestock can put you on the road to stardom.

But I had missed one thing on my list: the livestock competition. I hurried to the livestock pavilion but it was late and the goats already muzzled to keep them from eating their bed of wood shavings. In other pens were pigs: Chester Whites, Spotted, Landrau, Hampshire, Berkshire, and Duroc; a full half-dozen more kinds of pigs than I knew existed. Signs above the cows told me that they were Brahman, Simbrah, Beefmaster, Red Brangus, and Santa Gertrudis cattle. While reading about their characteristics, I was intercepted by a young handler who was eager to help.

I reflected on my good fortune. Two hours earlier I was trapped inside a house of mirrors on the Midway and now a little farmer was revealing to me the mysteries of methane gas. It turns out that poop from a healthy cow can generate enough methane gas to generate one kilowatt of power, enough energy to power an electric light.

Just be careful where you plug it in.

CONTACTS

www.weekendevent.com/statefairs.htm   www.statefairrecipes.com

For Lodging and Dining, see pp. 314–315

66. THE ALAMO
San Antonio, Texas

The odds were definitely against the defenders of the Alamo, a mission on the outskirts of circa 1836 San Antonio. For nearly two weeks fewer than 200 volunteers attempted to hold back thousands of trained Mexican soldiers to advance their drive for the independence of Texas.

Had they succeeded, we would celebrate how a small army achieved victory despite overwhelming odds. But that didn't happen. They didn't succeed. Every one of them died and so we remember them for their heroism. And we still remember the Alamo.

YOU SAY YOU WANT A REVOLUTION? WELL...

Wars are fought for a variety of reasons and sometimes for no reason at all, but in Texas in 1835 and 1836 a revolution was fought because the Texians and Tejanos (Texans of Hispanic descent) wanted their independence from Mexico. Mexican general Antonio López de Santa Anna, who called himself the "Napoleon of the West," was determined they wouldn't get it. Out of a complex situation between an established nation (Mexico), a breakaway republic (Texas), and the neighboring United States, a legend was created.

In 1830, when Anglo immigrants living in what is today's Texas, then a Mexican state, began to outnumber the native population by as much as ten to one, the Mexican government imposed a ban on immigration. Five years later, the Mexican government nullified a decade-old constitution that had guaranteed Texas representative government. That did it. On October 2, 1835, a group of newly arrived immigrants and native Texians and Tejanos began their fight for freedom by starting the Texas Revolution. They had passion and they had a cause, but the Texian Army was just a random assortment of citizen soldiers facing down Santa Anna's well-trained and well-equipped soldiers.

The iconic curved parapet atop the shrine wasn't built until 1850, 14 years after the battle.

By February 1836, Santa Anna had quashed uprisings in other parts of Texas and was at the frontier town of San Antonio. Perhaps the townspeople knew of his ruthlessness; how in central Mexico his men had looted the city of Zacatecas, executed thousands, and raped women. The residents of

San Antonio surrendered without a fight, but across the San Antonio River there was an insurgent army garrisoned at the Alamo. As far as they were concerned, this wasn't even Mexico anymore, but the provisional capital of the Republic of Texas.

Seeing that Santa Anna had raised the red flag of "no quarter," meaning no one would be spared, 26-year-old Lt. Col. William Travis laid out the options to the volunteers. The farmers, lawyers, surveyors, and frontiersmen, including Jim Bowie and former congressman Davy Crockett could surrender unconditionally, escape under cover of darkness, or fight. Counting on the arrival of reinforcements, they decided to fight. Travis telegraphed their decision by firing a cannon at Santa Anna's troops and the siege of the Alamo began.

Although the Alamo became a legend almost immediately, it wasn't always treated with respect. At one point, the Long Barrack was used as a general store and the shrine was a warehouse. It was only after the property was acquired by Daughters of the Republic of Texas 1905 that the complex received the care it needed.

Although couriers managed to sneak past Mexican patrols and deliver the messages from Travis, including one addressed "To the People of Texas and All Americans in the World," no one—not even the United States government—offered to send reinforcements. But from the town of Gonzales, 32 heroic men answered the call and managed to sneak into the compound to help.

For 12 days the Alamo was under siege. Before daybreak on the 13th day, the familiar recognized roar of Mexican cannon was replaced by shouts of "Viva Santa Anna!" Two waves of Mexican soldiers attacked the Alamo and were repelled before the third wave crashed over the walls. After Colonel Travis was killed, some defenders retreated into an area known as the Long Barrack while others sought shelter in the shrine. Neither could protect them against the Alamo's own cannon, which the Mexican troops simply wheeled around to blow down the doors.

After finishing off the defenders with muskets and bayonets, bodies were gathered and stacked into three large piles and burned. A handful of women and children and slaves coaxed out of hiding were given some change and some blankets and told to spread the word to rebellious Texans that what had happened at the Alamo could be their fate as well.

There would never be another Alamo, though. Just over a month later in San Jacinto, Gen. Sam Houston and his 800 volunteers defeated Santa Anna's 1,400 troops in a surprise attack, and the following day scouts captured Santa Anna himself. With his own freedom on the line, the general agreed to release Texas from Mexican domination and the Republic of Texas was born.

THE EXPERIENCE

It's natural to picture the Alamo as a small building in the middle of the desert, but it is now part of a massive walled compound that sits in the middle of downtown San Antonio. Credit goes to the Daughters of the Republic of Texas who have worked hard to keep it as authentic as possible.

The shrine, which has always been the focal point of the complex, is where most people start, either investing in a 45-minute audio tour or picking up a brochure for a self-guided visit. In the oak-shaded courtyard, rangers give frequent presentations.

Time your visit for the first Saturday of the month and you'll be there when the Alamo features displays of crafts and weapons and cooking from the period.

"A lot of people, young people in particular, think history is just taking a test," suggests Dr. Richard Winders, curator of the Alamo. "But when you see the place and can speak with someone there and have that personal experience, then it becomes real. So talk to the rangers. Ask them questions. Each of them has different interests and areas of expertise."

Outside the shrine, the complex includes a tranquil garden built as a WPA project in the 1930s and a museum within the Long Barrack that presents an easy-to-follow timeline of events leading up to the Texas Revolution. Displays of artifacts include jewelry, swords, spurs, fighting knives, muskets, and long rifles (including one used by Fess Parker, TV's Davy Crockett).

It's a period of history that remains a mystery for most, but the rangers and exhibits make the drama of what happened at the Alamo easy to grasp.

And impossible to forget.

CONTACTS

The Alamo
(210) 225-1391
www.thealamo.org

San Antonio Convention
and Visitors Bureau
(800) 447-3372
www.visitsanantonio.com

For Lodging and Dining, see p. 315
For Lodging and Dining, see p. 315

ROCKY MOUNTAIN WEST

Arizona, Colorado, Nevada, New Mexico, Utah

I'm not sure how the Rocky Mountains do it, how they manage to make you seem physically infinitesimal while simultaneously making you feel spiritually larger and more powerful.

It's this way, I think, because if you live in a world of strip malls, traffic, and subdivisions there's something freeing about this region. In a way, it's a geographical declaration of independence that allows you to travel anywhere you like, for hundreds of miles, without seeing a town or a billboard or encountering any distraction that interrupts this great American landscape.

The Grand Canyon. Aspen, Colorado. Albuquerque, New Mexico's Balloon Fiesta, which offers aerial views of the entire sweep of the Sandia Mountains and the mighty Rio Grande. If you feel your life needs a boost of grandeur, this is a fine place to find it.

67. ASPEN
Colorado

Like the Kentucky Derby, Groundhog Day, and the indictment of a congressman, there are certain events we can count on each year. One is the annual return of movie stars to Aspen. Their arrival focuses the attention of the nation on a tiny little town in the Rockies.

SILVER SERVICE

Based on what we read in gossip rags and showbiz mags, the living is easy in Aspen. Maybe a little too easy. Which actually makes it kind of nice to learn that, to its credit, Aspen really earned it. Back in 1885 about 12,000 people lived there because one of the world's largest silver veins ran right through town. In fact, one day a miner made a major find: a pure silver nugget weighing 2,350 pounds. It was stunning, incredible, and way too heavy to wear on a necklace.

At first, Aspen was a rough and rugged frontier town out in the wilderness of the Roaring Fork Valley. Miners would work underground all day before ending up under the table at the Hotel Jerome's saloon. There was money to be made and people were making it—at least until 1893, when the federal government demonetized silver. Almost overnight miners got the shaft and over the next four decades, Aspen's fortunes plunged because of influenza, fires, and departing residents. By the 1930s only 700 people called Aspen home, but a change came in the 1940s, when World War II veterans who had served in the Alps in the U.S. Army's 10th Mountain Division started prospecting for white gold: snow. The plan was to add to the one existing ski trail and turn Aspen into a resort.

Aspen's affinity for food and wine can rival its penchant for skiing. The annual Food & Wine Magazine Classic (www.foodandwine.com), in June, is a celebrity-filled homage to the best and brightest in the culinary industry.

The idea got a tremendous boost when vet Friedl Pfeifer's quest met the vision of Walter Paepcke, a cardboard box magnate (really) from Chicago who dreamed of transforming Aspen into a cultural center for mind, body, and spirit.

The town that struck out on silver struck gold with a new and ever-evolving blend of art, recreation, literature, cuisine, and film. The change also helped spark improvements to the town's infrastructure, and by 1963, Aspen finally got around to paving its streets. So this winter join the well-heeled, famous, and curious as you tool into Aspen to see the stars, visit the shops, and hit the slopes.

DO IT YOURSELF

A surprising fact about Aspen is that its high season isn't winter, but summer, when about 25,000 seasonal visitors join the town's 6,000 year-round residents. The part-timers show up to explore the alpine wilderness around Aspen, which is smack dab in the middle of the White River National Forest and at the base of the Elk Mountain Range. Aspen also has the good fortune to be at the confluence of Castle, Maroon, and Hunter Creeks and the Roaring Fork River, which runs through the center of town. If your wife's busy shopping, step outside and catch a trout.

Rock-climbing, trout fishing, rafting, kayaking, cycling, and hiking can fill weeks. Or you could just sit in the middle of the street and stare at the scenery. In winter, that scenery includes the likes of Antonio Banderas, Melanie Griffith, Kevin Costner, Michelle Pfeiffer, Michael Douglas, and dozens of other stars who live there part-time or full-time or just drop in for the season. Winter adds a shine to Aspen that rivals that of Beverly Hills or Palm Beach, with ultra-high-end boutiques that include Chanel, Dior, Louis Vuitton, Prada, and others. There are art galleries and upscale restaurants and even local favorites like the Little Nell, and the Hotel Jerome's J Bar.

Early evidence that Walter Paepcke succeeded in making Aspen a destination for mind, body, and spirit came in 1949, when Nobel Peace Prize winner Dr. Albert Schweitzer spoke there while making his first and only visit to the United States. Aspen's cultural institutions include the Aspen Music Festival & School, Aspen Institute, and the Aspen Ideas Festival.

After you've taken your shopping bags back to your chalet, make tracks for any of the local ski resorts—Snowmass, Aspen Highlands, Aspen Mountain (aka Ajax), or Buttermilk—where the mountains are packed with snow and the lifts are packed with people. From bunny slopes (easy) to double black diamonds (tricky) to quadruple double black diamonds squared (impossible), there's a range of downhill skiing challenges. In Aspen, those are only part of a winter mix that includes backcountry skiing, snowmobiling, snowshoeing, hut trips, and snow camping.

After shussing down mountains all day, at night join the crowd downtown for the après ski scene. Outside, the snow falls and holiday lights glow while you're warming up in one of the coolest towns in America.

CONTACTS
Aspen Chamber Resort Association
(970) 925-1940
(800) 670-0792
www.aspenchamber.org

For Lodging and Dining, see p. 316

68. MORMON TABERNACLE CHOIR
Salt Lake City, Utah

Whether it's a church choir, a gospel group, a lone guitarist, or an entire rock band, the music of worship can emphasize the message. Every Sunday morning in Salt Lake City, 360 members of the Mormon Tabernacle Choir are making sure they're getting their message across by lifting the spirits of both worshippers and visitors of all ages, cultures, and religions.

AMERICA ACQUIRES A CHOIR
In the early 19th century, Joseph Smith claimed that an angel named Moroni gave him golden plates inscribed with the word of God. It was a radical notion; radical enough that, in 1844, Smith was killed by a mob. After his death, Brigham Young stepped up to lead the new Church of Jesus Christ of Latter-day Saints. Now he just had to lead his flock to safety.

After the Choir's performance, join a tour around Temple Square, the 35-acre complex that is the heart of the Church's campus. The free tour includes stops at Brigham Young's home and the 28-story Church Office Building and its observation deck.

Already having been run out of other towns, Young was earning the nickname American Moses as he and his followers traveled west in groups. In each company, Young made sure there was a cooper to mend the wheels and a musician to lift flagging spirits. Music was such an integral part of the new church that, following publication of the Book of Mormon in 1830, the next official publication was the hymnbook in 1835.

Less than a month after arriving at their new home in Salt Lake City, church singers and musicians formed a choir that performed at a general conference on August 22, 1847.

Working from a design envisioned by Brigham Young (a hollowed-out eggshell viewed lengthwise) craftsmen spent four years building the Tabernacle, an auditorium that could hold 10,000 people. Its inspiration may have been unusual, but the execution of its design was exquisite. With trusses to shape the self-supporting dome of the structure, there was no need for pillars or posts to obstruct audience views. Acoustically, it was a masterpiece as well. From 170 feet away parishioners could hear a pin dropped at the pulpit. You can only imagine how impressed they were when they heard the church organ.

The original organ, built in 1867, featured 2,000 pipes. After five renovations, today there are an astounding 11,623 pipes. The organ has been a perfect complement to the Choir that was destined to become an American icon. The Choir has sung for ten presidents, beginning with William Howard Taft. They sang at the Chicago's World's Fair in 1893, the first of 13 fairs they would attend. Concert tours would take the Choir abroad to nearly 30 countries in South America, Europe, and Asia, and to music festivals across the United States. In 1929 came the premiere radio broadcast of the weekly program *Music and the Spoken Word,* which expanded the Choir's reputation. The half-hour program of choral music and inspirational words was later also broadcast on television and would become the world's longest continually running network program.

> **One of the most sought-after tickets in America is for the December Christmas Concerts at Temple Square. Tickets are free and distributed by random selection, but there are more than a million requests annually. Start checking *www.lds.org/events* around mid-October to sign up, or call *801-570-0080 or 866-LDS-TIKS.***

When President Johnson asked the Choir to sing at his inauguration, it was the first of five presidential inaugurations at which it would appear. When it performed at the 1981 inauguration of Ronald Reagan, his observation that it was "America's Choir" stuck. Its recordings have sold millions. Each Sunday, 360 men and women volunteer their voices to continue a tradition that first echoed across Salt Lake City in 1847.

DO IT YOURSELF

Each week there are two opportunities to hear the Mormon Tabernacle Choir live: on Sunday, and during the their Thursday-evening rehearsal that begins at 8 p.m. and lasts for 90 minutes. The Sunday performance is the spectacle, however, as it finds the Choir in their concert attire of tuxedos and gowns.

If you arrive on a Sunday morning between Labor Day and Memorial Day, the Mormon Tabernacle Choir sings in the Tabernacle itself. In the summer, during special Christmas programs, and at semiannual world conferences, they perform in the 21,000-seat Conference Center across the street.

The most popular of the Choir's recordings was its Grammy-winning 1959 rendition of "The Battle Hymn of the Republic."

Assuming it's Sunday and "in season," the Choir has been warming up for an hour when the doors open at 8:30 a.m. At 9:30 a.m., the live broadcast of *Music and the Spoken Word* begins. You may be surprised by the lack of a Mormon sermon. Instead, the morning is devoted to an ecumenical message delivered through a songbook of hymns, inspirational songs, the occasional Broadway show tune, and, quite likely, an organ solo.

Near the conclusion of the performance, the announcer shares the "spoken word," a message of inspiration crafted to close the program and to open the heart.

CONTACTS

Mormon Tabernacle Choir
(801) 240-4150 or (801) 240-3221
www.mormontabernaclechoir.org

Music and the Spoken Word
(information and radio listings)
www.musicandthespokenword.com

For Lodging and Dining, see pp. 316–317

69. SUNDANCE FILM FESTIVAL
Park City, Utah

Calling upon his own experience as an artist, actor, and director, Robert Redford puzzled over a way for up-and-coming directors to break through a top-heavy motion picture system and get their stories out. In the end, the answer was the Sundance Film Festival. Now a part of America's cultural calendar, it remains "dedicated to the discovery and development of independent artists and audiences." You should go.

ACTION!

Aside from starring roles in major motion pictures, respect from his peers, and several Academy Award nominations and wins, Robert Redford was a virtual unknown when he hooked up with some friends in Salt Lake City to present the Utah/US Film Festival in 1978. With Redford as chairman, the festival was meant to shine a spotlight on his adopted home state, encourage filmmakers to consider Utah for their next picture, and highlight the potential of independent films.

In 1981 the festival gained even more traction when Redford established the Sundance Institute—named after his character in *Butch Cassidy and the Sundance Kid*—in a stunning mountain location near Provo. By 1985 the Institute was running what would become known as the Sundance Film Festival, whose mission it was to discover new talent and assist independent filmmakers. In addition to giving the festival a boost by backing it with Redford's good name, organizers added an element of good timing when the September festival was moved to January to capture the benefits of Utah's popular ski season.

At the first Sundance Institute Filmmakers/Directors Lab, ten emerging filmmakers worked with leading writers and directors to develop their original independent film projects. From the start it was clear the summer labs and winter film festival would offer a different and more productive environment than filmmakers would find in Hollywood. Given a safe haven several hundred miles from the grind of LA, filmmakers had the advantage of working in a natural, casual setting as they pursued a creative vision true to their ideas.

In the past, Sundance has introduced the nation to independent filmmakers like Quentin Tarantino, Steven Soderbergh, and the Coen Brothers, and to movies like *Little Miss Sunshine, Reservoir Dogs, Saw,* and *Napoleon Dynamite.* The festival has long been known for a synergy that draws attention to brilliant new talent and then back to the festival itself. The combination of the festival's setting, its celebrity founder, and an overall atmosphere of sincerity continue to make Sundance a standout among film festivals.

Success comes at a price. In recent years, as outside forces started to turn the gathering of motion picture artists into a domestic version of the Cannes Film Festival, festival organizers have begun passing out buttons that reminded directors, corporations, showbiz reporters, major studios, and press-seeking celebrities to "Focus on Film."

Unless you happen to be a press-seeking celebrity or showbiz reporter, you'll appreciate the efforts of the Sundance Film Festival to keep the focus on film.

DO IT YOURSELF

While relatively young, today's Sundance Film Festival has evolved significantly from its early years and even farther from Thomas Edison's film festival, where all he showed was a clip of a man sneezing. Today at Sundance there are film culture events, panel discussions, youth programs, online exhibitions, and live music taking place in the festival's epicenter, Park City, as well as at satellite venues in Ogden, Salt Lake City, and Sundance.

The Sundance Institute relies on thousands of volunteers, who are needed at the Sundance Film Festival, as well as at summer workshops in film, theater, music, and documentaries. Check www.sundance.org for information on what positions are open and how to apply.

After you've reached Park City, you can find your feet at the festival's headquarters inside the Park City Marriott. A great place to begin, this is where you'll find schedules and information and hot coffee and Internet access at a café and lounge. The festival staff can also get you acquainted with the layout of the town, provide you with a transit map, and point out locations of festival information booths around town. They'll also steer you toward the free shuttle system to get you to the various theaters; they suggest going this route because there are very many people (an estimated 50,000) and very little parking.

Considering this isn't a drive-in film festival and your friends can't sneak you into showings in a car trunk, the key component of enjoying the festival is obtaining tickets. In 2008, 125 feature films from 34 nations were selected for presentation (culled from more than 3,600 submissions); from more than 5,100 entries juries chose 83 short films from 17 countries to be awarded with a screen test. There are a number of ways to get tickets for these presentations and festival organizers suggest a few ways to improve your odds. First is knowing your options.

Nearly everything is done online and you need to register to receive a "purchase timeslot" that randomly assigns buying times. After you're notified when you can buy, be ready to go online and buy tickets for an individual screening. You can also upgrade to a Festival Pass (around $300 to $3,000), which is like a Wonka Golden Ticket since the higher levels can get you into the Sundance House, Filmmaker Lodge, New Frontier on Main, the Sundance Music Café, and the Salt Lake City Café. Then there are various Ticket Packages that range in price from about $200 to $750.

If you just happened to stumble into town and want to catch a single flick, individual tickets are $15 and are available in advance, although some shows also offer day-of-show sales. For these, just be at the Main Box Offices in Salt Lake City or Park City by 8 a.m., when they release a limited number of tickets to that day's screenings. If that fails, there is also waitlist ticketing. Two hours before showtime, head over to the theater where your film is showing and sign up. With your number in hand, you have the freedom to roam around town before heading back a half-hour before the movie begins to see if any seats have opened up. Cash only.

The festival culminates with the Awards Ceremony, recognizing films selected by ballots submitted by festival attendees.

Before you leave, look around. Maybe you'll have the good fortune to bump into Robert Redford. He's a nice man. Talk to him. Show him some of the home movies you've made. He's impressed by the pacing, the editing, the artistic perspective you've applied to *Family Christmas '08*. He's so impressed he immediately arranges a private screening for studio reps, each of whom bids millions for distribution rights…

Redford's golden hair glistens as tears well up in the eyes of his newly discovered protégé. The camera pulls back to show snow-covered Park City at twilight. Music swells. Fade out.

CONTACTS

Sundance Film Festival
(435) 658-3456
www.sundance.org/festival
festival.sundance.org (no www.)

Sundance Institute
www.sundance.org

For Lodging and Dining, see p. 317

70. INDIAN POWWOWS
Albuquerque, New Mexico, and Across America

When it came to subduing native peoples, the American government was driven to steal their lands, languages, music, customs, and beliefs. The theft of their culture tamped down their pride. Attend a powwow and you'll see that ember of pride ignite into an inferno.

PRIDE AND PREJUDICE

One story traces the history of Indian powwows to the war dance societies of Southern Plains tribes. Others believe they were rooted in the dances

Indians were forced to perform as they were being sent to reservations. Although Indians from South Dakota, Montana, and the Northern Plains had been pushed off their ancestral land, audiences in the late 1800s could get a glimpse of their vanishing world by attending Wild West spectaculars presented by two of the most famous promoters in the nation, Buffalo Bill and Pawnee Bill. Sitting Bull and dozens of other Indians joined cowboys to show spellbound audiences (that included Queen Victoria and Pope Leo XIII) what they expected to see: Indians circling a wagon train; defeating General Custer; and dancing tribal dances.

If you're wowed by a pow-wow, consider delving deeper into tribal history. Go Native America (888-800-1876, www.gonativeamerica .com) works with a network of Indian guides on single and multiday tours that tie together Indian culture, politics, history, and spirituality.

When the curtain fell on these shows and the cowboys rode off into the sunset, the Indians returned to their reservations with some dances that were purely traditional and others recently enhanced with show business. At intertribal gatherings groups shared these dances and songs that celebrated their beliefs and values. If there were language differences, words were replaced by "vocables," rhythmic and tonal sounds introduced so the melody became one that everyone could sing. This sense of unity teaches us a good lesson. There's a whole lot of things America did wrong when it came to Indians, so one thing we can do right is learning what we nearly lost—and what we can do to preserve native Americans' heritage and history. A good place to start is a powwow.

DO IT YOURSELF

A few hundred words is a few hundred thousand shy of what's required to explain the history and spiritual aspects of America's Indian culture. A powwow will give you only a taste of this, but it's a good start because it'll whet your appetite to continue your education with a more in-depth tribal tour.

Powwows range in size and duration, lasting from a single day to several and drawing from a few hundred to several thousand guests. Each powwow begins with a much-anticipated event—the spectacular Grand Entry. Preceded by tribal music and participants carrying American and POW flags and eagle staffs of participating tribes, a parade of tribal chiefs, princesses, tribal elders, powwow organizers, and dancers enters.

"This is a Kodak moment," says Derek Matthews, organizer of America's largest powwow, the Gathering of Nations. "You always get chills during the Grand Entry."

Those chills may cause frostbite at the Gathering of Nations in Albuquerque, which takes place every April. More than 3,000 costumed Indian dancers and singers representing more than 500 tribes from across Canada and the United States parade into the arena to the sound of chants and the thundering rumble of drums—the foundation of a powwow. Elaborate ribbons, beaded and feathered headbands, chokers, armbands, fur, knee bands, medallions, bells, breastplates, shawls, breech cloths, fans, whistles, capes, and colorful feather hackles all contain special significance and symbolism. Their beauty is on full display when performers and contestants join in as many as 32 dance categories that are the focal point of a powwow.

Paul Gowder, creator of the comprehensive website www.powwows.com, offers a glimpse of the dances you'll see.

Grass Dancing
This is rooted in the days when a nomadic tribe's advance scouts would prepare a new site by rhythmically stomping down the grass.

Fancy Feather Dancing
Part of the dance includes steps for dancing around the drum, as well as a "contest step" that demands fast and intricate footwork and spinning.

Fancy Shawl Dancing
Female dancers wear their colorful shawls over their shoulders and gracefully dance, jump, and spin to mimic butterflies in flight.

Straight Dancing
To outsiders, this dance appears more formal, with closely matched dress and smoothly coordinated movements.

Northern Traditional
Modern adaptations of dances of Northern Plains tribes such as Sioux, Blackfoot, Crow, and Omaha, they are sometimes characterized as the reenactment of a warrior searching for the enemy.

The Gathering of Nations also includes the crowning of Miss Indian World, presented to the woman who displays the greatest knowledge of her tribe and its traditions.

Buckskin Dancing
Women circle the drum and bob slightly to its beat, letting the long fringes on their sleeves, their beaded purse, and their shawl sway in time.

Cloth Dancing

As with several other dances, there are northern and a southern styles to this slow and graceful ladies' dance.

Jingle Dancing

Legend says the dress used in this dance was seen in a medicine man's dream. His granddaughter became ill and his spirit guides told him to make a jingle dress and have her dance in it. She recovered. Today's jingle dresses are decorated with rolled up snuff can lids hung with ribbon and then sewn to the dress, which, during the dance, can sound like falling rain.

In addition to dancing, drumming circles are an integral part of a powwow, symbolizing the heartbeat of the Earth Mother.

From dances to drumming to crafts, a powwow can be a transformative experience, says the Gathering of Nations' Derek Matthews.

"Non-Natives come with the mindset that they really *want* to understand," he explains. "They ask about Indian outfits and engage dancers and drummers in conversation and new relationships are formed. A powwow is a way to bring people of all cultures together."

Better late than never.

FACTS AND SITES TO SEE

Gathering of Nations
(505) 836-2810
www.gatheringofnations.com

www.powwows.com

For Lodging and Dining, see p. 317–318

71. ALBUQUERQUE BALLOON FIESTA
Albuquerque, New Mexico

Each fall, one of the year's most pleasing visual samplers arrives special delivery from New Mexico. It is the sight of hundreds of balloons floating peacefully above the Sandia Mountains and the Rio Grande at Albuquerque.

Why are so many balloonists here and doing this? Because flying a balloon is fun, and it is beautiful. Isn't that reason enough?

PARADE FLOATS

At first, ballooning wasn't a sport or even a leisure activity. When it was created, it was a curiosity and then a science experiment. In 1783 the Montgolfier brothers held one of their first public demonstrations of balloon flight in Paris, but no one knew what effect the high-altitude ascent would have on passengers. Wise King Louis XVI suggested sending two criminals aloft, but a duck, a rooster, and a sheep got the nod instead.

After the crew of this barnyard Apollo XI survived, ballooning drifted into other areas over the next few centuries: aerial reconnaissance, fairground demonstrations, and weather forecasting.

Then, around 1960, balloonist and inventor Ed Yost responded to the Navy's request for a less expensive gas balloon by creating the prototype of the modern hot-air balloon, using a nylon envelope and an on-board butane burner in the gondola. Balloons were about to enter the leisure market.

Sid Cutter of Albuquerque's Cutter Flying Service bought one in 1971 and became so enamored that he and eight friends created the Albuquerque Aerostat Ascension Association (Quad A) to develop their ballooning skills. Cutter then floated the idea of helping celebrate the 50th anniversary of a local radio station by staging New Mexico's first hot-air balloon rally—with a goal of breaking the existing rally record of 19 balloons.

Sign up to be on a chase crew. When you do, be sure to arrive wearing close-toed shoes, and layer your clothing—it can be quite cold in the predawn darkness, but warms up rather quickly after sunrise. After you sign up, you'll be assigned to a launch site where you'll meet the pilot.

In April 1972, 20,000 fans and a single police officer gathered at the Coronado Shopping Center to witness the "KOB Birthday Bash & Balloon Race." The attempt fell seven balloons shy of the record. Still, spectators watching even 13 balloons drifting north were amazed at the sight of such large objects floating so tranquilly above Albuquerque. So where was the race? It was a "Roadrunner-Coyote" in which the "coyotes" took off several minutes after the launch of the lead balloon and tried to land as close to the "roadrunner" as possible.

By the time the balloons had landed, Cutter knew there would be another event. He just didn't know things were really about to take off. Don Kersten, president of the Balloon Federation of America, had just returned from a conference of the Federation Aeronautique Internationale (FAI) in Paris and it was his mission to locate a city capable of hosting the first World Hot Air Balloon Championship. Kersten was convinced it could be Albuquerque.

Quad A and Albuquerque jumped at the chance and everyone was amazed when the city was selected. Selected from a field of one, as it turned out. No other city had bothered to apply.

In February 1973, balloonists from 14 nations arrived for the Albuquerque International Balloon Fiesta, joined by ground crews and chase teams and thousands of fans. Competitions that challenged balloonists to rise and descend to predetermined heights were created. Cutter took to the skies in his specialty Wile E. Coyote balloon; Ed Yost sailed away in a polyethylene gas balloon; and Denny Floden of Flint, Michigan, won the title of world champion and the nickname Captain Phogg.

What began with just a few friends interested in the sport earned Albuquerque the title of "hot-air balloon capital of the world."

DO IT YOURSELF

Kathie Leyendecker, who's attended every Balloon Fiesta since the early 1970s, knows the best way to see it.

Be there.

"Be on the field," she insists. "There's no flight line so you can walk among the balloons and talk to pilots and be in the middle of everything. When I'm there, that's when the kid in me comes out to play. It's like being in the middle of a huge gumball machine."

Located about seven miles north of downtown Albuquerque, Balloon Fiesta Park is a 72-acre park the size of 54 football fields. It is from there that 700 balloons are launched nearly every single morning of the nine-day event.

Most pilots and ground crews are on hand before dawn, and balloonatics arrive early to watch the inflation from up close or from a spot on the bluffs. The first wave of 170 balloons usually takes off by 7 a.m., and once they're up and adrift, a second wave follows close behind, trailed by the third and final ascension around 8 a.m.

If conditions are right, some pilots will execute a "splash and dash," briefly dropping the gondola into the waters of the Rio Grande before taking off again.

After the balloons return at about 10 a.m., the Fiesta turns into one of the world's largest tailgate parties. People set up tents and grills; kids fly kites; and vendors sell balloon gifts and pins. Don't feel you have stay on the sidelines just because you arrived without a balloon.

"If you want to know about ballooning, talk to the pilots," says Leyendecker. "They love to talk about the magic and wonder and science of what they do."

Leyendecker points out that even first-time attendees can become part of a chase crew, a support team that follows a balloon by car to its anticipated landing site. That may lead to a free balloon flight from a grateful pilot.

"There are so many international pilots who come here without their regular chase crew," she says. "They absolutely rely on the assistance of volunteers, which is why there's a sign-up sheet at Chase Crew headquarters."

In addition to the mass ascensions there are other special events: the pilots' competition, for example, and flights reserved for balloons of special shapes—seeing scarecrows, flying cows, storks, or Darth Vader ascend is like watching a fantastic, floating fairy tale. And if you're impressed when a neighbor creates some sidewalk lumi-naries at Christmastime, arrive on one of the five evenings when pilots conduct a synchronized burn known as "the glow." As they ignite their burners, the envelopes of their balloons glow like enormous Easter eggs, lighted from within.

> **Why so early? Balloonists launch early in the morning when the air is cooler and more stable, which gives them more flying time.**

Time for the kid in you to come out and play.

CONTACTS

Albuquerque International Balloon Fiesta
(505) 821-1000
(888) 422-7277
www.balloonfiesta.com

For Lodging and Dining, see pp. 317–318

72. TOMBSTONE
Arizona

Nearly every old Western includes a scene that ratchets up the suspense: the showdown. Close-ups capture spurred boots stepping along a dusty street, a nervous hand fingering a holstered gun, and a furrowed brow beneath the brim of a wide cowboy hat. Scenes like these really happened in frontier towns like Tombstone. Still do.

AW, SHOOT

For a long stretch in the 20th century, Westerns were riding high. Nearly everyone knew Roy Rogers and Gene Autry and characters like Hoss, Matt

Dillon, and Miss Kitty. Viewers watched *Gunsmoke, Bonanza,* and *The Big Valley.* The Old West was so popular that people even knew that real-life characters like Doc Holliday and the Earps were involved in a shootout at the O.K. Corral, and that meant they knew all about Tombstone.

Well, almost. Television and movies didn't pay much attention to Ed Schieffelin, a wagoneer and amateur miner who arrived at Arizona's Fort Huachuca in 1877 before heading out to search for rare stones. A soldier noted that with Apache warriors outside, the only precious stone Schieffelin would find would be his tombstone. Schieffelin proved his instincts and sense of humor were intact when he discovered a rich silver strike at Goose Flats and named his claim Tombstone. The name stuck as the mining camp grew into a wild frontier town.

The world's largest rosebush is in Tombstone. Planted in 1885, the Lady Banksia rose covers 8,000 square feet and has a trunk 12 feet in circumference.

Within a few years as many as 15,000 miners, laborers, and businessmen rushed into Tombstone. For some it proved to be a deadly mix. This was still a remote and inhospitable desert town, and some people just didn't get along. That was best evidenced by the famous shootout at the O.K. Corral on the afternoon of October 26, 1881.

Law was on a long leash in Tombstone. Brothers Frank and Tom McLaury, brothers Ike and Billy Clanton, and Billy Claiborne used that to their advantage. They worked as ranchers and part-time petty criminals who called themselves the Cow-boys. Anxious to show the Cow-boys who was boss was town marshal Virgil Earp, his brothers Morgan and Wyatt, and their colleague Doc Holliday. The showdown was also fueled by rumors, perceived slights, personal grudges, and misunderstandings. When the principals met, about 30 shots were fired in half a minute. Ike Clanton and Billy Claiborne had the good sense to run away, but both McLaurys and Billy Clanton stuck around long enough to get killed, while Morgan, Virgil, and Doc were wounded. When the law won, the outcome was destined to go down in history.

For several years after the boys were buried alongside slow-on-the-draw cowboys, hanged prisoners, and lynching victims at the Boot Hill Cemetery, miners were digging up millions in silver and gold. But then subterranean waters flooded the mines and washed away the boom years. Tombstone came back, in a way, during World War I, when it produced manganese for the government, but by 1929 things were so bad the county seat was moved to nearby Bisbee. Tombstone's 200 residents still weren't ready to throw in the towel, though. The townspeople stabilized the town's historic district, showcased architectural treasures, and began prospecting for a sustainable commodity: tourists. Did it work? Well, in 1961 the town was named a National Historic Landmark District. Tombstone has also managed to bring members of the Starship *Enterprise* to town in an episode of *Star Trek;* had its name used on more than half a dozen feature films; and has even inspired the name of a frozen pizza.

DO IT YOURSELF

To reach Tombstone, go to Arizona, look in the direction of nowhere, and then head that way. When you find Tombstone about 70 miles southeast of Tucson you'll find it much as it was more than 100 years ago—with the facades of frontier businesses that included hotels, livery stables, saloons, and bordellos (which were usually coupled with the saloons). You'll also notice the fashion sense of the locals hasn't changed much over time. Tombstone is one of the few towns where adults can play dress-up, so residents saunter around town dressed like 1880s saloon gals, desperadoes, and lawmen.

If you've traveled to Tombstone specifically to see a re-creation of the Gunfight at the O.K. Corral, just make sure you're there between January 1 and December 31. Yes, it's so popular that they replay the battle twice a day, at 2 and 4 p.m. Heads up, pilgrim: It costs to enter the re-creation of the corral; the portrayal relies on reenactors who are definitely not actors; and the shootout itself lasts all of 30 seconds. If that's not enough to satisfy your thirst for shootouts, you'll be pleased to learn that there are gunfights at attractions all over Tombstone—more in one day than there are in New York City in a week.

Before shooting over to a shootout, head to the Visitors Center, where clerks will provide brochures and a map that lists the town's museums, shows, and showtimes. Then, get acquainted with the town and its history on a trolley or an old-fashioned stagecoach tour.

Take time to drop by some of the sites you saw on the tour, including the Good Enough Mine, the Crystal Palace Saloon, and the Bird Cage Theater, where a guide will direct your attention to bullet holes in the ceiling and stage and then point out where the madam put her gals on layaway. About a mile outside of town is the infamous Boot Hill Cemetery, which, some say, earned its name from the number of residents

Two movies that locals suggest watching before you arrive are *Tombstone,* starring Kurt Russell, and *Wyatt Earp,* starring Kevin Costner.

who died with their boots on. Some 26 men died in the town's 16 recorded gunfights, although it was a knife that took the life of a prostitute nicknamed Gold Dollar. How much she charged remains a mystery.

To witness Tombstone in the context that probably best reflects its glory (or gory) days, arrive on the third weekend in October. I'd sure love to meet the marketing genius who came up with the name of the town's annual celebration: *Helldorado*. Started in 1929, the event pays tribute to Tombstone's Wild West roots by giving the town both barrels with gunfights, street entertainment, fashion shows, and a carnival.

Tombstone wasn't just too tough to die—folks here really know how to live.

CONTACTS

Tombstone Chamber of Commerce　　www.tombstoneweb.com
(520) 457-3929
(888) 457-3929
www.cityoftombstone.com

For Lodging and Dining, see pp. 318–319

73. GRAND CANYON
Arizona

When you stand at the rim of the Grand Canyon and look across some 4,000 square miles of what is essentially nothing, the view seems surreal. All the postcards you've seen and all the pictures your friends have shared are now right in front of you, but magnified a billion times. In a way, all of this is a visible reminder of what happens when you leave the water running.

WATER WORKS

In extraordinarily simple terms, millions and millions of years ago what would someday be called the Colorado River was flowing over the Colorado Plateau. It kept flowing and began to erode the rocks and minerals beneath it. Simultaneously, mountains were being pushed up, volcanic activity was occurring, and the land was gouged, stretched, tugged, and expanded into what you see today. Although we'll hardly notice any changes in our lifetime, the canyon is still taking shape. Every day and every season, the natural forces of water, heat, and wind are carving out fantastic new bluffs and buttes.

Considering this is still a work in progress, we can assume it was a slightly different canyon that Garcia López de Cárdenas saw in 1540. According to history and legend, the captain in Francisco Vasquez de Coronado's expedition discovered the Grand Canyon (and the Pueblo Anasazi who were there to greet him could vouch for that). He thought he could cross it, but the canyon is 277 miles long, as much as 18 miles wide, and has an average depth of a mile, so de Cárdenas turned back. It wasn't until 1869 that the geologist and explorer John Wesley Powell began to figure things out. The one-armed Civil War veteran led a team through the Grand Canyon via the Colorado River on a three-month expedition.

In 1893, the Grand Canyon was given federal protection as a Forest Reserve and later as a National Monument. After the National Park Service was created in 1916, it would take another three years for the Grand Canyon to become a national park. Fewer than 45,000 people visited that first year, but now about five million of us make the trek annually to stand along its rim, explore its depths, and marvel at its grandeur.

DO IT YOURSELF

The first time I truly *saw* the Grand Canyon was the second time I was there. The first time, I couldn't fathom what I was looking at. The next time around I took a helicopter tour and, when the pilot pointed at a tiny pebble at the bottom of the canyon and said it was the size of an 8,000-square-foot house, I started to understand.

The Grand Canyon experience can be approached many different ways. There are hiking trails and mule rides to the bottom of the canyon, airplane and helicopter tours, whitewater rafting expeditions, and camping. You'll most likely arrive at the South Rim, which has the Grand Canyon Village and its hotels, restaurants, and visitors center. At the Canyon View Information Plaza, you can pick up maps and see displays, like the scale model that shows your size in relation to the canyon's depth, to wit: You're only as tall as the thickness of a paper match, a little more if you're wearing heels.

A truly American image is the line of tourists heading into the canyon on mules. To arrange your excursion, call Grand Canyon Mule Trips (303-297-2757, www .xanterra.com). These can be rigorous trips; there is a weight limit of 200 pounds.

From the Village, it's an easy walk over to popular Mather Point on the Rim Trail, a paved walkway that extends for several miles along the canyon. It's also a level walk to other vantage points like Yavapai Point, Trailview Overlook, Maricopa Point, Powell Point, and Hopi Point. And don't be afraid to branch out. Noticing that most travelers tended to cluster around the same areas, I just walked a few dozen yards away and was instantly alone and able to focus on the canyon in luxurious solitude.

Even if you hate going to the movies while on vacation, make an exception and see *Grand Canyon: The Hidden Secrets,* a National Geographic IMAX movie presented in Tusayan. Call 928-638-2203 or visit *www.explorethecanyon.com.* It'll blow your socks off and prepare you for your trip to the canyon.

If you're an average hiker, you'll find it relatively easy to hike to the bottom of the canyon—although walking back up is extremely arduous. Mule rides are an alternative, ranging from a few hours long to overnight trips to the rustic, no-frills Phantom Ranch on the canyon floor. If you do reach the depths of the canyon, you'll be able to see up close what folks a mile overhead view as just a tiny trickle. The Colorado River is big. It averages 300 feet wide and up to 100 feet deep and is the primary force that carved the canyon. Nearly two dozen outfitters lead rafting trips down the river, and the experience can range from a pleasant sojourn to a hair-raising explosion through whitewater. Some last a day; other, wilderness trips last much longer.

In addition to its immense proportions, another marvelous aspect of the Grand Canyon is the many ways it can be framed. Drive several miles along East Rim Road and you'll reach an overlook called Desert View and its 70-foot-tall Watch Tower, opened in 1933. You can climb to the top of this observation station for one of the most impressive views yet as you sight down the length of the canyon from 7,522 feet above sea level.

It's a fantastic sight. And it's right here in our own backyard.

CONTACTS

Grand Canyon National Park
General Visitor Information
(928) 638-7888
www.nps.gov/grca

Backcountry Information Center
(928) 638-7875

Grand Canyon River Trip
Information Center
(928) 638-7843
(800) 959-9164
www.nps.gov/grca

For Lodging and Dining, see p. 319

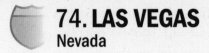

74. LAS VEGAS
Nevada

After a brief flirtation with wholesomeness, in 2003 Las Vegas decided instead to remind visitors that "what happens in Vegas, stays in Vegas." Turned out that was the clarion call for hedonists and expense account execs on business trips. Although Las Vegas turns Puritanism on its head, you can't argue with excess.

VIVA LAS VEGAS

In the early 1900s, settlers, farmers, and miners who had been in Las Vegas for decades were continuing their quest to carve out a town in the middle of the desert. Even though their city had a head start, by the 1930s it seemed that they'd be rolled over by nearby Boulder City. That was where construction workers were busy building Boulder Dam (later named Hoover Dam). But Las Vegas had an ace up its sleeve: Bugsy Siegel.

The mobster had gone to Las Vegas and seen that gambling was legal and women were tender. With Nevada's liberal gaming laws and legal prostitution, the city would be a perfect setting for him and his friends. Casinos like Hotel Nevada (today the Golden Gate Hotel) had been there for decades, but Siegel upped the ante by creating the glitzy Flamingo. It was a smart bet, but one Siegel should never have made. Less than a month after the resort opened in December 1947, the Flamingo was running deep in the red and shut down. Six months later, Bugsy was rubbed out.

Siegel left in his wake a Disneyland for adults: a place where vice was nice and where entertainers could enjoy days that lasted all night. Organized crime had found a home as well. In the '50s and '60s larger and more elaborate resorts were built. Sinatra put his stamp of approval on the city when the Rat Pack came to town, while billionaire Howard Hughes, with Kleenex boxes on his feet and *Ice Station Zebra* on the television, sat naked in a suite at the Desert Inn and masterminded the creation of a new era of grand Las Vegas resorts.

> A monorail connects many of the major hotels along the Strip. An all-day pass costs about ten bucks. Check *www.lvmonorail .com* for information.

By the 1970s, a force more powerful than the mob muscled its way in. Corporations arrived and began building resorts; in the 1980s many of the aging icons were purchased and then imploded to clear the way for enormous city-states such as the Bellagio, Venetian, Mirage, and Treasure Island. To attract travelers who weren't interested in gambling, the resorts booked stage extravaganzas that added to the appeal of Vegas with must-see entertainment like Siegfried and Roy, Elton John, Celine Dion, and the multiple personalities of Cirque du Soleil.

Overshadowed by the shows and slots are the city's adventures and excursions. In town or nearby are helicopter tours, indoor skydiving, dune buggy rentals, and motorcycle racing schools. Hoover Dam is only 30 minutes away and Red Rock Canyon is a short drive west. The local visitors' bureau has information.

In the 1990s the city tried to clean up its image by repositioning itself as a family-friendly destination, but no one was buying it. Cooler heads prevailed and played up the town's strengths as Sin City, the place where sex, gambling, entertainment, gambling, and sex were not only tolerated, but celebrated.

Some say Las Vegas is a modern-day Sodom, while others believe it's a contemporary Gomorrah. Either way, it's an experience.

DO IT YOURSELF

It's scientifically impossible to tell you the right way to experience Las Vegas, and I know that because my friend's a scientist and he told me. I believe him because Las Vegas is a nonstop city with unlimited entertainment. Depending on your age, interests, and desires, there are infinite ways to take it on. Since I can't tell you *how* to do it, I'll tell you where to start.

The Strip.

A section of Las Vegas Boulevard, this is the main artery of the city, where an endless parade of people cruise or stroll past the latest multibillion-dollar resorts. If stage shows are outside your budget, wander along the Strip and you'll find some resorts presenting synchronized water, light, and fireworks shows with great views right from the sidewalk. Then, after you get your bearings, head inside. Most new resorts feature a theme, so when you step inside the Venetian you'll be able to take a gondola ride down a canal. Over at the Mirage, you'll feel you've walked into a rain forest when you enter the lobby. The Luxor places you in ancient Egypt, while Caesar's Palace fast forwards you into ancient Rome. Within minutes you can travel from New York New York to Monte Carlo to Paris to Rio—each a resort hotel and each using art and design to sustain the illusion that you've left Las Vegas. Some hotels, like the MGM Grand, avoid themes while others, like the Bellagio, appeal to guests who desire elegance. Glass artist Dale Chihuly's exquisite "Fiori di Como," composed of over 2,000 hand-blown glass flowers, presides over the Bellagio's lobby to help that hotel make its case.

I haven't mentioned casinos yet, and one thing that disappoints some visitors is finding there's no gambling there. On the other hand, there's plenty of *gaming*. Either way, you'll probably lose your money. Again I can't tell you which casinos are the best, but I can tell you that all casinos share certain traits: None has clocks or windows and each is filled with the din of electronic slot machine bells, chimes, and tones. For serious gamblers, finding the "loosest slots in town" is an important consideration and some believe they have the best luck in the casinos of Fremont Street, the original Glitter Gulch. Located about six miles north of the Strip, that is where you'll find the classic casinos of Old Las Vegas: the Four Queens, the Golden Nugget, Binion's Horseshoe, and the charming Golden Gate Hotel.

If you're unfamiliar with the rules of certain games, many casinos offer instructional classes. Ask the hotel concierge.

There is one sure bet in Las Vegas. Resorts learned they could attract tourists by offering the finest in A-list entertainment. Tom Jones, the Blue Man Group, Bette Midler, Cher, Cirque du Soleil's surreal shows, and the phenomenal Wayne Brady (a one-man Rat Pack) are just a handful that have taken the stage.

It's sad Bugsy Siegel didn't live to see what he started. His city hit the jackpot.

CONTACTS

Las Vegas Convention and
Visitors Authority
www.visitlasvegas.com

www.vegas.com

For Lodging and Dining, see pp. 319–320

75. MISS AMERICA
Las Vegas, Nevada

Even after its popularity dimmed during its final years in Atlantic City, the Miss America pageant could never really go away. Why not? It's the nation's original reality show.

LANDING ON BOARDWALK

In Atlantic City in 1921, business tended to drop off following Labor Day, so some newspapers needed a gimmick to boost circulation. City fathers also needed a way to convince tourists to stay put. So the two forces came up with a gem of an idea: They would get attractive women in bathing suits to compete in a beauty pageant. With far too much feminine pulchritude to display in just one day, the first Fall Frolic was a two-day contest won by the curvaceously challenged Margaret Gorman, who showed off her 30-25-32 figure to win the Golden Mermaid title, although in mid-reign she was given the less fishy title Miss America.

It was a promising start, but within a few years things started to fall apart with rumors of a rigged contest, the reality of heavy debt, and the burden of the Great Depression. By the 1940s, the Miss America pageant had found its feet. In 1954 it became permanently rooted in the American landscape when ABC put it on the air and attracted 27 million viewers, who waited anxiously to see the newly crowned winner beaming as she sashayed down the runway, serenaded by emcee Bert Parks's baritone rendition of "Miss America!"

Until 1949, winners had their title suffixed with the year of their victory (a simple procedure done on an outpatient basis). Afterward, dates were advanced to the following year, which meant there was no Miss America 1950. If you ever meet a woman claiming to be Miss America 1950, contact the authorities.

By the late 1960s, Miss America's traditional tribute to femininity was going head to head with women's liberation and changing times. There was a demonstration at the 1968 pageant (protestors crowned a sheep the pageant winner). It took until 1970 to welcome the pageant's first black contestant, Iowa's Cheryl Adrienne Browne. Vanessa Williams, Miss America 1984, was asked to turn over her crown to runner-up Suzette Charles after nude photos were made public. The photos, of course, were of Williams, not Charles.

The television audience was also drifting away. After 2004, ABC dropped the telecast. In 2006, pageant officials decided to drop Atlantic City. The pageant was relocated to Las Vegas and the contest was moved from September to January, which gave Deidre Downs, Miss America 2005, four extra months to keep the title. But the contest's most significant and successful change occurred when TLC, which was now broadcasting the pageant, teamed up with the Miss America Organization to create "Miss America: Reality Check," in which viewers could see the process of competition and the real women behind the sparkling gowns. In 2008, nearly 20 million viewers tuned in to witness the crowning of their...*Miss America!*

DO IT YOURSELF

Although the Miss America pageant is telecast on only one evening, you can triple your viewing pleasure by attending in person and purchasing tickets for the three evenings of preliminary competition. They showcase evening wear, swimsuits, an onstage question, and the contestant's talent—which usually includes singing, dancing, twirling, or changing the rings on an 1,800-horsepower diesel engine. It is on those evenings that judges determine which contestants will be awarded a place among the semifinalists.

If you're here early, you may even meet some of the contestants. A day or so before the final I bumped into Miss Iowa, who, in her sweats and flip-flops, seemed more comfortable than cosmopolitan. I remarked on her casual appearance.

"None of us on stage is perfect," explained Diana Reed. "The audience sees perfection but what it doesn't see are the smoke and mirrors. There's a lot of illusion. There's taping here, gluing there, padding here, bronzing there….You have to look like a million bucks on three hours' sleep.

"That's part of being the All-American Girl," she continued. "Not only can you walk on a stage in a bikini or gown and look absolutely stunning, you can hang out wearing a ponytail and kick back and relax with people one on one. I think that's what makes an all-around person and someone you want to get to know and someone you want to represent America."

Miss Iowa had my vote.

With her words in mind, I was astounded at the amount of makeup and spritz and glitter and mousse and gel—and that was just in the lobby when I arrived for the pageant. Silver-haired gentlemen in tuxes and ties escorted sophisticated ladies with polished teeth and spiked heels. It was only 4 p.m. and I was in a flashback to every wedding reception I'd ever attended. Once inside the hall I thumbed through a program that featured a fantastic amount of information about the pageant itself as well as a photo and biography of each contestant. While it's natural to handicap the field, after reading their bios I wanted everyone to win.

When the competition kicked off on live television, the pageant seemed to become a political convention. When Miss Kansas stepped to center stage,

According to a gentleman who designs dresses for pageant contestants, dress for Miss Kansas will be more conservative than the "fashion forward" styles of Miss California. Incidentally, many of these dresses sell for north of $4,000, which begs the question: If these ladies are competing for a $20,000 scholarship, couldn't they simply invest that money? A few gowns could pay for medical school.

her Kansan fans waved paper sunflowers; Georgians held up paper peaches when Miss Georgia appeared; Floridians applied tanning butter. Soon, 16 ladies were chosen as finalists.

Knowing the talent portion will likely be the most watched performance of their lives, the contestants make it worth the price of admission. Minutes later they're back to display additional assets in the swimsuit competition.

When they reappear in evening wear it's clear that the 1960s' hoop skirts and helmet hair are out, and when the final eight are left they face what may be the most excruciating part of the competition: the interview. If you find it hard to carry on a conversation with a tech support guy in India, try answering a tricky question in front of 4,000 people.

After the judges' votes were tallied came the moment the contestants, their families, and 20 million viewers were waiting for. The emcee counted down the finalists in reverse order and each eliminated contestant displayed the grace and class you've come to expect. Soon only two ladies were left. When the runner-up was announced and the winner was named, there was one of the longest shrieks of joyful excitement you've ever heard.

It was me.

CONTACTS AND SITES TO SEE

Miss America Organization
www.missamerica.org

For Lodging and Dining, see pp. 319–320

PACIFIC COAST, HAWAII, & ALASKA

Alaska, California, Hawaii, Oregon, Washington

If you were limited to exploring just one section of the U.S.A., this region would likely provide the greatest range of experiences. Head along the Pacific Coast from the Mexican border to Canada and you'll find enough diversions to keep you busy for the rest of your life.

It's not just the sights that are magical—an abundance and awareness of nature make this region a delight to visit. You'll feel it from the depths of Death Valley to the vineyards of Napa Valley. Head north and you'll find America's frontier wilderness in Alaska, where residents are ready to show you how powerful sled dogs and iconic bald eagles keep them warm with pride. Across the waters in Hawaii, the appeal is more exotic, with luaus and surfing balanced against the tragedy of Pearl Harbor.

If you ever fear that America is too homogenized, just think of the Pacific Coast, Alaska, and the Hawaiian Islands. Then go there.

76. SPACE NEEDLE
Seattle, Washington

When directors enter film school, I bet one of the first things they learn is that nifty little trick about setting a scene. The Eiffel Tower tells the audience the action is in Paris; Big Ben means the scene's in London; the Statue of Liberty is used for New York; and the St. Louis Ar—well, you get the picture. So when you watch *Frasier, Grey's Anatomy,* or *Sleepless in Seattle,* what do you see? Right. The Space Needle.

DESIGN ON A DINER

Flashes of brilliance (like those in this book) are often first jotted down on a scrap of paper. Space Needle was one of those ideas.

It was 1959, just three years before the grand opening of the Century 21 Exposition, known to history as the Seattle World's Fair. Edward E. Carlson, then president of Western International Hotels, was at a diner noodling sketches on a placemat, hoping to create a centerpiece that would symbolize the event.

Having seen Germany's Stuttgart Tower and aware of the postmodern styles inspired by the dawn of the Space Age, Carlson sketched out what looked like a balloon on a tether: a design that was visually impressive, but architecturally impractical. Still, it would give architects and engineers a place to start.

Five successful Seattle businessmen formed a group called the Pentagram Corporation and hired a team of architects, designers, and engineers to conjure up ways to get the job done. As revisions were made, the shape of Carlson's tower went from a balloon on a tether to a sleek tower capped with a five-level flying saucer–shaped deck and narrow antennae. Leading the design team was architect John Graham who also deserves credit, or blame, for creating the nation's first shopping mall.

The New Year's Eve celebration at the Space Needle attracts thousands for a display of fireworks, synchronized to music and shot from dozens of different firing locations on the tower.

Although everyone agreed on the design, there was still no place to put the structure and just thirteen months before the fair opened. At the last minute, the backers bought a $75,000 parcel of land surrounded by the fairgrounds. To create the tower's foundation, contractors excavated a pit 30 feet deep and 120 feet square. In a single day they dumped into the pit the contents of 467 cement trucks. The foundation weighed 5,850 tons, almost twice the weight of the Space Needle itself.

Engineers created a structure that could withstand a wind velocity of 200 miles per hour and earthquakes reaching 9.0 on the Richter scale. The center of gravity was located just five feet above the ground. Atop that workers fashioned 7.4 million pounds of steel into the shape of the Space Needle and fastened it to the foundation with 72 30-foot-long bolts.

Each of the three elevators uses seven cables (one would be enough) and all are replaced annually. Even if they were all clipped, a governor brake would lock the elevator on the tracks.

With futuristic visions as its guiding light, the Pentagram Corporation approved colors for the finished structure: Astronaut White (the legs), Orbital Olive (the core), Reentry Red (the halo), and Galaxy Gold (for the sunburst and pagoda roof). No one, apparently, suggested jetpacks to replace the elevators. Incredibly, the $4.5 million Space Needle was built in just 407 days and, at the time, was the tallest building west of the Mississippi.

When the World's Fair opened on April 21, 1962, visitors were pleased with the tower and amazed by its revolving restaurant. The Space Needle played a major role in introducing to the world the Golden Age of Centrifugal Dining. Sparked by curiosity, amazement, or hunger pangs, 20,000 people would be lifted to its summit every day. Over the course of the fair, more than two million people rode to the top.

So who's visited the Space Needle since? Who hasn't? Kelsey Grammer's been here, and so have Mike Myers and Demi Moore and Vanna White, and John Travolta, Michael Douglas, Tim Robbins, and Paul Reiser. In 1962, Elvis Presley was there to play Mike Edwards, an unemployed cropduster pilot, in *It Happened at the World's Fair*.

More than 45 million people have visited since opening day, and 1.3 million visitors arrive each year to enjoy the view. Some even use it as a launching pad for either a parachute jump or a marriage since locals agree it's a romantic place to get engaged.

And it all started with a sketch on a placemat.

DO IT YOURSELF

If you have any trouble finding the 605-foot Space Needle, first ask directions and then make an appointment for an eye exam. You should be able to see it from miles away.

You can bypass the 848 steps via three elevators that race skyward at ten miles per hour, and while that may not sound fast, it's as fast as rain falls and even faster than snow falls, so if it's snowing as you're descending, the snow seems to be falling up.

You'd think it'd take an enormous engine to spin the SkyCity restaurant, but the whole thing turns with the assistance of just a 1.5-horsepower motor.

About 43 seconds after the elevator takes off, you'll exit at the Observation Deck at 520 feet. Most visitors spend about an hour there, hooking up with guides who offer free tours several times an hour. On a clear day you can see Mount Baker, about 130 miles away, as well as downtown Seattle, Mount Rainier, Puget Sound, and Lake Washington. Some folks claim they can even see their house from there.

And they live in Kansas.

CONTACTS

Space Needle and SkyCity Restaurant
(206) 905-2100
(800) 937-9582
www.spaceneedle.com

For Lodging and Dining, see pp. 320–321

77. CABLE CARS
San Francisco, California

There's something quite pleasing about San Francisco's cable cars. There's tradition, for one. They were named a National Historic Landmark in 1964. But there's something more. Maybe it's the sense of determination these squat little cars suggest. When they scale some of San Francisco's most demanding hills they seem to achieve the impossible and we, as Americans, can take pride in their accomplishment. Could that be it?

Nah. We just like them because they're so darn cute.

THE HILLS ARE ALIVE

No one likes to see an overburdened beast of burden, and that's what Andrew S. Hallidie saw on the streets of San Francisco in 1869. In this city of staggering hills, horses (as well as people) had their work cut out for them even if they just wanted to take a walk around the block. A 17-degree grade on Nob Hill posed a challenge, but that was just a hill of beans compared to the 21-degree pitch of Hyde Street.

It would take him four years but Hallidie, who made his living manufacturing metal rope, tinkered around with a way to take horses out of the harness and help people up the hills. By 1873 he had a system he thought would work. On August 2 a few folks got up in the middle of the night and headed to Nob Hill to see if his invention—a streetcar tugged along by a cable running beneath the street—would work. It did. In time, eight companies expressed their gratitude by starting 22 cable car routes in the city.

"Streetcars were fine in cities with level surfaces," explains cable car expert Judson True. "But cable cars were perfect for San Francisco. This was much better than having horses drag carriages up and down these hills."

But the Great Earthquake of 1906, as well as more powerful and efficient buses, threatened the future of the city's cable cars. By the end of World War II, San Francisco's cable car business was hanging by a thread. But in 1947, a feisty resident, Freidel Klussman, rallied women's civic clubs to form the Citizens Committee to Save the Cable Cars. The cable cars would stay.

An event that should be featured on ESPN is the cable car bell ringing contest that's held in Union Square each summer. Along with the professional bell ringing contest, celebrities will often compete on behalf of local nonprofit organizations for bell-ringing glory.

In 1982 it was determined the cable car system needed a comprehensive 20-month, $60 million restoration. Cable car fanatics alone donated $10 million. Pavement stretching across nearly 70 blocks was picked up and cleaned out to make room for brand-new cables, tracks, turntables, and utility lines. The city also rebuilt the cable car barn and spiffed up the entire fleet. Following this extreme makeover, hundreds of thousands of fans and footsore pedestrians came out to witness the return of the cable car in 1984.

A quarter-century after their restoration, they're still rolling.

DO IT YOURSELF

When you get to San Francisco you may be all hopped up to hop on a cable car, but wait just a minute. For now, consider holding off on dessert and starting at the Cable Car Museum and the car barn and powerhouse at the corner of Mason and Washington streets.

This is where it all begins. From a catwalk above, you can peer down into a Rube Goldberg–inspired nest of humongous gears, pulleys, and 11 miles of flowing wrapped steel rope that pulls the cars up and down the hills. The museum also showcases one of Hallidie's originals—a sporty little 1873 model—as well as scale models of some of the 57 different types of cable cars that once scooted across San Francisco.

Why "gripman"? Because in over a century of nearly continuous use, there has only ever been one grip woman.

Where are you headed? Wherever you want. Despite having only three lines, the system extends farther than you'd imagine. The route is shaped roughly like a Y—a *very* rough Y. Both the Powell-Mason Line, which heads all the way to Fisherman's Wharf, and the Powell-Hyde Line, which ends at Aquatic Park near Ghiradelli Square, roll through residential districts and into popular tourist areas. The California Line, the longest, runs across the bottom of the Y from the Financial District through Chinatown, then over Nob Hill to stop at Van Ness Avenue.

It won't take long to understand why Freidel Klussman and the gals stood up for cable cars. While you'd be hard-pressed to find anything entertaining about a New York City cab ride, riding a cable car is like being in a rolling theater that stars a cast of two. The cable car gripman operates levers that get the car going and slow it down. He's also the one who rings the gleaming brass bell, which, each year, gives him a chance to compete in the Muni Cable Car Bell Ringing Contest. His supporting cast is the cable car conductor who somehow manages to work his way through the passengers and around the car to collect fares, check tickets, and assist in working the back brake when needed. It's a masterful presentation and reveals why the dynamic duo is considered the public transportation system's elite.

As your advance team, I highly recommend that at one point you cling to a rail and stand on the running board as you watch the pavement whiz by at 9.5 miles per hour. At the end of the line, hop off and watch how operators whirl the cable car around on a turnaround that looks like a massive lazy Susan.

While you could pay for an individual one-way ticket (currently $5), an all-day pass is just $11 and gives you free rein to string out your own extended tour of the city. As the owner of an all-day pass, you also get something else: the night. Once the sun falls into the Pacific, city lights create a fluid tapestry stretching from the highest hills to the waters of San Francisco Bay. As the pavement continues to pass by at a steady clip, it's all yours: the quiet city streets, the Golden Gate Bridge, and the cheerful clang of the cable car bell ringing in the night.

CONTACTS

San Francisco Visitor
Information Center
900 Market Street
(415) 391-2000
www.onlyinsanfrancisco.com

Cable Car Museum
(415) 474-1887
www.cablecarmuseum.org

www.sfcablecar.com
www.cablecarmuseum.org

For Lodging and Dining, see p. 321

For Lodging and Dining, see p. 321

78. GOLDEN GATE BRIDGE
San Francisco, California

The loveliest bridges in America are the ones that seem to be in the proper place. Covered bridges are right at home in New England, and there's nowhere else the sturdy Brooklyn Bridge should be than crossing the wide East River. San Francisco's breathtaking Golden Gate Bridge does even better. In addition to being in the right place, it's a masterpiece of design, style, form, and function.

BRIDGE OVER TROUBLED WATERS

After Joseph Strauss determined that he would build a bridge across San Francisco Bay, only one obstacle stood in his way.

San Francisco Bay.

Look at a map of northern California and you'll notice that for about 600 miles, it's the only significant dent in the coastline. Confronting the irresistible force of the Pacific Ocean is the power packed inside 500-square-mile San Francisco Bay. With 16 rivers flowing into the bay, there's a whole lot of energy exploding where the twain meet. When the tidal surge peaks at the Golden Gate Strait, the flow is three times greater than that of the Amazon River and 14 times greater than the flow of the Mississippi. Wind gusts can surpass 60 miles per hour, howling through the mouth of the bay as fog

> **More than 40 million vehicles cross the bridge each year.**

shrouds everything in a blanket of gray. Other than this, it was a perfect place to build a bridge.

People had proposed bridges here before, but the price and challenge drove them off. Strauss wasn't deterred. In addition to the skills of his Chicago-based engineering firm, he had vision and tenacity. Turns out he needed every ounce of it.

After he arrived in San Francisco in 1917, Strauss tried for 13 years to convince city, state, and federal officials that his suspension bridge could—and should—be built. In the end, Strauss won by going around politicians and to the voters of a half-dozen Bay-area counties who were anxious to see a bridge connect northern San Francisco to Marin County. Their desire for the project was heightened with a little help from the Great Depression. With people scrambling for work, they approved bonds for the $35 million bridge by a three-to-one margin. Picking up the tab for the materials was Amadeo Giannini, founder of the Bank of America.

Another battle Joseph Strauss had to fight was with the U.S. Navy, which wanted to see a black bridge with yellow stripes. Others wanted it painted carbon black and steel gray. Strauss pressed for "International Orange," a color chosen by the bridge's designer, Irving Morrow, which would blend in with the surroundings and be more visible in the fog.

By January 5, 1933, everything was in place for construction to begin, and it was soon apparent that the years Strauss spent preaching the need for a bridge may have been the easy part. The same elements that created a treacherous pass—the wind, the cold, the fog, the fierce tides—were still there, but now workers were having to battle them every day to plant two 746-foot-tall towers into the bedrock some 300 feet beneath the waves. They also had to string two main cables that contained not just a single strand, but 80,000 miles of individual strands—enough to circle the Earth more than three times. Close to a million tons of steel and concrete anchored six lanes of traffic crossing 1.7 miles of the Pacific Ocean and giving ships below 220 feet of clearance. Over the course of four years, 11 men died—ten in one accident. Another 19 men became members of the "Halfway to Hell Club" after falling toward certain death before landing in a safety net strung beneath the span.

On May 27, 1937, a few hundred thousand pedestrians crossed and inaugurated the newly completed red-orange bridge. When vehicles began motoring over it the following day, officials really had nothing special planned except a symphony of sirens triggered at noon when Franklin Roosevelt pressed a telegraph key at the White House. Well, that plus a serenade of car horns, foghorns, ships' whistles, church bells, people cheering, and 400 planes flying overhead.

Since opening day, the bridge has been closed only briefly for wind gusts, special maintenance, and when special guests like Roosevelt and, later, Charles de Gaulle, dropped by.

Maybe they'll do the same when you show up.

DO IT YOURSELF

Sure, it's just a bridge but it may take several hours for you to get your fill of it. It's just that pretty.

There are a dozen different ways to see it, and one of the most popular is on San Francisco Bay at historic Fort Point, part of the Golden Gate National Recreational Area. From here, you'll see the Golden Gate Bridge framed against the hills of the Marin Headlands.

After you've seen it from the shore, hop in your jalopy, look for US 101, and head north. Right before you reach the bridge, watch for the last exit within the city and pull off to your right. This is the 1938 Roundhouse, a full-service visitors area with dozens of photo ops.

Either from here or at an overlook on the north side of the bridge, consider leaving the car and crossing the bridge on foot. En route you can see Alcatraz prison sitting in the middle of San Francisco Bay and, twenty stories down beneath your feet, the bay itself. You can also cycle across; bike rental businesses at Pier 39 (Fisherman's Wharf) offer a deal for riders to pick up a bicycle, pedal across the bridge, and ride into Sausalito before returning via ferry.

When you drive across, you won't pay a toll heading north so consider your first trans-Pacific trip free.

According to a bridge spokesman, the weather has a tendency to catch people off guard. Summer months can be foggy and windy and are not the best time to see the Golden Gate Bridge. Try September or October.

At the end of the bridge, watch for a turnout to your right that leads to Vista Point, another overlook where you can snap more bridge photos from a new angle. From here you're only one exit and a few miles away from the charming village of Sausalito. To the west (your left) are the Marin Headlands and a twisty road that leads into the hills and to another magnificent shot of the bridge, this time with the spans framing the heart of San Francisco.

Don't be in a hurry to get back. It took Strauss and his team four years to build this. Spend some time here and you'll have images and memories that will last far longer.

CONTACTS

San Francisco Visitor
Information Center
900 Market Street
(415) 391-2000
www.onlyinsanfrancisco.com

www.goldengatebridge.org

For Lodging and Dining, see p. 321

79. NAPA VALLEY
California

I've been to many places in America, but I can't recall any as fertile and picturesque as Napa Valley. Rolling in on a motorcycle, I noticed the soft low hills, green creeksides, and groves bursting with almonds, avocados, and black walnuts. And there were grapes. Miles and miles and miles of grapes.

THE VINTAGE VALLEY

It's natural for anyone arriving in Napa Valley to claim they discovered it, but credit is due to the Wappo who, quite astutely, recognized the special qualities of the region. When they arrived around 6,000 B.C., they were unaware that a volcano named Mount Konocti had erupted millions of years earlier. What they did know was that if they mixed the ash it had left on the valley floor with the naturally heated mineral water from percolating underground springs, they had made-to-order mud baths. They called the valley either Ta La Ha Lu Si (beautiful land) or Colaynomo (oven place), and they were right on both counts.

Like nearly every spot in America where there were Indians, there were new settlers—in this case, mainly Spanish and Mexican soldiers and missionaries—who wanted them out. Arriving in the valley in 1823, Mexican missionary Padre Jose Altimira wrote that several thousand Wappo Indians were in the area, enjoying the blessings of abundant food, fresh water, and a temperate climate. That enviable lifestyle sparked the interest of others who wanted what the natives had. When the Gold Rush brought hordes of miners to nearby San Francisco in the late 1840s, quicksilver mines and lumber mills soon displaced the Wappo. The tribe's consolation prize? In a bow to the Wappo, their language led to the name *Napa*—land of plenty.

It was soon the land of plenty of Anglos. In the 1860s, Gold Rush millionaire Sam Brannan found the healing mineral waters in the northern part of the valley and envisioned a western version of New York's Saratoga Springs. He was so excited about his idea that during a sales pitch he vowed it would become the "Calistoga of Sarifornia!" The name Calistoga was a perfect marketing gimmick and it stuck.

Tourists could board boats in chilly San Francisco and take a three-hour pleasure cruise up the Napa River to the town of Napa. Steam trains to Calistoga zipped tourists along the 30-mile-long valley. It seemed like paradise, but soon it was paradise lost. In 1875 one of the largest silver mines was tapped out after just three years; in 1893 a disease crippled grapevines and fledgling wineries; and from 1920 to 1933 Prohibition dismantled the wine industry. Some vintners tried to see the glass as half full and began selling their product as sacramental wine.

A few things helped rescue Napa Valley. First, in the early 20th century farmers had planted more than a half million fruit and nut trees in the county so a backup industry was already blooming. Second, in 1933 people realized Prohibition was stupid and in time Napa's wine industry bounced back. Today there are nearly 400 wineries pressing grapes into service for the world's oenophiles. Among these are legends like Charles Krug, Robert Mondavi, and Beringer.

But even if the main industry was a chain of radiator repair shops, you would still want to go there. It is that beautiful.

According to the Napa Valley Vintners, there are some things you need to know about wine:

- One barrel of wine equals roughly 20 cases, which equals 1,200 glasses.

- A ton of grapes makes about 720 bottles of wine, or 60 cases.

- One vine annually produces between four and six bottles of wine, or between 20 and 30 glasses.

- Each bottle of wine contains about 2.8 pounds of grapes.

- There are between 15 and 45 clusters of grapes per vine.

- One acre of land holds between 900 and 1,300 vines.

DO IT YOURSELF

There are no towering condos there; no eight-lane highways either; just peace and prosperity. Some of this can be traced back to 1968, when citizens gained protection for more than 438,000 acres as an agricultural preserve. One thing that may strike you is the area's European feel, with reminders of the Greek Peloponnese, Swiss Alps, and Italy's Tuscan region.

When you arrive in the southern end of the valley, stop at the Napa Visitors Center. Pick up the official guidebook, which is full of detailed maps and information on winery tours, tasting room experiences, and the varietals of wine.

> **There are more than 330 wineries in Napa Valley, nearly a hundred of which are open for tastings.**

"You have to look at Napa Valley as a playground for your taste buds," suggests David Turgeon of the Napa Destination Council. "Definitely visit the larger wineries, but it's really fun to go to small wineries as well. Tastings are important, but it's also important to appreciate how the wine got to where it is. What ends up in the glass is all a result of what comes from the earth, the types of vines, the weather, and the care the vintner has given the grapes. The growers are passionate about what they produce so you'll want to spend several days here to take in the entire experience."

After the vineyards, explore. Most communities present fine galleries, upscale dining, and intriguing boutiques. Expand your range and motor over to Lake Berryessa and beautiful neighboring valleys like Alexander and Sonoma.

At day's end, many travelers drop to the southern end of the valley and stay the night in Napa. I've found great pleasure in the smaller town of Calistoga. In this comfortable walking town are hot mineral baths dating from the town's earliest days as a resort, small restaurants and wine bars, local saloons, massage studios, and soothing mud baths.

But wherever you go, just about everything you see or do in Napa Valley reminds you that what brought the Wappo here brought you here as well.

CONTACTS

Napa Visitors Center
1310 Napa Town Center
(707) 226-5813
www.legendarynapavalley.org

Napa Valley Vintners Association
(707) 963-3388
www.napavintners.com

Sonoma County Wineries Association
(707) 586-3795
www.sonomawine.com

Alexander Valley Wine Growers
(888) 289-4637
www.alexandervalley.org

For Lodging and Dining, see pp. 321–322

80. YOSEMITE
California

In the late '60s, a sci-fi show called *Land of the Giants* followed space travelers from Earth who landed on an alternate Earth where everything was 12 times normal size. That's how you may feel in Yosemite. Everything—the trees, the mountains, the waterfalls—seems abnormally huge.

THE BIG VALLEY

The nomadic tribes that first arrived about 4,000 years ago knew that Yosemite was a special place. So did the Ahwahnechee, who were living there in the early 1800s, and so did the gold prospectors who tried to shove the Ahwahnechee out in the mid-1800s.

It was President Lincoln who, in 1864, "held for public use, resort and recreation…inalienable for all time" Yosemite Valley and the Mariposa Grove of giant sequoias. Three thousand miles away in Washington, Lincoln relied on evidence of Yosemite's grandeur provided by an increasing number of explorers, artists, and photographers including landscape designer Frederick Law Olmsted, who was astounded by the scope of beauty here. But even with Lincoln's John Hancock, the new state park lacked sufficient reach to fully protect the region from possible industrial encroachment.

In the following decades, naturalist John Muir rallied other concerned conservationists to help create Yosemite National Park. In 1890, their efforts were rewarded. The new park preserved nearly 1,200 square miles of forests, fields, valleys, and mountains; 240 species of birds; 80 species of mammals; and 1,400 species of flowering plants.

If you plan to fish at Yosemite, you need a fishing license, available at the Sport Shop in Yosemite Valley, the Wawona Store, and the Tuolumne Meadows Store. If you want to take the first step toward tackling El Capitan, sign up for climbing lessons by calling the Mountaineering School at *(209) 372-8344.*

So who was ready to take it all in? At first, the focus was on the rich—folks who could afford to embark on a weeklong expedition from San Francisco and then travel on horseback to stay for several more days at grand lodges inside Yosemite Valley. Despite the work of engineers, rangers, and naturalists, it was not a place suitable for casual tourists.

A half century later, new roads, lodging, and services were ready for post-WWII families able to afford autos and vacations. Like other national parks, Yosemite became a favorite destination for the middle class. And everything our parents and grandparents enjoyed during the '50s is still worth seeing today.

DO IT YOURSELF

Getting there is almost as much fun as being there. *Almost.* Highways leading into the park from the four points of the compass all deliver an abundance of wonderful central California scenery, so even if you got stranded by a flat, you wouldn't mind too much.

Approaching from the southeast, I drove up from the town of Lone Pine near Sequoia National Park and entered Yosemite at Lee Vining. If the sun is dropping or the weather is dicey when you arrive, consider staying there since it'll take a few hours to reach the heart of the park via some twisty and tricky roads best avoided after dark.

Roads revealing breathtaking scenery take you to Yosemite Village, the park's "downtown." At the visitors center, park rangers can help map out a day that might include anything from fishing and camping to cookouts, photography classes, and nature talks. While the park may be best enjoyed by tossing the schedule and lying in a hammock, odds are you'll be motivated to explore.

At the Ansel Adams Gallery in Yosemite Village, you'll find posters of works by the legendary nature photographer and original prints by other gifted artists and photographers.

I opted for a tour to help me get my bearings and learn a little more about the park's botany, geology, and forestry. Armed with maps, brochures, and schedules from the visitors center, I boarded a tram for a two-hour Valley Floor Tour that covered 26 miles and took in park highlights including El Capitan, a nearly vertical 3,000-foot-tall rock wall that justifies your purchase of a wide-angle lens. The few specks of pepper on the wall are climbers, and the sprinkling of parsley beside them are, in reality, 80-foot-tall pine trees.

El Capitan puts things in perspective, but it is only one of Yosemite's highlights. Guides will tell you about the meadows that hold 80 percent of the park's flowers and show you justifiably famous sights like Bridalveil Fall, Half Dome, Yosemite Falls, North Dome, and Sentinel Rock.

The full-day Glacier Point Tour and Grand Tour also cover Glacier Point and Mariposa Grove, with its 2,500-year-old sequoias. If you ever doubt that the world lacks wonder, spend some quiet time here and just look at these trees.

After getting a sense of place from a tour, pick up your walking stick and head out on your own. There are 800 miles of hiking trails at Yosemite and on maps they are rated according to degree of difficulty. Choosing the equivalent of a bunny slope, I found a quiet forest trail near Bridalveil Fall. An outdoorsman in the Tony Randall sense, now I felt like Grizzly Adams. I could hear the crunching leaves beneath my feet, the whisper of wind in the boughs, the random plop of acorns and pinecones as they dropped, and the feel of rough bark on trees that had probably never felt a human hand.

The magic never flagged. Not once.

CONTACTS

Yosemite National Park
(209) 372-0200
www.nps.gov/yose

For Lodging and Dining, see p. 322

81. DEATH VALLEY
California

Death Valley.

Even the name is stark. It conveys visions of lost prospectors stumbling toward a mirage, bleached cow skulls half-buried in the sand, and lonely miles of eerie emptiness. The Valley, though, is not completely empty or desolate. It is a wondrous place that offers a graphic lesson in proportion.

It is immense, and you are not.

HOT AND BOTHERED

If you had been out for a walk through Death Valley on July 10, 1913, you would have enjoyed clear skies and a temperature that reached 134 degrees.

That was the hottest day ever recorded there.

Then again, nearly every day there is hot. You could cross the entire nation and you won't be able to find a place as low, as dry, or as hot as this. When you're at its deepest point, you're 282 feet below sea level. If you're here on an average July day, wear a sunbonnet

Some families of the Timbisha tribe, whose ancestors arrived there 1,000 years ago, still live in the valley at Furnace Creek.

because it will be hovering around 117 degrees. You may be able to find some shelter in the shade of the Panamint Range to the west or the Amargosa Range to the east, but overall it is just plain hot and dry and void.

It's mighty impressive that Death Valley is 282 feet below sea level, but it doesn't come close to the Dead Sea, which has a record depth of 1,371 feet below sea level.

The entire valley was once submerged—part of a chain of inland seas in the middle of the Pleistocene era. When the water evaporated, it left behind huge quantities of salt and borax which, about 1.5 million years later, helped develop an industry.

But why is this place so dadgum hot? When you combine the depth of the valley, its long and narrow outline, and the steep mountains that surround it, and then include sunlight that is seldom blocked by clouds, the valley absorbs and radiates more heat than college students at Cozumel.

What heat is reflected never quite manages to rise above the mountain peaks, so it cools and then falls back to the desert floor, heating up and rising again. It's a massive circulating hair dryer. There's little chance for a refreshing rain either. It can take more than six years for some parts of Death Valley to get a foot of water.

But it didn't faze the Timbisha Shoshone Indians, who lived there during seasonal migrations. It was the prospectors who traveled across this region in the mid-1800s who dubbed it Death Valley. While few of them stuck around, their spiritual descendants returned in the 1880s to mine the borax that the Pleistocene Era had left behind. If you're old enough to recall a television program called *Death Valley Days,* you'll recall the sponsor—20 Mule Team Borax—a laundry additive that paid tribute to the miners who excavated borax and moved it to the nearest railroad spur line via mule-drawn wagons.

Since the miners cleared out, just a few folks have moved in, including Japanese internees during World War II. Although it is still one of the loneliest places on the planet, there is a strange beauty there.

DO IT YOURSELF

One of the biggest mistakes of my life was assuming I could travel the 200 or so miles from Las Vegas, Nevada, to Lone Pine, California, in less than four hours. The only thing in my way was Death Valley.

A Floridian, I was unaware that valleys are valleys because they lie between mountains. I managed a teeth-grinding ascent over the Amargosa Range and then, with night upon me, faced an even more nerve-racking attempt to navigate pitch-black hairpin turns and sheer precipices of the Panamint and then Inyo Mountains. Keep that in mind when planning your adventure. Avoid traveling after dark and allow yourself a surplus of time because what lies between those mountain ranges is incredible.

At 3.3 million acres, Death Valley is big—bigger than Connecticut—and there's far more to see than you'd expect. To prepare, there are three visitors centers. The main one is at Furnace Creek, where you can stop or call in advance to learn from rangers what activities might pique your interest.

Seeing this on a motorcycle only emphasized the majesty and grandeur of Death Valley. The deeper I went into the valley, the more unusual it became. In some places the land was so flat and empty that I could see a lone object a good 20 miles down the road. At Zabriskie Point, a short loop road led in and out of 20 Mule Team Canyon, and the main road led to a most unexpected find, the four-star Furnace Creek Resort (see p. 322). Even less expected was the Amargosa Opera House at the intersection of Death

More than 1,000 kinds of plants live in Death Valley National Park. The roots of some plunge to a depth of 60 feet to seek water.

Valley Junction at 190 and 127. In 1967, the ramshackle remnants of the Pacific Coast Borax Company's office space and hotel was restored by New York dancer Marta Becket. To this day the opera house and hotel continues to welcome guests and present shows.

Dimensions seemed to change. I spied the headlights of oncoming cars but the cars were still a good ten miles away. I was completely lost in the environment, riding across the desert floor and around slow, sweeping curves when I realized I was in the basin of Death Valley. Trusting I could get the bike to start again, I shut it off, removed my helmet, and felt like I had landed on another planet.

With an early sunset on its way, I would have to navigate more dark and dangerous mountain roads. I was scared to death but it was worth it. In the depths of Death Valley there was no noise or people or activity. There was *nothing*. That was nice.

CONTACTS

Death Valley National Park
(760) 786-3200
www.nps.gov/deva

For Lodging and Dining, see page 322

82. ROSE BOWL
Pasadena, California

Come New Year's Day some of us have just three things on our to-do list: sober up, start the diet, and watch the Rose Bowl. Of the three, watching America's oldest college bowl game is easily the most enjoyable—and exciting.

HOW TO GROW A ROSE BOWL

Considering how the first Tournament of Roses football game turned out, it's a testament to sportsmanship that there's still a game today. In 1902, the players of Stanford University were taking a 49-0 shellacking by the University of Michigan. So at the end of the third quarter, Stanford decided to play to its strengths by refusing to come out for the fourth quarter.

Courtesy shuttle buses to the stadium pick up at the corner of Fair Oaks Avenue and Holly Street and run from mid-morning to a few hours after the game is over.

Following the Drubbing of '02, Stanford players headed back to class and organizers of the Tournament of Roses returned to more popular and competitive events such as ostrich races and Roman chariot races. Really. Football wouldn't regain its foothold until 1916, and when it did, it received a hero's welcome. A 57,000-seat horseshoe-shaped stadium was built in Pasadena and completed in 1922. On January 1, 1923, the new stadium became home to a new football game: the Rose Bowl. Making its first appearance since 1902, Pop Warner's Stanford team showed up in 1925 to battle Knute Rockne's Notre Dame (Stanford lost), returned in 1927 against Alabama (and tied); and then gave it one more good ol' college try versus Pittsburgh and won (!) in 1928.

From the start, the game and the Rose Bowl Stadium became American institutions, so much so that since opening day the stadium's repeated expansions have nearly doubled seating capacity. In addition to being the nation's first bowl game, the Rose Bowl racked up other firsts. It was the first to be broadcast live on radio from coast to coast (1927); the first college football game televised locally (1948) and nationally (1952); and the first broadcast by satellite to Europe (1968).

Fantastic football is only part of the reason why the Rose Bowl has been sold out every year since 1947. Kicking off Game Day is the Rose Bowl Parade, a perfect way to start the new year.

DO IT YOURSELF

Southern California is not a bad place to be on New Year's Day—especially if you have a ticket to the game. It's been a sellout every year since 1947, with most tickets going to the competing universities and the rest available to the public in early December. For a price, you can raise the odds of getting a ticket to 100 percent by purchasing an "official tour package," which secures your seat and includes lodging, event tickets, visits to float-decorating sites, some meals, and transportation.

> After the Japanese attacked Pearl Harbor three weeks before the 1942 Rose Bowl, the fear of an attack on a stadium filled with 90,000 people prompted Rose Bowl officials to move the game to Durham, North Carolina.

Get the year off to a great start by watching the legendary Rose Parade. The surface of each float's framework is covered in natural flowers or greenery, and while I don't have proof, I bet this is probably America's best-smelling parade. It's certainly one of the oldest. Since 1890, the parade has rolled through Pasadena with floats, marching bands, equestrians, color guards, dancers, twirlers, and entertainers who march more than five miles in about two and a half hours. From the sidewalks, crowds receive a year's worth of entertainment for free, plus a chance to wave at an A-List Grand Marshal—at one time or another, Walt Disney, President Dwight D. Eisenhower, Shirley Temple, Bob Hope, Hank Aaron, and Kermit the Frog.

With kickoff scheduled for just after 2 p.m., countless tailgate parties—some of them elaborate events sponsored by corporations—fill the Rose Bowl's parking lot. But even if you're in the middle of the best tailgate party ever—even if Aerosmith drops by to perform a private acoustic set—don't miss the pregame ceremonies.

The Rose Parade Grand Marshal, at midfield with representatives of the Pacific-10 and Big Ten champion teams, flips a coin to determine which team kicks and which receives. The Rose Queen and her Royal Court smile and wave; a marching band fills the stadium with sound; a color guard displays the flags; and military jets scream past in a breathtaking flyover. Other than that, there's not much to see.

> The Rose Bowl Game is always scheduled for January 1, unless that happens to be a Sunday. If so, the game and parade are held on Monday, January 2.

At halftime, the marching bands take the field to create a swirl of motion and movement and patterns. Fans still recall the day in 1973 when Ohio State failed in their attempt to complete a dodecahedron.

With the champion of the Big Ten Conference competing against the champion of the Pacific-10 Conference, the second half should be even more exciting than the first. And even if you don't attend either school or have the slightest interest in who comes out on top, you still have four action-packed quarters of a gridiron classic, and a heck of a way to start the new year.

CONTACTS

Tournament of Roses
(626) 449-4100 (information)
(213) 365-3675 (tickets)
www.tournamentofroses.com

For Lodging and Dining, see pp. 322–323

83. DISNEYLAND
Anaheim, California

Parents sometimes have those awkward moments when they take their kids to a place they recall as fun and amusing and find it is now boring and decrepit. The kids are disappointed, and the parents feel old.

Walt Disney was a parent who wanted time to stand still. He wanted to create a place that captured the memories of his youth; a place where parents and kids could enjoy a day...together.

And so he built Disneyland.

DADDY'S DAY

By the mid-1950s Walt Disney's potent combination of intuition, instinct, and innovation had managed to confound his critics (and creditors) for a quarter-century. In 1928 he had added sound to a cartoon and become famous, and in 1937 he had transformed animation into art in *Snow White and the Seven Dwarfs* and become rich enough to build his own motion picture studio. It was merely a prelude to what would come next.

For years, Saturdays had been "Daddy's day" for Walt Disney and his daughters, Sharon and Diane. At a small amusement park in Beverly Hills the girls would ride ponies or go on the merry-go-round while Walt sat alone on a bench and wondered why amusement parks weren't clean and why there was nothing for parents and children to do together.

The idea stuck with him. He visited Tivoli Gardens in Copenhagen; went to Oakland, California, to see Children's Fairyland; and attended a Chicago railroad fair that featured themed villages. The idea was taking shape by the early 1950s, but it would require capital. Over a weekend, Disney and artist Herb Ryman created a park on a groundbreaking "hub and spoke" design, with avenues leading to uniquely themed lands that celebrated adventure, fantasy, the future, and the American frontier. The investors signed on. Next, Walt learned that a fledgling network, ABC Television, was looking for an audience and programming. Coincidentally, Walt was looking for an audience and money. Through *Disneyland*, a weekly program, ABC could show original and existing Disney films and Walt could introduce viewers to the new park taking shape in southern California.

> **As you walk along Main Street U.S.A., look at the names painted above the shops. They're the names of notable Disney executives and performers.**

Construction began on July 18, 1954. When Disneyland opened exactly one year and $17 million later, it would change the way Americans were entertained. And it all started with an idea on Daddy's day.

DO IT YOURSELF

For starters, Disneyland is more than just the original Disneyland Park. There are a few hotels, the Downtown Disney entertainment complex, and a retro-theme park called California Adventure. But you'll want to see the original first. And to be sure you do, get an early start. Not only will it give you more time to enjoy the day, but you'll also be able to knock out the major attractions before other guests arrive.

> **Finding "hidden Mickeys"— the tri-circle image that reveals the famous mouse— has become a passion for Disneyphiles. You'll find "hidden Mickeys" tucked away at every Disney destination, although you can take a shortcut and find them at *www.hiddenmickeys.org*.**

An authentic steam locomotive circles the park. Walking through the arches beneath the station creates a splendid grand opening. As you enter Town Square, before you is a charming portrayal of the turn of the 20th century, with barbershop quartets and marching bands, popcorn wagons, horse-drawn streetcars, and horseless carriages—and Main Street, U.S.A. filled with old-fashioned ice cream parlors, magic shops, candy shops, and the Emporium. One thing you won't find is litter on the ground. It's picked up by "cast members"— employees—who are uncommonly friendly and courteous. Why not? Consider where they work.

At the far end of Main Street, U.S.A., Sleeping Beauty Castle is the centerpiece and focal point of the entire park—a fantasy medieval castle that attracts visitors and draws them deeper into the park. This is the hub of the park's "hub and spoke" design, and the paths that spread out from there will take you to the park's different lands. Since most guests turn to their left, I'd suggest you veer off to your right into Tomorrowland, whose retro-futuristic look seems a little like Fritz Lang's *Metropolis*. This is where you'll find the thrill rides Space Mountain and Star Tours, and other favorites like Buzz Lightyear Astro Blasters, the Finding Nemo Submarine Voyage, and Honey, I Shrunk the Audience.

Disney's California Adventure opened in early 2001, built atop what used to be the Disneyland parking lot. More entertaining than a parking lot, this is a tribute to the golden age of amusement parks of nearly a century ago and includes many thrill rides and roller coasters. And don't miss Downtown Disney, a collection of shops and nightclubs that should keep you up past Cinderella's bedtime.

Next door, in Fantasyland, you'll find the elaborate It's a Small World, twirling teacups at the Mad Tea Party, Dumbo the Flying Elephant, Snow White's Scary Adventures, the Matterhorn bobsleds, and the lovely King Arthur Carousel. Toon Town, a small detour inspired by the 1988 hit *Who Framed Roger Rabbit,* separates Fantasyland from Frontierland and its major attractions: the Big Thunder Mountain Railroad roller coaster, Tom Sawyer Island, the Mark Twain Riverboat, and the Golden Horseshoe Review.

At New Orleans Square are two classics, the Haunted Mansion and Pirates of the Caribbean. Next door, Critter Country is where you'll find Splash Mountain, a water flume ride, and the Many Adventures of Winnie the Pooh. Call me a sentimental old fluff, but as an old Jungle Cruise skipper, my favorite is Adventureland, where you'll find the wonderfully entertaining Jungle Cruise, Tarzan's Treehouse, the Enchanted Tiki Birds, and the thrilling Indiana Jones Adventure, which ties in skeletons, mummies, explosions, and the ubiquitous rolling boulder.

You've now circled the park, but you haven't seen it all. Each day there is a parade and live stage shows and each evening throughout the summer and on holidays there are fantastic fireworks and the magical sight of Tinkerbell soaring around the glittering spires of Sleeping Beauty Castle.

But amid all this beauty and fantasy and magic, perhaps the most amazing sight at Disneyland is this: Parents and children are having fun…together.

CONTACTS

Disneyland
(714) 781-4565 (recording)
(714) 781-7290 (person)
www.disneyland.com

www.justdisney.com
www.disneyheaven.com
www.mouseplanet.com

For Lodging and Dining, see p. 323

84. BEVERLY HILLS
California

Of all the cities in the nation that exude flair, I'm pretty certain that Beverly Hills is the exudingest. The name itself is enough to ignite images of beautiful people, Spanish-Mediterranean mansions, Grecian columns surrounding crystal blue swimming pools, and towering palms standing over wide avenues. Guess what? They're really there.

...AND THEY MOVED TO BEVERLY

Beverly Hills's streak of good fortune began in the Cretaceous Era, when three canyons—Franklin, Coldwater, and Benedict—were formed. A few million years later the canyons helped direct precious water to a spot that the native inhabitants, the Tongva, considered a sacred site. They called it the Gathering of the Waters. Later, the Spanish called it El Rodeo de las Aguas, and today locals refer to it as the Intersection of Beverly Drive and Sunset Boulevard.

> Why Beverly Hills? The name was inspired by Beverly Farms, MA.

Although the water provided the Tongva with a lush oasis, it wasn't enough to save them from an outbreak of smallpox introduced by the Spanish settlers. With the tribe nearly wiped out, cowboys and ranchers and then land speculators like Edward Preuss moved in. Preuss bought enough acreage to sell five-acre lots at ten bucks a pop (they're more now) until drought forced him out.

Success would have to wait until 1906 when Burton Green and the Rodeo Land and Water Company began turning the area into a residential area. In 1912, the Beverly Hills Hotel—which served the few residents as an inn, theater, community center, and church—opened for business, and in 1914 Beverly Hills was incorporated.

The new city rose in tandem with the fledgling motion picture industry. Movie stars and moguls like Douglas Fairbanks, Mary Pickford, Gloria Swanson, Charlie Chaplin, John Barrymore, Buster Keaton, Clara Bow, Rudolph Valentino, and Jack Warner built elaborate mansions. By the 1930s the city had amassed enough clout to fight annexation by Los Angeles, and under the leadership of honorary mayor Will Rogers, Beverly Hills received a new City Hall and U.S. Post Office in the 1930s. But these civic improvements paled beside two changes that would come after World War II.

First, there was shopping. At the epicenter of fame and fashion was Rodeo Drive. Then, starting in the 1950s, the nation could tune into shows that glamorized the lifestyle of residents in programs like the *Jack Benny Show, Beverly Hillbillies, Beverly Hills 90210,* as well as movies including *Beverly Hills Cop* and *Pretty Woman.* A century after it became a city, Beverly Hills remains America's real-life gold standard in the pursuit of wealth, power, fame, and prestige.

DO IT YOURSELF

It'll take a little preparation, but I believe the best way for you to experience Beverly Hills is to become rich and famous, and then buy a home here. If you've already made travel plans, skip that step and drop by the Chamber of Commerce to pick up a map that details confirmed celebrity gathering places. If you have trouble spotting a real celebrity, you can either sprinkle some Botox on the ground or embark on a Hollywood sightseeing tour.

Bristol, Charlotte, Daytona, Indianapolis...Beverly Hills? During the 1920s the Beverly Hills Speedway was well known for its races, which were broadcast across the United States.

Starline Tours' "Tour of Movie Stars Homes" departs from Grauman's Chinese Theatre on Hollywood Boulevard and passes the homes of nearly six-dozen current and former stars. Note that the higher the wall, the more famous the star.

There are other options to consider. A narrated trolley tour scoots down Rodeo Drive and to local sites like the Beverly Hills Hotel. Also, sidewalk vendors throughout Hollywood and Beverly Hills sell maps of the stars' homes for a self-guided tour.

One sight many tourists seek is the Clampett Mansion, featured in the *Beverly Hillbillies.* Following an exhaustive and fruitless search, I discovered that to see it you have to head to Bel Air and find the Kirkeby Mansion. As a consolation prize, Beverly Hills has opened the gardens of the 55-room Greystone Mansion, built in 1928 for a hotel magnate, for a glimpse of an authentic estate. With advance notice, rangers will conduct tours of the mansion itself for large groups.

Few of us can afford property here, but if you head to Rodeo Drive you can own your own free parking space for two hours. There are just a few blocks of shops here—but what shops! Put on your sunglasses, clutch a chihuahua under your arm, and drop by Cartier, Gucci, Chanel, Tiffany's, and other exclusive boutiques. Stroll down to the south end of the block and drop by the Beverly Wilshire hotel. There, and at the Beverly Hilton and Beverly Hills Hotel, you can dine in one of several restaurants. Just keep one eye on the prices and one eye open for them movie stars.

CONTACTS

Beverly Hills Visitors Center
239 S. Beverly Drive
(310) 248-1015
www.lovebeverlyhills.org

Starline Tours
(323) 855-7000 (Beverly Hills)
(800) 959-3131 (Hollywood and
Stars' Homes)
www.starlinetours.com

Rodeo Drive
www.rodeodrive-bh.com

Trolley Tours
www.beverlyhills.org

For Lodging and Dining, see pp. 323–324.

85. ACADEMY AWARDS
Hollywood, California

One evening each February, a billion people around the world (it's always a billion) stay home from the movies to watch a television show *about* the movies. Does it really matter to us who won for Best Sound Mixing or for Best Foreign Language Film? Not necessarily, but for a few hours at least, the nation is riveted to the tube and privy to a world of limousines, paparazzi, evening gowns, glamour... and suspense.

SHOW TIME!

Nearly every American profession and pastime has an awards ceremony of some sort. Somewhere, someone—perhaps even your best friend, physician, or clergyman—has won honors for (and these are real) "Best Pincushion" or

"Fastest Grocery Bagger" or "Best Use of Brick in a Music Video." But at the pinnacle of all merit competitions is the Academy Awards.

The curious fascination fans have with movie stars has been going strong since Edison first filmed a man sneezing and Charlie Chaplin, Mary Pickford, and Douglas Fairbanks addressed millions during a World War I bond drive. What would really rocket America's devotion to the movies and its stars came a few years later. On May 16, 1929, to be exact.

> An Oscar is 13.5 inches tall, weighs 8.5 pounds, and stands on a five-spoked reel of film that signifies the original branches of the Academy: Actors, Writers, Directors, Producers, and Technicians.

If you happened to be in Hollywood that night and had five bucks to spare, you could have bought a ticket and joined about 250 celebrities and motion picture insiders at a small banquet in the Blossom Room of the Hollywood Roosevelt Hotel. This was the Academy of Motion Pictures Arts and Sciences' very first Academy Awards presentation.

There wasn't much edge-of-your-seat suspense, as winners had been announced three months earlier—so master of ceremonies Douglas Fairbanks only handed out the trophies. But whether it was Fairbanks's charisma or the sight of so many celebrities in one place, the event was such a hit that a radio station broadcast the event live the following year. The Academy also did a little fine-tuning and added a degree of drama by withholding the names of the winners. Starting in 1930, the Academy would issue results to newspapers in advance—but only on the condition they agreed to hold the results until 11 p.m. on awards night. This all worked perfectly until 1940, when stars arriving at the gala banquet found that the *Los Angeles Times* had already released the winners' names in its evening edition. The aftershock of the leak helped create an iconic staple of the Academy Award: the sealed envelope.

> So the cameras don't pick up an empty seat when a celebrity heads to the stage (or to powder her nose), "seat fillers" are used to sit in for a moment. These trained professionals are immediate family of Academy staff and members of the legal and accounting firms.

Whether the event was staged at hotels or theaters or auditoriums, the public always seemed to want more. On March 19, 1953, they got it when Bob Hope emceed the first televised broadcast. Even though the stars have changed and the ceremonies have ping-ponged between the Shrine Auditorium and the Dorothy Chandler Pavilion before settling in at the Kodak Theatre in 2002, one constant has been the fans. And that could mean you.

DO IT YOURSELF

To improve your chances of being ushered inside the Kodak Theatre to witness the Academy Awards presentation, you should either buy your own motion picture studio or star in a blockbuster picture. If neither of these options is viable, the best you can hope for is joining about 600 people who have literally won the lottery to be awarded a spot in the bleachers for the celebrities' arrival.

Hollywood & Highland Center, a $600-million retail and entertainment complex next to Grauman's Chinese Theatre on Hollywood Boulevard, is the home of the 3,300-seat Kodak Theatre. When the awards made this venue their home in 2001, people who had once camped out on the sidewalks for days learned that they wouldn't have to do this anymore.

For about one week each September, the Academy website opens up a special subsite where you can submit your application and then wait for the random drawing. If you win the golden ticket, you'll be ever-so-close to the celebs. How close? Close. The bleachers are right above the red carpet, so your calls of "Hey, George Clooney!" or "Hallie, I love you!" or "Ron Howard! Can you turn *USA 101* into a movie?" can be heard above the snapping of cameras. You may even lure a celebrity over to chat and sign an autograph.

Why the name Oscar? A few legends surround the name of the golden statuette, but the most plausible seems to be the one that involves an Academy's executive secretary, Margaret Herrick. When she saw the golden figure in 1931, she said it reminded her of her uncle Oscar Pierce. A reporter overheard the comment and ran it in the paper.

If you're in the stands, you are allowed to leave for restroom breaks and to stretch your legs, but be back by around 3:30 p.m. when the first limousines begin to arrive, although some Hollywood insiders claim that the flood of A-List celebs won't show up until around 4:30 p.m. From their limos (or hybrid cars), they'll begin the red carpet walk, stopping every few feet to trade quips with an entertainment reporter, show off their dresses or borrowed jewelry, or perhaps wave at you in the stands.

The flurry of film fanaticism is over all too soon. By 5:30 p.m. the stars have all arrived and are tucked inside the theater. Where do you go from here? Fans in the stands are invited across the street to the El Capitan Theatre for a private screening of the awards show that is also being watched by a billion other people. Always a billion.

CONTACTS

Academy of Motion Picture Arts
and Sciences
(310) 247-3000
www.oscars.org
www.oscars.org/bleachers
Registration, which lasts a week,
begins in late September. Winners are
notified in October.

www.seeing-stars.com
One of the best sites for all things
Hollywood.

For Lodging and Dining, see pp. 323–324

86. PEARL HARBOR
Oahu, Hawaiian Islands

Hours after Japanese aircraft and submarines attacked America's Pacific Fleet, Franklin Delano Roosevelt announced that December 7, 1941, was a "date which will live in infamy." The world knows it as Pearl Harbor Day.

HEROES AND HORRORS

It was a quiet Sunday morning on Oahu, where the battleships, cruisers, and destroyers of the U.S. Pacific Fleet were moored at Pearl Harbor. For many of the sailors stationed in this tropical paradise, Pearl Harbor was a dream duty assignment.

At the University of Arizona, the student union is shaped like the bow of the USS *Arizona*.

For a determined faction of the Japanese military, it was a perfect target.

Japan was already at war with China. It had moved into Manchuria and French Indochina, and was eager to invade the Dutch East Indies for oil and other resources. Knowing the United States would counter aggression with even stricter embargoes and, perhaps, force, hawks within the Japanese military and civilian government agreed that a preemptive strike was justified—and necessary. They pressured their colleagues until any objections were overwhelmed, and eventually even convinced the Emperor that an attack was needed.

For nearly a year pilots were trained and intelligence was collected.

CONTACTS

Academy of Motion Picture Arts
and Sciences
(310) 247-3000
www.oscars.org
www.oscars.org/bleachers
Registration, which lasts a week,
begins in late September. Winners are
notified in October.

www.seeing-stars.com
One of the best sites for all things
Hollywood.

For Lodging and Dining, see pp. 323–324

86. PEARL HARBOR
Oahu, Hawaiian Islands

Hours after Japanese aircraft and submarines attacked America's
Pacific Fleet, Franklin Delano Roosevelt announced that December 7,
1941, was a "date which will live in infamy." The world knows it as Pearl
Harbor Day.

HEROES AND HORRORS

It was a quiet Sunday morning on Oahu, where the battleships, cruisers, and
destroyers of the U.S. Pacific Fleet were moored at Pearl Harbor. For many
of the sailors stationed in this tropical paradise, Pearl Harbor was a dream
duty assignment.

For a determined faction of the Japanese military,
it was a perfect target.

**At the University of
Arizona, the student union
is shaped like the bow of
the USS *Arizona*.**

Japan was already at war with China. It had
moved into Manchuria and French Indochina, and
was eager to invade the Dutch East Indies for oil and
other resources. Knowing the United States would
counter aggression with even stricter embargoes and, perhaps, force, hawks
within the Japanese military and civilian government agreed that a preemptive strike was justified—and necessary. They pressured their colleagues
until any objections were overwhelmed, and eventually even convinced the
Emperor that an attack was needed.

For nearly a year pilots were trained and intelligence was collected.

DO IT YOURSELF

To improve your chances of being ushered inside the Kodak Theatre to witness the Academy Awards presentation, you should either buy your own motion picture studio or star in a blockbuster picture. If neither of these options is viable, the best you can hope for is joining about 600 people who have literally won the lottery to be awarded a spot in the bleachers for the celebrities' arrival.

Hollywood & Highland Center, a $600-million retail and entertainment complex next to Grauman's Chinese Theatre on Hollywood Boulevard, is the home of the 3,300-seat Kodak Theatre. When the awards made this venue their home in 2001, people who had once camped out on the sidewalks for days learned that they wouldn't have to do this anymore.

For about one week each September, the Academy website opens up a special subsite where you can submit your application and then wait for the random drawing. If you win the golden ticket, you'll be ever-so-close to the celebs. How close? Close. The bleachers are right above the red carpet, so your calls of "Hey, George Clooney!" or "Hallie, I love you!" or "Ron Howard! Can you turn *USA 101* into a movie?" can be heard above the snapping of cameras. You may even lure a celebrity over to chat and sign an autograph.

Why the name Oscar? A few legends surround the name of the golden statuette, but the most plausible seems to be the one that involves an Academy's executive secretary, Margaret Herrick. When she saw the golden figure in 1931, she said it reminded her of her uncle Oscar Pierce. A reporter overheard the comment and ran it in the paper.

If you're in the stands, you are allowed to leave for restroom breaks and to stretch your legs, but be back by around 3:30 p.m. when the first limousines begin to arrive, although some Hollywood insiders claim that the flood of A-List celebs won't show up until around 4:30 p.m. From their limos (or hybrid cars), they'll begin the red carpet walk, stopping every few feet to trade quips with an entertainment reporter, show off their dresses or borrowed jewelry, or perhaps wave at you in the stands.

The flurry of film fanaticism is over all too soon. By 5:30 p.m. the stars have all arrived and are tucked inside the theater. Where do you go from here? Fans in the stands are invited across the street to the El Capitan Theatre for a private screening of the awards show that is also being watched by a billion other people. Always a billion.

Under the command of Adm. Isoroku Yamamoto, the Kido Butai (Striking Force) carrier battle group sailed toward a staging position northwest of Hawaii. Even though the first wave of attacking aircraft was detected by radar operators at Pearl Harbor, the planes were misidentified as six B-17s flying in from the American mainland.

Most Americans believed that any Japanese strike would occur thousands of miles away, in the Philippines. At 7:48 a.m. that Sunday many of the sailors and citizens who watched the first wave of Japanese fighters, dive bombers, and torpedo planes sail overhead thought it was merely military maneuvers. It was a deadly mistake.

When word went out, "Air raid Pearl Harbor—this is not a drill," defenders ill-prepared for a direct attack on home turf had to deal with ammunition held under lock and key and figure out ways to protect thousands of sailors aboard battleships, cruisers, and destroyers, as well as other high-value targets. To ensure there would be no counterattack, Japanese pilots strafed Hickam Airfield, Wheeler Field, and Bellows Field, where planes were parked wingtip to wingtip. Midget Japanese submarines were dispatched as well, with some breaching the mouth of the harbor and firing their torpedoes while others were sunk by patrolling warships.

During two aerial attack waves, displays of American heroism would lead to the presentation of 14 Medals of Honor. But when the last of the 353 Japanese planes flew away 90 minutes after the attack began, approximately 2,400 soldiers, sailors, and civilians were dead or dying; 1,139 were wounded; and 21 vessels—including five battleships—were crippled or completely disabled. Of the American fatalities, nearly half of the total—1,177 men—were from a shell that hit the forward magazine and exploded the USS *Arizona*.

To give himself an out, Admiral Yamamoto insisted the attack begin a half-hour *after* Japan told the U.S. that peace negotiations were over. But by the time personnel at the Japanese Embassy finished transcribing the 5,000-word message, planes were already bombing Pearl Harbor.

But the Japanese failed to dismantle one thing: America's fighting spirit. Following the attack, Admiral Yamamoto observed, "I fear all we have done is to awaken a sleeping giant."

THE EXPERIENCE

Besides the USS *Arizona*, three other battleships were sunk and four more were damaged, along with three cruisers, three destroyers, a minelayer, and

188 aircraft. The USS *Arizona* Memorial, operated by the National Park Service, honors everyone lost on that day.

The ten-ton anchor from the doomed ship is on display at the Visitor Center, where you receive a numbered ticket for a scheduled shuttle boat to the Memorial. Be there early if you can. With 1.5 million visitors arriving each year, the 4,500 tickets issued each day are usually distributed early. Before you go to the Memorial, you'll see a 23-minute documentary film on the attack. For more in-depth understanding, you can rent a narrated audio tour featuring WWII Navy vet Ernest Borgnine.

> Symbolism is omnipresent at the memorial. Peaks at the ends and a dip in the middle represent pre- and postwar pride interrupted by national depression; the seven windows on each wall symbolize the date, with the total—21—representing a 21-gun salute.

When you reach the Memorial, you may be moved by its eerie stillness. The sunken ship is in fact an active U.S. military cemetery, with the bodies of many of the 1,177 men still entombed in the wreckage. When vessels of the United States Navy, Coast Guard, Merchant Marine, and foreign countries enter Pearl Harbor, crews "man the rails," standing at attention at the ship's guard rails to salute the USS *Arizona* and her fallen crew.

As you step onto the Memorial, you walk upon what is essentially a floating bridge that spans the hull of the battleship. An opening in the floor looks through a few feet of clear water and over the deck of the ship that, to this day, continues to seep a trickle of oil. The "tears of the *Arizona*," they say, will continue to flow until the last survivor has passed away. At the far end, the Shrine Room is highlighted by a marble wall bearing the names of all those killed aboard this ship.

Take a few moments and read their names. If you arrive with flowers, leis, or wreaths, you can pay your respects by dropping them into the water as a salute to the men who awoke that morning to the sound of bullets and bombs—and never awoke again.

A simple gesture of peace to offset the thought of war.

CONTACTS

World War II Valor in the Pacific National Monument
(808) 422-3300
www.nps.gov/usar

www.gohawaii.com
www.visit-oahu.com

For Lodging and Dining, see pp. 324–325

87. SURFING
Hawaii, California, and Along America's Coasts

Of sports that convey the essence of Zen, surfing may top the list. Or tetherball. Maybe its appeal is its simplicity. All you need is a surfboard and a wave to enjoy a pastime that's part sport, part recreation, and totally natural. Totally.

There are waves breaking along coastlines around the continental United States, but to reach the beach whose history is attached to surfing, you'll have to head about 2,500 miles off the west coast and rip the curl on the shores of Hawaii.

DUKE IS KING

Credit Beach Boys genius Brian Wilson for linking the shores of southern California into the legend of surfing. Following the release of a string of surfing related songs in the early 1960s, much of the world believed that surfing had originated off the coast of Malibu.

It's true that surfers were riding the waves in the '60s, but, to be fair, it was the 1760s. To be even more fair, surfing probably goes back as far as the 1500s or even earlier and originated in Polynesia. The first record of surfing written by a European was in 1779 when Capt. James King, during a British exploratory tour of the Hawaiian Islands, wrote in his journal of as many as 30 Hawaiians "taking each a long narrow board, rounded at the ends" and setting out from shore.

Surfer slang is as cool as the surf culture. (For example, "aggro" means hardcore aggressive surfing; a "cavefish" is a surfer who lacks a tan; and "ba roos" means extremely cool or awesome.) Visit www.rippinh2o.com for the best of the rest.

For those who made it past the breaking waves, the pleasure was waiting for the large third wave in a set that would lift the men and their boards back toward the shore, often to safety— but sometimes to a painful landing on the rocks. King concluded his entry: "The boldness and address, with which we saw them perform these difficult and dangerous manoeuvres, was altogether astonishing, and is scarcely to be credited."

The spectacle was astonishing to westerners who were deathly afraid of deep water. For Hawaiians, though, surfing was an integral part of the culture. Carved into lava rock on the islands are ancient petroglyphs of surfers, who relied on surfing to retain their strength and agility. Native islanders sang chants that celebrated the most impressive feats of surfers but, unlike the Beach Boys' efforts, none of these tunes ever cracked the Top Ten.

There were many rituals associated with surfing, from the cutting of the wood to its shaping and coloring. But the rites of surfing displeased the New England missionaries who, after their arrival in 1820, worked to get Hawaiians on the straight and narrow. Convinced that surfing was an extension of heathen voodoo, the missionaries pretty much killed the pastime. Thankfully, in the early 1900s their influence was eclipsed by the legendary swimming and surfing prodigy Duke Kahanamoku.

If you're a passionate surfer or surfing fan, attend the three competitions that comprise the Triple Crown of Surfing, all but one of which take place on the north shore of Oahu in the winter. Men compete at the Reef Hawaiian Pro at Haleiwa Ali'i Beach Park; the O'Neill World Cup of Surfing at Sunset Beach; and the Billabong Pipeline Masters at the Banzai Pipeline. Visit www.triplecrownofsurfing.com.

In 1905 the teenager helped organize the surfing club Hui Nalu (Club of the Waves), which accelerated the sport's resurgence. When he wasn't competing as an Olympic swimmer—at four games—Kahanamoku traveled the world to share the excitement of surfing. And in southern California in 1910, a developer named Henry Huntington enlisted Irish-Hawaiian George Freeth to demonstrate surfing at the opening of a local railroad. Within minutes, Californians were taken by surfing's beauty and grace. When Kahanamoku arrived a few years later, he helped establish Huntington Beach as the capital of southern California surfing.

Technological improvements began making surfing easier. Breakthroughs included new materials—balsa wood and fiberglass boards; boards shortened from 16 feet to a more manageable 8 feet or less; and skegs that, like rudders, made surfboards more stable and maneuverable. It was a cool sport. Legends who rode the big waves were featured in magazine spreads, and movies like 1959's *Gidget* and 1966's *The Endless Summer* inspired a nation of amateur surfers. Soon, kooks and grommets everywhere could see themselves riding the waves.

DO IT YOURSELF

Why surf? Once you catch a wave that's right for you, you'll know. It's an extreme sensation that heightens your awareness. You may have looked at the ocean before, but when you are waiting on your board, you actually *see it*. When the right wave comes along, you are in tune with it and then you become a part of it. Your mind and body focus only on the wave's curl and shape as you aim for the part of the tide that'll sustain your ride. In a word, *bitchin'*.

Cocoa Beach, Florida, bills itself as the "small wave capital of the world," which is kind of like a hotelier advertising the "world's cheapest luxury inn." Still, if you're a *kook* (a beginner), this may be a good place to start because right on Cocoa Beach is Ron Jon's, the world's largest surf shop. It's open 24 hours a day in case you're inspired to attack a gnarly wave at 3 a.m. They also offer a surfing school to teach the basics: how to paddle to the breaks, judge the right wave, and catch it back to shore. With a bit of coordination, even beginners can grasp the rudiments of surfing in a day.

Stage two may take you to Huntington Beach, California (aka Surf City, USA), where surfers cluster like ducks near the breaks at the Huntington Beach Pier. Many local surf shops offer lessons and one lesson is to avoid Huntington Beach Pier. The shops direct novices to less crowded areas and after you've learned to catch the perfect wave, you can paddle over to the Pier and hang with the locals.

To experience the thrills that hooked Duke Kahanamoku, paddle out to Oahu. On the waves off Waikiki, the biggest challenge is avoiding other beginners and their loose boards, but there are many surf schools and board rentals there. If, after about five years, you feel ready for a bigger challenge, head to Oahu's Waimea Bay on the north shore. In the wintertime, the waves start to peak there and at nearby Sunset Beach and Banzai Pipeline. Since these beaches are where some of the world's largest waves are crashing, they attract some of the world's most skilled and experienced big wave surfers.

In the summer at Huntington Beach, the U.S. Open of Surfing draws nearly half a million fans to watch 600 top surfers in action at a festival that also features outdoor concerts and competitions including skateboarding, freestyle bicycling, and inline skating. Check *www .usopenofsurfing.com* for details.

If you don't have the experience to surf these monsters, have the common sense to avoid them. From the shore, spectators live vicariously through the feats of extraordinary athletes. After being towed out to the breaks by motorized wave runners, surfers wait for waves as large as *30 feet* to lift them up, put them in the curl, and rocket them in as they perform, in the words of Captain King, "dangerous manoeuvres, altogether astonishing, and scarcely to be credited."

CONTACTS

Space Coast Office of Tourism
(Cocoa Beach, Florida)
(321) 433-4470
(877) 572-3224
www.space-coast.com

Huntington Beach, California
(714) 969-3492
www.surfcityusa.com

Oahu Visitors Bureau
(808) 524-0722
(877) 525-6248
www.visit-oahu.com

www.surfrider.org
www.surfline.com
www.isurfing.com
www.surfermag.com
www.surfguru.com
www.mavsurfer.com
www.ronjons.com
www.bigwaveshawaii.com

For Lodging and Dining, see pp. 324–325

88. LUAUS
Hawaiian Islands

Given a choice to move to Hawaii, wrap ourselves in sarongs, wear leis, drink coconut milk, and hang out at a luau, most of us would probably quit work and catch the first steamship west. Well, we do have that choice because luaus are still a part of Hawaiian culture. But before you submit your resignation, learn a bit about their history and presentation. After that, you can tell your boss aloha.

FEAST MEETS WEST

Remember long-ago Thanksgivings when the relatives would come over? The dining room table was reserved for the grown-ups while the children (anyone between the ages of 3 and 18) ate at a folding table. That's kind of how it was in Hawaii before luaus made the scene. Because of religious restrictions, prior to 1819 Hawaiian men and women ate separately. Even some foods, like pork, bananas, coconuts, and certain types of fish were off-limits to women. They weren't even given a folding table.

If you're traveling to Hawaii in peak season (December–March), book your luau well in advance.

A major change came in 1819, when King Kamehameha II (short for

Kalani Kaleiaʻimoku o Kaiwikapu o Laʻamea i Kauikawekiu Ahilapalapa Kaliʻi Kauinamoku o Kahekili Kalaninui i Mamao ʻIolani i Ka Liholiho) introduced *ʻAi Noa,* which abolished *kapu,* the strict system of religious taboos. With that, he was able to sit down to dinner with his mom and could also invite other women over to dine with him at a royal feast. The feasts were called *ʻaha ʻaina,* and one of the favorite dishes at these communal gatherings was a mixture of taro leaves and chicken baked in coconut milk. That dish was called *luau*; by the mid-1800s, the feast itself had adopted this name.

Those luaus sound as good as movies make them look. Around a centerpiece made of ti leaves, ferns, and native flowers, platters of roasted meat, sweet potatoes, dried fish, and dried meat were served, while bowls of poi (mashed taro) were set out and covered with leaves. The kitchen staff solved the problem of selecting just the right silverware by not using any. Whether diners were eating poi, pork, fish, chicken, or dog, every food was finger food.

In 1847, the son of King Kamehameha II—his buddies called him King Kamehameha III—proved the banana hadn't fallen far from the tree when he hosted one of the largest luaus in history. While other ingredients were later introduced to luaus, on the grocery list for this one were 271 hogs, 3,125 salt fish, 1,820 fresh fish, 2,245 coconuts, 482 large gourds filled with poi, and 4,000 taro plants.

Luaus seemed custom made for the genial Kalakaua, a Hawaiian king of the late 19th century. Kalakaua was such a fan of parties and dances that on his 50th birthday, in 1886, 1,500 friends (who were fed in shifts of 500) came over for his celebratory luau. Known as the "Merrie Monarch," he wrote the state song of Hawaii, helped revive the sport of surfing, and popularized the ukulele. He even brought back the Hawaiian art of hula dancing.

In many ways, today's luaus haven't strayed too far from the days of King Kalakaua. The only difference is that you'll be there.

> Ancient hula dancing, *kahiko,* is accompanied by chanting and traditional percussion instruments. The hula that evolved under Western influence is called *ʻauana* and is accompanied by song and instruments such as ukulele, guitar, and bass. The motions of a hula dancer are meant to tell a story. In 1978, a determined dancer interpreted Leo Tolstoy's *Anna Karenina* in a marathon hula lasting 33 hours.

DO IT YOURSELF

Hawaii isn't like the rest of America, and that's not a slam at all—it's just my observation that they ran the table when it came to claiming beautiful scenery. Tropical flowers, stunning beaches, rolling waves…all of this is a backdrop to what may be the most exotic meal of your life.

Don't expect any breakfast luaus. Most luaus start around dusk; many are held in the open air on the beach, while others are hosted in fragrant tropical courtyards, at indoor theaters, or in amphitheaters. Reference a few of the websites below and, with a little sleuthing, you can learn which luaus offer touches you like, such as a lei greeting or an oceanfront setting. You won't have to worry about hula dancers—they are standard at every luau.

> **Local families will host luaus for notable occasions such as special birthdays, weddings, or graduations.**

Now that you've starched and pressed your favorite Hawaiian shirt and put on your Bermuda shorts, here's how your evening may unfold. After a lei greeting, tropical drinks, and entertainment, two natives (or two hourly employees dressed like what tourists think natives look like) conduct the Imu Ceremony, when a pig that has been slowly roasting beneath a layer of ti and banana leaves for most of the day in a traditional underground pit, the Imu, is unearthed and taken to the kitchen for preparation.

In addition to Kalua pig, you'll feast on *laulau* (fish or chicken wrapped in ti leaves), lomi salmon (salted fish marinated in lemon juice, tomatoes, and onions), ahi poki (ahi tuna marinated in seaweed, chilies, and nut oils), rice, plantains, yams, breadfruit, sweet potatoes, and nut relish. You'll have a chance to cleanse your palate with poi—the remnants of the taro plant root that has been beaten, cooked, and watered down to a bland, soft paste.

Throughout, you'll listen to traditional Hawaiian tunes performed on ukulele and steel guitar; feel the heat from fire dancers; and see hula dancers conducting the most incredible navel maneuvers since the voyage of Teddy Roosevelt's Great White Fleet. Chances are that some audience members will also be invited to demonstrate their hula skills.

At the end, the entertainers go into overdrive, wrapping up the event with a spectacular finish. Luau? No. Lu-wow!

CONTACTS

www.hawaii-luaus.com
www.mauihawaiiluau.com
www.hawaiiluaufacts.org

For Lodging and Dining, see pp. 324–325

89. BALD EAGLES
Alaska, Florida, and Minnesota

Nearly every schoolkid knows that as the nation was being built, the Founding Fathers had narrowed the choice of our national bird down to two contestants: the wild turkey and the bald eagle.

Despite getting nearly everything right, Benjamin Franklin got this one wrong. He lobbied for the turkey, but in the end the vote, rightfully, went to the bald eagle. Whether it's perched on the arm of a handler or, better yet, flying free in a wide-open sky, its dignity, power, and presence is a soaring reflection of America.

BALD EAGLES ON THE BRINK

To be fair, members of the Continental Congress weren't the only ones who were captivated by the bald eagle. Native American tribes revered the bird as a sacred object, and their headdresses and fans were adorned with bald eagle feathers. To this day, many tribes use naturally molted eagle feathers for religious rites and as rewards for outstanding achievements.

Which makes it all so hard to believe that just a few decades ago, bald eagles were on the brink of extinction. In addition to loss of habitat and, incredibly, hunters who kept them in their sights, a toxic pesticide called DDT was being indiscriminately sprayed in fields and forests. After its residue washed into waterways, it flowed up the food chain. Fish that were affected by the polluted water were eaten by eagles, which laid eggs too fragile to withstand the weight of the nesting parent. By the early 1960s, the estimated total of bald eagles in the Lower 48 had fallen to 450 nesting pairs.

If you live in Florida or spend any time there, contact the Audubon Society's Birds of Prey Center in Maitland *(407-644-0190 or www.audubonofflorida.org)* for information about joining the Bald Eagle Watch Program.

In 1967 the bald eagle was placed on the list of endangered species and by 1972 DDT had been banned. After conservationists, environmentalists, and the government teamed up, the bald eagle population more than doubled. By mid-1995, the United States Fish and Wildlife Service felt the population had reached the point where it could change the bird's status from endangered to threatened. Its numbers have continued to grow to an estimated 11,000 nesting pairs in the Lower 48, and an estimated 50,000 nesting pairs in Alaska alone.

On June 28, 2007, the change in fortune prompted another change in its status when the bald eagle was taken off the list of threatened species.

Although the decision led to concern that it would lead to open season on the icon, the Bald and Golden Eagle Protection Act will remain a deterrent.

America can justifiably look at the resurrection of the bald eagle as a success story.

And every American should look at a bald eagle.

DO IT YOURSELF

First off, the bald eagle is amazing. It lives in nests that could double as dorm rooms, averaging about ten feet deep and eight feet across and weighing as much as a ton. These nests are the birthplace of eaglets that earn their reputation as the fastest-growing bird in America by leaping from four ounces to ten pounds in ten weeks. By then they are fully grown and ready to leave the nest.

Thanks to relatively undeveloped wilderness, plentiful lakes, and an abundant supply of fish, more bald eagles live in Alaska than anywhere else. Adjacent to the Tongass National Forest, a salmon-spawning stream called Eagle Creek attracts eagles year 'round, but especially in late June when as many as 300 bald eagles perch along the stream and in the branches of trees for the all-you-can-eat buffet.

When they catch a thermal—an uplift of warm air—they'll accelerate with each beat of their eight-foot wingspan and soar as fast as 45 miles per hour. How do such large birds move so quickly? The secret may be in their aerodynamic shape as well as hollow bones that help reduce their weight. You've heard about their eyesight? It's sharp. Their vision is up to ten times keener than yours, which means they can spot a rabbit from as far as three miles away.

There are a few ways to improve your own odds of actually seeing a bald eagle from just a few feet away, and that involves traveling to Alaska, Minnesota, or Florida, which, respectively, have America's highest bald eagle populations. Florida has the advantage of the Eagle Watch program, in which a group of volunteer citizen-scientists monitor the state's eagle populations. You can be one of them. Trained in eagle behavior, volunteers are assigned to watch the nests and share their observations with state and federal wildlife agencies.

"It doesn't take much time to check on a nest," says the Audubon Society's Linda White, coordinator of the program. "We provide a training manual; volunteers attend a training workshop and then go to nests to observe the birds."

Whether or not you're part of an organized program, White suggests that when watching nests, you should bring a pair of binoculars or a spotting scope and tripod. Considering the depth of the nests, she advises staying a few hundred feet away to gain a better view of the eagles' behavior.

If you'd rather not wait in the Florida woods, head to the National Eagle Center in Wabasha, Minnesota. Below Lake Pepin, a five-mile stretch of the Mississippi River narrows into a channel that creates warmer waters that attract up to 300 bald eagles a day between December and March (with enough eagles sticking around the rest of the year to make it worth a visit anytime).

> The law limits the use of bald or golden eagle feathers to spiritual use by individuals of certifiable Native American ancestry.

The center, a nonprofit educational institution, points out that in the 1960s only a single nesting pair lived along the 260 miles between Wabasha and Rock Island, Illinois. Today there's an estimated 175 active pairs. At the center, the team will bring out rescued eagles that have become their goodwill ambassadors and will explain the significance bald eagles have to both Native American and modern American cultures.

While it admittedly takes some effort, you can also travel to Haines, Alaska, for the world's largest gathering of bald eagles. During the Alaska Bald Eagle Festival (and even when the festival's over) as many as *3,000* bald eagles cluster along eight miles of riverfront. To see one bald eagle is a thrill. To see thousands is a dream.

You'll find them scoping out a river filled with salmon and deciding which they'll have for dinner. When an eagle spies the catch of the day, it will swoop down and skim just above the surface before thrusting its feet forward and dropping its razor-sharp talons into the stream. Moments later, it's beating its wings to fly away with its newly acquired cargo.

I'd like to see a wild turkey do that.

CONTACTS

Alaska Bald Eagle Festival
Haines, Alaska
(907) 766-3094
www.baldeaglefestival.org

Audubon Society
www.audubon.org

National Eagle Center
Wabasha, Minnesota
(651) 565-4989
www.nationaleaglecenter.org

Juneau Raptor Center
Juneau, Alaska
907-586-8393
www.juneauraptorcenter.org

For Lodging and Dining, see pp. 325–326

90. THE IDITAROD
Alaska

There are a lot of tough sports out there, but none tougher than the Iditarod Trail Sled Dog Race. In fact, more people have climbed Mount Everest than have ever wrapped up this race.

JUST SAY SNOW

Where there's gold, there are people willing to do whatever it takes to get it. Prospectors proved this in Alaska when several major gold strikes (and about 30 minor ones) cropped up between the 1880s and 1920s. Since each was in a remote and frozen section of an already remote territory, prospectors had to resort to the rugged Iditarod Trail, a route first carved out by Native American Inupiaq and Athabaskans.

Roughly 1,000 miles of wilderness separated Knik and Seward from the gold that was hidden near Nome, and to reach it men had to rely on the SUVs of the day: dogsleds. Powered by a 20-dogpower engine, the musher and his team could haul a half-ton of freight, mail, and passengers to Nome on a hard three-week slog.

Things changed in the 1920s. Gold was nearly tapped out and airplane travel took off as bush pilots proved they could move men and supplies faster and over greater distances. Apart from hauling supplies between native villages and patrolling the Alaskan wilderness during World War II, dog teams kept losing ground to new inventions like snowmachines.

Arrive early in Anchorage and plan to attend the Musher Drawing Banquet, which is held the Thursday before the race. It costs about $65 and it's when all the mushers draw for their bib numbers to determine when they'll leave the starting line.

By the mid-1960s few Alaskans recalled the importance of sled dog teams. Fortunately, Dorothy Page was one who did. In 1967, to commemorate the centennial of the purchase of Alaska from Russia, the armchair historian envisioned a way to celebrate sled dogs, the Iditarod Trail, and the pioneering spirit of Alaska. Her idea for an Iditarod Race was seconded by musher Joe Redington, Sr., and Norman Vaughan, who had once been a dog wrangler for Adm. Richard Byrd in Antarctica. Thanks to musher clubs and volunteers, the Susitna Valley portion of the long-neglected Iditarod Trail was cleared in time for a 25-mile version of the Iditarod Trail Sled Dog Race in 1967 and again in 1969. By 1973 the decision to run an even longer race gathered support after the U.S. Army cleared the entire trail as part of winter exercises. Although the length of the race increased dramatically, from 25 to more than 1,000 miles, 22 of the 34 mushers made it through.

DO IT YOURSELF

Since the race relies on nearly 2,000 volunteers, many attendees have signed up online to participate in a free two-and-a-half-hour training class to become a "certified dog handler."

"You learn how to move the teams into the chute and to the starting line," explains Iditarod spokesman Chas St. George. "But you're not really *leading* them to the line. They're so ready to race that they end up pulling you along."

The race kicks off at the corner of 4th Avenue and D Street in Anchorage on the first Saturday in March at 10 a.m. After an honorary musher departs, approximately 75 mushers are waiting to take off at two-minute intervals. Dogs are barking and baying; people are cheering; and announcers are giving brief bios of the racers before the countdown releases them to tear off down the avenue. This is where you'll notice that some folks have super-sized their experience by hitching a ride aboard a competition dog sled. How'd they do it? They bid for the privilege in an online auction (held between October 1 and January 31) and for around $2,000 the winning Idita-Riders get to climb into the sled baskets for an 11-mile ride through Anchorage.

In 1925, a diphtheria epidemic swept across Alaska and threatened the Inuit children of remote Nome. A Pony Express–type relay of dog teams was organized to deliver serum. Gunnar Kaasen followed his lead dog, Balto, through an 80-mph blizzard to Nome in time to save hundreds of lives. A statue of Balto can be found in New York's Central Park.

Saturday's ceremonial start leads to Sunday's "restart" in the Matanuska-Susitna Valley at Willow Lake. This is when the clock officially starts ticking for the field of contenders. The first musher departs at 2 p.m. and glides past a long, long corridor of cheering and waving supporters, many of whom have traveled the 70 miles from Anchorage to be there. After the mushers pass the crowd, they disappear into the Alaskan wilderness.

While you're back at your cozy bed and breakfast, these mushers are on their way to Nome. In the first 182 miles they'll travel from 77 feet to 3,177 feet above sea level as they head into and then through the heart of North America's largest mountain range, the Alaska Range. Carrying a heavy sleeping bag, ax, snowshoes, and food for themselves and their dogs, they'll pass remote villages and sleep in temperatures that can drop to 60 below. They'll race through white forests and across frozen rivers and encounter moose and bears and face blizzards and whiteouts. Mushers will coach their teams of canine athletes and become their vet techs, their nutritionists, and group leaders. They'll cross the Yukon Delta and then the Gold Coast of the Seward Peninsula before racing toward the finish line in Nome, where everyone is waiting.

The Iditarod Trail was designated one of the first four National Historic Trails in 1978.

When a musher and his team are spotted on the outskirts of town, the city fire siren wails and thousands of residents and tourists drop what they're doing and rush to Front Street to welcome the team. People do this day and night until the last musher and his team have arrived. Later, about 750 mushers, officials, and members of the general public will gather at the Nome Awards Banquet to watch the winning mushers receive their cash prizes and trophies and hear their tales from the trail.

After it's all over, some mushers will hang up their parkas and look back on a successful run, while others will say farewell forever to a race they couldn't complete. Some are already looking forward to next March and one more chance to conquer America's Last Great Race.

CONTACTS

Iditarod Race Headquarters
(907) 248-MUSH (6874)
www.iditarod.com

For Lodging and Dining, see p. 326

ACROSS AMERICA

What can I say? Since I was a kid I've had a desire to explore America, and since I've been an adult I have—and have done what I can to coax people to do the same.

If you're old enough to recall Charles Kuralt, you'll remember how he gently guided his audience to the people and places that we all should know but were too busy to see. While it wasn't intentional, it turns out that most of the selections here—classic American pastimes and events such as drive-in theaters, quilting bees, pie-baking contests, and touching naturalization ceremonies—reflect the spirit of Kuralt's favorite places because these are all simple things that everyone of any age can witness and experience.

For extra credit, tie it all together by taking to the roads or rails on a cross-country trip. As you see and experience the things in this and the preceding chapters, understand that they were chosen because they are, arguably, uniquely American and therefore a part of us.

Which means they are meant for you.

91. BARBERSHOP QUARTETS
Across America

At a barbershop quartet concert I recall one of the performers slipping in a note of encouragement. "If you can sing *'Happy Birthday,'*" he said, "then you can sing barbershop."

Well, that leaves me out. But for anyone who's mastered the tune, there are thousands of people who would love to harmonize with you. Why not? The American-born style of barbershop is about the pure joy of singing. It also brings to mind an era when folks frolicked on the shores of Coney Island; rode bicycles built for two; and enjoyed country drives in their merry Oldsmobiles.

FOUR ON THE ROOF

Most of us are familiar with the distinct sound and harmonies of barbershop, but few of us, I'd wager, realize it didn't really take off until the late 1930s. And who knew that barbershop, like jazz, was quite possibly the creation of African Americans?

The music was the result of informal singalongs in the late 1800s at gathering spots that actually did include barbershops. References to the style were already being made in African-American communities in the early 1900s, but barbershop's great leap forward wouldn't come until 1938 when a tax attorney named, incredibly, Owen Cash, helped bring barbershop quartet singing into the mainstream with the formation of the Society for the Preservation and Encouragement of Barber Shop Quartet Singing in America. Later, to save time and ink, the famed S.P.E.B.S.Q.S.A. would be abbreviated to the Barbershop Harmony Society.

At the group's first gathering on April 11, 1938, 26 charter members met in Tulsa, at the Tulsa Club of the Alvi Hotel. Their spontaneous rooftop barbershop singing drew the police, who told the singers to keep it down. How could they resist singing?

The Barbershop Harmony Society's takes seriously its role of promoting and safeguarding the heritage of the singing style. Its website has digitized downloadable recordings of international competitions going back more than a decade. To find your favorite barbershop songs, visit www.harmonymarketplace.com.

With a lead, tenor, baritone, and bass and the sound of the elusive "barbershop chord," barbershop was like audio onomotopoeia—it sounded just like it should.

The nostalgic singing style matched the Rockwell caricature of four jovial white men singing old-fashioned tunes with clear lyrics and simple melodies. Barbershop was a hit; in fact it was so much fun that it couldn't be contained by a single gender. In 1945, another Tulsan, Edna Mae Anderson, created the Sweet Adelines so women could harmonize with their own a cappella quartets. Eventually, barbershop couldn't be contained by America. Today there are barbershop quartets in New Zealand, Australia, Britain, Ireland, Holland, Saudi Arabia, Sweden, Scandinavia, Germany, Japan, South Africa, and other countries. If the members don't speak English, they learn the songs phonetically.

The four-part harmonies first performed in minstrel shows, on vaudeville stages, in barbershops, and on a rooftop in Tulsa now spread goodwill around the world. Makes you wonder how successful the Beatles could have been if they had they only recorded "Coney Island Baby."

DO IT YOURSELF

Thanks to the effort of the Barbershop Harmony Society, Sweet Adelines International, and Harmony Incorporated (a sister organization), there are thousands of barbershop quartets and choruses performing across the nation at venues including churches, schools, hospitals, and senior centers. The B.H.S. also hosts 32 district conventions a year (16 in the spring, and 16 in the fall) so odds are there'll be one near you. These conventions feature classes as well as competitions, with a good-natured mood from start to finish.

"On Saturday night, some districts will host 'Sing with the Champs,'" explains Todd Wilson of the Barbershop Harmony Society. "For about $25 that goes to charity, a fan can get up and sing with their favorite group."

The Osmond Brothers got their start singing barbershop on *The Andy Williams Show*. Other practitioners of the art form include Harry Truman, Bing Crosby, Irving Berlin, Frank Sinatra, Burl Ives, Gordon Lightfoot, Victor Borge, Dick Van Dyke, and Groucho Marx.

That is, of course, if they know the words.

"Of course they know the words!" Wilson insists. "These people are *fans*. They may have the group's CDs and videos and if they want to sing 'I'm Looking Over a Four-Leaf Clover' then they'll know the words. Some people nail it. *Just nail it.* They've studied all four parts because they may be avid followers of a particular group. And when the song is over, they'll get a faux gold medal and a Polaroid signed by the entire group."

(NOTE: Bono, if you are reading this, please include a "Sing with the Champs" segment on U2's next tour. Thx, Gary)

Some of the trickiest and most impressive singalongs take place in the A.H.S.O.W. Rooms, where members of the Ancient Harmonious Society of Woodshedders work on new tunes.

One of the biggest four-part harmony hits ever was "Mr. Sandman" by the Chordettes of Sheboygan, Wisconsin. It made the charts in 1954.

"Early barbershop had no written arrangements," explains Wilson. "People would buy a piano score and study it and stand around and try to create harmonies. That's what happens in the A.H.S.O.W. Rooms. One person will know the melody and sing it, and the others have to join in and figure out their harmonies to a song they've never heard before. It's spontaneous harmonizing by ear. If you're a good woodshedder, you can do it."

To really leap into barbershop, arrange your vacation days to coincide with the annual international convention of the B.H.S., which is held in early July. While you may think you'll only see men in striped vests and handlebar mustaches, many barbershoppers are now GQ-looking men in their 20s singing current—for barbershop anyway—songs released in the 1960s.

Of course, nearly every quartet is expected to know the "polecats," traditional favorites like "Down by the Old Mill Stream," "Let Me Call You Sweetheart," "My Wild Irish Rose," "Sweet Adeline," "Wait 'til the Sun Shines, Nellie," and "You Tell Me Your Dream (I'll Tell You Mine)." The songs give complete strangers the chance to meet new friends by harmonizing on a song everyone knows.

Singing and making new friends. Pretty nice way to live your life.

CONTACTS

Barbershop Harmony Society
(615) 823-3993
(800) 876-SING
www.barbershop.org

Sweet Adelines International
www.sweetadelinesintl.org

Harmony Incorporated
www.harmonyinc.com

Ancient Harmonious Society of Woodshedders
www.harmonize.com/ahsow

For Lodging and Dining, see "Across America" p. 285

92. CROSS-COUNTRY ROAD TRIPS
Across America

Most of us lose track of how large America really is because we can cross it from coast to coast in less than six hours. If you want to avoid America, take a plane. But if you have a desire to see it—really see it and understand it and appreciate the diversity that's invisible at 40,000 feet and 600 miles per hour—get in your car and go.

DRIVE TIME

In 1903, Dr. Horatio Nelson Jackson took up a $50 bet from members of San Francisco's University Club. Jackson insisted it was possible to drive across America by automobile—and he'd be the first to do it. On May 23, he climbed into his 20-horsepower Winton touring car with his co-driver, Sewall Crocker, and headed out of San Francisco.

A few weeks later he picked up a bulldog named Bud in Idaho, and just over two months after starting out, the trio rode triumphantly into New York City.

To understand how extraordinary Jackson's journey was, keep in mind there was hardly anyplace to buy gas between San Francisco and New York; there were no roadside hotels; no chain restaurants; no television; no radio; and, most incredibly, only 150 miles of paved roads in the entire nation. That would soon change.

> If you don't belong to the American Automobile Association, join. Part of your membership includes roadside assistance and trip planning. Go to *www.aaa.com.*

After Jackson's triumph, the boom of the automobile industry completely reshaped how Americans viewed their nation: With a car you could go virtually anywhere. The Automotive Age also changed the nation itself. Cars needed roads so paved roads were built. They needed gasoline so service stations opened. Drivers needed food so roadside restaurants were created. Drivers also needed a place to rest so motor courts and then motels and then hotels were built. By the 1950s, the Interstate Highway System was bypassing two-lane rural roads to create webs of asphalt between major cities, national borders, and both coasts.

We have the good fortune to live in a nation that is designed for road trips. So if you can spare the time and work up the passion, all you need to do is gas it up and hit the road.

DO IT YOURSELF

Yes, I know gas is expensive and so are hotels and restaurants and attractions. And, yes, I know time is tight and you're not sure if you can collect enough sick leave or vacation days to pull it off. But trust me, if you do it right one thing is certain: At the end of your own road trip you'll have completed a journey that you will never forget. In fact, you may even be so impressed by what you've seen that these voyages of discovery will become a regular part of your life. I sure hope so.

Even with several cross-country trips under my wheels, I keep making new discoveries. On a road in Kansas, I stopped the engine at the top of a hill and was the only one looking out over 600 square miles of farmland. In a small California town I met a gold prospector and his mule. There have been great little diners with cozy booths, drives through canyons, and times when I've yielded to a moose or a grizzly bear. Best of all were the long, lonely drives with the windows down and cold air rushing in. The sky would be bright blue and I'd fly down a two-lane road slung between two mountain ranges.

These long journeys will give you back a special freedom. Freedom from *routine*. Each day most of us follow the same route to work and then follow the same route back. Road trips are for improvising. Since every road between your driveway and the rest of the nation is yours to explore, a journey from Rhode Island to Oregon can include a side trip to Mississippi or maybe North Dakota or Michigan. Why? Simply because you have the desire to go there.

One more thing you should know. Long ago I learned not to worry about getting lost because I knew I could always find my way back. Gradually I discovered I usually didn't want to go back. Out west, wrong turns have literally taken me to mountain peaks where I could see nothing but magnificence. Once I missed a turn-off and was hopelessly lost when, in the middle of nowhere, I found a clear mountain stream bordered by shade trees and a place to park. It was a great place for a nap and I awoke to the sound of songbirds and rushing water. A GPS can't find that for you.

There are thousands of books that will help you discover America. Before you head out, check out a few especially suited for a road trip:

Road Trip USA **by Jamie Jensen (***www.roadtripusa.com***); *Roadfood* by Jane and Michael Stern (***www.roadfood.com***); and *Great American Motorcycle Tours* by Gary McKechnie (***www.motorcycleamerica.com***)—a personal choice, this is my book about 25 back-road excursions that are especially suited for great motorcycle runs.**

Deciding how to arrange your own cross-country road trip—or one that boomerangs from the Midwest and touches a coast before returning—is up to you and depends on your time, your interests, and your bank account. But make the investment. The return will be worth it when you speak with someone who has a different accent or you chance upon a festival or meet a guide or ranger or docent who will educate you about some city or landscape, historic site, or work of art.

The first time you pull out of your driveway, you'll feel the magic because on a freewheeling cross-country road trip, you won't be taking the journey as much as the journey will be taking you.

CONTACTS

American Automobile Association   www.roadsideamerica.com
www.aaa.com

American Motorcyclist Association
www.ama-cycle.org

For Lodging and Dining, see "Across America" p. 285

93. DRIVE-IN THEATERS
Across America

About once an hour, technicians come up with a new entertainment system that, like grandfather clockwork, makes your old one obsolete. Even though drive-in theaters have been supplanted by nearly every technology available (including pencil sharpeners and shadow puppets), there's something uniquely American about pulling into a large field lorded over by a huge sheet of white and knowing that you're upholding a tradition that's been around since the 1930s.

SCREEN TEST

Even though America was entrenched in the Great Depression, one thing Americans didn't scrimp on was entertainment. At the same time, the nation was firmly in the grasp of the Automobile Age and people still liked to drive. That's when Richard Hollingshead, Jr., decided that, as with chocolate and peanut butter, there was a sacred obligation to marry these two disparate things.

Hollingshead envisioned a wide area where cars could park on an incline while passengers watched a movie. He created various parking patterns to test sight lines and experimented with different sound and projection systems, and in 1932 was awarded U.S. Patent 01909537 for his breakthrough idea of a drive-in theater.

Within a year drive-ins had spread across the country. But it was after World War II that drive-ins went into overdrive. By 1958 there were as many as 5,000 American drive-in theaters across the nation, and while the idea still appealed to the original target audience (families), teenagers who managed to wheedle the keys from the old man discovered that a darkened drive-in encouraged practical hands-on biology lessons.

Citing the sexual promiscuity that ran rampant at drive-ins, critics once dismissed them as "passion pits." Those critics were notorious loners who wished they had been invited to drive-ins.

It was inexpensive entertainment until the pricing system shifted from per car to per person. Aside from the risk of death by carbon monoxide poisoning, some moviegoers wondered why anyone should pay an extra two bucks when you could sneak four people into the movie inside the trunk. There were even some cheapskates who avoided drive-ins entirely by getting out their binoculars and watching the movie from a nearby hill. They had a point. In the 1970s, dialogue became less important as theater owners started showing cheap exploitation films filled with sex, gore, horror, or the entire drive-in trifecta. It was in 1972 that I asked Santa for a pair of binoculars.

Despite improvements in sound quality (soundtracks were picked up on the car radio), and assorted add-ons such as playgrounds and miniature golf to keep the crowds coming, it was hard for drive-in operators to compete with new forms of entertainment or ignore offers of quick cash for large parcels of real estate.

While drive-ins won't see the type of widespread popularity they once enjoyed—there are roughly 500 left in the world, 400 of those in America—a resurgence that began in the late 1990s has found passionate fans preserving the art.

"Enough drive-ins closed that people started worrying that they would be wiped out," explains drive-in historian Jennifer Sherer Janisch. "There was a renewed interest as people realized, 'Hey, here's something we almost lost and we want to keep it around.' A lot of people who enjoyed the drive-in wanted it for their kids and grandkids."

So when you pull into a traditional drive-in and enjoy the type of entertainment that thrilled viewers in the 1950s, it's a cozy little peek at the past—plus you can climb into the backseat and make out like a rooster.

DO IT YOURSELF

There's really not too much to know about going to a drive-in. You'll need a car, mostly, but you also need to know where to find one. For that, you can drive across the country and look for screens the size of the Lincoln Memorial or you can save time and gas by visiting a few of the websites below for continuously updated lists.

Of course you'd look out of place if you simply drove into a drive-in unprepared, so Jennifer Sherer Janisch and her brother Kipp Sherer created one of the genre's premium sites—*www.drive-ins.com*—where, as a testament to their love of these theaters, they offer suggestions to enhance your evening at the theatre. Among their tips:

> Jennifer Sherer Janish hit the nail on the head with her observation about the appeal of the drive-in: "The drive-in represents a simpler time, even to people who did not experience the drive-in heyday first hand. Parents want to give their children something from the carefree childhood that they had."

- In case you want to sit outside your car, bring lawn chairs, blankets, pillows, a sleeping bag, a portable radio (and extra batteries), and bug spray.

- Obey proper horn-honking etiquette (whatever that means).

- Make sure to put your key in the accessories position, and start your engine occasionally to avoid a dead battery.

- Support your local drive-in by eating at the concession stand.

- Last but not least, thank the staff for a lovely evening.

CONTACTS

www.drive-ins.com
www.driveintheater.com
www.driveinmovie.com

For Lodging and Dining, see "Across America" p. 285

94. LUMBERJACK CONTESTS
Across America

Is a lumberjack contest exciting? Well, even when lumberjacks are featured on rolls of paper towels, they already seem larger than life. Wait'll you watch 'em blasting chunks of wood out of a log or scurrying up a perfectly vertical tree and you'll swear you're watching Superman.

BUDDIES HACK IT

The same way cowboys applied the skills they used during the workday to create rodeo, a century ago lumberjacks turned their talents into sport.

At lumber camps across the Midwest and Pacific Northwest, loggers looked forward to Sunday, when they could stop chopping down trees and sawing logs so they could start chopping down trees and sawing logs.

"On Saturday they'd get rowdy and that led to bragging," explains Arden Cogar, Jr., a third generation lumberjack from West Virginia. "So on Sundays they started setting up competitions within their camps to see who could chop the fastest or use a crosscut saw the best or climb a tree the quickest—all of the things that are found in competitions today."

After contests had exhausted competition among a camp's own lumberjacks, they branched out to neighboring lumber camps and pretty soon everyone knew who was really the best logroller or tree chopper. After that, fairs and carnivals persuaded lumberjacks (and a growing number of "lumber jills") to show off their own brand of woodworking. In the late 1920s, the Rhododendron Festival in West Plains, West Virginia, hosted one of the first public lumberjack contests. Other festivals took root around the Great Lakes and the Pacific Northwest.

During World War II, the sport languished. But, by the late 1940s, lumberjacks out of the military were back in the woods and ready to compete. With the creation of the Lumberjack World Championships in Hayward, Wisconsin, in 1960, the contests reached the mainstream. Now shown on weekend sports programs, what had begun as a friendly competition was transformed into a commercial enterprise. Athletes swapped out their workday tools for specialized axes, saws, and chain saws. In 1994 a group of lumberjacks and athletes created the United States Axemen's Association to promote the sport, codify events, and ensure that the competitors were recognized and respected as athletes.

Are they? Just wait'll you see a human meat cleaver make a toothpick out of a tree trunk.

DO IT YOURSELF

There are approximately 200 opportunities to catch a lumberjack competition during the summer, with most events held in conjunction with local or state fairs. The three leading tournaments are the Webster County Woodchopping Festival (Webster Springs, West Virginia); the Lumberjack World Championships (Hayward, Wisconsin); and the New York State Woodsmen Field Day (Boonville, New York), where you'll be present at the coronation of the world's best Lumber Jill.

Promoters are well aware of the public's diminished attention span so many events are based on speed. At some events, spectators may be invited to test their own skills at heaving a three-pound axe into a bull's-eye on a tree trunk 20 feet away. A few pitches later they appreciate the physical demands that draw lumberjacks into the sport in the first place.

"I sit on my ass 60 hours a week," explains Cogar, who makes his living as an attorney. "After arguing cases for ten hours, there is nothing more satisfying than putting up a block of wood and beating the everlasting crap out of it."

To that end, axemen at every contest engage in a standard series of events. When you head to a lumberjack tournament, here's a sample of what you'll see:

Where are these athletes coming from? Believe it or not, most learn the sport in college. In forestry programs at state-funded schools, Woodsman Teams gives members a chance to learn how to compete in traditional lumberjack contests.

Single Buck

Using a one-man bucking saw, contestants are challenged to cut through a 20-inch pine log. World record time: 10.78 seconds. Teams pair up for the Double Buck, working each end of a single saw to slice through the log. Men have done this in as fast as 4.77 seconds. In the Women's Single Buck, a member of the fairer sex is turned loose on a 16-inch pine log. One hearty competitor sliced through hers in a record time of 11.61 seconds.

Underhand Block Chop

Wielding a five-pound axe, contestants stand astride a horizontal aspen log a foot thick and just over two feet long. Then they "beat the everlasting crap out of it" until they've chopped smack dab through it—which they can do in about 16 seconds. A similar event, the Standing Block Chop, is nearly identical but the lumberjack stands beside a vertical log as he beats on it. In the women's events, the logs are 11 inches in diameter.

Jack and Jill Sawing

A man and woman work both ends of a bucking saw to sever a chunk of 20-inch white pine. The feat, recommended by some counselors as a way to add zest to a marriage, has been performed in a record 6.17 seconds.

Logrolling

One of the coolest competitions to watch is also one of the most difficult to master. In contests for men and women, "birlers" step onto a floating log, dig into it to get it rolling, and then rapidly start-stop-reverse the spinning log until the challenger is so dazzled by the other's fancy footwork that he loses his balance and falls into the water. If no one falls within the time limit, contestants move to smaller logs until one takes a bath.

60- and 90-Foot Speed Climb

Men who will one day be reincarnated as squirrels latch onto a harness, hold a steel-cored climbing rope, and don special spurred boots to shimmy up vertical poles. Their mission is to be the first to ring a bell at the top of the pole and then drop like lead to the ground. An amazing spectacle, the 60-foot record is 12.33 seconds, and a climbing fool mastered the 90-foot model in 19.87 seconds.

Hot Saw

A sawyer places his hands on a 20-inch pine log and on the command "Go!" grabs a chain saw, revs it up, and does three complete swipes through the log. How long can it take to cut through five feet of wood? Six minutes? Seven? Nope. *5.55 seconds*. Guaranteed to get your adrenaline going.

Like I said…*Superman*.

CONTACTS

Webster County Woodchopping Festival
Webster, West Virginia
(304) 847-7666
www.woodchoppingfestival.com

Lumberjack World Championships
Hayward, Wisconsin
(715) 634-2484
www.lumberjackworldchampionships.com

New York State Woodsmen Field Day
Boonville, New York
(315) 942-4593
www.nyswfd.com

Lumberjack Days Festival
Stillwater, Minnesota
(651) 430-2306
www.lumberjackdays.com

For Lodging and Dining, see "Across America" p. 285

95. MONSTER TRUCK RALLIES
Across America

What's loud, ugly, violent, and demands the cessation of any logical thought?

No, not the *Jerry Springer Show*.

It's a Monster Truck Rally, and it's a far sight more entertaining than anything on trash television. For several hours these rallies deliver 100 percent USDA entertainment as a motorcade of massive trucks thunder through the dirt and run roughshod over a pyramid of automobiles.

So when's it coming to your town?

Sunday! Sunday! Sunday!

HE CREATED A MONSTER

Cars are a motorized expression of masculinity. For decades, hordes of men and a handful of women have souped 'em up and tricked 'em out to make them larger, louder, faster, stronger, and cooler than any other ride on the road. Cars have never ceased becoming bigger and badder. It happened in the '50s with hot rods and in the '60s with muscle cars, paving the way for a groundbreaking behemoth called Bigfoot. It was the first truck that could do something frivolous like, say, crush other trucks.

America's monster truck movement started in the mid-'70s when St. Louis native and car buff Bob Chandler's passion for off-roading often found him rattling home in his damaged Ford F-250. In the parts and repair shop he opened primarily for his own benefit, he gave his truck a larger engine—which needed stronger axles, which demanded bigger tires, which counted on extensions for added elevation. Then, using technology that had previously been applied only to military vehicles, he installed a device that allowed him to steer his truck from the rear axle. Now Chandler had a 4x4x4—a four-wheel truck with four-wheel drive and four-wheel steering. Even in this heavy-duty machine, though, he continued leaving broken axles and engine parts in his wake. When a friend said the damage was the result of his "big foot," Chandler's unusual truck gained an unforgettable name.

It takes as long as a year and as much as $250,000 to make a Bigfoot truck.

A 1981 videotape showing Bigfoot passing two cars caught the attention of a promoter—because Bigfoot passed the two cars by *driving over them*.

Chandler was invited to repeat this feat at a show in Columbia, Missouri, but he was reluctant. With the crowd screaming for action, Chandler put it in drive. Bigfoot was an instant superstar.

The first public car crush in world history inspired others to follow suit. Rednecks and motorheads nationwide slapped massive tires, extenders, and shocks on their trucks and raced to the closest arena to crush a few cars. Although Bigfoot has faced competition from copycat competitors, it has always remained first in the hearts of Americans. Riding atop 10-foot-high tires previously used on an Arctic snow train, the current model stands nearly 16 feet tall, is more than 20 feet across, and weighs more than 38,000 pounds, which earn it the honor of being the "world's tallest, widest, and heaviest monster truck."

What Bigfoot spawned is now presented at arenas across the country in national and regional events created by various organizations. Even if you own box seats at the opera, once you attend a monster truck rally you won't deny that it's a thrilling, high-octane, mega-decibel, all-American spectacle of dirt-throwing, hill-jumping, and drag-racing.

And they'll crush cars. Lots of them.

DO IT YOURSELF

Each year there are about 500 monster truck rallies presented across the U.S., Canada, and Mexico. At my first rally, the Winter Southern Monster Truck Showdown in Florida, I was surprised to see so many guests wearing camouflage, which books of etiquette suggest is frowned upon after Labor Day.

It takes about three gallons of methanol racing fuel for each 250-foot run.

Many rallies feature a preshow Pit Party that allows fans to meet the drivers, take snapshots, and see their favorite 1,200- to 2,000-horsepower monster trucks up close. Styles can range from a simple truck body perched atop massive tires to a lovely 15-foot fiberglass human skull. But since drivers manning trucks like Gunslinger, Wild Thang, and Grave Digger are vying for cash prizes and trophies, they're anxious to get the show going.

The musical prelude—say, a medley of singalong southern rock standards—announces the arrival of the monster trucks, which enter the arena like gladiators. The music, combined with the racket produced when they rev their engines, sounds—as someone once described a Dylan concert—like a squadron of B52s flying through a cathedral. For a sneak preview of the show, one truck may drive up to and then atop a Chevy Caprice to squash it like a scrap of aluminum foil. Next, the real fun begins. Two trucks line up, and then rocket over a mound of cars, the spectacle blending thunderous exhaust, flying dirt, and the unique visual of a 10-ton truck achieving a near vertical position. If a driver feels he has disappointed the audience, he makes amends by backing over the cars he has just cleared.

For hours, trucks line up, rocket over cars, crush a few. Then a tractor hauls out more cars, which are soon crushed as the cycle of destruction continues.

At the Southern Showdown, intermission was followed by a sight more stirring to me than the launch of *Apollo 11*. In the center of the arena a car was dumped beside a van, which was shoved next to a motor home roughly twice the height of Gunslinger. Based on physics, it should have been impossible for the smaller truck to ascend and crush the motor home, but it did. Repeatedly. Then, for good measure, Gunslinger floored it into a wheelie to crush the car and van as well. To top it all off, another hour of freestyle racing followed: Drivers jumped hills, kicked up dirt, and attacked and crushed cars from various angles.

An ambassador of goodwill, Bigfoot has traveled to many nations including Aruba, Australia, Brazil, Canada, Great Britain, Iceland, Ireland, Japan, New Zealand, Scotland, Thailand, and Venezuela.

It was all so inspiring I could hardly sleep. The next morning I ordered a set of 10-foot tires for my '99 minivan.

CONTACTS

Monster Truck Racing Association
www.mtra.us

United States Hot Rod Association
www.ushra.com

Southern Monster Truck Showdown
www.southernmonstertruckshowdown.com

For Lodging and Dining, see "Across America" p. 285

96. NATURALIZATION CEREMONIES
Across America

Ready to offer our nation their best are thousands of foreign-born citizens who share a common goal: becoming American citizens. Applicants renounce their homelands and pledge their allegiance to America. If your faith in this nation ever wavers, attend a naturalization ceremony.

CIVICS LESSON

Today, the United States Citizenship and Immigration Services (USCIS) is charged with administering the tests to determine if a person qualifies to become a citizen, while the FBI conducts background checks to address the issue of character.

Those foreign-born residents who want to become Americans must study hard to learn a citizen's rights and responsibilities. They learn about landmark Supreme Court decisions and the meaning of founding documents like the Declaration of Independence and the Constitution of the United States. When they've passed their tests and have successfully completed a background check, they attend a naturalization ceremony.

DO IT YOURSELF

Naturalization ceremonies take place regularly throughout the nation; finding one near you requires contacting the USCIS. It may be a simple judicial ceremony with just a few applicants or an epic administrative event held at a historic site like Monticello or aboard the USS *Constitution*. A judicial ceremony was the kind I witnessed.

To see the type of questions immigrants petitioning for citizenship are required to answer, go to www.uscis.gov and click on Education and Resources. You'll find a study guide to help applicants improve their knowledge of U.S. history and the structure of our government.

About 60 people gathered at the federal courthouse outside Courtroom 3-A. There was an Indian man who looked to be in his late 70s; young Asian women; and some men from the Middle East, among others. Some were dressed casually, while others, like the tiny old woman in a formal dress and pearl necklace, had dressed painstakingly for the occasion.

I watched applicants seated on benches with their families, and others standing alone. Every few minutes, the bailiff would usher applicants into the courtroom. The judge's bench was empty for now.

A clerk then entered and informed the applicants of the process; how they would be asked to stand when the judge entered; raise their right hand and repeat the oath; how they would repeat the Pledge of Allegiance following the oath. They were also told that if their culture or religion didn't allow them to swear an oath to the country, they didn't have to. No one, as it turned out, would opt out of this step.

A woman told me that, before I arrived, some applicants had been removed from the process. She wasn't sure if it was merely paperwork or something else, but she saw the effect it had on the applicants who remained.

"Some of them come from countries where the authorities could just take things from you," she whispered. "They're not sure if the same thing can happen to them now."

Their worries would soon be over. Seconds later the judge entered and shared a few words. He remarked that in this one room, in this one city, there were 60 applicants from 38 countries. He explained that the applicants had learned essential facts about American history and had been found to be of good moral character. He added that if they were called upon, they would serve their country.

An agent of the USCIS requested that the judge approve their petition for citizenship and the judge agreed. Next the clerk asked the applicants to stand when their homeland was named. When she said "Egypt," one man stood. Then Nigeria, Iran, Colombia... An entire family might stand when they heard Venezuela or Malaysia or Sweden.

When every nation had been called, the clerk read the Oath of Renunciation and Allegiance, and each applicant raised his or her right hand and repeated the oath.

> **The Oath of Renunciation and Allegiance**
>
> "I hereby declare on oath that I absolutely and entirely renounce and abjure all allegiance and fidelity to any foreign prince, potentate, state, or sovereignty...; that I will support and defend the Constitution and the laws of the United States against all enemies foreign and domestic...; that I will bear arms on behalf of the United States when required by law...; and that I take this obligation freely without any mental reservation or purpose of evasion. So help me God."

And that was it. Now they were Americans. Singers from a local church had requested a few minutes to sing "My Country 'Tis of Thee." They then asked their fellow countrymen to join them in "God Bless America." Most new citizens sang along, as did family members, guests, the judge, the court clerks, the bailiff, and even officials from the Immigration and Naturalization Service. Many people were crying.

The judge addressed the 60 new citizens from 38 countries. He told them that he knew that this ceremony followed a long and difficult journey and that he was proud to have taken part in it. He offered to stay for picture-taking as the new Americans received their certificates of citizenship, and then he added a parting thought: "America is no longer just your home. It is your country."

CONTACTS
United States Citizenship and Immigration Services
(800) 375-5283
www.uscis.gov

For Lodging and Dining, see "Across America" p. 285

97. PIE-BAKING CONTESTS
Across America

I bet you didn't know that the United States has a national pie council, but it does. The American Pie Council is committed to "preserving America's pie heritage and promoting Americans' love affair with pies." It also "raises awareness, enjoyment, and consumption of pies" by encouraging folks like you to buy a pie, bake a pie, or attend a pie-baking contest at a county or state fair. Yes, this is a good thing.

FLOUR POWER
It was the American Pie Council (APC) that lobbied Congress to create National Pie Day, so in return here's what you can do for it: Mark your calendar for January 23, the day that you and your 300 million fellow Americans are requested to, and this is no joke, "pie it forward" by spreading goodwill through sharing pie with loved ones and strangers alike.

Why pie? Longevity, for one thing. There are pie recipes dating from the 1300s. In 1590, Robert Green mentioned fruit pies in *Arcadia* ("thy breath is like the steame of apple-pyes"). Pies were featured in Dutch masterpieces in the 1600s, and Puritans would read into each pie symbols of Christ's manger and the gifts of the Magi. In a theological setback, in 1644 the British pie-baking trade had to go underground for 16 years after Oliver Cromwell declared that eating pie was a pagan form of pleasure.

Novices usually get knocked out by simple mistakes. If an apple pie tastes too much like cinnamon, that's not a good pie. Judges are looking for a balanced flavor.

Across the Atlantic, apple pies eventually became associated with America, but whatever the flavor, the pastry's image always seemed to tie in with the national personality. It's easy to picture a farmer's wife putting a pie on a windowsill to cool or a Midwest matron passing a piece of pie to a soldier on a train or contestants lined up along a picnic table engaged in a blueberry pie-eating battle.

"Pies bring back good memories," explains Linda Hoskins, executive director of the APC. "Pies involve family history, with parents and grandparents passing down not just recipes, but techniques such as rolling and crimping. And bakers have inherited treasured kitchen items like their special rolling pins and pie plates. No one ever has a sad story about pies. Pies always bring happy memories."

This comforting image of pies resonates across America, especially at fairs where women (mostly) can be found beneath a tent pitting their pies against one another's. It seems like an easy road to a wall of blue ribbons, but contestants claim baking a pie is an art, not a science. Emily Lewis, the winner of several national first place and best-of-show awards, entered her first pie-baking contest at Ohio's Lucas County Fair in 1987.

"There are so many factors involved," she sighs. "Every time you bake a pie the fruit can react differently with other fruit and make it too dry or too moist or too sweet or sour and it may not be sweet enough or maybe it can be too juicy or even too runny, even if you've used the same thickener!"

> **If you do bake, *enter*. There are no qualifying heats in the national contest, so you can just submit your recipe (which needs to adhere to certain parameters) as well as your entry fee (between $15 and $35) and then go to Florida with at least one pie to display and one to devour. You can enter in as many categories as you desire. Head to *www.piecouncil.org* for applications.**

Smarting from the unpleasant thought, Lewis dusts off her apron, catches her breath, and shares what judges look for in the perfect pie. Different qualities score different points, with overall impression, appearance, and creativity each accounting for 20 percent of the score, while taste, which could be the equivalent of a pastry's swimsuit competition, accounts for a full 40 percent.

Who's baking the best pies in America? The bakers who believe their pies are ready to compete in the major leagues fire up their ovens each April at the American Pie Council/Crisco National Pie Championships.

DO IT YOURSELF

Over the course of three days, more than 125 bakers whip up nearly 900 pies at the National Pie Championships—with commercial bakers competing on the first day; amateur bakers showcased on the second; and the junior chefs and specialty pie shops competing on the third.

I like the second day because many of these ladies have traveled long distances carrying with them their favorite whisks, beaters, measuring cups, thermometers, and rolling pins. Some have even hauled along home-grown ingredients like blueberries, strawberries, and even pumpkins. Many are staying in rental condos that provide a fully-equipped kitchen, but every contestant shudders at the quirks of an unfamiliar oven.

Even if you don't bake, you can participate in the festival as a volunteer. In exchange for performing tasks such as cutting pies, taking tickets, or perhaps being deputized as part of the "pie police" and checking for wristbands, you'll receive a free T-shirt and a ticket to the Never-Ending Pie Buffet.

If all goes right, by Saturday morning they amateur bakers have grown to love their ovens and have arrived at the competition with perfectly fresh pies. If not, they have three hours to use American Pie Council ovens to create an entry in one of 15 categories, including apple, chocolate, and cherry as well as nut, pumpkin, custard, fruit/berry, and peanut butter.

While the contestants are busy baking, you and about 20,000 others can enjoy the festival, which is centered around the Never-Ending Pie Buffet. For about ten bucks, you can feast on pies by more than a dozen commercial pie makers and top it off with as much ice cream as you wish. The festival also includes pie-eating contests, baking demonstrations, vendor exhibits, games, and live entertainment, followed that afternoon by the day's highlight: the announcement of the winners. While you were rooting around the buffet, the judges were making their decisions. You'll be there when four first place winners recoup $200 of the money they spent to get there, and watch as one contestant is honored with $5,000 for the pie deemed Best of Show.

It's as American as apple pie.

CONTACTS

American Pie Council
www.piecouncil.org

www.statefairrecipes.com

For Lodging and Dining, see p. 306

98. QUILTING BEES
Across America

If the average person were handed an armload of fabric scraps, he or she would probably look for an average trash can. This is where quilters prove they are above average. Combining nimble fingers, flying needles, keen eyesight, and a creative eye, participants at an old-fashioned quilting bee turn those scraps into a traditional work of American art.

IT'S SEW EASY

Probably not a single day goes by that you spend a single minute thinking about quilts. Neither do I, and that's kind of unusual considering that quilts are almost literally sewn into the fabric of America. While today we socialize by sending text and e-mails and occasionally even seeing our friends in person, in the 1800s a decent quilting bee could combine all three of these things (except the texting and e-mails).

From about 1830 to 1870 quilting was in its heyday in America for several reasons, and number one was economics. Prior to the Industrial Age, it was far less expensive to create a warm bedcover out of used scraps and old clothing than to pay exorbitant prices for British goods.

Fabric was more plentiful in port cities, but as Americans headed west, anything would do. Worn clothes were snipped into pieces, sorted by size and shape, and sewn onto a plain fabric backing. But some folks had better scraps than others, so neighbors created ad hoc social networks to compare and trade scraps. Quilting started to evolve from a practical necessity to a social outlet, especially in newly settled areas where loneliness was a fact of life. The lady of the house would nearly complete a few quilts on her own and then invite her friends over to add the finishing touches. Provided an interloper didn't mess up a quilt and cause a ruckus, it was possible that by late afternoon several quilts could be completed so the women could stop quilting and start cooking.

During the Great Depression, grain companies learned that sales increased when they made their feed sacks with impressive designs and colors. Families could later use those feed sacks to make dresses and quilts.

By the early 20th century, fabric was plentiful and sewing affordable, and new patterns and dyes appeared frequently. Although quilting was knocked back in the Jazz Age, it was resurrected out of necessity during the Great

Depression. It peaked again in a big way starting in 1971, when New York's Whitney Museum of American Art launched an exhibition that led to a four-year world tour of antique American quilts, reminding Americans that quilting was a native American craft that had matured into a true art form.

DO IT YOURSELF

Dedicated quilters have such a devotion to the craft that they've made it quite easy for outsiders to get started. Just contact your local quilt shop (yes, Virginia, there *are* local quilt shops), which will have a list of local quilting groups and guilds. After finding out when they meet, go. Chances are what you'll see isn't too far removed from the quilting bees of your imagination.

The AIDS quilt was started as a way to remember victims of the epidemic. Started in 1987, today it consists of nearly 6,000 blocks (comprising more than 44,000 individual memorial panels) and weighs about 54 tons.

There are more than two hundred members of the Lake County Quilting Guild in Mount Dora, Florida; on a Tuesday morning I witnessed about a hundred of them arriving with tote bags filled with material, scissors, thread, templates, and small sewing machines. Within minutes they were selecting patterns, fabrics, and batting before piecing together swatches with stab stitches and rocking stitches.

Work on quilt designs like a "grandmother's garden" may consume *two years* of quilting for a final product that can fetch a few thousand dollars. But money is not the objective for the women, who work on their projects in a large room filled with conversation and laughter.

What will hook you about a quilting bee?

"Quilting is one of those things you can do yourself or with a group to enjoy its social aspects," explains Connie Davidson, president of the National Quilting Association. "It's also a way to express your creativity. You can create a quilt to donate to charity or sell for profit or simply for the pure pleasure of creating something for yourself or to pass down to your children or your grandchildren—things that are homemade have never gone out of style."

CONTACTS

National Quilting Association
(614) 488-8520
www.nqaquilts.org

www.quiltingbeehive.org
www.quilthistory.com
www.quiltnational.com
www.quiltfest.com

For Lodging and Dining, see "Across America" p. 285

99. RINGLING BROTHERS AND BARNUM & BAILEY CIRCUS
Across America

It takes a lot of brass to bill your presentation as "The Greatest Show on Earth." But who could dispute the fact that the Ringling Brothers and Barnum & Bailey Circus deserves the title? It packs a month's worth of entertainment into each three-hour performance.

"The circus awakens every sense in you," a performer told me. "That's why it's timeless. When you watch the circus, it is a beautiful escape. You don't think about the housing market or mortgages or bills. And then it's over so quickly…"

Actually, the show is never really over. Once you see it, it will stay with you forever.

LORDS OF THE RING

The Ringling Brothers weren't the first to organize a circus. The Romans did it 2,000 years earlier. The brothers weren't even the first to put on a popular American circus. There were circuses in the U.S. more than a century before theirs. They didn't even come up with the motto "The Greatest Show on Earth." That was Phineas T. Barnum.

But five of the seven Ringling brothers of Baraboo, Wisconsin—Al, Alf T., John, Otto, and Charles—just happened to be top-notch organizers and promoters. The circus they created in 1884 had become a "railroad circus" by the end of the decade. Their Ringling Brothers United Monster Shows, Great Double Circus, Royal European Menagerie, Museum, Caravan, and Congress of Trained Animals kept gaining in popularity—although their business cards were the size of a dinner table.

In 1919 the surviving Ringlings, John and Charles, combined their circus with those of the late P.T. Barnum and James Bailey. Television was three decades away and movies were still silent so the Ringlings, especially John, cleaned up. In fact, John became one of the richest men in the world.

The Depression took its toll on the circus, as did World War II. But the government realized the circus was good for morale and provided special dispensation for Ringling's circus to use trains to travel the nation. It even let it use a special fire retardant solution to coat its tents. But in 1944 a fire broke out at a matinee in Hartford, Connecticut, and the Big Top burned to the ground, taking with it 167 people. Ringling never declared bankruptcy, but spent the next eight years paying off settlements.

Even as movies and television pulled people out of the stands, fans still knew stars like Emmett Kelley and the Flying Wallendas. But times were changing and the circus had to as well. In July 1956, Ringling folded its tents and moved into indoor venues, and a decade later a Ringling advance man named Irvin Feld teamed up with his brother and a Texas judge and bought the circus outright. They developed the Clown College so old clowns could teach their skills and secrets to promising young acolytes. Successful grads joined the circus, while dropouts entered Congress. (Surely, I jest.) Then, in 2006, the traditional three-ring circus was switched to a one-ring stage.

One ring or three, it's still the Greatest Show on Earth!

DO IT YOURSELF

Even if the Ringling Circus doesn't arrive in your town in a grand procession, the rest is pure tradition. Arrive early for the Animal Open House to see elephants, tigers, lions, goats, porcupines, and miniature horses waiting for their moment in the spotlight. Inside the arena, before the show, you're invited to the floor to meet tightrope walkers, jugglers, balancing acts, clowns, showgirls, and animal trainers. You can try on circus costumes (including the ringmaster's jacket), and maybe compete in a tug of war with an elephant (you'll lose).

Some fine circus museums to visit:

Circus World in Baraboo, WI (www.circusworld museum.com), is the original home of the Ringling Brothers; Ringling Circus Museum in Sarasota, FL (www.ringling.org), features an incredible miniature circus on the grounds of John Ringling's majestic estate; and the Barnum Museum in Bridgeport, CT (www .barnum-museum.org), pays tribute to the promotional genius of P.T. Barnum.

At showtime the ringmaster announces in his best ringmaster's voice, *"WELCOME TO THE GREATEST SHOW ON EARTH!"* as all the show people you've just met fly out of the portal carrying flags or standing on galloping horses or tumbling or running out on stilts and doing backflips. There are motorcycles and elephants and dogs catching Frisbees and 40 feet above the floor a woman suspended by her hair spins like a top. While this is a grand finale for any other show, at Ringling there are still three hours to go.

Next come performances that are outlandish, cartoonish, and heart-stopping. Cossacks leap on and off galloping horses. Next, a pot-bellied pig unrolls a red carpet for a goat astride a miniature horse. Then, there's a drag race of Bombastic Bouncers astride hyper-inflated inner tubes. My attention diverted,

I missed the motorcyclist going for a spin up a narrow high wire and then performing a handstand at the top.

Hour after hour the performers never let up. A tiger trainer arrives with a menagerie of big cats and finishes his act without requiring emergency care or having to clean up a hairball. Acrobats walk on a wire no wider than their thumbs and toss in a back flip for kicks. Super Silva, who earlier rode his motorcycle up the wire, now jogs up an inclined wire and then drops below it to *walk upside-down.* That could only be followed by a bellhop clown standing on his head and playing "What a Wonderful World" on a trumpet. The grand finale brings in every performer for an extravaganza of clowns, motorcycles, dogs, goats, motorcyclists, aerialists, and bouncing inner tubes.

With the phrase *panem et circenses*—bread and circuses—the Roman satirist Juvenal described how the imperial class placated the masses by appealing to their desires rather than their civic duty.

As the audience departs, you can see kids holding balloons and know that they're wondering how they can join the circus. Their parents? They're wondering if they can stop payment on the Harvard tuition check and apply those funds to Clown College.

CONTACTS

www.ringling.com
www.circusweb.com

For Lodging and Dining, see "Across America" p. 285

100. SQUARE DANCING
Across America

If you were living in the 1850s and somehow had the ability to travel to the present, you'd be hard pressed to comprehend the changes that had taken place in fashion, transportation, technology, and architecture. If someone took you to a square dance, though, you'd feel right at home.

SQUARE ROOTS

Picture two popular movie scenes: One is a European royal ball in the late 1700s, with dancers gracefully and meticulously executing each carefully memorized step.

Fade to Scene Two. As the caller announces the dance, Rhett Butler and Scarlett O'Hara line up for the Virginia Reel. *That's* what square dancing brought to America.

"Americans were too busy to learn dance steps," explains Jim Mayo, author of *Step by Step Through Modern Square Dance History.* "So they needed guidance. The caller was a uniquely American contribution to the square dance. Basically he was the dance teacher—the prompter—who would cue the dancers and prompt their memory of the next step."

The National Square Dance Convention is held each year during the last weekend of June.

By the mid-1800s the caller had been established as part of American square dancing, which was a rather large umbrella that included the "Kentucky Running Set" (a dance done in circles that could be as large as the room) and "contra" dances along lengthwise lines perfect for dances like the aforementioned Virginia Reel.

And then…nothing happened. Well, almost nothing and that pleased Henry Ford. Because square dances looked about the same in 1925 as they had in 1850, their long tradition appealed to Ford, who was absolutely fascinated by square dancing.

The story goes that Ford vacationed at the Wayside Inn in Sudbury, Massachusetts, where a dance instructor named Benjamin Lovett taught square dances. Because Lovett was under contract to the inn, he declined Ford's offer to relocate to Michigan. Ford worked around the problem by buying the inn, and with it Lovett's contract. Ford then built a Dearborn, Michigan, dance hall resplendent with teakwood floors and crystal chandeliers, and brought Lovett to lead lessons there.

Ford wasn't finished. During the Roaring '20s, he broadcast square dances over the radio and distributed recorded square dance music and calls to schoolchildren—as well as to his Ford Motor Company executives.

Not every square dance club has a dress code, but if one suggests "traditional square dance attire" you may want to sport some western-style duds.

According to Mayo, square dancing's real seismic shift came after World War II. Better sound equipment made it possible for callers to change the routine as it was being danced. The result was the dance floor equivalent of jazz improvisation as callers created a huge variety of dance patterns. New square dance clubs were formed, meanwhile, that sustained the popularity of both traditional and modern square dancing.

One survey by the International Association of Square Dance Callers found that an estimated 30 million Americans have participated in square dancing, and its popularity has traveled far beyond our borders. There are more than 12,000 square dancers in Japanese clubs, and there are tens of thousands more weaving the ring at clubs in Germany, England, Scandinavia, Australia, and New Zealand.

Why are so many people around the world promenading across the floor? When you start to do-si-do, you'll find out that dancing's only a part of it.

DO IT YOURSELF

Before you attend your first square dance, it's good to know that you're not just there to dance.

"Square dances are a marvelous way to build friendships," Mayo explains. "I have lifelong friends I met while square dancing 40 years ago. Plus it's a nice combination of using your mind and your body. You are dancing and moving and listening to the calls and responding to an always-changing assemblage of terminology."

Mayo's take is backed up by Jerry Reed, executive director of the International Association of Square Dance Callers.

"It's disappointing if people just picture an old barn and hillbillies when they think of a square dance," Reed suggests. "Square dancing is actually very sophisticated. You have to be moving and thinking all the time. Once you start dancing all your worries just leave your mind—you can't concentrate on anything else but the dancing."

Reed's right. While a dedicated and dyed-in-the-wool caller can really mix things up with a repertoire of as many as 500 calls, a typical square dancer should be familiar with about roughly 60 to 70 calls. Don't let the numbers keep you away—square dancers want you around. "I can't imagine a stranger coming in who is not welcomed enthusiastically," says Mayo.

Square dance callers are blessed with verbal gifts on a par with auctioneers. Typical callers work weekend dances and rake in as much as $500 a month, while a handful who work areas that are popular with retirees may call three to four dances a day and gross $100,000 a year.

Over the course of the evening you and your partner will have dozens of chances to follow the lead of the caller who may urge you to "Allemande left with your left hand" and then "back to the partner for a right and left grand," all to the melody of a traditional Appalachian fiddle tune. Then again, you could be dancing to "Over the Rainbow." Really.

Most likely, your first square dance won't be your last. The whirl of activity, the music, the mental and physical energy you've tapped into, the friendships you've made… All of it is pure old-fashioned American fun. So what's next? All you have to do is bow to your partner, then bow to your corner…

And promenade home.

CONTACTS

United Square Dancers of America
www.usda.org

Square Dance Magazine
www.squaredancemagazine.com

www.dosado.com
The largest site with links to local clubs.

National Square Dance Convention
www.nsdcnec.com

For Lodging and Dining, see "Across America" p. 285

101. TRAIN JOURNEYS
Across America

We're so accustomed to driving cars that most of us have forgotten the thrill of riding the rails. When you're on a train you're exploring with complete freedom. Freedom from reading maps, freedom from buying gas, and the freedom to knock out the miles as you sleep. Outside, the scenery rolls past like a life-sized American documentary.

MAKING TRACKS

As far back as the 1830s, the Baltimore and Ohio Railroad was shuttling passengers across the eastern countryside, but it wasn't until 1869 that the Union-Pacific Railroad connected both coasts. Following that monumental feat of engineering, railroads would hold a monopoly on cross-country travel until 1903. That's when Dr. Horatio Nelson Jackson, his mechanic friend Sewall Crocker, and Jackson's dog Bud completed a road trip from San Francisco to New York in a little over two months.

Still, trains remained the preferred choice for long-distance travel. In 1925 the Seaboard Air Line Railroad began persuading people, especially rich people, to travel south, as Miami's land boom took off. The company's Orange Blossom Special was a luxury liner that chuffed straight down the Atlantic Coast to the sunny shores of Miami Beach.

Beginning in 1936, the Atchison, Topeka and Santa Fe Railway offered ordinary folks and Hollywood celebrities a lift from Chicago to downtown Los Angeles's Union Station aboard the Super Chief, known as the "train of the stars." Traveling some 2,200 miles in about 40 hours, the Super Chief epitomized a golden age of American passenger rail travel.

A complex series of factors precipitated the decline of rail travel, Even before America entered the Jet Age, the Orange Blossom Special ceased service—in 1953—and the Super Chief made its last run in 1971, after the route was adopted by a new government-owned corporation, Amtrak. But the most significant element was the Boeing 707. When it took off in 1958, passengers could slice about 36 hours off a 40-hour train ride.

Although the Orange Blossom Special and Super Chief left the landscape years ago, Amtrak continues to operate trains that follow the paths they blazed. The Silver Star and Silver Meteor depart New York's Penn Station and travel along the Atlantic seaboard. The Southwest Chief runs between Chicago and Los Angeles.

While Amtrak has been battered by many of the same issues that forced its predecessors out of business, its trains and an assortment of private sightseeing trains and luxury lines are still chugging along, maintaining the magic of American rail travel.

DO IT YOURSELF

Americans in Europe are amazed that an entire continent can be theirs via a Eurail pass that, for one price, offers virtually unlimited rail travel. Only a few Americans realize Amtrak's 15-, 30-, and 45-day USA Rail Passes are our domestic equivalent.

I warmed up for an extended train tour by embarking on a 900-mile overnight between Florida and Washington, D.C., on Amtrak's Auto Train (which returned excitement to travel with the conductor actually shouting "Aaaaaall aboard!").

The amount of space in the massive Superliner cars led me to believe I had mistakenly entered First Class, but there was no mistake. The train was far more spacious and impressive than any other mode of transportation I could recall.

The scenery matched the setting. When the train's plodding start gave way to a healthy 60 miles per hour, I was at the window watching scrub oaks, cemeteries, and small-town backyards sail by. I listened to the long, lonely call of the train whistle as we rounded long curves in the tracks, and then roamed the length of the train, finding kids playing cards, babies napping, and adults socializing in the lounge.

Amtrak's USA Rail Pass may be one of the best values in America. Passes are available for 15-, 30-, and 45-day windows, offering up to 8, 12, and 15 separate travel segments, respectively. Sleeping berths are extra.

After reaching our cruising altitude (20 feet above sea level), we were called to a multicourse dinner, which far surpassed an airline's standard fare of peanuts and crackers. Complementing the meal was civilized, entertaining conversation with fellow passengers who quickly became new friends.

After dinner, a movie played in the lounge, but I chose to settle down with a good book. A few cars away, some passengers had upgraded to the sleeper car but I was content with my comfortable reclining seat.

Closing the book and flipping off the light, I wondered what other train passengers were seeing that night as they were riding the rails across America—and realized that, whatever it was, one day I'd see it, too. I'd be riding across Kansas and through Oregon and in the Adirondacks, knocking out the miles and following the great tradition of American rail travel.

CONTACTS

Amtrak
(800) 872-7245 (USA-RAIL)
www.amtrak.com

Alaska Railroad Corporation
(907) 265-2494
(800) 544-0552
www.alaskarailroad.com

Green Mountain Railroad (Vermont)
(800) 707-3530
(802) 463-3069
www.rails-vt.com

**Great Smoky Mountains Railway
(North Carolina)**
(800) 872-4681
www.gsmr.com

**Shasta Sunset Dinner Train
(Mount Shasta, California)**
(530) 964-2142
www.shastasunset.com

Napa Valley Wine Train (California)
(707) 253-2111
(800) 427-4124
www.winetrain.com

Grand Canyon Railway (Arizona)
(800) 843-8724
www.thetrain.com

For Lodging and Dining, see "Across America" p. 285

LODGING AND DINING

ACROSS AMERICA

Across America, lodging and dining choices are as varied as the sites, people, and icons you'll encounter. Each city below includes a range of options—but there are certainly many more to consider. Chain hotels and restaurants are always easy to find (but often overdone), so consider local choices. Contact the local chambers of commerce or convention and visitors bureau locations and websites for information.

If a chain hotel is your only option, the following information will help you on your search:

Choice Hotels International
www.choicehotels.com
1-877-424-6423

Wyndham Hotels and Resorts
www.wyndham.com
877-999-3223

Marriott Hotels
www.marriott.com
1-888-236-2427

Holiday Inn Hotels and Resorts
www.holidayinn.com
1-888-HOLIDAY (465-4329)

Best Western International Hotels
www.bestwestern.com
1-800-780-7234

Hotels by Hilton
www.hilton.com
1-800-HILTONS (445-8667)

Accor Hotels
www.accorhotels.com
1-800-515-5679

NORTHEAST

CAPE COD-MAINE COAST
(Clambake-Lobsterbake)

LODGING–Cape Cod
Chatham Bars Inn
297 Shore Road
Chatham, MA
(508) 945-0096
(800) 527-4884
www.chathambarsinn.com
If you can swing it, this Cape Cod icon is the place to stay since it's elegant, indulgent, and covers acres of oceanfront.

Crowne Pointe Historic Inn
87 Bradford Street
Provincetown, MA
(508) 487-6767
(877) 276-9631
www.crownepointe.com
Provincetown's only AAA four-diamond property. Exceptional amenities and attentive staff.

Annabelle Bed & Breakfast
4 Grove Street
Sandwich, MA
(508) 833-1419
www.annabellebandb.com
An exceptionally appointed six-room bed and breakfast. Pulls out all the stops when it comes to creature comforts, service, and innovative dishes.

A Little Inn on Pleasant Bay
654 South Orleans Road
South Orleans, MA
(508) 255-0780-(888) 332-3351
www.alittleinnonpleasantbay.com
European-style inn overlooking exquisite Pleasant Bay and offering hospitality and impeccable guest service to match the view.

DINING–Cape Cod

Captain Linnell House
137 Skaket Beach Road
Orleans, MA
(508) 255-3400
www.linnell.com
One of Cape Cod's most romantic and sophisticated dining experiences.

Osteria la Civetta
133 Main Street
Falmouth, MA
(508) 540-1616
www.osterialacivetta.com
Artfully presented Northern Italian entrées and an extensive wine list.

The Red Inn
15 Commercial Street
Provincetown, MA
(508) 487-7334
www.theredinn.com
Small, award-winning restaurant that offers an ever-changing seasonal menu and views of Provincetown Harbor.

Quahog Republic
161 Leeward Road
Bourne, MA
(508) 759-9390
(866) 759-9390
www.quahogrepublic.com
Authentic Cape Cod lobster rolls and seafood savored by locals (and visitors) at a down-home waterfront restaurant.

LODGING–Maine Coast

Samoset Resort
20 Warrenton Street
Rockland, ME
(207) 594-2511
(800) 341-1650
www.samosetresort.com
The grand resort's oceanfront location and expanse offers breathing room, elegance, and peace.

Towne Motel
68 Elm Street
Camden, ME
(207) 236-3377
(800) 656-4999
www.camdenmotel.com
In the heart of town and close to the harbor. Includes a light continental breakfast.

The Belmont Inn
6 Belmont Avenue
Camden, ME
(207) 236-8053
(800) 238-8053
www.thebelmontinn.com
Wraparound porches, a great sitting room, breakfasts on the porch. Larger rooms with a homey feel.

DINING–Maine Coast

Cappy's
1 Main Street
Camden, ME
(207) 236-2254
www.cappyschowder.com
Active and lively local hangout, with clam chowder, sandwiches, lobster, and microbrews.

Waterfront Restaurant
40 Bayview Street
Camden, ME
(207) 236-3747
www.waterfrontcamden.com
Comfortable, unpretentious meals at the harbor. Lobster, steak, and an oyster bar. The full bar is open until the customers go home.

BOSTON, MA
(Colonial Boston, Boston Marathon)

LODGING

Boston Harbor Hotel
70 Rowes Wharf
(617) 439-7000
www.bhh.com
Five-star service. A waterfront location as extraordinary as its rooms and hospitality.

Fairmont Copley
138 St. James Avenue
(617) 267-5300
www.fairmont.com-copleyplaza
Opened in 1912 and seems to have been transported directly from Paris. At the finish line of the Boston Marathon.

Boston Omni Parker House Hotel
60 School Street
(617) 227-8600
(800) 843-6664
www.omnihotels.com
Historic 1885 hotel on the Freedom Trail. Home of the famous Parker House rolls, Boston

Cream Pie, and $30 million 2008 restoration and renovation.

Fifteen Beacon Hotel
15 Beacon Street
(617) 670-1500
www.xvbeacon.com
In a Beaux Arts building atop Beacon Hill, with fireplaces in 60 individually designed guest rooms.

The Green Turtle
Shipyard Quarters Marina, 13th Street, Charlestown
(617) 337-0202
www.greenturtlebb.com
Here's something interesting: a floating bed & breakfast located in the historic Charlestown Navy Yard. Expansive views of the Boston Harbor skyline with amenities of a modern inn.

The Inn @ St. Botolph
99 St. Botolph Street
(617) 236-8099
www.innatstbotolph.com
Trendy 16-suite boutique hotel set on a quiet street in historic Back Bay. Within easy proximity of the city's most renowned sights and districts.

DINING
Union Oyster House
41 Union Street
(617) 227-2750
www.unionoysterhouse.com
Here since 1826, UOH is considered the nation's oldest continuously operating restaurant. Five different dining areas each have their own personality. Seafood, of course, is a specialty.

The Oak Room
Fairmont Copley Plaza
138 St. James Avenue
(617) 267-5300
www.fairmont.com-copleyplaza
Elegant Old World dining in a classic hotel dining room.

B&G Oysters Ltd.
550 Tremont Street
(617) 423-0550
www.bandgoysters.com
South End neighborhood oyster bar. Lobster rolls and an amazing selection of fresh oysters.

Vinoteca Di Monica
143 Richmond Street
(617) 227-0311
In the heart of Boston's Little Italy District, Monica's pasta is handmade at the nearby trattoria. A marathon-eve tradition.

Locke-Ober
3 Winter Place
(617) 542-1340
www.lockeober.com
A landmark restaurant rich in tradition and impervious to trends. Classic seafood dishes, an oysters—and a (business casual) dress code!

The Barking Crab
88 Sleeper Street
(617) 426-2722
www.barkingcrab.com
The feel of the coastal clam shack in the heart of the city.

Jasper White's Summer Shack
50 Dalton Street
(617) 867-9955
www.summershackrestaurant.com
Traditional New England dishes from clambakes to pan-roasted lobster, ice cold beer, and corn dogs.

PLYMOUTH, MA
(Plymouth Rock)

LODGING
John Carver
25 Summer Street
(508) 746-7100
(800) 274-1620
www.johncarverinn.com
In the heart of historic Plymouth on the site of the original Pilgrim settlement. Walk to the *Mayflower II* and Plymouth Rock.

Radisson Hotel Plymouth Harbor
180 Water Street
(508) 747-4900
www.radisson.com-plymouthma
On the waterfront, with 175 rooms—within walking distance to nearly all attractions.

Pilgrim Sands on Long Beach
150 Warren Avenue
(508) 747-0900
(800) 729-7263
www.pilgrimsands.com

Outside the town, on the water, and across from Plimoth Plantation. Private beach.

Best Western Cold Spring
188 Court Street
(508) 746-2222
(800) 678-8667
www.bwcoldspring.com
On five landscaped acres in central Plymouth, with views of Cape Cod Bay. Complimentary breakfast.

DINING
East Bay Grille
173 Water Street
(508) 746-9751
www.eastbaygrille.com
On Plymouth's Town Wharf, offers fresh seafood, pasta, and steaks in a warm casual environment. Spacious dining room, lively bar area, and scenic outdoor patio.

Cabbyshack
Town Wharf
(508) 746-5354
www.cabbyshack.com
The area's largest outdoor deck for dining, cocktails, and entertainment. Indoor-outdoor bar.

Woods Seafood
Town Wharf
(508) 746-0261
www.woodsseafoods.com
On the Town Wharf overlooking Plymouth Harbor and *Mayflower II.* Serving the freshest seafood; lobster "in the rough," fried clams, fish and chips.

STOCKBRIDGE, MA
(Norman Rockwell Museum)

LODGING
Red Lion Inn
30 Main Street
Stockbridge
(413) 298-5545
www.redlioninn.com
The most legendary lodging in Stockbridge (since the 1700s) offers 108 rooms right in the heart of town.

Cranwell Resort
55 Lee Road (Route 20)
Lenox
(413) 637-1364
(800) 272-6935
www.cranwell.com
Gilded Age 107-room Tudor mansion surrounded by an 18-hole golf course. Spa, pool, fitness areas, fine dining.

Blantyre
16 Blantyre Road
Lenox
(413) 637-3556
www.blantyre.com
A 24-room Relais & Chateaux classic that has earned five stars from Mobil. Unstuffy perfection.

Garden Gables Inn
135 Main Street
Lenox
(413) 637-0193
(888) 243-0193
www.lenoxinn.com
In neighboring Lenox, five secluded and peaceful acres provide a buffer from the real world.

Lodging Services
For more lodging options:
Berkshire Visitors Bureau (413-743-4500, 866-444-1815, www.berkshires.org);
Lenox Chamber of Commerce (413-637-3646, www.lenox.org-lodging);
Berkshire Lodging Association (413-528-4006, www.berkshirelodging.com).

DINING
Once Upon a Table
34 Main Street
Stockbridge
(413) 298-3870
The downtown restaurant was captured in Rockwell's painting "Main Street at Christmas."

Firefly
71 Church Street
Lenox
(413) 637-2700
www.fireflylenox.com
International cuisine served in a luminescent atmosphere.

Wheatleigh
Hawthorne Road
Lenox
(413) 637-0610
www.wheatleigh.com
Upscale dining in a Gilded Age mansion.

Dakota
1035 South Street
(413) 499-7900
Located between Lenox and Pittsfield on Route 7. Big food in a big Pacific Northwest setting.

NIAGARA FALLS, NY

LODGING

The Seneca Niagara Hotel
310 Fourth Street
(877) 873-6322
www.senecaniagaracasino.com
The largest hotel in western New York, with 486 deluxe rooms, 86 corner suites, and 22 one-bedroom suites.

The Red Coach Inn
2 Buffalo Avenue
(716) 282-1459
www.redcoach.com
A lovely English Tudor–style inn directly across from the rapids and the state park.

Hillcrest Inn
1 Hillcrest Street
(716) 278-9676
www.hillcrestniagara.com
An elegant, Georgian mansion on a bricked, private street. Quiet seclusion within walking distance of the falls and most attractions.

DINING

Top of the Falls Restaurant
Niagara Falls State Park
(716) 278-0340
www.niagarafallsstatepark.com
The park's signature restaurant is romantic, classy, and only a short walk to the falls.

The Western Door
310 Fourth Street
(877) 873-6322
www.senecaniagaracasino.com
This upscale steakhouse is in the Seneca Niagara casino.

The Como Restaurant
2220 Pine Avenue
(716) 285-9341
www.comorestaurant.com
Since 1927, this is the Italian-American choice in Niagara Falls, with traditional dishes of Old Italy.

COOPERSTOWN, NY
(Baseball Hall of Fame)

LODGING

Otesaga Resort Hotel
60 Lake Street
(607) 547-9931
(800) 348-6222
www.otesaga.com
Since 1909, this Federal-style hotel has reflected a genteel era. Overlooks Otsego Lake, "Glimmerglass" of James Fenimore Cooper's *Leatherstocking Tales*.

Inn at Cooperstown
16 Chestnut Street
(607) 547-5756
www.innatcooperstown.com
Built in 1874 and completely restored in 1985, the inn (which would be at home in Bedford Falls) offers distinctive accommodations in the heart of Cooperstown.

Cooperstown B&B
88 Chestnut Street
(607) 547-2532
www.cooperstownbandb.com
Homestyle accommodations and hospitality, within walking distance of downtown and its one stoplight.

DINING

Alex & Ika Restaurant
149 Main Street
(607) 547-4070
www.alexandika.com
Tucked-away gem often touted as one of the region's best culinary destinations. International dishes, impressive wine and beer lists.

Hoffman Lane Bistro
2 Hoffman Lane
(607) 547-7055
www.hoffmanlanebistro.com
Serving "hall of famer" items such as classic meat loaf over mashed potatoes with gravy, as well as pasta and sautéed and grilled items.

Doubleday Café
93 Main Street
(607) 547-55468
Long time Main Street fixture serving basics at breakfast, lunch, and dinner. Daily specials for every meal.

Fly Creek Cider Mill & Orchard
288 Goose Street
Fly Creek
(607) 547-9692
www.flycreekcidermill.com
About three miles from Cooperstown, the Mill features mill-made fudges, pies, and more than 40 kinds of salsas, cheeses, spreads, wine, pulled pork sandwiches, cider, and cider slushies.

WEST POINT, NY

LODGING
The Thayer Hotel
674 Thayer Road
(845) 446-4731
(800) 247-5047
www.thethayerhotel.com
Set on a hill overlooking the Hudson River, the historic Thayer is the only full-service hotel on the Hudson River from the George Washington Bridge to Albany.

Bear Mountain Inn
Bear Mountain State Park
(845) 786-2731
www.bearmountaininn.com
A cozy and rustic inn just four miles from West Point and within a lovely and tranquil state park.

Holiday Inn Express
1106 Route 9W
Fort Montgomery
(845) 446-4277
www.hiexpress.com
A practical lodging option about three miles from West Point.

Cromwell Manor
174 Angola Road
Cornwall
(845) 534-7136
www.cromwellmanor.com
A romantic and beautiful 12-room inn on acres of landscaped property 5 miles from West Point.

Garrison House
915 Route 9W
Fort Montgomery
(845) 446-2322
www.thegarrisonhouse.com
A seven-room B&B in a historic 1700s house overlooking Garrison Pond.

DINING
Canterbury Brook Inn
331 Main Street
Cornwall
(845) 534-9658
www.thecanterburybrookinn.com
Traditional Swiss dishes served in European style beside a lovely brook.

Painter's Tavern
266 Hudson Street
Cornwall
(845) 534-2109
www.painters-restaurant.com
Located in a restored mansion, a local favorite for its eclectic nouvelle cuisine, intriguing artwork, and moderate prices.

The River Bank
Three River Avenue
Cornwall
(845) 534-3046
www.theriverbank.biz
An eclectic ethnic mix of nouvelle cuisine in a historic (and converted) bank.

NEW YORK, NY
(Empire State Building, Times Square New Years, Broadway, Statue of Liberty, Macy's Thanksgiving Day Parade)

LODGING
The Waldorf-Astoria
301 Park Avenue
(212) 355-3000
(800) 925-3673
www.waldorfastoria.com
The Waldorf was created in 1893 and joined the neighboring Astoria in 1897. Since then it's been America's gold standard for elegant hotels.

The Plaza Hotel
Fifth Avenue at Central Park South
(212) 759-3000
(888) 850-0909
www.fairmont.com-theplaza
If it's good enough for the Beatles, it'll be good enough for you. A timeless New York landmark since 1907.

The St. Regis New York
2 East 55th Street at Fifth Avenue
(212) 753-4500

www.stregis.com-newyorkcity
A refined atmosphere, gracious service, and butler service (!) rank this among New York's top hotels.

The Jumeirah Essex House
160 Central Park South
(212) 247-0300
www.jumeirahessexhouse.com
Luxurious New York lodging since 1931, with a recent $90 million renovation to restore its art deco heritage. Incredible Central Park and Manhattan views, style, and 24-hour concierge.

Hudson Hotel
356 West 58th Street
(212) 554-6000
www.hudsonhotel.com
Close to Central Park and the theater district, with Philippe Starck design touches including chartreuse-lit escalators. Hip and utterly cool.

The Bowery Hotel
335 Bowery
(212) 505-9100
www.theboweryhotel.com
135 modern rooms, but with warmth, in the NoHo District near the East Village.

The Inn at Irving Place
56 Irving Place
(212) 533-4600
www.innatirving.com
In historic Gramercy Park, two renovated landmark town houses (circa 1834) were combined into a city-centered inn. No name on the building, just a number that ushers you into a bygone era.

Times Square & Broadway

There are more than 16,000 rooms in the vicinity of Times Square and Broadway in large hotel chains, boutique hotels, and even youth hostels. Some, but certainly not all of these, include the **Renaissance New York** (714 Seventh Avenue at W. 48th Street, 212-765-7676, www.renaissance-hotels.com); **DoubleTree Guest Suites** (1568 Broadway, 212-719-1600, www.doubletree,com); and the **Marriott Marquis** (1535 Broadway, 212-398-1900, www.marriott.com).

DINING

Tavern on the Green
Central Park at West 67th Street
(212) 873-3200

www.tavernonthegreen.com
The heavenly 1870 Victorian Gothic retreat tucked into Central Park is an oasis of peace, tranquillity, and elegance. Indoor and outdoor dining rooms are filled with topiaries, flowers, and greenery.

Le Cirque
One Beacon Court
151 East 58th Street
(212) 644-0202
www.lecirque.com
The convergence of New York food, fashion, art, and culture.

Sarabeth's
40 Central Park South
(212) 826-5959
www.sarabethscps.com
Comfort foods in a stylish New York City setting.

Carnegie Delicatessen
854 Seventh Avenue at 55th Street
(800) 334-5606
www.carnegiedeli.com
Their motto? "We cure, bake, smoke, and pickle our own. That says it all." Well, that and they have huge sandwiches.

Times Square & Broadway

Restaurants around Times Square include TGI Friday's, Bubba Gump Shrimp House, Sbarro Pizza, Foley's Fish House, and Olive Garden.

MID-ATLANTIC

HERSHEY, PA

LODGING
Hershey Lodging
(800) HERSHEY (437-7439)
www.hersheypa.com
Among your choices in town are the **Hotel Hershey** (100 Hotel Road), a four-diamond, four-star resort that brings to mind the style and elegance of a Mediterranean villa. The **Hershey Lodge** (University Drive) is larger than the hotel, and is a family-friendly resort and meetings retreat. The toll-free number will put you in touch with a reservation service with access to

these on-site and approximately 20 area properties. On-property guests receive free shuttles and early access to Hersheypark and Chocolate World, as well as reduced admission to Hershey Gardens and the Hershey Story museum.

DINING

The Circular Dining Room
100 Hotel Road
(800) 437-7439
www.hersheypa.com
Inside the Hotel Hershey, the dining room is consistently voted one of the best restaurants in Central Pennsylvania.

The Hershey Pantry
801 East Chocolate Avenue
(717) 533-7505
www.hersheypantry.com
Downhome dishes served during breakfast, lunch, and dinner.

Hershey's Chocolate World
Near the park, the family-friendly food court serves sandwiches and salads and also features the second-floor Kit Kat Cafe.

LANCASTER COUNTY, PA
(Amish Country)

LODGING

Intercourse Village B&B Suites
Main Street
Intercourse
(717) 768-2626
(800) 664-0949
www.amishcountryinns.com
Clean, comfortable, and close to everything.

AmishView Inn & Suites
3125 Old Philadelphia Pike (Route 340)
Bird-in-Hand
(866) 735-1600
www.amishviewinn.com
At the Plain & Fancy Farm complex, right in the heart of all the scenery and activity of Pennsylvania Dutch Country.

Bird-in-Hand Village Inn & Suites
2695 Old Philadelphia Pike (Route 340)
Bird-in-Hand
(800) 665-8780
www.bird-in-hand.com
Upscale country lodging in a quaint

village setting, with 24 uniquely decorated guest rooms and suites in four preserved historic buildings.

The Inn at Leola Village
38 Deborah Drive (Route 23)
Leola
(877) 669-5094
www.theinnatleolavillage.com
AAA four Diamonds, this wonderful property features 63 guest rooms and suites housed within six authentic, carefully restored Dutch Country homes and workplaces.

Harvest Moon B&B
311 East Main Street
New Holland
(888) 824-3763
www.harvestmoonbandb.com
Turn-of-the-century B&B nestled in the charming village of New Holland, with classically-trained chefs as your hosts.

The Hurst House B&B
154 East Farmersville Road
Ephrata
(800) 603-9227
www.hursthousebandb.com
Elegant Victorian mansion, located on top of the Katza Buckle (Cat's Back Hill) overlooking hundreds of beautiful Amish and Old Order Mennonite farms.

Lancaster Arts Hotel
300 Harrisburg Avenue
Lancaster
(866) 720-2787
www.lancasterartshotel.com
A converted warehouse, now with deluxe accommodations with unique surroundings featuring original works of art.

DINING

Restaurant Mazzi
46 Deborah Drive (Route 23)
Leola
(717) 656-8983
www.restaurantmazzi.com
Located at The Inn at Leola Village, this casual but elegant restaurant serves rustic Italian- and French-influenced cuisine.

Effie Ophelia
230 North Prince Street
Lancaster

(717) 397-6863
www.effieophelia.com
Upscale intimate bistro with ever-changing menus
featuring seasonal Lancaster County products.

Amish Dining
Choices of dining are plentiful, and each of
these restaurants serve the big food Amish
Country is known for: **The Plain & Fancy Farm**
(Route 340, 717-768-4400, www.plainand
fancyfarm.com); **Bird-In-Hand Family Restaurant** (2760 Old Philadelphia Pike (Route 340),
Bird-In-Hand, 717-768-1500, www.bird-in-
hand.com); **Stoltzfus Farm Restaurant** (Route
772 East, 717-768-8156, www.stoltzfusfarm
restaurant.com); **Miller's Smorgasbord** (Rte. 30,
717-687-6621, www.millerssmorgasbord.com).

WILLIAMSPORT, PA
(Little League World Series)

Peter Herdic House and Inn
411 West Fourth Street
(570) 326-0411
www.herdichouse.com
Classic Gilded Age Victorian home with large,
well-appointed rooms, just blocks from downtown. Friendly hosts.

Genetti Hotel and Suites
200 West Fourth Street
(570) 326-6600
(800) 321-1388
www.genettihotel.com
Historic downtown hotel. Traditionally-styled
guest rooms and suites.

Holiday Inn Downtown
100 Pine Street
(570) 327-8231
www.holidayinn.com-williamsportpa
Safe chain choice in the heart of downtown.
145 guestrooms.

DINING
Peter Herdic House
407 West Fourth Street
(570) 322-0165
www.herdichouse.com
Creative gourmet dining in a romantic setting at
sister property of Victorian inn. Impressive wine list.

33 East
33 East Third Street

(570) 322-1900
www.33east.com
Surprisingly trendy restaurant with internation-
ally-inspired entrées and chic lounge.

Bullfrog Brewery
229 West Fourth Street
(570) 326-4700
www.bullfrogbrewery.com
Local favorite corner microbrewery as well as a
fine dining restaurant and social lounge.

GETTYSBURG, PA
LODGING
Gettysburg Hotel
1 Lincoln Square
(717) 337-2000
www.hotelgettysburg.com
Right on the town square, this is a legend in
the city. Here since 1797, it became nationally
known when President Eisenhower (who lived
in Gettysburg) used it as the base of operations
for him and his staff.

James Getty's Hotel
27 Chambersburg Street
(717) 337-1334
(888) 900-5275
www.jamesgettyshotel.com
A clean, well-situated, and well-equipped
11-room boutique hotel great for groups. The
5-room suites include a kitchenette.

Brickhouse Inn
452 Baltimore Street
(717) 338-9337
(800) 864-3464
www.brickhouseinn.com
First-rate B&B midway between downtown and
Visitors Center. Extraordinary breakfasts served
on the backyard patio.

Inns of Gettysburg
(717) 624-1300
(800) 586-2216
www.gettysburgbedandbreakfast.com
Consult for a substantial list of local B&Bs and
their locations.

DINING
Dunlap's
90 Buford Avenue
(717) 334-4816

www.dunlapsrestaurant.com
A local favorite for home cooking as it's been done for decades.

The Dobbin House
89 Steinwehr Avenue
(717) 334-2100
www.dobbinhouse.com
Six historic dining rooms with meals delivered by servers in colonial dress.

The Lincoln Diner
32 Carlisle Street
(717) 334-3900
An actual old-fashioned 24-hour diner serving big breakfasts and hearty dinners.

General Pickett's
571 Steinwehr Avenue
(717) 334-7580
Made-from-scratch soups, breads, and down-home entrées.

PUNXSUTAWNEY, PA
(Groundhog Day)

LODGING
Pantall Hotel
135 East Mahoning Street
(814) 938-6600
(800) 872-6825
www.pantallhotel.com
Built in 1888 the downtown icon offers rooms for under $100 (which leap to around $500 at Groundhog Day).

Punxsutawney B&Bs
Consider the **Jackson Run Bed and Breakfast** (363 Jackson Run Road, 814-938-2315, www.jacksonrun.com); **Plantation Bed and Breakfast** (20652 Route 119, 814-939-7371, www.plantationgetaway.com); or **Victorian Tudor Suite** (202 Pine Street, 814-938-9059, www.victoriantudorsuite.com).

Community Center Crash Pad
220 North Jefferson Street
(814) 938-1008
On Groundhog Day Eve spend about five bucks and settle down on the floor in your sleeping bag.

DINING
Mary's Place Restaurant
17080 Route 36

(814) 938-2962
www.meetatmarys.com
Italian, steak, and seafood dishes served in a historic home.

Nick's Corner Lunch
265 North Findley Street
(814) 938-4020)
A Punxsutawney institution. Try the hamburger on a hot-dog bun with special sauce.

Punxy Phil's Family Restaurant
116 Indiana Street
(814) 938-1221
Marvel at murals of Phil in a family restaurant that serves great diner food.

The Groundhog Banquet
Punxsutawney High School
(800) 752-7445
Contact the Chamber of Commerce for tickets and information about this coveted social event.

VALLEY FORGE, PA

LODGING
The Mainland Inn
17 Main Street
Mainland
(215) 256-8500
www.themainlandinn.com
Features a British-style tavern and Zagat-rated fine dining in a historic inn.

William Penn Inn
1017 DeKalb Pike
Gwynedd
(215) 699-9272
www.williampenninn.com
Pennsylvania's oldest continually operating country inn.

Crown Plaza Valley Forge
260 Mall Boulevard
King of Prussia
(610) 265-7500
www.cpvalleyforge.com
More than two hundred luxurious guest rooms and ten spacious suites for travelers.

Normandy Farm Hotel
1431 Morris Road
Blue Bell
(215) 616-8500

www.normandyfarm.com
Famous local landmark is an ideal setting for meetings, special occasions, or quick getaways.

Hotel Fiesole
4046 Skippack Pike
Skippack
(610) 222-8009
www.hotelfisole.net
European flair and sophistication with Old World charm and modern amenities.

Shearer Elegance
1154 Main Street
Linfield
(610) 495-7429
(800) 861-0308
www.shearerelegance.com
Quaint bed and breakfast in an 1897 22-room Victorian mansion.

Great Valley House of Valley Forge
1475 Swedesford Road
Malvern
(610) 644-6759
www.greatvalleyhouse.com
The 300-year-old stone farmhouse is now a bed and breakfast just five minutes from Valley Forge National Park.

DINING
Creed's Seafood and Steaks
499 North Gulph Road
King of Prussia
(610) 265-2550
www.creedskop.com
Excellent service and a diverse selection of dishes.

Trinacria Ristorante Italiano
1016 DeKalb Pike
Blue Bell
(610) 275-0505
www.trinacria-pa.com
Zagat-rated among America's top Italian restaurants.

Coleman Restaurant
Route 202 & Morris Road
Blue Bell
(215) 616-8300
www.normandyfarm.com
Chef Jim Coleman cooks up classic recipes from the Pennsylvania countryside.

G-Lodge Restaurant
1371 Valley Forge Road

Phoenixville
(610) 933-1646
Homemade fare in a cozy setting.

The Mainland Inn
17 Main Street
Mainland
(215) 256-8500
www.themainlandinn.com
Features a British-style tavern and Zagat-rated fine dining in a historic inn.

William Penn Inn
1017 DeKalb Pike
Gwynedd
(215) 699-9272
www.williampenninn.com
Pennsylvania's oldest continually operating country inn.

WASHINGTON CROSSING, PA

LODGING
Washington Crossing Inn
Routes 532 & 32
(215) 493-3634
www.washingtoncrossinginn.com
An elegant Federal-style lodge from the 1930s, located directly across from the park.

Inn to the Woods B&B
150 Glenwood Drive
Washington Crossing
(215) 493-1974
www.inn-bucks.com
Seven uniquely appointed guest rooms in a serene setting near the banks of the Delaware River.

Inn at Bowman's Hill
518 Lurgan Road
New Hope
(215) 862-8090
www.theinnatbowmanshill.com
A luxurious hideaway on a landscaped estate outside New Hope center. Features a tropical waterfall and orchid conservancy.

Logan Inn
10 West Ferry Street
New Hope
(215) 862-2300
www.loganinn.com
Charming 18th-century country inn and a steak

and seafood restaurant in the center of historic New Hope.

The Temperance House
5 South State Street
Newtown
(215) 860-9975
www.temperancehouse.com
A historic country inn about 15 minutes from Washington Crossing. Features a fantastic restaurant.

DINING
Marsha Brown
15 South Main Street
New Hope
(215) 862-7044
www.marshabrownrestaurant.com
A refined Creole kitchen and lounge designed in a centuries-old stone church located in the heart of New Hope.

Triumph Brewing Company
400 Union Square
New Hope
(215) 862-8300
www.triumphbrewing.com
A sophisticated restaurant-brewpub featuring eclectic contemporary American dishes and handcrafted freshly brewed beer.

Wildflowers Garden Restaurant
8 West Mechanic Street
(215) 862-2241
www.wildflowersnewhope.com
Serves traditional as well exotic Thai dishes that don't cost a fortune. A lovely riverside setting in downtown New Hope.

PHILADELPHIA, PA
(Colonial Philadelphia, Army-Navy Football Game)

LODGING
Penn's View Inn
14 North Front Street
(215) 922-7600
(800) 331-7634
www.pennsviewhotel.com
A short walk from Independence Mall, an independent (and very nice) European-style boutique hotel in the heart of Old City Philadelphia.

Sheraton Society Inn
One Dock Street
2nd and Walnut Streets
(215) 238-6000
www.sheraton.com-societyhill
A family and pet-friendly two-story hotel in the historic district.

Hyatt Regency Philadelphia at Penn's Landing
201 South Columbus Boulevard
(215) 928-1234
www.pennslanding.hyatt.com
Beautiful, modern building on Philadelphia waterfront. Great views from every room.

Loews
1200 Market Street
(215) 569-8300
www.loewshotels.com
One of the nation's first skyscrapers, the former bank building is now a sleek, masculine, modern hotel.

Sofitel
120 South 17th Street
(215) 387-8000
www.sofitel-philadelphia.com
The former Philadelphia Stock Exchange building is now a great escape for romantic getaways. French elegance, American style.

DINING
Campo's
214 Market Street
(215) 923-1000
www.camposdeli.com
Creative sandwiches, good cheesesteaks—great prices and food in a casual setting.

Serrano
20 South Second Street
(215) 928-0770
www.tinangel.com
Warm and cozy atmosphere with international cuisine.

Fork-Fork Etc.
306 Market Street
(215) 625-9425
www.forkrestaurant.com
Elegant American bistro helped jump-start the Old City restaurant scene.

Buddakan
325 Chestnut Street

(215) 574-9440
www.buddakan.com
A temple of modern Asian cuisine with creative takes on Japanese, Chinese, Vietnamese, Thai, and Indian fare in a striking, theatrical setting.

Jim's Steaks
400 South Street
(215) 928-1911
www.jimssteaksphilly.com
Perhaps the best-known purveyor of the Philly cheesesteak sandwich. Here since 1939, and with three other locations.

Tony Luke's Old Philly Style Sandwiches
39 East Oregon Avenue
(215) 551-5725
www.tonylukes.com
Another world-famous steak shop. Old-World, real Philly.

Tequilas
1602 Locust Street
(215) 546-0181
www.tequilasphilly.com
Dramatic decor and delicious Mexican cuisine, sangria, and margaritas.

WASHINGTON, D.C.
(Arlington National Cemetery, Washington, D.C.)

LODGING
Willard Continental Washington
1401 Pennsylvania Avenue, NW
(202) 628-9100
(800) 827-1747
www.washington.interconti.com
A landmark hotel rich in tradition, elegance, and style.

Marriott Wardman Park
2660 Woodley Road, NW
(202) 328-2000
(800) 228-9290
www.marriott.com-wasdt
The largest hotel in Washington, D.C., is located atop a private landmark estate.

Hotel Palomar
2121 P Street, NW
(202) 448-1800
(877) 866-3070
www.hotelpalomar-dc.com

A wonderful mix of stylish sophistication and artistic expression.

The Liaison Capitol Hill
415 New Jersey Avenue, NW
(202) 638-1616
www.affinia.com
Guest rooms feature a contemporary design yet residential feel.

DC Guesthouse
1337 10th Street NW
(202) 332-2502
www.dcguesthouse.com
Located in an 1867 mansion that's accented with loads of charm.

DINING
1789 Restaurant
1226 36th Street, NW
(202) 965-1789
www.1789restaurant.com
Serves the finest regional game, fish, and produce in a country inn atmosphere.

Ben's Chili Bowl
1213 U Street, NW
(202) 667-0909
www.benschilibowl.com
Attracts celebrities as well as real people with a half-century of incredible food, atmosphere, and rich history.

Old Ebbitt Grill
675 15th Street, NW
(202) 347-4801
www.ebbitt.com
A political power spot and D.C.'s oldest bar.

ALEXANDRIA, VA
(Mount Vernon)

LODGING
Best Western Mount Vernon
8751 Richmond Highway
(703) 360-1300
www.bestwestern.com-mtvernonalexandria
Renovated in 2007, 132-room chain hotel three miles from Mount Vernon. Complimentary continental breakfast.

Quality Inn Mount Vernon
7212 Richmond Highway
(703) 765-9000

www.alexandriaqualityinn.com
Pet-friendly 89-room hotel with several complimentary services including phone calls, Wi-Fi,
and breakfast.

Travelers Motel
5916 Richmond Highway
(703) 329-1310
www.budgethostalexandria.com
Family owned and operated affordable motor
lodge-style motel.

DINING
Mount Vernon Inn
George Washington's Mount Vernon
(703) 780-0011
www.mountvernon.org
Colonial atmosphere and meals. Six dining
rooms where lunch is served daily by colonial-
costumed servers. Dinners by candlelight.

Mike's Italian Restaurant
8368 Richmond Highway
(703) 780-5966
www.mikesitalianrestaurant.com
Family-owned restaurant serving authentic Italian since 1975. A casually elegant local favorite.

WILLIAMSBURG, VA
(Colonial Williamsburg)

LODGING
Williamsburg Inn
136 East Francis Street
(800) 447-8679
www.history.org
Where Queen Elizabeth II stays when she's in
town (seriously). Elegance enhanced by a spa,
golf course, tennis, and four-star dining.

Williamsburg Lodge
310 South England Street
(800) 447-8679
www.history.org
Across from the Inn, this comfortable
Federal-style lodge is also within walking
distance of town.

Colonial Cottages
(800) 447-8679
www.history.org
Several historic colonial cottages have been
renovated and are perfectly suited for couples
and families who prefer a bit of privacy.

DINING
Regency Room
136 East Francis Street
(757) 229-2141
www.colonialwilliamsburgresort.com
In the Williamsburg Inn, culinary classics in an
elegant setting, coat and tie required for men at
Sunday jazz brunch and dinner.

Williamsburg Lodge Restaurant
310 South England Street
(757) 229-2141
American cuisine with contemporary southern
and Chesapeake influences. Seafood buffet every
Friday night.

Williamsburg Taverns
www.colonialwillamsburgresort.com
Christiana Campbell's, Shields Tavern, and the
King's Arms were actual taverns in the 1700s and
dishes are based on historic menus—all served in
candlelit dining rooms and presented by servers in
colonial dress. Christiana's was Washington's favorite.

SOUTHEAST

LOUISVILLE, KY
(Kentucky Derby)

LODGING
Seelbach Hilton Hotel
500 South Fourth Street
(502) 585-3200
www.seelbachhilton.com
Located in the heart of downtown, Louisville's
grand hotel was the inspiration for the Mulbach
Hotel in *The Great Gatsby*.

The Brown Hotel
335 West Broadway
(502) 583-1234
www.brownhotel.com
Classic English Renaissance architecture in a
historic AAA four-diamond downtown hotel.

The 21C Museum Hotel
700 West Main Street
(502) 217-6300
www.21chotel.com
A boutique hotel offering southern-style hospitality and contemporary art throughout galleries
and public space.

Louisville Inns
In historically preserved neighborhoods, Louisville innkeepers have converted many of the city's old Victorian mansions into bed and breakfasts, including the business-friendly **1888 Historic Rocking Horse Manor** (1022 South 3rd Street, 502-583-0408,www.rockinghorse-bb.com), the **Inn at the Park Bed & Breakfast** (1332 South 4th Street, 502-637-6930, www.innatpark.com) which overlooks Central Park, and the **Dupont Mansion Bed & Breakfast** (1317 South 4th Street, 502-637-6930, www.dupontmansion .com). For information on Old Louisville and inns visitwww.oldlouisville.org.

DINING
Jack Fry's
1007 Bardstown Road
(502) 452-9244
www.jackfrys.com
This upscale American bistro features live jazz and a convivial atmosphere. A Louisville institution.

Lynn's Paradise Café
948 Barret Avenue
(502) 583-3447
www.lynnsparadisecafe.com
Super-duper funky and fun decor matched with fine southern cooking.

Equus
122 Sears Avenue
(502) 897-9721
www.equusrestaurant.com
Classic cooking with a heavy emphasis on traditional flavors and seasonal ingredients.

Derby Dining
In addition to sampling a mint julep, the Derby's entrée of choice is burgoo. The thick stew of meats and vegetables including potatoes, beans, and spices is a classic Kentucky dish. Top it off with a Derby Pie, a chocolate and walnut tart in a pie shell— often flavored with pecans, chocolate chips, and Kentucky Bourbon.

OWENSBORO, KY
(Bluegrass Festival)

LODGING
Helton House Bed & Breakfast
103 East 23rd Street
(270) 926-7117

www.bbonline.com-ky-helton-index.html
A gracious charmer of another era graced with oak millwork, antiques, richly appointed bedrooms, and a "treetop" sun porch.

River House Bed & Breakfast
1510 Riverview Drive
Lewisport
(270) 295-4199
www.lastsummer.com-rhbb
Fifteen miles east of Owensboro, this modern Inn overlooks the Ohio River. Relaxed atmosphere, beautiful grounds, and private quarters.

Chain Choices
Owensboro features several franchise hotels including a Ramada Inn (270-685-3941), Days Inn (270-684-9621), Fairfield Inn (270-688-8887), Hampton Inn (270-926-2006), Holiday Inn Express (270-685-2433), Comfort Suites (270-683-4128), and Sleep Inn (270-691-6200).

DINING
Moonlite Bar-B-Q Inn
2840 West Parrish Avenue
(270) 684-8143
www.moonlite.com
Moonlite slow-cooks meats in their custom-built, hickory-fired pits. An Owensboro tradition since 1963.

Niko's Italian Cuisine
2200 East Parrish Avenue
(270) 852-1628
www.nikositalian.com
A local favorite, affordable Italian cuisine.

Famous Bistro
102 West 2nd Street
(270) 686-8208
www.famousbistro.com
Mediterranean and world cuisine served in a quaint downtown building with an intimate feel.

Colby's Fine Food & Spirits
201 West Third Street
(270) 685-4239
Casual dining in a historic downtown building complete with original tin ceilings.

KITTY HAWK, NC

Oceanfront Hilton Garden Inn
5353 North Virginia Dare Trail

(252) 261-1290
www.hiltongardeninn.hilton.com
On the Atlantic Ocean near Wright Brothers
National Memorial, Jockey's Ridge State Park,
and the Cape Hatteras National Seashore.

Tranquil House Inn
405 Queen Elizabeth Avenue
Manteo
(252) 473-1404
www.1587.com
On the waterfront in tranquil downtown Manteo. Styled like the stately Outer Banks inns of
the 19th century.

The Inn on Pamlico Sound
49684 NC Highway 12
Buxton
(252) 995-7030
(866) 995-7030
www.innonpamlicosound.com
Casually elegant waterfront 12-room bed and
breakfast on the banks of the Pamlico Sound
on Hatteras Island, near the Cape Hatteras
Lighthouse. Indoor and outdoor waterfront
fine dining.

Sanderling Resort & Spa
1461 Duck Road
Duck
(252) 261-4111
www.thesanderling.com
Spreads from the Atlantic Ocean to serene
Currituck Sound. Secluded ocean beaches and
luxurious spa.

DINING
Elizabeth's Café & Winery
1177 Duck Road
Scarborough Faire Shoppes
Duck
(252) 261-6145
www.elizabethscafe.com
Indulgent fine dining, but you're at the
beach, so leave the tie at home. Exquisite
food preparation.

Kelly's Outer Banks Restaurant & Tavern
U.S. Highway 158 Bypass, Milepost 10.5
Nags Head
(252) 441-4116
www.kellysrestaurant.com
Fresh, locally caught seafood served with a
mixture of local history, nostalgia, live music,
and dancing.

Basnight's Lone Cedar Café
Nags Head Causeway
Nags Head
(252) 441-5405
www.lonecedarcafe.com
A hallmark of down-home cooking and southern coastal cuisine on the Outer Banks. Overlooks beautiful Roanoke Sound.

Jolly Roger
Virginia Dare Trail, Milepost 6.5
Kill Devil Hills
(252) 480-3241
www.jollyrogerobx.com
Popular breakfast spot across the beach near
Wright Brothers National Memorial.

MOUNT AIRY, NC
(Mount Airy/Mayberry)

LODGING
The Andy Griffith Home Place
711 Haymore Street
(336) 789-5999
Believe it or not, the small home where Andy grew
up is now open for overnight guests. Decor consists of actual furnishings from the Griffith family.

The Mayberry Motor Inn
501 Andy Griffith Parkway North
(336) 786-4109
www.mayberrymotorinn.com
The old-fashioned motor lodge has a Mayberry
squad car out front, standard rooms, and a pool.

Hampton Inn
2029 Rockford Street
(336) 789-5999
www.hamptoninn.com
Familiar and comfortable and within a mile of
downtown Mount Airy.

Sobotta Manor Bed and Breakfast
347 West Pine Street
(336) 786-2777
www.sobottamanor.com
An elegant 1932 English Tudor manor in a
parklike setting, within walking distance to
downtown restaurants and shopping. Full
breakfast included.

DINING
Pandowdy's Restaurant
243 North Main Street

(336) 786-1993
Stylish dining, Mount Airy style, with super steaks and southern hospitality.

Cross Creek Country Club
1129 Green Hill Road
(336) 789-5131
www.crosscreekcc.com
Clubhouse provides the perfect setting and country views.

Barneys
206 North Main Street
From famous "Barneys Burgers" to home-cooked "meat and two veggies" specials.

Snappy Lunch
125 North Main Street
(336) 786-4931
www.thesnappylunch.com
An old-fashioned diner serving old-fashioned diner foods. Their specialty? The legendary pork chop sandwich.

Goobers 52
458 Andy Griffith Parkway
(336) 786-1845
www.goobers52.com
A contemporary hangout with a laidback, funky atmosphere and signature servings of lobster Reuben's, barbecued salmon sandwiches, and Black Jack burgers.

GATLINGBURG, TN
(Great Smoky Mountains National Park)

LODGING
Gatlinburg Inn
755 Parkway
(865) 436-5133
www.gatlinburginn.com
Historic, old-fashioned seasonal inn that's been a favorite of celebs. Lovely landscaping—and "Rocky Top" (Tennessee's state song) was written in room 388.

Lodge at Buckberry Creek
961 Campbell Lead Road
(865) 430-8030
(866) 305-6343
www.buckberrylodge.com
A 45-room Adirondack-style lodge on 26 acres. Regional cuisine, a creekside pavilion for outdoor gatherings, and stunning views of the Smokies.

Foxtrot B&B
1520 Garrett Lane
(888) 436-3033
www.thefoxtrot.com
Chalet-style cedar and stone inn with four luxurious guest rooms and spectacular views of Mt. Leconte and the Great Smoky Mountains.

DINING
Bennett's
714 River Road
(865) 436-2400
www.bennetts-bbq.com
Huge, rustic restaurant with numerous awards for best ribs, beef, pork, and chicken. Pig out on an endless soup and salad bar.

Howard's Restaurant
976 Parkway
(865) 436-3600
www.howards-gatlinburg.com
In town since 1946. Seductive creekside setting and southern dishes like fried catfish, trout, gourmet burgers, 20-ounce T-bone (serves two).

Smoky Mountain Brewery & Restaurant
1004 Parkway
(865) 436-4200
www.smoky-mtn-brewery.com
Designed like a lodge, and with a far-flung menu of wood-roasted steaks, pizzas, fresh breads, burgers, and handcrafted beers.

Peddler Steakhouse
820 River Road
(865) 436-5794
Specializing in naturally aged steaks cut to your specification at your table and grilled over real Tennessee hickory charcoal.

No Way Jose's
555 Parkway
(865) 430-5673
www.nowayjosescantina.com
Popular local Tex-Mex cantina right on the Parkway and with an outdoor café on the riverfront.

CHARLESTON, SC
(Fort Sumter)

LODGING
Wentworth Mansion
149 Wentworth Street
(843) 853-1886

(888) 466-1886
www.wentworthmansion.com
Twenty-one beautiful and dramatic rooms
and suites with hand-carved marble fireplaces,
crystal chandeliers, and intricate woodwork
from 1886. Charleston's only AAA five-
diamond hotel.

1843 Battery Carriage House Inn
20 South Battery
(800) 775-5575
www.batterycarriagehouse.com
A romantic and highly popular inn at "The
Battery" next to Charleston Harbor. Silver tray
breakfast delivered your room.

Mills House Hotel
115 Meeting Street
(843) 577-2400
www.millshouse.com
Opened in 1853, earned a place on Conde
Nast's Gold List of the World's Best Hotels.
Boutique hotel with a 19th-century Charleston charm.

DINING
Oak Steakhouse
17 Broad Street
(843) 722-4220
www.oaksteakhouserestaurant.com
Italian-inspired steakhouse fare within a historic
bank building. Martinis and a well-edited selection of Old and New World wines complement
the flavors of steaks, chops, seafood specialties,
and vegetarian dishes.

Dixie Supply Cafe & Bakery
62 State Street
(843) 722-5650
Specializing in Low-Country cuisine. Breakfast
sandwiches, biscuits, wraps and pastries, the classic
Dixie Burger, custom boxed lunches, great desserts.

Jim 'n Nicks Bar-B-Q
288 King Street
(843) 577-0406
www.jimnnicks.com
Made from scratch BBQ slow-cooked over hickory wood then finished on an authentic brick
pit. From grilled catfish to homemade pies.

Fleet Landing Restaurant
186 Concord Street
(843) 722-8100
www.fleetlanding.net

Classic and contemporary southern seafood
fare. Enjoy views from the wrap-around deck
and maritime chic dining room.

NASHVILLE, TN
(Grand Ole Opry)

LODGING
The Gaylord Opryland Resort
2800 Opryland Drive
(615) 889-1000
(866) 972-6779
www.gaylordopryland.com
Surprisingly elegant hotel adjacent to the Grand
Ole Opry, with lush indoor gardens, winding
rivers and pathways, and sparkling waterfalls.

Hermitage Hotel
231 Sixth Avenue North
(615) 244-3121
(888) 888-9414
www.thehermitagehotel.com
Holds the prestigious Mobil Travel Guide five-
star rating and a AAA five-diamond rating.

Mulberry House
111 Clifton Lane
(615) 473-8437
www.mulberryhousenashville.com
Spacious and secluded contemporary guest
cottage with original art and stylish accents.

DINING
Watermark Restaurant
507 12th Avenue South
(615) 254-2000
www.watermark-restaurant.com
The downtown restaurant is known for its warm
atmosphere, fine dining, and excellent service.

Loveless Café
8400 Highway 100
(615) 646-9700
www.lovelesscafe.com
Popular with locals, celebrities, and world travelers for its quaint country charm and genuine
country cooking.

Jack's Bar-B-Que
416 Broadway
(615) 254-5715
www.jacksbarbque.com
Nashville's BBQ king serves mouthwatering
pork, beef, turkey, ribs, chicken, and other

southern cuisine slathered with award-winning sauces.

The Standard at the Smith House
167 Eighth Avenue North
(615) 254-1277
www.thestandard.com
Serves fresh, uniquely southern dishes in Nashville's oldest town house.

MEMPHIS, TN
(Graceland)

LODGING
The Peabody Hotel
149 Union Avenue
(901) 529-4000
www.peabodymemphis.com
The Memphis legend sits in the heart of town, fancy as ever. The ducks march at 11 and 5.

Heartbreak Hotel
3677 Elvis Presley Boulevard
(901) 332-1000
www.elvis.com
A short walk to Graceland, this themed and fun hotel has retro furnishings, a heart-shaped swimming pool, and several Elvis-themed suites.

Lauderdale Courts
252 North Lauderdale
(901) 523-8662
www.lauderdalecourts.com
Believe it or not, you can sleep in the small apartment (#328) where Elvis grew up.

DINING
Chez Philippe
149 Union Avenue
(901) 529-4188
The Peabody Hotel's signature restaurant epitomizes exquisite dining with impeccable service and French cuisine. Memphis's only Mobil four-star restaurant.

The Rendezvous
52 South Second Street
(901) 523-2746
This subterranean BBQ pork parlor features scads of memorabilia, celebrity photos, and platters of rubbed ribs, mustard-based coleslaw, pork shoulder sandwiches, lamb riblets, and chicken in a dozen dining rooms.

Arcade Restaurant
540 South Main Street
(901) 526-5757
One of Elvis's favorite eateries, the Arcade is also Memphis's oldest restaurant. Home cooking a few blocks from Beale Street. Ask to sit in the Elvis booth.

CLARKSDALE, MS
(Mississippi Delta)

LODGING
Big Pink Guesthouse
312 John Lee Hooker Lane
(662) 313-0321
www.bigpinkguesthouse.com
Deep South inn that pays tribute to its writers and musicians.

Delta Cotton Company
0 Blues Alley
(662) 645-9366
www.groundzerobluesclub.com
Cool apartments located above Morgan Freeman's world-famous Ground Zero blues club.

DINING
Madidi
164 Delta Avenue
(662) 627-7770
www.madidires.com
Fine dining, exquisite art, co-owned by Morgan Freeman.

Resthaven Restaurant
419 State Street
(662) 624-8601
An assorted choice of Italian, Greek, and Lebanese dishes to die for.

Abe's BBQ
616 State Street
(662) 624-9947
A Clarksdale must for BBQ, ribs, tamales, and history.

Hick's Hot Tamales
305 South State Street
(662) 624-9887
(888) 404-4257
www.hickstamales.com
Family-owned and -operated eatery serving homemade corn-shucked hot tamales, ribs, catfish, BBQ, and homemade sausage.

Ground Zero Blues Club
0 Blues Avenue
(662) 621-9009
www.groundzerobluesclub.com
Catfish, fried grits, sammiches, fried green
tomatoes, and burgers.

NEW ORLEANS, LA
(Mardi Gras)

Hotel Inter-Continental
444 St. Charles Avenue
(504) 525-5566
www.ichotelsgroup.com
Four blocks from the French Quarter, the hotel
is located on the "uptown" parade route and
features front-row grandstand viewing for the
passing parades.

Soniat House
1133 Chartres
(504) 522-0570
www.soniathouse.com
Historic boutique hotel with balconies and
a courtyard located on the quiet side of the
French Quarter, within walking distance of the
hottest music clubs and great restaurants.

Columns Hotel
3811 St. Charles Avenue
(504) 889-9308
(800) 445-9308
www.thecolumns.com
Boutique hotel located on the uptown parade
route; features a front porch veranda with views
of the passing streetcars.

Hotel Monteleone
214 Royal Street
(504) 708-4668
www.hotelmonteleone.com
The French Quarter's oldest hotel is historic,
haunted, and a bit pricey. Just two blocks from
parades, it features the Carousel Bar, one of the
city's most unique spots for a cocktail.

Hubbard Mansion Bed and Breakfast
3535 St. Charles Avenue
(504) 897-3535
www.hubbardmansion.com
Five-room inn in an elegant Greek Revival
home, furnished with period antiques and heir-
looms. On the Uptown parade route.

DINING
Emeril's
800 Tchoupitoulas
(504) 528 9393
www.emerils.com
www.chow.com
Flagship restaurant of one of the city's most
famous chefs, lives up to its reputation every
day. Dining room is handsome and waitstaff
is top-notch.

Brigtsen's
723 Dante Street
(504) 861-7610
www.brigstens.com
In the Riverbend. Serves upscale modern Creole
Acadian cuisine in a Victorian cottage.

Camellia Grill
626 South Carrollton Avenue
(504) 309-2679
Old-style diner beloved by locals. Some of the
best omelettes in town at any hour of the day.
Worth the wait in line for breakfast, lunch, or
dinner. Take the streetcar.

Johnny's Po-boys
511 St. Louis Street
(504) 524-8129
www.johnnyspoboy.com
Popular with locals, city politicians, and celebs.
The busy, crammed lunch counter is where the
family has been slinging po-boys since 1950.

Mother's
401 Poydras Street
(504) 523-9656
www.mothersrestaurant.net
Classic New Orleans home cooking including
jambalaya, etouffe, red beans and rice, gumbo,
oversized po-boys, fried seafood, and breakfast
all day. Worth the wait.

CHATTANOOGA, TN
(Rock City)

DINING
St. Johns
1278 Market Street
(423) 266-4400
www.stjohnsrestaurant.com
Locally owned downtown restaurant serving
four-star fine dining.

Back Inn Café
412 East 2nd Street
(423) 265-5033
www.bluffviewartdistrict.com
A renovated Colonial Revival mansion is the setting for upscale global cuisine with an extensive wine list.

Big River Grille & Brewing Works
222 Broad Street
(423) 267-2739
www.bigrivergrille.com
All-American food in a downtown microbrewery.

LODGING
Sheraton Read House
827 Broad Street
(423) 266-4121
(800) 691-1255
www.readhousehotel.com
Historic Georgian property in the heart of downtown Chattanooga.

The Chattanoogan Hotel & Urban Resort
1201 South Broad Street
(877) 756-1684
www.chattanooganhotel.com
Downtown, high-end urban resort, exquisite rooms and suites, outstanding restaurants, and a full-service spa.

Chattanooga Choo Choo
1400 Market Street
(423) 266-5000-(800) 872-2529
www.choochoo.com
Historic 1903 landmark, 24-acre vacation and convention complex in the heart of downtown Chattanooga.

TITUSVILLE, FL
(Kennedy Space Center)

LODGING
Holiday Inn Cocoa Beach Resort
1300 North Atlantic Avenue (A1A)
Cocoa Beach
(321) 783-2271
(800) 206-2747
www.hi-cocoa.com
Two adjacent beachfront hotels connected by a promenade park create a tropical sanctuary just right for families. Also offers a restaurant, snack bar, tennis, pool, shuffleboard, volleyball, and children's programs.

Wakulla Suites Resort
3550 North Atlantic Avenue (A1A)
Cocoa Beach
(321) 783-2230
(800) 992-5852
www.wakullasuites.com
The two-story tiki-style motel is clean, comfortable, and just off the beach. Completely furnished suites (with kitchens) sleep six and are great for families.

Jetty Park
400 East Jetty Road
Cape Canaveral
(321) 783-7111
www.portcanaveral.org
A sprawling park at the south side of Port Canaveral features restaurants, a grocery store, bicycle and fishing gear rentals, marine shops, a 4.5-acre beach—and 126 campsites for tents and RVs. Great place to watch a launch.

DINING
The Surf
2 South Atlantic Avenue
Cocoa Beach
(321) 783-2401
www.thesurfbarandgrill.com
Relive NASA's glory days by ducking into the restaurant where the Mercury 7 astronauts and their successors hosted their prelaunch dinners.

Dixie Crossroads
1475 Garden Street
(321) 268-5000
www.dixiecrossroads.com
A full slate of seafood choices fill up an extensive menu (plus corn fritters dusted with powdered sugar). A local legend that's always packed.

Atlantic Ocean Grille
Cocoa Beach Pier
Cocoa Beach
401 Meade Avenue
(321) 783-7549
On a pier 500 feet over the Atlantic, dine in style on super fresh seafood served broiled, blackened, grilled, or fried. The neighboring Boardwalk is an open-air bar on the pier.

Lone Cabbage Fish Camp
8199 State Road 520
(321) 632-4199
Cocoa

www.twisterairboatrides.com
Several miles inland, this is a Florida Cracker favorite, a down-home diner right on the St. Johns River. Catfish, frogs legs, alligator meat, burgers, hot dogs, and airboat rides.

ORLANDO, FL
(Black Gospel, Pie-Baking Contests)

LODGING
Walt Disney World
Lake Buena Vista
(407) 824-4500
www.waltdisneyworld.com
There are literally thousands of rooms available at the massive resorts, from modestly priced options to elaborate suites.

Grand Bohemian
325 South Orange Avenue
Orlando
(407) 313-9000
(866) 663-0024
www.grandbohemianhotel.com
A gorgeous and artistic downtown boutique hotel with a lively lounge.

Courtyard at Lake Lucerne
211 North Lucerne Circle East
(407) 648-5188
www.orlandohistoricinn.com
A collection of diverse and historic inns in the heart of Orlando, with the 1883 Dr. Phillips House, the I.W. Phillips House, the Norment-Parry Inn, and the art deco Wellborne Suites.

DINING
Victoria and Albert's
Grand Floridian Resort
Walt Disney World
(407) 934-3463
www.waltdisneyworld.com
Disney's signature restaurant. Intimate, formal, and the only AAA five-diamond rating in Central Florida.

California Grill
Contemporary Resort
Walt Disney World
(407) 934-3463
www.waltdisneyworld.com
Atop one of Disney's iconic hotels, offering a California-style dining experience and adding brilliant views of the Magic Kingdom.

Sonny's BBQ
7423 South Orange Blossom Trail
Orlando
(407) 859-7197
www.sonnysbbq.com
Big, down-home, affordable meals focused on BBQ, with huge portions of beans, coleslaw, catfish, and corn on the cob. Several locations in Orlando.

MIAMI BEACH, FL

LODGING
The Delano
1685 Collins Avenue
(305) 672-2000
(800) 697-1791
www.delano-hotel.com
Pricy, surreal, and always hip.

Indian Creek Hotel
2727 Indian Creek Drive
(305) 531-2727
www.indiancreekhotel.com
A Pueblo Deco oasis far from the buzz of Ocean Drive.

Miami River Inn
118 SW South River Drive
(305) 325-0045
(800) 468-3589
www.miamiriverinn.com
A bed and breakfast sanctuary in the heart of downtown on the tranquil Miami River.

DINING
Joe's Stone Crab Restaurant
11 Washington Avenue
(305) 673-0365
www.joesstonecrab.com
Before SoBe, Joe Be. A local legend since the early 1900s. Serves tons of stone crab claws daily between November and July.

11th Street Diner
11th Street and Washington Avenue
(305) 534-6373
www.eleventhstreetdiner.com
A 24-hour working-class diner in a cosmopolitan city.

Van Dyke Café
846 Lincoln Road
(305) 534-3600

www.thevandykecafe.com
Great food and even better service, both inside and at their trendy sidewalk café on Lincoln Road Mall.

KEY WEST, FL

LODGING
Casa Marina Resort & Beach Club
1500 Reynolds Street
(305) 296-3535
www.casamarinaresort.com
Originally built by railroad magnate Henry Flagler, the renovated and upgraded resort maintains the glorious lobby area with an Old World feel.

Marquesa Hotel
600 Fleming Street
(305) 292-1919
(800) 869-4631
www.marquesa.com
This gem, on the National Register of Historic Places, has been rated a AAA three-diamond hotel since the early '90s.

La Mer Hotel-Dewey House
504-506 South Street
(305) 296-6577
www.southernmostresorts.com
Two waterfront sister properties, the Victorian house features rooms with whirlpool tubs, private balconies or verandas, and an afternoon tea.

Key West Collection
For a wide range of lodging options, contact the Key West Welcome Center (800-284-4482, www.keywestwelcomecenter.com) or the Key West Information Center (305-292-5000 or 888-222-5145, www.keywestinfo.com), who both offer free assistance to locate lodging.

DINING
Mangoes Restaurant
700 Duval Street
(305) 292-4606
On the quiet side of Duval Street, with signature mushroom martini appetizers, a mango snapper entrée, and mango colada cocktails.

Blue Heaven Restaurant
729 Thomas Street
(305) 296-8666
A Key West institution in historic Bahama Village. Hemingway memorabilia throughout

(he officiated boxing matches there). Big breakfasts (homemade blueberry pancakes, lobster eggs benedict), lunch, and dinners.

Turtle Kraals
231 Margaret Street
(305) 294-2640
www.turtlekraals.com
At the historic seaport with a great view of boats, catamarans, and tall ships. Down-home seafood and other specialties, it's a local favorite.

MIDWEST

AKRON, OH
(Soap Box Derby)

LODGING
Sheraton Suites Akron Cuyahoga Falls
1989 Front Street
Cuyahoga Falls
(330) 929-3000
(800) 325-5788
www.sheratonakron.com
An all-suite property overlooking the river falls.

Quaker Square Inn at the University of Akron
135 South Broadway Street
(330) 253-5970
www.quakersquare.com
Located on the site of the original Quaker Oats factory, featuring circular "Silo" rooms.

The Inn at Brandywine Falls
8230 Brandywine Road
Northfield
(888) 467-1812
www.innatbrandywinefalls.com
Six rooms allow you to commune with the Cuyahoga Valley National Park, Ohio's only national park.

DINING
Ken Stewart's Grille
1970 West Market Street
(330) 867-2555
www.kenstewartsgrille.com
Gourmet cuisine with an exceptionally sophisticated eclectic flair.

Menches Brothers Restaurant
Canal Park, 300 South Main Street

(330) 375-1717
www.menchesbros.com
Recognized as the creators of the hamburger,
this restaurant anchors the National Hamburger
Festival celebrated each summer in Akron.

Swensons
40 South Hawkins Avenue
(330) 864-8416
www.swensonsdriveins.com
Car-side service is featured at this newly remod-
eled Akron landmark.

Vegiterranean
21 Furnace Street
(330) 374-5550
www.thevegiterranean.com
Akron-native Chrissie Hynde of the Pretenders
co-owns this vegan eatery.

CLEVELAND, OH
(Polka Fest)

LODGING
Cleveland Marriott Downtown
127 Public Square
(216) 696-9200
www.clevelandmarriottdowntown.com
The Marriott plays host to the Polka Festival
Thanksgiving weekend.

Doubletree Hotel Cleveland Downtown Lakeside
1111 Lakeside Avenue
(216) 241-5100
www.clevelanddowntownlakeside.doubletree.com
A modern (and reasonable) choice overlooking
Lake Erie.

Crowne Plaza Cleveland City Centre
777 St. Clair Avenue
(216) 771-7600
www.clevelanddowntownhotel.com
Upscale 472-room hotel with walking distance
of downtown attractions including the Rock
and Roll Hall of Fame.

DINING
Sokolowski's at University Inn
1201 University Road
(216) 771-9236
www.sokolowskis.com
Traditional Polish comfort foods and Cleveland
memorabilia reflecting three generations of
family history.

Sterle's Slovenian Country House
1401 East 55th Street
(216) 881-4181
www.sterlescountryhouse.com
Delicious German food and live polka music
on weekends.

Der Braumeister
13046 Lorain Avenue
(216) 671-6220
www.derbraumeister.net
A rustic watering hole and restaurant serving up
fine German and Belgian brews.

Melt Bar + Grilled
14718 Detroit Avenue
(216) 226-3699
www.meltbarandgrilled.com
More than 20 different takes on the All-American grilled cheese.

Great Lakes Brewing Company
2516 Market Avenue
(216) 771-4404
www.greatlakesbrewing.com
Eco-friendly restaurant and brewery with handcrafted beers named after local historical figures
and events

DETROIT, MI
(Greenfield Village)

LODGING
The Dearborn Inn
20301 Oakwood Boulevard
(313) 271-2700
www.dearborninnmarriott.com
Near Greenfield Village, this is a lovely 222-room
Federal-style inn built in 1931 by Henry Ford.

The Ritz Carlton-Dearborn
300 Town Center Drive
(313) 441-2000
www.ritzcarlton.com
308 well-appointed guest rooms only minutes
from the Village. Two restaurants, two ballrooms.

The Inn on Ferry Street
84 East Ferry Street
(313) 871-6000
www.theinnonferrystreet.com
Four restored Victorian homes and two carriage
houses in the East Ferry Street Historic District
of Midtown, 20 minutes from Dearborn.

DINING

Greenfield Village serves hearty park meals (gumbo, huge sandwiches, fried chicken) while at the **Golden Eagle Tavern** the bartender will whip up a cherry effervescent or phosphate, and serve you a salmagundi, a salad of chopped meat, anchovies, eggs, onions, and oil and vinegar.

Ciao
1024 Monroe Street
(313) 274-2426
www.ciaodearborn.com
Upscale Italian is served in Dearborn. Warm, relaxed, yet refined ambience.

MILWAUKEE, WI
(Harley-Davidson)

LODGING
Pfister Hotel
424 East Wisconsin
(414) 271-8222
(800) 558-8222
www.pfister-hotel.com
A local legend since it opened in 1893, this is as elegant as a grand downtown hotel should be.

The Intercontinental
139 East Kilbourn Avenue
(414) 276-8686
www.intercontinentalmilwaukee.com
Four stars on the shores of Lake Michigan. Contemporary style in the downtown business and theater district.

Iron Horse Hotel
500 West Florida Street
(888) 543-4766
www.theironhorsehotel.com
A Harley-themed luxury boutique hotel that opened downtown in 2008.

DINING
Lake Park Bistro
3133 East Newberry Boulevard
(414) 962-6300
www.lakeparkbistro.com
Traditional French dining with fresh ingredients. Outstanding views of Lake Michigan.

Sobleman's Pub & Grill
1900 West St. Paul Avenue
(414) 931-1919

www.milwaukeesbestburgers.com
A popular neighborhood blue-collar burger joint, with great (naturally) hamburgers.

Harley-Davidson Museum
6th and Canal Streets
(877) 436-8738
www.h-dmuseum.com
There are two dining options in the museum: the full-service 150-seat Motor, and faster food at Café Racer.

OSHKOSH, WI
(Oshkosh Air Show)

LODGING
Commercial Lodging
More than 600,000 visitors from 75 countries flock to Oshkosh during the air show, and most chain hotels sell out well and advance and require minimum stays of several days which is why most folks opt for private homes (below).

Private Housing Hotline
(920) 235-3007
www.visitoshkosh.com
The town's hotels sell out quickly, so families open their homes to travelers—for a fee.

DINING
Fratellos Waterfront Brewery & Restaurant
1501 Arboretum Drive
(920) 232-2337
www.supplerestaurantgroup.com-fratellos
Handcrafted microbrews and dining inside at multitier seating areas or outside on the patio overlooking the Fox River.

LaSure's Café
1570 Ripon Lane
(920) 231-5227
The food's so good you'll think your mom's in the kitchen.

Acee Deucee Lounge
667 West 8th Avenue
(920) 235-1453)
Tip a pint with aviation icons and locals in this historic AirVenture hangout.

MINNEAPOLIS, MN
(Mall of America)

LODGING
Minneapolis Depot
225 Third Avenue South
(612) 375.1700
www.thedepotminneapolis.com
Historic train station–turned–hotel features an indoor skating rink in the winter.

Nicollet Island Inn
95 Merriam Street
(612) 331-1800
www.nicolletislandinn.com
Built in 1893, the romantic oasis in the city is within walking distance of the funky northeast Minneapolis shopping district.

Chambers
901 Hennepin Avenue
(612) 767-6900
(877) 767-6990
A luxury art hotel with 60 guest rooms in a trendy Minneapolis neighborhood. Boutique hotel that combines art, culinary, and design influences.

DINING
La Belle Vie
510 Groveland Avenue
(612) 874-6440
www.labellevie.us
Elegant and upscale; almost perfect dining. Smaller portions served in the intimate wine bar.

Hell's Kitchen
80 South 9th Street
(612) 332-4700
www.hellskitcheninc.com
Known for breakfast and the bold tag line "Damn good food." Try the homemade peanut butter or the bison sausage.

INDIANAPOLIS, IN
(INDY 500)

LODGING
The Brickyard Crossing Golf Resort and Inn
4400 West 16th Street
(317) 241-2500
www.brickyardcrossing.com
The 108 rooms fill up quickly, but if you get in you'll be close to the track. Really close: It's about ten yard to the grandstands. Even their Pete Dye–renovated golf course is nearby—14 holes are outside the track, 4 are inside.

Conrad Indianapolis
50 West Washington Street
(317) 713-5000
www.conradindianapolis.com
Hilton's luxury brand. Private access to Circle Centre mall.

The Canterbury Hotel
123 South Illinois Street
(317) 634-3000
www.canterburyhotel.com
This 99-room boutique property is located in the heart of downtown.

The Villa Inn
1456 North Delaware Street
(317) 916-8500
www.thevillainn.com
Quaint castle-looking B&B in a historic downtown Indianapolis neighborhood, a stone's throw from the President Benjamin Harrison home.

DINING
Café Patachou
4911 North Pennsylvania Street
(317) 925-2823
www.cafepatachou.com
A health-conscious breakfast spot. All fresh midwestern ingredients and organic products.

R Bistro
888 MA Avenue
(317) 423-0312
www.rbistro.com
True farm-to-table eatery open for lunch and dinner, with the menu changing daily.

St. Elmo Steak House
127 South Illinois Street
(317) 635-0636
www.stelmos.com
Landmark in downtown Indianapolis since 1902, touting the largest wine cellar in the state.

ST. LOUIS, MO
(Gateway Arch, Anheuser-Busch)

LODGING
Westin St. Louis
811 Spruce Street
(314) 621-2000
www.starwoodhotels.com
In the historic Cupples Station section of the

city, near the historic courthouse and Gateway Arch. Features spa and health club.

St. Louis Union Station Marriott
1820 Market Street
(314) 621-5262
www.marriott.com
Located at the restored and historic Union Station, a St. Louis landmark. Architectural elegance and adjacent to plentiful shopping and dining.

Drury Hotel and Plaza at the Arch
2 South 4th Street
(314) 231-3003
(800) 378-7946
www.druryhotel.com
Just a few steps to the Gateway Arch, the former hat manufacturing building is now a very nice hotel run by very friendly people. Great (and free) breakfasts, friendly family atmosphere.

DINING
Tony's Restaurant
410 Market Street
(314) 231-7007
The restaurant has a warm upscale ambiance. Service is top notch. Tony's received AAA five-diamond status.

Sweetie Pie's
9841 West Florissant Avenue
(314) 521-9915
Named St. Louis's best soul-food restaurant.

Big Sky Café
47 South Old Orchard Avenue
Webster Groves
(314) 962-5757
Classic old favorites are updated and enlivened at this colorful and laid-back restaurant.

BRANSON, MO

LODGING
Hilton Branson Convention Center
200 East Main Street
(417) 336-5400
www.bransonconventioncenter.hilton.com
In the heart of historic downtown Branson and across from sister property, the Hilton Promenade and the Branson Landing retail and entertainment district on Lake Taneycomo.

Hotel Grand Victorian
2325 West Highway 76
(417) 336-2935
www.hotelgrandvictorian.com
Centrally located on the 76 Strip, within walking distance of most shows, restaurants, and attractions. Gazebo pool house, whirlpool, fireplace, free breakfast.

Big Cedar
612 Devil's Pool Road
Ridgedale
(800) 225-6343
www.big-cedar.com
Ten miles south of Branson, large lakefront resort with golf. Rooms range from wilderness lodge rooms to cottages and log cabins.

Bradford House
296 Blue Meadows Road
(888) 488-4445
www.bradfordhouse.us
Twenty-room Victorian-style bed and breakfast a short drive from the Highway 76 Strip and Silver Dollar City.

DINING
Candlestick Inn Restaurant and Lounge
Candlestick Road off E76
(417) 334-3633
Established in 1962 and still serving American eclectic cuisine with a European flair in the warm atmosphere of the Candlestick Inn. Great views of Lake Taneycomo and downtown Branson.

Bleu Olive
204 North Commercial Street
(417) 332-2538
www.bleuolive.com
Surprisingly trendy Mediterranean grille.

BillyGails
5291 State Highway 265
(417) 338-8883
Local favorite for unpretentious meals, quirky style, and an unusual setting—a converted filling station.

Sons of the Pioneers Chuckwagon Dinner Show
Shepherd of the Hills Outdoor Theatre
5586 West Highway 76
(417) 334-4191
(800) 653-6288
Cool, clear harmonies by one of the West's most

famous groups, accompanied by chicken, beef, corn on the cob, and other authentic "Old West" dishes.

Danna's BBQ
7930 East Highway 76
(417) 334-9541
www.dannssbbq.com
Tain't fancy, but a local-favorite BBQ joint serving great ribs, pulled pork, smoked chicken, and specialties like the "fat burger" and "garbage burger."

HANNIBAL, MO

LODGING
Garth Woodside Mansion
11069 New London Road
(573) 221-2789
(888) 427-8409
www.garthmansion.com
Gorgeous Victorian home on a 39-acre estate. Large rooms, grand architecture, large breakfasts, and plenty of country privacy.

LulaBelle's
111 Bird Street
(573) 221-6662
www.lulabelles.com
The former brothel is now one of Hannibal's finest dining and lodging establishments. Inviting bed and breakfast accommodations upstairs.

Quality Inn & Suites
120 Lindsey Drive (Highway 36)
(573) 221-4001
www.qualityinn.com
A practical choice that welcomes guests with a full hot buffet breakfast and indoor aquatic and fitness facility.

Hannibal's Inns
"Millionaire's Row" includes several bed and breakfasts including the **Dubach Inn** (221 North 5th, 573-355-1167, www.dubachinn.com); **Reagan's Queen Ann** (313 North 5th Street, 573-221-0774 or 888-221-1251, www.reagans queenanne), and **Garden House B&B** (301 North 5th Street, 573-221-7800 or 866-423-7800, www.gardenhousebedandbreakfast.com).

DINING
The Woodside Restaurant at Garth Mansion
11069 New London Road
(573) 221-2789
(888) 427-8409

www.garthmansion.com
At the estate of the Garth Woodside Mansion. Meals with an emphasis on fine Missouri cuisine crafted using herbs and ingredients from local farmers and purveyors.

Ole Planters Restaurant
316 North Main Street
(573) 221-4410
Family-owned restaurant with daily specials, plate lunches with three vegetables, BBQ, chicken fried steak, and homemade pies.

Star Dinner Theatre
215 South Main Street
(573) 221-7771
A 1906 vaudeville theatre that entertains guests with tasty dinners and a classic movie shown on a big screen.

GREAT PLAINS

KEYSTONE, SD
(Mount Rushmore)

LODGING
Custer State Park
13389 U.S. Highway 16A
Custer
(605) 255-4772
(888) 875-0001
www.custerresorts.com
Rates range widely at this stunningly gorgeous 73,000-acre park depending on whether you stay at a cabin, hotel, or lodge. Calvin Coolidge made the State Game Lodge and Resort his summer White House.

Alex Johnson
523 Sixth Street
Rapid City
(605) 342-1210
(800) 888-2539
www.alexjohnson.com
Historic hotel has welcomed six presidents since 1927. Looks the same as it did during the Coolidge administration.

K-Bar-S Lodge
434 Old Hill City Road
Keystone
(866) 522-7724

www.kbarslodge.com
Magnificent lobby, huge rock fireplace, western style, and views of Mount Rushmore. Sixty-four rooms on 45 wooded acres.

French Creek B&B
Custer
(605) 673-4790
(877) 673-4790
www.frenchcreekranch.com
Sophisticated yet comfortable, western hospitality year-round in the heart of the Black Hills.

Custer Mansion B&B
(605) 673-3333
(877) 519-4948
www.custermansionbb.com
A charming place to visit, a wonderful place to stay.

DINING
Corn Exchange
727 Main Street
Rapid City
(605) 343-5070
www.cornexchange.com
An amazing bistro in downtown Rapid City. Fine dining not far from Mount Rushmore.

Firehouse Brewing Company
610 Main Street
Rapid City
(605) 348-1915
www.firehousebrewing.com

Alpine Inn
225 Main Street
Hill City
(605) 574-2749
www.alpineinnhillcity.com
European style in the heart of the hills. Great steaks.

Sage Creek Grille
611 Mount Rushmore Road
Custer
(605) 673-2424
Fresh food made to order, and rustic breads. Daily dinner specials.

Custer State Park
www.custerresorts.com
Lodges at Custer State Park feature dining rooms for breakfast, lunch, and dinner. **Tatanka Dining Room** at Blue Bell Lodge (605-255-4535);

Legion Lake Dining Room (605-255-4521); **Lakota Dining Room** at the Sylvan Lake Resort (605-574-2561); and the **Pheasant Dining Room** (605-255-4541) at the State Game Lodge.

CHEYENNE, WY
(Rodeo)

LODGING
Nagle Warren Mansion
222 East 17th Street
(307) 637-3333
(800) 811-2610
www.naglewarrenmansion.com
An 1888 Victorian home restored to yesterday's luxury with today's comforts. Named the West's best B&B by *True West* magazine.

The Historic Plains Hotel
1600 Central Avenue
(307) 638-3311
(866) 275-2467
www.theplainshotel.com
Classic boutique property that's been a downtown fixture since 1911.

The Little America Hotel and Resort
2800 West Lincolnway
(307) 775-8400
(800) 445-6945
www.littleamerica.com-cheyenne
A full-service hotel-resort featuring a nine-hole executive golf course and Olympic-size outdoor swimming pool.

DINING
Albany Restaurant
1506 Capitol Avenue
(307) 638-3507
www.albanycheyenne.com
A local favorite since 1942. Old-fashioned American food, and a bar to boot.

Luxury Diner
1401 West Lincolnway
(307) 638-8971
Funky and down-home restaurant in an old railroad car. Quite popular with locals.

Poor Richard's Restaurant
2233 East Lincolnway
(307) 635-5114
www.poorrichardscheyenne.com
Fine continental dining.

YELLOWSTONE, WY
(Yellowstone National Park)

LODGING
Park Lodging
(866) 439-7375
www.xanterra.com
www.travelyellowstone.com
Old Faithful Inn, the park's landmark hotel, is a towering log structure with a wide-open lobby highlighted by a 500-ton stone fireplace. Other lodging options, from hotels to cabins to campgrounds, are available throughout the park.

DINING
Park Dining
(307) 344-7311
www.travelyellowstone.com
Dining options range from cafeterias and snack bars to grocery stores and delis. The large hotels (Mammoth Hot Springs Hotel, Old Faithful Inn, Grant Village, Canyon Lodge, and Lake Yellowstone Hotel) have dining rooms, and there are also Old West cookouts you reach via horseback.

CROW AGENCY, MT
(Little Bighorn)

LODGING
American Inn
1324 North Crawford Avenue
Hardin
(406) 665-1870
(800) 582-8094
www.hardinamericaninn.com
A 43-room motel with pool and waterslide, fine for families. Free continental breakfast. In Hardin, 15 miles from Little Big Horn.

Western Motel
830 West 3rd Street
Hardin
(406) 665-2296
www.westernmotel.net
Family-owned and operated motel with clean, comfortable rooms.

Super 8
201 West 14th Street
Hardin
(406) 665-1700

Chain option in town, with free Internet and continental breakfast.

DINING
Purple Cow
1485 North Montana Highway 47
(406) 665-3601
Hardin
Family-style restaurant with homemade steaks, chicken, sandwiches, pies, soup, bread, and rolls at breakfast, lunch, and dinner.

Merry Mixer
317 North Center Street
(406) 665-3735
Hardin
Decades-old family-owned restaurant, serving steaks, hamburgers, and chicken dishes.

Lariat Country Kitchen
721 North Center Avenue
(406) 665-1139
Hardin
Country folks, country food, country setting. Cute and quaint with a local coffee club that makes you feel right at home.

DALLAS, TX
(Dealey Plaza, Texas State Fair)

LODGING
Adolphus
1321 Commerce Street
(214) 742-8200
www.hoteladolphus.com
Opened in 1912, this has earned the right to be named the "Grand Dame of Dallas Hotels." The service matches the landmark's architectural splendor, which has been called "the most beautiful building west of Venice."

The Joule
1530 Main Street
(214) 261-4491
www.luxurycollection.com-joule
Renovated 1920s downtown Dallas bank is now a luxury boutique hotel

Bailey's Uptown Inn
2505 Worthington Street
(214) 720-2258
www.baileysuptowninn.com
Mid-priced bed and breakfast in the trendy uptown district.

DINING

Stephan Pyles
1807 Ross Avenue
(214) 580-7000
www.stephanpyles.com
"New Millennium" southwestern cuisine served in a super modern, yet warmly inviting, setting in the Dallas Arts District.

All Good Café
2934 Main Street
(214) 742-5362
www.allgoodcafe.com
Diner-style food with Texas favorites. Live music on the weekends.

Mi Cocina
3699 McKinney Avenue
(469) 533-5663
www.mcrowd.com-micocina.shtm
Flavorful cuisine with tastes from the Lone Star state and across the border. Assorted margarita flavors make this a local hangout during happy hour.

SAN ANTONIO, TX
(The Alamo)

LODGING

Menger Hotel
204 Alamo Plaza
(210) 223-4361
www.mengerhotel.com
Across the alley from the Alamo. Built in 1859, it's only improved with age and reflects its rich heritage with displays, a spa, gardens, historic bar, and restaurant.

Hotel Valencia
50 East Houston Street
(210) 227-9700
(866) 842-0100
www.hotelvalencia-riverwalk.com
A 213-room contemporary luxury hotel on the Riverwalk in downtown San Antonio. Stylish Old World palazzo with modern conceptual design.

Grand Hyatt San Antonio
600 East Market Street
(210) 224-1234
www.hyatt.com
On the Riverwalk, a blend of modernism and Latin culture.

The Watermark Hotel & Spa
212 West Crockett Street
(866) 605-1212
www.watermarkhotel.com
The city's only Mobil four-star hotel and spa, with 99 luxury hotel rooms and suites on the Riverwalk.

Drury Plaza
105 South St. Mary's Street
(210) 270-7799
www.druryhotels.com
The lobby features 50-foot ceilings, travertine flooring, and stained-glass windows—this was once the Alamo Bank. The 24-story skyscraper was renovated to maintain its historic character while creating modern comforts.

The Havana Inn
1015 Navarro
(210) 222-2008
(888) 224-2008
www.havanariverwalkinn.com
Built in 1914, the building has the air of an Italianate villa. Its 28 rooms and suites have eclectic antiques and historic photographs, creating a turn-of-the-century Old Havana feel.

DINING

Mi Tierra Cafe & Bakery
218 Produce Row
(210) 225-1262
www.mitierracafe.com
Started in 1941 as a three-table café, this is now a popular 24-hour destination with a cool bar, bakery, and strolling musicians.

Taco Haven
1032 South Presa
210-533-2171
www.tacohaven.info
Welcome to Taco Haven of San Antonio, one of south Texas's finest in authentic Mexican food.

Boudro's
421 East Commerce
(210) 224-8484
www.boudros.com
A distinctive menu of Texas and southwestern specialties. Sidewalk tables right on the Riverwalk.

Riverwalk
On a casual stroll you'll come across numerous restaurants, most of them featuring waterfront sidewalk cafés.

ROCKY MOUNTAIN WEST

ASPEN, CO

LODGING

Hotel Jerome
(970) 920-1000
330 East Main Street
www.hoteljerome.com
Aspen's crown jewel since 1889. Comfortably elegant accommodations, impeccable dining and service, and a sophisticated yet relaxed ambience.

St. Regis Aspen
315 East Dean Street
(970) 920-3300
www.stregis.com-aspen
Luxury hotel at the base of Aspen Mountain, with 179 guest rooms and suites, 20 with fireplaces. Superb staff and seductive spa.

Sky Hotel
709 East Durant Avenue
(970) 925-6760
www.theskyhotel.com
Trendy luxury hotel; a hotspot on the town's see-and-be-seen scene. Ski-in access.

The Little Nell
675 East Durant Avenue
(970) 920-4600
(888) 843-6355
www.thelittlenell.com
Vibrant, fashionable choice that's not stuffy. Boutique style rooms with ski-in-ski-out convenience.

Hotel Lenado
200 South Aspen Street
(970) 925-6246
(800) 321-3457
www.hotellenado.com
Rustic mountain lodge with 19 distinctive rooms next to Whitaker Park.

Mountain House Lodge
905 East Hopkins
(866) 920-2550
www.mountainhouselodge.com
An unusual find: location, hospitality, and value—24 rooms near downtown. Complimentary breakfast.

DINING

Cache Cache
205 South Mill Street
(970) 925-3835
www.cachecache.com
Modern American bistro with classical French cuisine, emphasis on table and wine service (a 5,000-bottle inventory).

Piñons
105 South Mill Street
(970) 920-2021
www.pinons.net
Traditional American cuisine influenced by local products. Leather, suede and lodgepole decor evokes the casual western elegance of Aspen. The windows frame picturesque Aspen Mountain.

Little Annie's Eating House
517 Hyman Avenue
(970) 925-1098
www.littleannies.com
For hamburgers, stews, chili, and sandwiches.

Boogies Diner
534 East Cooper Ave
(970) 925-6610
Burgers, grilled cheese, and basic fares make this a good choice for families.

SALT LAKE CITY, UT
(Mormon Tabernacle Choir)

LODGING

The Grand America Hotel
555 South Main Street
(801) 258-6000
(800) 304-9346
www.grandamerica.com
Five-diamond downtown hotel with 775 spacious guest rooms, which includes 395 suites. Includes a world-class spa, indoor and outdoor pools, views of the Rocky Mountains.

Hotel Monaco
15 West 200 South
(810) 595-0000
(877) 294-9710
www.monaco-saltlakecity.com
Seductive and stylish rooms and suites set in a meticulously refurbished, landmark 14-story building.

Inn on the Hill
225 North State Street
(801) 328-1466
www.innonthehillslc.com
Elegant historic manor home near
downtown Salt Lake City. Views of the
city or intimate gardens that surround
this sanctuary. Complimentary continental
breakfast.

DINING
Cucina Toscana
307 West Pierpont Avenue
(801) 328-3463
www.cucina-toscana.com
Several dining experiences in several dining
rooms. Authentic Tuscan fare in a visually dramatic atmosphere.

Squatters Pub Brewery
147 West Broadway
801-363-2739
www.squatters.com
Big boisterous brewery (and burgers). Eco-
friendly and hip.

The Garden Restaurant
15 East South Temple
(801) 539-3170
www.diningattemplesquare.com
The 10th-floor restaurant is themed to the
Mormon Tabernacle Choir.

PARK CITY, UT
(Sundance Film Festival)

LODGING
Hotel Park City
2001 Park Avenue
(435) 200-2000
www.hotelparkcity.com
Service-oriented upscale 100-suite lodge.
Contemporary American cuisine served in
the lodge restaurant.

Old Town Guest House
1011 Empire Avenue
(435) 649-2642
(800) 290-6423, ext. 3710
www.oldtownguesthouse.com
Charming four-unit bed and breakfast
close to downtown. Wilderness decor with
lodgepole pine furniture. Great for outdoor
enthusiasts.

Silver Boutique Queen Hotel
632 Main Street
(800) 447-6423
www.silverqueenhotel.com
Boutique hotel featuring twelve one- and two-
bedroom condominium-style rooms. Perfect
downtown location, offers rooftop deck and
hot tub.

Washington School Inn
543 Park Avenue
(435) 649-3808
(800) 824-1672
www.washingtonschoolinn.com
Lodge in a historic 1889 schoolhouse by the
Wasatch Mountains. Fifteen modern rooms,
two with wood-burning fireplaces.

DINING
350 Main
350 Main Street
(435) 649-3140
www.350main.com
Eclectic choice of contemporary fusion cuisine,
blending American, Latin, Asian, and Caribbean tastes.

Purple Sage
434 Main Street
(435) 655-9505
www.purplesageparkcity.com
American Western cuisine served in an upscale
restaurant. Beef dishes a specialty.

The Eating Establishment
317 Main Street
(435) 649-8284
www.theeatingestablishment.net
Casual and cozy family-favorite. Comfort food
line up of breakfasts, burgers, fish and chips,
salads, sandwiches, and barbecued pork, beef,
or chicken.

ALBUQUERQUE, NM
(Indian Powwow, Balloon Fiesta)

LODGING
Nativo Lodge
6000 Pan American Freeway NE
(505) 798-4300
(888) 628-4861
www.nativolodge.com
A nice complement for the Gathering,
with Native American influenced–decor.

Conveniently located, easy to get to, with a great rate.

Albuquerque Marriott Pyramid North
5151 San Francisco Road NE
(505) 821-3333
(800) 627-7468
www.marriott.com-abqmc
Perfect location for Balloon Fiesta. Large hotel with easy access to interstate. Book early.

Sandia Resort & Casino
30 Rainbow Road NE
(505) 798-3978
(877) 272-9199
www.sandiacasino.com
Resort close to Balloon Fiesta Park with spa, golf, dining, gorgeous view of the balloons.

Chocolate Turtle B&B
1098 West Meadowlark Lane
Corrales
(505) 898-1800
(877) 298-1800
www.chocolateturtlebb.com
Beautiful Southwestern architecture and landscaping complement this B&B in the neighboring village of Corrales.

Isleta Casino and Resort
11000 Broadway Boulevard SE
(505) 244-8171
www.isleta-casino.com
Resort owned by the Isleta Pueblo. Spa, golf, casino, family entertainment.

Downtown Historic Bed & Breakfasts
207 High Street NE
(505) 842-0223
www.albuquerque bedandbreakfasts.com
Gorgeous B&B properties with a hint of mystery and fascinating histories. Minutes from Gathering of Nations.

DINING
Pueblo Harvest Café
2401 12th Street NW
Indian Pueblo Cultural Center
(505) 843-7270
(866) 855-7902
www.indianpueblo.com
Albuquerque's only Native American–owned restaurant, featuring Sunday brunch, musical entertainment on weekends.

Tiwa Steakhouse
11000 Broadway, SE
(505) 244-8188
(800) 460-5686
www.isleta-casino.com
Fine dining at the Isleta Casino and Resort.

Tucanos Brazilian Grill
110 Central Avenue, SW
(505) 246-9900
www.tucanos.com
Brazilian churrasco tradition of grilling, with seasoned meats cooked on skewers over open-flame grills and sliced onto your plate.

Sadie's of New Mexico
6230 Fourth Street, NW
(505) 345-5339
www.sadiesofnewmexico.com
Local favorite with hot chile, delicious salsa, huge portions. Great hidden find.

Sandiago's Mexican Grill at the Tram
38 Tramway Loop NE
(505) 856-6692
www.sandiapeak.com
High-altitude eatery, with gorgeous view of the city. Perfect at sunset.

Sunshine Café
1134 Mountain Road NW
(505) 242-1499
www.sunshinecafe.biz
Great café to sit at and watch the sky dotted with hot-air balloons. Serves locally grown produce and homemade products.

Corn Maiden
1300 Tuyuna Trail
Santa Ana Pueblo
(505) 867-1234
(800) 554-9288
www.tamaya.hyatt.com
Southwestern-infused dishes, gorgeous views of the Sandia Mountains, especially at sunset.

TOMBSTONE, AZ

LODGING
Katie's Cozy Cabins
16 West Allen Street
(520) 559-0464
www.cabinsintombstone.com

Kitchenettes, lofts, and separate bedrooms with bunk beds, cable TV-DVD player, and porches with swings.

Larian Motel
410 East Fremont Street
(520) 457-2272
www.tombstonemotels.com
Large rooms, free coffee, refrigerators available. One block from historic Allen Street.

Tombstone Sagebrush Inn
320 East Bruce Street
(520) 457-3211
www.tombstonesagebrushinn.com
Two blocks to the historic district. John Wayne stayed here!

Stampede RV Park
201 West Allen Street
(520) 457-3738
www.tombstone-stampede.com
Walking distance of historic district. Fifty spaces, tent sites, and B&B cabins available.

DINING

The Depot Steakhouse-Johnny Ringo's Bar
60 South 10th Street
(520) 457-3404
Featuring homemade Sonoran Mexican cuisine and steaks.

World Famous Crystal Palace Saloon
436 East Allen Street
(520) 457-3611
www.crystalpalacesaloon.com
"Good whiskey, tolerable water"—along with burgers, ribs, pizza, and steaks.

Nellie Cashman Restaurant
127 South 5th Street
(520) 457-2212
Full service, family-style restaurant serving homemade meals in one of Tombstone's historic buildings.

Six Gun City
128 South 5th Street
(520) 457-3827
www.6guncity.com
The only show in Tombstone with food, drinks, and live western music.

GRAND CANYON, AZ
(Grand Canyon National Park)

LODGING

Grand Canyon National Park Lodges
(303) 297-2757
(928) 638-7888
(888) 297-2757
www.xanterra.com
www.grandcanyonlodges.com
The park's signature lodging experience is the El Tovar. Only a few steps from the rim, it opened in 1905 and features the distinctive stone-and-timber design, concierge and room service, and fine dining at the on-site restaurant. Visit the website for other lodges and camping information.

Grand Hotel
State Highway 64
Tusayan
(928) 638-3333
(888) 634-7263
www.gcanyon.com
In the style of an Old West national park resort, housed in an attractive and spacious hotel.

DINING

Grand Canyon National Park Dining
(928) 638-2631
Call for complete information of dining choices within the park, although the dining room at the El Tovar is the only restaurant that requires reservations.

Canyon Star
Tusayan
(928) 638-3333
(888) 634-7263
www.gcanyon.com
Inside the Grand Hotel. Serves large portions of hand-carved steaks and turkey and includes nightly entertainment.

LAS VEGAS, NV
(Las Vegas, Miss America Pageant)

LODGING
Resorts
There are billions of dollars worth of grand resorts; with most along the Strip. Here are some: **Luxor** (3900 Las Vegas Blvd., 702-262-4000, 800-288-1000, www.luxor.com); **New York New York** (3790 Las Vegas Blvd., 702-740-6969, 800-693-6763, www.nynyhotelcasino.com); **MGM Grand** (3799 Las Vegas Blvd., 702-891-1111, 800-929-1111, www.mgmgrand.com); **The Mirage** (3400 Las Vegas

Blvd., 702-791-7111, 800-627-6667, www.
mirage.com); **Treasure Island** (3300 Las Vegas
Blvd., 702-894-7111, 800-944-7444, www.
treasureisland.com); **Monte Carlo** (3770 Las
Vegas Blvd., 702-730-7777, 800-311-8999,
www.monte-carlo.com), **Caesars Palace** (3570
Las Vegas Blvd., 702-731-7110, 800-634-6001,
www.caesars.com); **Excalibur** (3850 Las Vegas
Blvd., 702-597-7777, 800-937-7777, www.
excaliburcasino.com); **Mandalay Bay** (3950 Las
Vegas Blvd., 702-632-7777, 877-632-7000,
www.mandalaybay.com); **Venetian** (3355 Las
Vegas Blvd., 702-414-1000 or 888-283-6423,
www.venetian.com).

Hard Rock Hotel
4455 Paradise Road
(702) 693-5000
(800) 473-7625
www.hardrockhotel.com
Hits the jackpot with its rock and roll attitude
and collectibles.

La Quinta
3970 South Paradise Road
(702) 796-9000
Just a few blocks from the action, it also has a pool.

Golden Gate Hotel and Casino
1 Fremont Street
(702) 385-1906
(800) 426-1906
www.goldengatecasino.net
The oldest hotel in Vegas, and still kinda cute.
Down on historic Fremont.

DINING
Alex at Wynn
3131 Las Vegas Boulevard
(702) 770-7000
(888) 320-7123
www.wynnlasvegas.com
High-style, pricey dining room with crystal
chandeliers and mahogany wood. Prix fixe
menus and seasonal tasting options.

Joel Robuchon at MGM Grand
3799 Las Vegas Boulevard South
(702) 891-7925
www.mgmgrand.com
High roller favorite paying tribute to 1930s
Paris in a stylish and intimate 64-seat restaurant.

Village Seafood Buffet at The Rio
3700 West Flamingo Road

(702) 777-7777
As much prawns, salmon, king crab, snow crab,
shrimp, and lobster as you can handle—along
with unlimited desserts.

Cravings at The Mirage
3400 Las Vegas Boulevard South
(702) 791-7223
Chefs prepare international meals at eleven
cooking stations, from a raw bar to dim sum,
bruschetta bread to rotisserie chicken.

PACIFIC COAST-HAWAII-ALASKA

SEATTLE, WA
(Space Needle)

The Fairmont Olympic Hotel
411 University Street
(206) 621-1700
www.fairmont.com-seattle
Since opening in 1924, the Fairmont Olympic
Hotel has combined traditional warmth with
21st-century convenience and personalized
service.

Inn at the Market
86 Pine Street
(206) 443-360
(800) 446-4484
www.inatthemarket.com
Located in Seattle's famous Pike Place Market
with views of the city skyline or Puget Sound.

Inn at Harbor Steps
1221 First Avenue
(206) 748-0973
(888) 728-8910
www.inatharborsteps.com
This Four Sisters Inn blends the modern luxuries and sophisticated services of a boutique
hotel with the traditional amenities and architecture of a B&B.

DINING
SkyCity Restaurant
(206) 905-2100
(800) 937-9582
www.spaceneedle.com
Atop the Needle, this warm and elegant

restaurant is the world's oldest revolving restaurant. Make a complete circuit every 47 minutes.

Rover's
2808 East Madison Street
(206) 325-7442
www.rovers-seattle.com
Pacific Northwest cuisine refined by a French accent, using traditional French techniques to bring out flavors of the region's freshest ingredients.

Campagne
86 Pine Street
(206) 728-2800
www.campagnerestaurant.com
In the Pike Place Market, serving dishes inspired by the cuisine of southern France, but with fresh produce, seafood, and game of the Pacific Northwest.

5 Spot
1502 Queen Anne Avenue North
(206) 285-7768
www.chowfoods.com-five
Big flavored comfort foods and kitsch from all points of the U.S. Menus inspired by the nation's cultural roots and history and found on kitchen tables across America.

SAN FRANCISCO, CA
(Golden Gate Bridge, Cable Cars)

The Ritz-Carlton
600 Stockton Street
(415) 296-7465
www.ritzcarlton.com
Luxury hotel featuring 336 guest rooms and suites, all improved with a $12.5 million renovation. Mobil five-star fine dining.

Hotel Vitale
8 Mission Street
(415) 278-3700
(888) 890-8688
www.hotelvitale.com
Modern luxury hotel with stunning views of the bay. On-site spa with rooftop soaking tubs, penthouse-level yoga studio, and signature restaurant.

Hotel Drisco
2901 Pacific Avenue
(415) 346-2880
www.jdvhotels.com

One of several boutique hotels represented by a single company. Like Hotel Drisco, most are based on the California lifestyle experience: fresh, inventive, and casual.

DINING
The Dining Room at The Ritz-Carlton
600 Stockton Street
(415) 296-7465
www.ritzcarltondiningroom.com
Elegantly crafted dishes present a unique and exciting dining experience.

The Beach Chalet Brewery and Restaurant
1000 Great Highway
(415) 753-5260
www.beachchalet.com
In Golden Gate Park. Ocean and garden views, handcrafted beer, full bar and a modern American menu with seaside accents for breakfast, lunch and dinner.

Fisherman's Wharf
www.fishermanswharf.org
Lots of restaurants and stands that serve fresh seafood, most notably dungeness crab and clam chowder served in a sourdough bread bowl. Thirteen bayview restaurants at Pier 39 (www.pier39.com).

NAPA VALLEY, CA

LODGING
Solage Calistoga Resort & Spa
755 Silverado Trail
Calistoga
(866) 942-7442
www.SolageCalistoga.com
An "Upvalley" gem where cosmopolitan luxuries take on a comfortable, enlightened attitude.

The Carneros Inn
4048 Sonoma Highway
Napa
(888) 400-9000
www.thecarnerosinn.com
In the beautiful Napa Carneros winegrowing region, a luxurious retreat designed to make absolutely everything feel better.

The Zinfandel Inn Bed & Breakfast
800 Zinfandel Lane
St. Helena
(707) 963-3512
www.zinfandelinn.com

An elegant stone inn known as the "castle in the vineyards".

DINING

The French Laundry
6640 Washington Street
Yountville
(707) 753-0088
www.frenchlaundry.com
Thomas Keller's legendary Michelin three-star masterpiece.

The Culinary Institute of America at Greystone
Wine Spectator Restaurant
2555 Main Street
St. Helena
(707) 967-1010
www.ciachef.edu-California
One of the Napa Valley's best is part of the Culinary Institute of America's western campus. Great ambiance, wine country cuisine and an all-California wine list.

Oxbow Public Market
610-644 First Street
Napa
(707) 226-6529
www.oxbowpublicmarket.com
A riverfront market hall with more than 20 artisan food and wine vendors, restaurants, and retail shops.

YOSEMITE, CA
(Yosemite National Park)

LODGING

Ahwahnee
(209) 372-1407
Built in 1927, this is the premier choice. The majestic lodge is breathtaking in design, superb in service, and costly in rates.

Yosemite Lodging Options
(801) 559-5000
www.yosemitepark.com
Yosemite accommodates nearly every budget, with rooms offered from canvas tents to cabins to motel-style lodges. For campground reservations call (877) 444-6777 or visit www.recreation.gov.

DINING
Ahwahnee

(209) 372-1489
The baronial dining room seems as large as the park itself, and the menu features items you would expect in the mountains of California.

DEATH VALLEY, CA
(Death Valley National Park)

LODGING

Furnace Creek Resort
(760) 786-2345
www.furnacecreekresort.com
A luxurious resort in the middle of Death Valley? Yes. Great views and the world's lowest golf course.

Amargosa Hotel
(760) 852-4441
www.amargosa-opera-house.com
Quirky hotel. How quirky? They still do a cabaret show in the middle of nowhere. Basic, but here.

Death Valley Inns
Stovepipe Wells (760-786-2387, www.stovepipewells.com) features 83 motel rooms, an RV park, gas, a general store, swimming pool, and saloon. The **Panamint Springs Resort** (775-482-7680, www.deathvalley.com) is a traditional 15-room motel a few miles from the base of the Inyo Mountains.

DINING

Furnace Creek Inn
(760) 786-3385
www.furnacecreekresort.com
The Inn Dining Room offers fine dining at breakfast, lunch, and dinner with stunning views of the desert salt pans and the majestic Panamint Mountains.

PASADENA, CA
(Rose Bowl)

LODGING

The Langham, Huntington Hotel & Spa
1401 South Oak Knoll Avenue
(626) 568-3900
(800) 591-7481
www.pasadena.langhamhotels.com
A AAA five diamond, this Pasadena landmark hotel features Michelin-rated dining, spa, and salon.

Saga Motor Hotel
1633 East Colorado Boulevard

(626) 795-0431
(800) 793-7242
www.thesagamotorhotel.com
On Old Route 66 (now Colorado Boulevard) and on the Rose Parade route. Spacious rooms with a country feel and the best complimentary continental breakfast in town.

The Bissell House
201 Orange Grove Avenue
(626) 441-3535
(800) 441-3530
www.bissellhouse.com
Located minutes from Pasadena and voted one of the Top 10 romantic inns of 2006 by American Historic Inns.

DINING
Maison Akira
713 East Green Street
(626) 796-9501
www.maisionakira.com
Fine French cuisine with a Japanese flair.

JJ Steak House
88 West Colorado Boulevard
(626) 844-8889
www.jjsteakhouse.net
Located in Old Pasadena, it offers the finest quality steaks and seafood.

Pie N Burger
913 East California Boulevard
(626) 795-1123
www.pienburger.com
A Pasadena institution since 1963; offering the best burgers and pies in town.

ANAHEIM, CA
(Disneyland)

LODGING
Disneyland
(714) 956-6425
www.disneyland.com
Disney has several lodging options including the Disneyland Hotel, the original resort when the park first opened. The Grand Californian is a re-creation of a grand lodge in the Arts and Crafts style.

Hilton Anaheim
11777 Harbor Boulevard

Garden Grove
(714) 703-9100
www.hiltongardeninn.com
Outside of downtown, the traditional offerings of the Hilton chain.

Hotel Ménage
1221 South Harbor Boulevard
(888) 462-7275
www.hotelmenage.com
Modern luxury boutique hotel in a chic environment.

DINING
Anaheim White House
887 South Anaheim Boulevard
(714) 772-1381
Exceptional service and award-winning classic Northern Italian cuisine and a hidden gem in Anaheim.

La Casa Garcia
531 West Chapman Avenue
(714) 740-1108
Authentic Mexican food with no frills, just the real deal.

Bar Louie Tavern & Grill
321 West Katella Avenue
(714) 495-4170
www.barlouieamerica.com
Hip neighborhood restaurant and bar specializing in oversized sandwiches and artfully created jumbo martinis. Also pastas, entrées, beers, and microbrews.

Downtown Disney
www.downtowndisney.com
A wide array of fast-food eateries, sit-down restaurants, food kiosks, and clubs near the gates of Disneyland.

BEVERLY HILLS, CA
(Acadamy Awards, Beverly Hills)

LODGING
Beverly Hills Hotel and Bungalows
9641 Sunset Boulevard
(310) 276-2251
www.thebeverlyhillshotel.com
"The Pink Palace" is a luxury, five-star hotel in the center of Beverly Hills that is surrounded by 12 acres of lush, tropical gardens; exotic flowers; and private walkways.

The Beverly Hilton
9876 Wilshire Boulevard
(310) 274-7777
www.beverlyhilton.com
Opened in 1955 by Conrad Hilton. Combines
Hollywood excitement and Beverly Hills elegance.

Beverly Wilshire, A Four Seasons Hotel
9500 Wilshire Boulevard
(310) 275-5200
fourseasons.com-beverlywilshire
A Four Seasons hotel in the heart of Beverly
Hills. Steps from renowned Rodeo Drive. The
historic hotel buzzes with vitality from dramatic
renovations that blend tradition and trend.

Avalon Hotel
9400 West Olympic Boulevard
(310) 277-5200
www.avalonbeverlyhills.com
Sophisticated hideaway set around a dramatic
pool terrace with private cabanas. From intimate guest rooms to expansive suites.

Mosaic Hotel
125 S Spalding Dr
(310) 278-0303
www.mosaichotel.com
Luxurious accommodations in a relaxed, comfortable setting surrounded by a heated garden and pool.

Luxe Rodeo Drive
360 N. Rodeo Drive
(310) 273-0303
www.luxehotelrodeodrive.com
A glamorous location coupled with deluxe
amenities including in-room spa service and
a rooftop restaurant and bar.

Maison 140 Beverly Hills
140 South Lasky Drive
(310) 281-4000
www.maison140beverlyhills.com
A one-of-a-kind hotel puts an eastern spin on
classic French elegance.

DINING
CUT
9500 Wilshire Blvd
310.276.8500
www.wolfgangpuck.com
Ranked as one of 2007's best new restaurants
Wolfgang Puck presents a modern take on the
classic steakhouse featuring a sidebar and posh
"ultra lounge."

Spago
176 North Canon Drive
(310) 385-0880
www.wolfgangpuck.com
Flagship restaurant of the Wolfgang Puck Fine
Dining Group. Seasonal menus showcase the
best of California's produce and products.

Nate'n Als
414 North Beverly Drive
(310) 274-0101
www.natenal.com
Famous delicatessen in the heart of Beverly
Hills. Since 1945 serving smoked fish, corned
beef brisket, pastrami, and matzo ball soup.

The Farm of Beverly Hills
439 North Beverly Drive
(310) 273-5578
www.thefarmofbeverlyhills.com
Downtown comfort food haven. An indoor-
outdoor fireplace in the bar and patio and a
private dining room for 25. Innovative American cuisine at breakfast, lunch, and dinner.

Muse
225 North Canon Drive
(31) 860-7800
www.montagebeverlyhills.com
Choose to dine from the chef's personal menu
or try a specially prepared wine pairing dinner
in this intimate dining room.

HONOLULU, HI
(Pearl Harbor, Surfing, Luaus)

LODGING
Moana Surfrider
2365 Kalakaua Avenue
(808) 922-3111
www.Moana-Surfrider.com
In the heart of Waikiki Beach, the oceanfront
Moana Surfrider introduced the world to
Hawaiian hospitality in 1901. Often referred
to as the "first lady of Waikiki."

The Royal Hawaiian
2259 Kalakaua Avenue
(808) 923-7311
www.royal-hawaiian.com
Built in 1927, the iconic Royal Hawaiian
Hotel is known as the "pink palace of the
Pacific." Known as an exclusive enclave for
luxury and romance.

Hotel Renew
129 Paoakalani Avenue
(808) 687-7700
www.hotelrenew.com
Dramatic lighting, striking artwork, and elegant guest rooms with an intimate atmosphere created in the spirit of wellness, ease and comfort.

Manoa Valley Inn
2001 Vancouver Drive
(808) 947-6019
www.manoavalleyinn.com
This historic country Inn is an Oahu landmark in an exclusive area of Honolulu. Built in 1912, it provides a luxurious and quiet getaway for visitors and local residents.

DINING
Alan Wong's Restaurant
1857 South King Street
(808) 949-2526
www.AlanWongs.com
Unique tastes of Hawaiian regional cuisine are a direct reflection of the diversified cultures living in the islands.

Side Street Inn
1225 Hoapaka Street
(808) 591-0253
Regulars knock back icy beers while watching sports on TV, dining on some of the best down-home food in the Islands.

Ono Hawaiian Food
726 Kapahulu Avenue
(808) 737-2275
Portions are big and includes such menu items as kalua pig, lomilomi salmon, chicken long rice, poi, pipikaula (seasoned beef jerky), and haupia (coconut) pudding.

Duke's Waikiki
2335 Kalakaua Avenue
(808) 922-2268
www.dukeswaikiki.com
World-famous restaurant named for Hawaii's favorite son, Duke Kahanamoku. With Diamond Head in the distance, you can overlook the spot where Duke rode his largest wave—a 30-foot-swell named Bluebird.

HAINES, AK
(Bald Eagles)

Hotel Halsingland
(907) 766-2000
(800) 542-6363
www.hotelhalsingland.com
Victorian-era hotel offers all the amenities of a modern stay in historic surroundings.

Captain's Choice Motel
(907) 766-3111
(800) 478-2345
www.capchoice.com
Panoramic views of the ocean water of the Lyn Fjord. Rooms are luxurious, quiet, and comfortable. Complimentary continental breakfast.

Lynn View Lodge
(907) 766-3713
www.lynnviewlodge.com
Just over three miles from downtown Haines, across from Tanani Beach and with great views of the Lynn Canal, Chilkat Mountains, Taiya Point, and Taiyasanka Harbor.

Fort Seward B&B
39 Mud Bay Road
(907) 766-2009
(877) 617-3418
www.ftsewardlodge.com
Near downtown Haines and historic Fort William H. Seward. Affordable accommodations, inviting restaurant, and popular saloon.

DINING
Commander's Room at Hotel Halsingland
(907) 766-2000
(800) 542-6363
www.hotelhalsingland.com
Seafood harvested from local waters with a range of robust, complex dishes that focus on the layering of intense flavors and textures.

Bamboo Room-Pioneer Bar
(907) 766-2800
Since 1953, a home away from home for many locals and visitors. All-American menu, famous halibut and chips, and friendly service.

Lighthouse Restaurant
Main and Front Street
(907) 766-2442
Bright and light restaurant in a saloon-style building. Specializing in fusion of seafood and Hawaiian dishes.

Chilkat Restaurant and Bakery
5th Avenue and Dalton Street
(907) 766-3653
Basic fare including hamburgers, soup, and bakery-prepared turnovers, croissants, muffins, and more.

ANCHORAGE, AK
(Iditarod)

LODGING
Copper Whale Inn
440 L Street
(907) 258-7999
(866) 258-7999
www.copperwhale.com
Fourteen-room downtown inn that survived the 1964 earthquake. Stunning views across Cook Inlet to the Alaska Range and convenient access to the 11-mile Coastal Trail.

The Hotel Captain Cook
939 West 5th Avenue
(907) 276-6000
(800) 843-1950
www.captaincook.com
Anchorage's luxury hotel. All guest rooms and suites present majestic and panoramic views of the Cook Inlet or Chugach Mountains. Three restaurants; martini, wine, and gourmet coffee bars.

Historic Anchorage Hotel
330 East Street
(907) 272-4553
www.historicanchoragehotel.com
anchoragehotel@alaska.com
Offers a glimpse into the past with the amenities of a modern hotel.

DINING
The Marx Bros. Café
627 West 3rd Avenue
(907) 278-2133
www.marxcafe.com
Specializes in innovative contemporary cuisine featuring fresh Alaskan seafood and quality meats. Quaintly elegant.

Snow City Café
1034 West 4th Avenue
(907) 272-2489
www.snowcitycafe.com
Urban and funky downtown cafe is a local hot spot for breakfast and lunch.

Glacier BrewHouse
737 West 5th Avenue
(907) 274-2739
www.glacierbrewhouse.com
Fresh Alaskan seafood, rotisserie grilled meats, and award-winning hand crafted ales.

HONORABLE MENTIONS

CERTAINLY THERE ARE far more than 101 sites and events that are unique to, and reflective of, America, and paring them down to the collection in this book was a tricky task. But by consulting with historians, travelers, and fellow writers, I settled on what you see here. Hopefully these 101 are enough to give you a good sense of the nation and get you started on your travels.

I'm sure you'd like to see what other entries were in the running, as well as contact information when available.

Alcatraz
San Francisco
www.nps.gov/alcatraz

Apollo Theater
253 West 125th Street
New York City (Harlem)
(212) 531-5300
www.apollotheater.org

Auto Assembly Line
Detroit

Ball of Twine
Cawker City, Kansas

Barbeques
Southeast

Brooklyn Bridge
New York City

Camping
Across America

Cajun Fais Do Do
Louisiana

Carnegie Hall
881 Seventh Avenue
(212) 247-7800
New York City
www.carnegiehall.org

Carter Family Fold
Hiltons, Virginia
(276) 386-6054
www.carterfamilyfold.org

Cattle Drives
American West

Cherry Blossoms
Washington, D.C.

Chesapeake Bay Crabs
Maryland

Coal Mine
West Virginia

Coca-Cola Headquarters
www.worldofcoca-cola.com

Coney Island
1208 Surf Avenue
Brooklyn
(718) 372-5159

Cotton Fields
Mississippi

Corn Palace
Mitchell, South Dakota
(605) 996-6223
www.cornpalace.org

Covered Bridges
New England

Cruise-Ins
Across America

Erie Canal
New York
www.eriecanal.org

First McDonald's
400 North Lee Street
Des Plaines, Illinois
(847) 297-5022

Fly Fishing
American West

Four Corners
New Mexico

Fourth of July
Across America

Friday Night Football
Texas

Goodyear Blimp
Akron, Ohio
www.goodyearblimp.com

Grauman's Chinese Theatre
Hollywood, California
www.manntheaters.com

Harpers Ferry
West Virginia
www.nps.gov/hafe

Harvard-Yale Football
Massachusetts-Connecticut

Hog Calling Contests
Southeast

Honky Tonks
Texas

Hoover Dam
www.usbr.gov/lc/hooverdam
Nevada-Arizona

International Storytelling Center
116 West Main Street
(423) 753-2171
(800) 952-8392
Jonesborough, Tennessee
www.storytellingcenter.com

Las Vegas Weddings
Nevada

Lighthouses
Coastal America

Maple Tree Tapping
Vermont

March Madness (basketball)
Across America
www.ncaa.com

Monticello
Charlottesville, Virginia
www.monticello.org

Muscle Beach
Venice, California
www.musclebeachvenice.com

NASCAR
Across America
www.nascar.com

National Spelling Bee
Washington, D.C.
www.spellingbee.com

Newport Mansions
Rhode Island
www.gonewport.com

Nudist Camps
Across America

Pikes Peak
Colorado

Polar Bear Clubs
Coney Island; Across America

Political Primaries
Across America

Radio City Music Hall
New York City
(212) 307-7171
www.radiocity.com

Return of the Swallows
Capistrano, California
www.sanjuancapistrano.org

Rock & Roll Hall of Fame
Cleveland, Ohio
(216) 781-7625
www.rockhall.com

Roller Derby
Across America

Route 66
Chicago-Los Angeles

Salem
Massachusetts
www.salemweb.com

Spring Break
Coastal America

Springfield
Illinois
www.springfield.il.us

St. Augustine
Florida
www.oldcity.com

St. Patrick's Day
Boston, New York

Sturgis
South Dakota
www.sturgis.sd.us

Super Bowl
Across America
www.superbowl.com

Surf Ballroom
(site of Buddy Holly's last concert)
460 North Shore Drive
(641) 357-6151
Clear Lake, Iowa
www.surfballroom.com

Today Show
New York City
http://today.msnbc.msn.com/

Tuskegee Institute
Alabama
www.tukegee.edu

United States Naval Academy
Annapolis, Maryland
www.usna.edu

Wall Street
New York City

World Series
Across America

Wrestling
Across America

ACKNOWLEDGMENTS

AMERICA IS FAR TOO large and diverse to create a book like this on my own. It took a contingent of hundreds of writers, historians, educators, and tourism officials to help create *USA 101*. Of course, there are also editors and proofreaders and designers at National Geographic I've never met but who pitched in to ensure this book was at its best. With so many people to credit, I've divided everyone by their favorite Miss North Dakotas of the '40s, '50s, and '60s.

Kitty Page (Miss North Dakota 1949)

Nancy Howell, Larry Porges, Scott Stuckey, Richard Snow, Leslie Allen, Emily Lewis, Jason Howell, Linda Hoskins, Candace Davis, Karen Baker, Mary Jude, Michelle Neal, Laura Shaffer, Dan Rogers, Lesley Bellus, Marty Stuart, Deana Ivey, Renee Monforton, Francisca Ovalle, Joel Cliff, Janet Wall, Cara O'Donnell, Cindy Hampton, Jay Smith, Amy McWethy, Peggy Williams, James Mahon II, Bob Early, Jeff Iula, Debbie Hunsicker, John Percy, Jr., Moira Henderson, Aaron Tuell, Carolyn McCormick, Wit Tuttle, Anne Marie Houppert, Kevin Whaley, Jim Bainbridge, Barbara Brown, Bailey Fucanan, Teni Melidonian, David Flitner, Sharon Rogers, Paul Gowder, Sue Schoening, Kate Boomer, Delia Meier, Sue O'Leary.

Helen Kofhage (Miss North Dakota 1958)

Rebecca Rodgers, Josie Gulliksen, Mindy Bianca, Tammy Hamilton, Connie McNamara, Walter Yeldell, Bob Rutan, Orlando Veras, Kim Heminger, Ray Smith, Ellen Mazzer, Megan Rapp, Henry Sweets, Bonnie King, Joni Moss, Mimi Tilton, Wendy Hielsberg, Brittani Von Ruden, Ann Claffie, Juan Flores, John McClintock, Carla Barry-Austin, Tara Wilson, Erika Dowell, Liz Puro, PJ Santos, Shannon Corrigan, Sarah Chapman, Chris Gahl, Alicia Malone, Katie Chapman, Abby Crooks, Charlene Williams, Rose Whitehouse, Maie Smith, Shari Closter, Bill Wiemuth, John Schieneman, Gary Mack, Neil Vandegrift, Katie Boomer, Lee Whittlesey, Lisa Simmons, Larry Meehan, Stacy Shreffler, Derek Matthews, Cindy Marquez, Adrian Cogar, Christine DeCuir, Mary Beth Romig, Jackie Reed, Evelynn Bailey, Dee Dee Poteet, Symmie Newhouse, Sara Fieberg.

Denise Fledderman (Miss North Dakota 1966)

Buddy Seiner, Cara Schneider, Donna Schorr, Jennifer Nagle, Liz Sullivan, Carl Whitehill, Phyllis Hammond, Veleisa Patton, Lisa Bowden, Frank Smith, David Mandapat, Mary Currie, David Fantle, Darren Rudloff, Jason Fink, Pat Holmes, Shawn Stinson, Scott Barrick, Willie J. Williams, Stacey Yates, Susan Dallas, Darren Rogers, Jocelyn Aframe, Kaitlin Horst, Bob Moore, Tarrah Lee Curtis, Susan Hawvermale-Cayea, Michelle Greco, Kathy Burrows, Heather Middleton, Donna Andrews, Connie Stelter, Rick Sylvain, Heather Bryant, Sue Gooding, Karl Nakagawa, Virginia Snyder Lee, Ashley Akin, Megan Mayo, Kathie Leyendecker, Stacey Fox, Jennifer Sherer Janisch, Paul Cripps, Kappi Allen, Karen Miller, Debbie Reynolds, Bill Troppman, Gabrielle Gray, Lori Stepansky, Shannon Marcak.

Wanda Lou Lowry (Miss North Dakota 1967)

Kimberli Partlow, Samantha Fryberger, Gina Rokas, Barbara Haselow, David Turgeon, Cameron Zotter, Barry Moreno, Betty Ann Collings, Rick Hatcher, Jessica Icenhour, Shannon Marcak, Angela Jackson, Tanya Houseman, Michelle Fusco, Richard Winders, Pat Bock, Jim Mayo, Bridget English, Jerry Reed, Larry Needle, Patrick Muncie, Linda White, Scott Mehus, Erin Lett, Tony Paraino, Scott Goodkin, Anita Turner, Wendy Raney, Anthony Wynn, Lisa Hasenbalg, John Kearns, Craig Muder, Judson True, Laurie Potteiger, Bob McCaw, Melissa Wood, Holly Dougherty, Tracey Berry, Annie Watts Dockter, Chas St. George, David Letterman.

INDEX